Scott Foresman
SCIENCE

Series Authors

Dr. Timothy Cooney
*Professor of Earth Science and
  Science Education*
Earth Science Department
University of Northern Iowa
Cedar Falls, Iowa

Michael Anthony DiSpezio
Science Education Specialist
Cape Cod Children's Museum
Falmouth, Massachusetts

Barbara K. Foots
Science Education Consultant
Houston, Texas

Dr. Angie L. Matamoros
Science Curriculum Specialist
Broward County Schools
Ft. Lauderdale, Florida

Kate Boehm Nyquist
Science Writer and Curriculum Specialist
Mount Pleasant, South Carolina

Dr. Karen L. Ostlund
Professor
Science Education Center
The University of Texas at Austin
Austin, Texas

Contributing Authors

Dr. Anna Uhl Chamot
*Associate Professor and
  ESL Faculty Advisor*
Department of Teacher Preparation
  and Special Education
Graduate School of Education
  and Human Development
The George Washington University
Washington, D.C.

Dr. Jim Cummins
Professor
Modern Language Centre and
  Curriculum Department
Ontario Institute for Studies in Education
Toronto, Canada

Gale Philips Kahn
Lecturer, Science and Math Education
Elementary Education Department
California State University, Fullerton
Fullerton, California

Vincent Sipkovich
Teacher
Irvine Unified School District
Irvine, California

Steve Weinberg
Science Consultant
Connecticut State
  Department of Education
Hartford, Connecticut

Scott Foresman

Editorial Offices: Glenview, Illinois • Parsippany, New Jersey • New York, New York
Sales Offices: Parsippany, New Jersey • Duluth, Georgia • Glenview, Illinois
Carrollton, Texas • Ontario, California
www.sfscience.com

Content Consultants

Dr. J. Scott Cairns
National Institutes of Health
Bethesda, Maryland

Jackie Cleveland
Elementary Resource Specialist
Mesa Public School District
Mesa, Arizona

Robert L. Kolenda
Science Lead Teacher, K-12
Neshaminy School District
Langhorne, Pennsylvania

David P. Lopath
Teacher
The Consolidated School District
of New Britain
New Britain, Connecticut

Sammantha Lane Magsino
Science Coordinator
Institute of Geophysics
University of Texas at Austin
Austin, Texas

Kathleen Middleton
Director, Health Education
ToucanEd
Soquel, California

Irwin Slesnick
Professor of Biology
Western Washington University
Bellingham, Washington

Dr. James C. Walters
Professor of Geology
University of Northern Iowa
Cedar Falls, Iowa

Multicultural Consultants

Dr. Shirley Gholston Key
Assistant Professor
University of Houston-Downtown
Houston, Texas

Damon L. Mitchell
Quality Auditor
Louisiana-Pacific Corporation
Conroe, Texas

Classroom Reviewers

Kathleen Avery
Teacher
Kellogg Science/Technology Magnet
Wichita, Kansas

Margaret S. Brown
Teacher
Cedar Grove Primary
Williamston, South Carolina

Deborah Browne
Teacher
Whitesville Elementary School
Moncks Corner, South Carolina

Wendy Capron
Teacher
Corlears School
New York, New York

Jiwon Choi
Teacher
Corlears School
New York, New York

John Cirrincione
Teacher
West Seneca Central Schools
West Seneca, New York

Jacqueline Colander
Teacher
Norfolk Public Schools
Norfolk, Virginia

Dr. Terry Contant
Teacher
Conroe Independent
School District
The Woodlands, Texas

Susan Crowley-Walsh
Teacher
Meadowbrook Elementary School
Gladstone, Missouri

Charlene K. Dindo
Teacher
Fairhope K-1 Center/Pelican's Nest
Science Lab
Fairhope, Alabama

Laurie Duffee
Teacher
Barnard Elementary
Tulsa, Oklahoma

Beth Anne Ebler
Teacher
Newark Public Schools
Newark, New Jersey

Karen P. Farrell
Teacher
Rondout Elementary School
District #72
Lake Forest, Illinois

Anna M. Gaiter
Teacher
Los Angeles Unified School District
Los Angeles Systemic Initiative
Los Angeles, California

Federica M. Gallegos
Teacher
Highland Park Elementary
Salt Lake School District
Salt Lake City, Utah

Janet E. Gray
Teacher
Anderson Elementary - Conroe ISD
Conroe, Texas

Karen Guinn
Teacher
Ehrhardt Elementary School - KISD
Spring, Texas

Denis John Hagerty
Teacher
Al Ittihad Private Schools
Dubai, United Arab Emirates

Judith Halpern
Teacher
Bannockburn School
Deerfield, Illinois

Debra D. Harper
Teacher
Community School District 9
Bronx, New York

Gretchen Harr
Teacher
Denver Public Schools - Doull School
Denver, Colorado

Bonnie L. Hawthorne
Teacher
Jim Darcy School
School District #1
Helena, Montana

Marselle Heywood-Julian
Teacher
Community School District 6
New York, New York

Scott Klene
Teacher
Bannockburn School 106
Bannockburn, Illinois

Thomas Kranz
Teacher
Livonia Primary School
Livonia, New York

Tom Leahy
Teacher
Coos Bay School District
Coos Bay, Oregon

Mary Littig
Teacher
Kellogg Science/Technology Magnet
Wichita, Kansas

Patricia Marin
Teacher
Corlears School
New York, New York

Susan Maki
Teacher
Cotton Creek CUSD 118
Island Lake, Illinois

Efraín Meléndez
Teacher
East LA Mathematics Science
Center LAUSD
Los Angeles, California

Becky Mojalid
Teacher
Manarat Jeddah Girls' School
Jeddah, Saudi Arabia

Susan Nations
Teacher
Sulphur Springs Elementary
Tampa, Florida

Brooke Palmer
Teacher
Whitesville Elementary
Moncks Corner, South Carolina

Jayne Pedersen
Teacher
Laura B. Sprague
School District 103
Lincolnshire, Illinois

Shirley Pfingston
Teacher
Orland School District 135
Orland Park, Illinois

Teresa Gayle Rountree
Teacher
Box Elder School District
Brigham City, Utah

Helen C. Smith
Teacher
Schultz Elementary
Klein Independent School District
Tomball, Texas

Denette Smith-Gibson
Teacher
Mitchell Intermediate, CISD
The Woodlands, Texas

Mary Jean Syrek
Teacher
Dr. Charles R. Drew Science
Magnet
Buffalo, New York

Rosemary Troxel
Teacher
Libertyville School District 70
Libertyville, Illinois

Susan D. Vani
Teacher
Laura B. Sprague School
School District 103
Lincolnshire, Illinois

Debra Worman
Teacher
Bryant Elementary
Tulsa, Oklahoma

Dr. Gayla Wright
Teacher
Edmond Public School
Edmond, Oklahoma

Activity and Safety Consultants

Laura Adams
Teacher
Holley-Navarre Intermediate
Navarre, Florida

Dr. Charlie Ashman
Teacher
Carl Sandburg Middle School
Mundelein District #75
Mundelein, Illinois

Christopher Atlee
Teacher
Horace Mann Elementary
Wichita Public Schools
Wichita, Kansas

David Bachman
Consultant
Chicago, Illinois

Sherry Baldwin
Teacher
Shady Brook
Bedford ISD
Euless, Texas

Pam Bazis
Teacher
Richardson ISD
  Classical Magnet School
Richardson, Texas

Angela Boese
Teacher
McCollom Elementary
Wichita Public Schools USD #259
Wichita, Kansas

Jan Buckelew
Teacher
Taylor Ranch Elementary
Venice, Florida

Shonie Castaneda
Teacher
Carman Elementary, PSJA
Pharr, Texas

Donna Coffey
Teacher
Melrose Elementary - Pinellas
St. Petersburg, Florida

Diamantina Contreras
Teacher
J.T. Brackenridge Elementary
San Antonio ISD
San Antonio, Texas

Susanna Curtis
Teacher
Lake Bluff Middle School
Lake Bluff, Illinois

Karen Farrell
Teacher
Rondout Elementary School,
  Dist. #72
Lake Forest, Illinois

Paul Gannon
Teacher
El Paso ISD
El Paso, Texas

Nancy Garman
Teacher
Jefferson Elementary School
Charleston, Illinois

Susan Graves
Teacher
Beech Elementary
Wichita Public Schools USD #259
Wichita, Kansas

Jo Anna Harrison
Teacher
Cornelius Elementary
Houston ISD
Houston, Texas

Monica Hartman
Teacher
Richard Elementary
Detroit Public Schools
Detroit, Michigan

Kelly Howard
Teacher
Sarasota, Florida

Kelly Kimborough
Teacher
Richardson ISD
  Classical Magnet School
Richardson, Texas

Mary Leveron
Teacher
Velasco Elementary
Brazosport ISD
Freeport, Texas

Becky McClendon
Teacher
A.P. Beutel Elementary
Brazosport ISD
Freeport, Texas

Suzanne Milstead
Teacher
Liestman Elementary
Alief ISD
Houston, Texas

Debbie Oliver
Teacher
School Board of Broward County
Ft. Lauderdale, Florida

Sharon Pearthree
Teacher
School Board of Broward County
Ft. Lauderdale, Florida

Jayne Pedersen
Teacher
Laura B. Sprague School
District 103
Lincolnshire, Illinois

Sharon Pedroja
Teacher
Riverside Cultural
  Arts/History Magnet
Wichita Public Schools USD #259
Wichita, Kansas

Marcia Percell
Teacher
Pharr, San Juan, Alamo ISD
Pharr, Texas

Shirley Pfingston
Teacher
Orland School District #135
Orland Park, Illinois

Sharon S. Placko
Teacher
District 26, Mt. Prospect
Mt. Prospect, IL

Glenda Rall
Teacher
Seltzer Elementary
USD #259
Wichita, Kansas

Nelda Requenez
Teacher
Canterbury Elementary
Edinburg, Texas

Dr. Beth Rice
Teacher
Loxahatchee Groves
  Elementary School
Loxahatchee, Florida

Martha Salom Romero
Teacher
El Paso ISD
El Paso, Texas

Paula Sanders
Teacher
Welleby Elementary School
Sunrise, Florida

Lynn Setchell
Teacher
Sigsbee Elementary School
Key West, Florida

Rhonda Shook
Teacher
Mueller Elementary
Wichita Public Schools USD #259
Wichita, Kansas

Anna Marie Smith
Teacher
Orland School District #135
Orland Park, Illinois

Nancy Ann Varneke
Teacher
Seltzer Elementary
Wichita Public Schools USD #259
Wichita, Kansas

Aimee Walsh
Teacher
Rolling Meadows, Illinois

Ilene Wagner
Teacher
O.A. Thorp Scholastic Acacemy
Chicago Public Schools
Chicago, Illinois

Brian Warren
Teacher
Riley Community Consolidated
  School District 18
Marengo, Illinois

Tammie White
Teacher
Holley-Navarre
  Intermediate School
Navarre, Florida

Dr. Mychael Willon
Principal
Horace Mann Elementary
Wichita Public Schools
Wichita, Kansas

Inclusion Consultants

Dr. Eric J. Pyle, Ph.D.
Assistant Professor, Science Education
Department of Educational Theory
  and Practice
West Virginia University
Morgantown, West Virginia

Dr. Gretchen Butera, Ph.D.
Associate Professor, Special Education
Department of Education Theory
  and Practice
West Virginia University
Morgantown, West Virginia

Bilingual Consultant

Irma Gomez-Torres
Dalindo Elementary
Austin ISD
Austin, Texas

Bilingual Reviewers

Mary E. Morales
E.A. Jones Elementary
Fort Bend ISD
Missouri City, Texas

Gabriela T. Nolasco
Pebble Hills Elementary
Ysleta ISD
El Paso, Texas

Maribel B. Tanguma
Reed and Mock Elementary
San Juan, Texas

Yesenia Garza
Reed and Mock Elementary
San Juan, Texas

Teri Gallegos
St. Andrew's School
Austin, Texas

Unit B
Physical Science

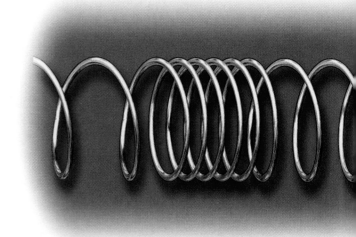

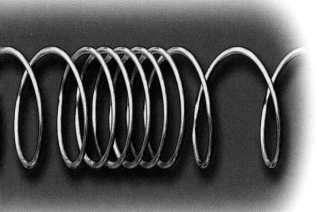

Unit C
Earth Science

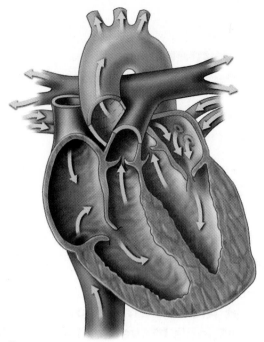

Unit D
Human Body

Your Science Handbook

Using Scientific Methods for Science Inquiry

Scientists try to solve many problems. Scientists study problems in different ways, but they all use scientific methods to guide their work. Scientific methods are organized ways of finding answers and solving problems. Scientific methods include the steps shown on these pages. The order of the steps or the number of steps used may change. You can use these steps to organize your own scientific inquiries.

State the Problem

The problem is the question you want to answer. Curiosity and inquiry have resulted in many scientific discoveries. State your problem in the form of a question.

Which clay boat design holds more marbles before sinking?

Formulate Your Hypothesis

Your hypothesis is a possible answer to your problem. Make sure your hypothesis can be tested. Your hypothesis should take the form of a statement.

◀ A wide boat with high sides holds more marbles.

Identify and Control the Variables

For a fair test, you must select which variable to change and which variables to control. Choose one variable to change when you test your hypothesis. Control the other variables so they do not change.

▲ Make one boat wide and the other boat narrow. Both boats will have high sides. Use the same amount of clay for each boat.

Test Your Hypothesis

Do experiments to test your hypothesis. You may need to repeat experiments to make sure your results remain consistent. Sometimes you conduct a scientific survey to test a hypothesis.

◀ Place marbles in the boat until it sinks. Repeat for the other boat.

Collect Your Data

As you test your hypothesis, you will collect data about the problem you want to solve. You may need to record measurements. You might make drawings or diagrams. Or you may write lists or descriptions. Collect as much data as you can while testing your hypothesis.

Number of marbles held	
Wide boat	ΗΗ ΗΗ I
Narrow boat	ΗΗ II

Interpret Your Data

By organizing your data into charts, tables, diagrams, and graphs, you may see patterns in the data. Then you can decide what the information from your data means.

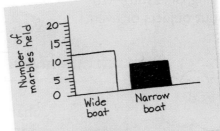

State Your Conclusion

Your conclusion is a decision you make based on evidence. Compare your results with your hypothesis. Based on whether or not your data supports your hypothesis, decide if your hypothesis is correct or incorrect. Then communicate your conclusion by stating or presenting your decision.

A wide boat design holds more marbles!

❓Inquire Further

Use what you learn to solve other problems or to answer other questions that you might have. You may decide to repeat your experiment, or to change it based on what you learned.

▼ Will the results be similar with aluminum foil boats?

Using Process Skills for Science Inquiry

These 12 process skills are used by scientists when they do their research. You also use many of these skills every day. For example, when you think of a statement that you can test, you are using process skills. When you gather data to make a chart or graph, you are using process skills. As you do the activities in your book, you will use these same process skills.

Observing

Use one or more of your senses—seeing, hearing, smelling, touching, or tasting—to gather information about objects or events.

I see..., I smell..., I hear..., It feels like..., I never taste without permission!

Communicating

Share information about what you learn using words, pictures, charts, graphs, and diagrams.

Classifying

Arrange or group objects according to their common properties.

◀ Rocks with one color in Group 1.

Rocks with two or more colors in Group 2. ▶

Estimating and Measuring

Make an estimate about an object's properties, then measure and describe the object in units.

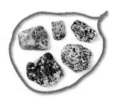

It's as heavy as a... It sounds like a... It must be shaped like a...

Inferring

Draw a conclusion or make a reasonable guess based on what you observe, or from your past experiences.

Predicting

Form an idea about what will happen based on evidence.

◀ *Predict what happens after 15 minutes.*

Making Operational Definitions

Define or describe an object or event based on your experiences with it.

An electromagnet is a coil of wire around a bolt that... ▶

Making and Using Models

Make real or mental representations to explain ideas, objects, or events.

◀ *It's different from a real bridge because... The model is like a real bridge because...*

Formulating Questions and Hypotheses

Think of a statement that you can test to solve a problem or to answer a question about how something works.

If you place a plant by a sunny window, the leaves will... ▶

Collecting and Interpreting Data

Gather observations and measurements into graphs, tables, charts, or diagrams. Then use the information to solve problems or answer questions.

The plant in the polluted water grew the slowest.

Identifying and Controlling Variables

Change one factor that may affect the outcome of an event while holding other factors constant.

Variables	
Change	Same
✓ Amount of fertilizer	✓ Temperature
	✓ Plant size
	✓ Water
	✓ Light
	✓ Soil

Experimenting

Design an investigation to test a hypothesis or to solve a problem. Then form a conclusion.

I'll write a clear procedure so that other students could repeat the experiment.

? Science Inquiry

Throughout your science book, you will ask questions, do investigations, answer your questions, and tell others what you have learned. Use the descriptions below to help you during your scientific inquiry.

> What kind of cup keeps liquid colder?

1 **Ask a question about objects, organisms, and events in the environment.**

You will find the answer to your question from your own observations and investigations and from reliable sources of scientific information.

2 **Plan and conduct a simple investigation.**

The kind of investigation you do depends on the question you ask. Kinds of investigations include describing objects, events, and organisms; classifying them; and doing a fair test or experiment.

3 **Use simple equipment and tools to gather data and extend the senses.**

Equipment and tools you might use include rulers and meter sticks, compasses, thermometers, watches, balances, spring scales, hand lenses, microscopes, cameras, calculators, and computers.

4 **Use data to construct a reasonable explanation.**

Use the information that you have gathered to answer your question and support your answer. Compare your answer to scientific knowledge, your experiences, and the observations of others.

5 **Communicate investigations and explanations.**

Share your work with others by writing, drawing, or talking. Describe your work in a way that others could repeat your investigation.

Question
what kind of cup
keeps liquid colder?
materials
thermometer
paper cup
clear plastic cup
plastic foam cup

Unit A
Life Science

Science and Technology
In Your World!

Eat the Cup Too?

Imagine drinking a milkshake, then eating the vanilla-flavored cup and straw! The plastic in the cup and straw are made from plant proteins and starches—so they are safe to eat. And there's no trash to throw away! You'll learn more about plants and their parts in **Chapter 1 Plant Structure and Function.**

These Critters Wear Cameras!

After watching a remora fish "hitchhike" a ride on the back of a shark, Greg Marshall invented the Crittercam, a video camera "backpack" that attaches to an animal. The videotapes give scientists a firsthand look at what animals do when humans aren't around. You'll learn more about the differences between types of animals in **Chapter 2 Animal Structure and Function.**

Farm in a Fishpond!

In a new farming method called "aquaponics," fish and plant crops grow side by side—in one pond or tank. It's a kind of mini-ecosystem. The plants filter and clean the water for the fish, while fish wastes provide nutrients for the plants. You'll read more about how habitats meet the needs of living things in **Chapter 3 Energy in Ecosystems.**

Uplink My Tracks!

How do you track an elephant migrating over land, a whale through the ocean, or a bird across two continents? Scientists now use weather satellites as part of a tracking system for threatened wildlife. Tiny transmitters, attached to the animals, send signals to satellites. The signals are then relayed to the computers of wildlife scientists. You'll learn more about animal migration and endangered wildlife in **Chapter 4 Surviving in the Environment.**

Where's the Food?

Imagine what life would be like without plants! There would be no trees, no fruit, no grains and no bread! Actually, there would be no food at all!

Chapter 1

Plant Structure and Function

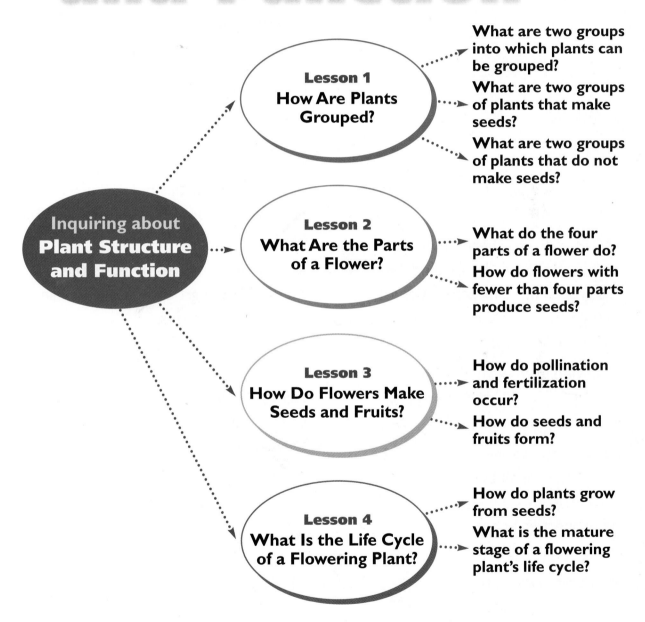

Inquiring about Plant Structure and Function

Lesson 1
How Are Plants Grouped?

What are two groups into which plants can be grouped?

What are two groups of plants that make seeds?

What are two groups of plants that do not make seeds?

Lesson 2
What Are the Parts of a Flower?

What do the four parts of a flower do?

How do flowers with fewer than four parts produce seeds?

Lesson 3
How Do Flowers Make Seeds and Fruits?

How do pollination and fertilization occur?

How do seeds and fruits form?

Lesson 4
What Is the Life Cycle of a Flowering Plant?

How do plants grow from seeds?

What is the mature stage of a flowering plant's life cycle?

Copy the chapter graphic organizer onto your own paper. This organizer shows you what the whole chapter is all about. As you read the lessons and do the activities, look for answers to the questions and write them on your organizer.

Classifying Seeds

Process Skills

- observing
- classifying
- communicating

Materials

- plastic bag of assorted beans
- paper
- colored pencils or crayons

Explore

1 Open the bag and place the beans on the paper.

2 **Observe** the beans. Begin to **classify** the beans by dividing them into two groups on your paper. Beneath each group, write the property that you used to describe it.

3 Divide each of the groups into two more groups. Write the property beneath each group.

4 Continue to divide groups of beans until they have all been classified individually by their properties. Write the properties beneath each bean.

5 Use colored pencils or crayons to make a drawing of each bean.

Reflect

1. What properties did you use to classify the beans? How else could you have classified the beans?

2. **Communicate.** Discuss the methods each group of students used to classify the beans.

? Inquire Further

How can you use the same method to classify plants that grow where you live? Develop a plan to answer this or other questions you may have.

Identifying the Main Idea

As you read for science, it is important for you to find the main idea. Sometimes these main ideas are stated directly. Look at "You will learn" on page A8. The three sentences here are the stated main ideas for the first lesson. As you read the lesson, however, the main ideas might be paraphrased or written in a slightly different way.

Example

In Lesson 1, the first stated main idea about plants is that there are "two groups into which plants can be grouped." In the lesson the main idea has been rewritten as: "Plants in one group make seeds. Plants in the other group do not make seeds."

Make a chart like this one for the rest of Lesson 1. Write the last two main ideas from "You will learn." As you read the lesson, decide whether these main ideas are stated or paraphrased. Write the main idea in the correct column of your chart.

Main Ideas	Stated	Paraphrased

Talk About It!

1. Where can you find the main ideas for each lesson in your book?

2. What two types of main ideas will you find in your book?

▼ *Have you ever wondered how plants that do not make seeds reproduce?*

You will learn:
- the two groups into which plants can be grouped.
- about two groups of plants that make seeds.
- about two groups of plants that do not make seeds.

Lesson 1

How Are Plants Grouped?

CDs, sports cards, or coins! You probably have a collection of these or other things. How do you store them so you can find what you're looking for easily? Maybe you put them into groups. Neat!

Grouping Plants

Notice the different kinds of plants in the pictures on these two pages. These are just a few of the thousands of plants that grow on the earth. As you can see, plants grow in many sizes and shapes.

Plants also grow in many different places. However, all plants are alike in one way. All plants use water, carbon dioxide, and energy from sunlight to make sugar. Then the plants use the energy in the sugar to grow.

◀ The vegetables that these children are planting are some of the many kinds of plants. What kinds of vegetables would you want to plant?

Learning about all the different kinds of plants could be hard. It is easier to learn about plants when you sort them into groups. All the plants in one group are similar in some ways. They are also different from plants in other groups.

Scientists group plants by the ways in which they are similar or different. One way that plants are similar or different is the way they make new plants, or **reproduce**. Scientists use this difference to group, or **classify**, plants into two large groups. Plants in one group make seeds. Plants in the other group do not make seeds.

Glossary

reproduce (rē′prə düs′), to make more of the same kind

classify (klas′ə fī), to sort into groups based on similarities and differences

Trees and cacti don't look much alike! But they are both kinds of plants that make seeds. ▶

Plants That Make Seeds

You can see that the sunflowers and the pine tree in the pictures look very different. However, they both belong to the large group of plants that make seeds. When their seeds are planted, the seeds grow into new plants. However, sunflowers and the pine tree make seeds in different ways.

Plants that make seeds can be sorted into two groups. Plants in one group have flowers. Plants in the other group do not have flowers.

You can see that the sunflower, with its bright yellow flowers, is a flowering plant. Flowering plants are the largest group of plants that make seeds. A cactus and a fruit tree are flowering plants. What other flowering plants have you seen?

Sunflowers make a lot of seeds. The seeds are good to eat. ▼

Pine trees belong to the group of plants that make seeds but do not have flowers. These plants are called **conifers.** They make seeds inside of cones. Most conifers are trees or shrubs and have needlelike leaves.

Glossary

conifer (kon′ə fər), a plant that makes seeds inside cones

▲ *It's amazing, but the small seeds formed in these pine cones grow into huge pine trees.*

Glossary

spore (spôr), a tiny cell that can grow into a new plant

Spores

The child is looking at the underside of a fern leaf. Each of the spots on the leaf is a cluster of spore cases. Each spore case is filled with tiny spores. ▼

Plants That Do Not Make Seeds

Have you ever walked through a forest and seen plants like the ones in the pictures? These plants belong to another large group of plants that reproduce in a similar way. Unlike the sunflower and pine tree, these plants do not make seeds.

Ferns and mosses are two kinds of plants that do not make seeds. They reproduce by forming tiny cells that can grow into new plants. Each tiny cell is called a **spore.** Look at the pictures and read to find out more about plants that do not make seeds.

Mosses

Mosses are small plants that do not have stems and roots that carry water to other parts of the plant. Mosses grow close to the ground and in shady, moist places. ▼

▲ *Mosses do have parts that are leaflike, but they do not have flowers or make seeds. Mosses produce spores in cases at the tips of short stalks. Each spore case holds hundreds of spores.*

Ferns

Unlike mosses, ferns are large plants that have roots, stems, and leaves. At one time, giant ferns covered much of the earth—even before the dinosaurs lived. Today, ferns grow in many places that are moist.
Like mosses, ferns do not have flowers or make seeds. Ferns produce spores. Unlike mosses, ferns produce spore cases on the undersides of their leaves. ▶

The pictures in the chart below review how to classify plants. What are two kinds of plants that make seeds? How would you classify the tulips at the bottom of the page? Use the chart to classify some plants that grow where you live.

Plant Classification

Plants that make seeds		Plants that do not make seeds	
Flowering plants 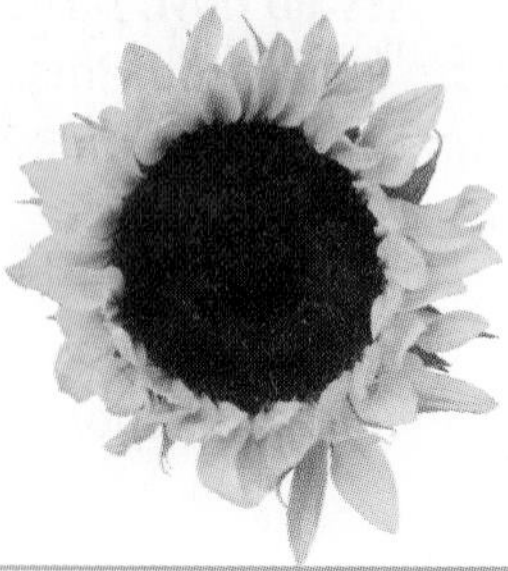	Conifers 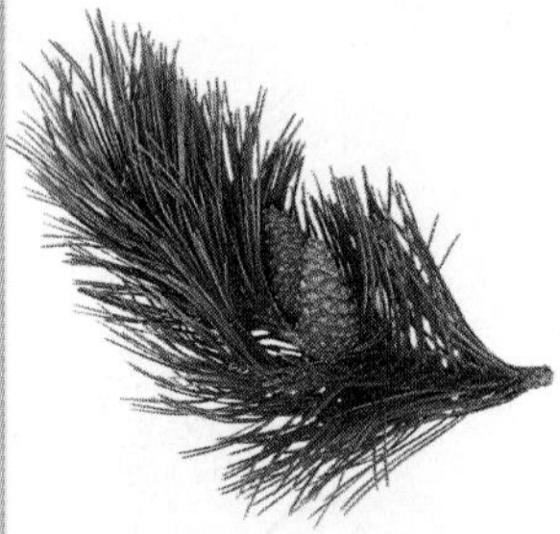	Ferns 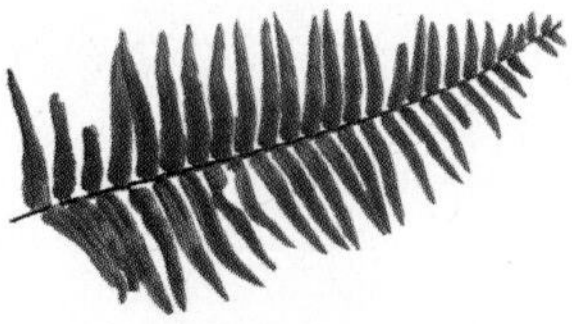	Mosses 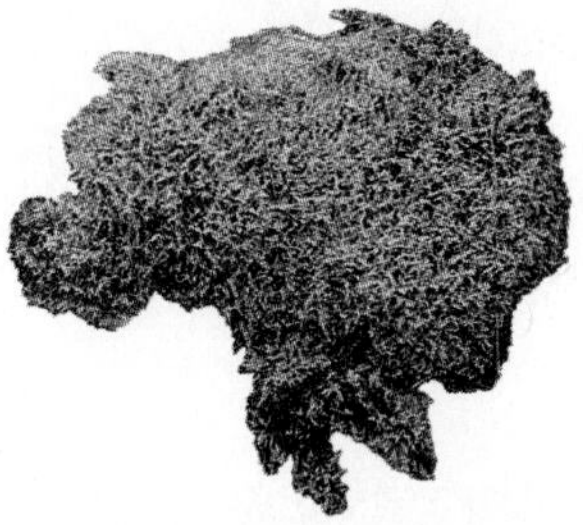

Lesson 1 Review

1. What is one way to classify all plants into two groups?
2. How do flowering plants and conifers differ in the way they make seeds?
3. How do plants that do not make seeds reproduce?
4. **Main Idea**
   What is the main idea of the second paragraph on page A12?

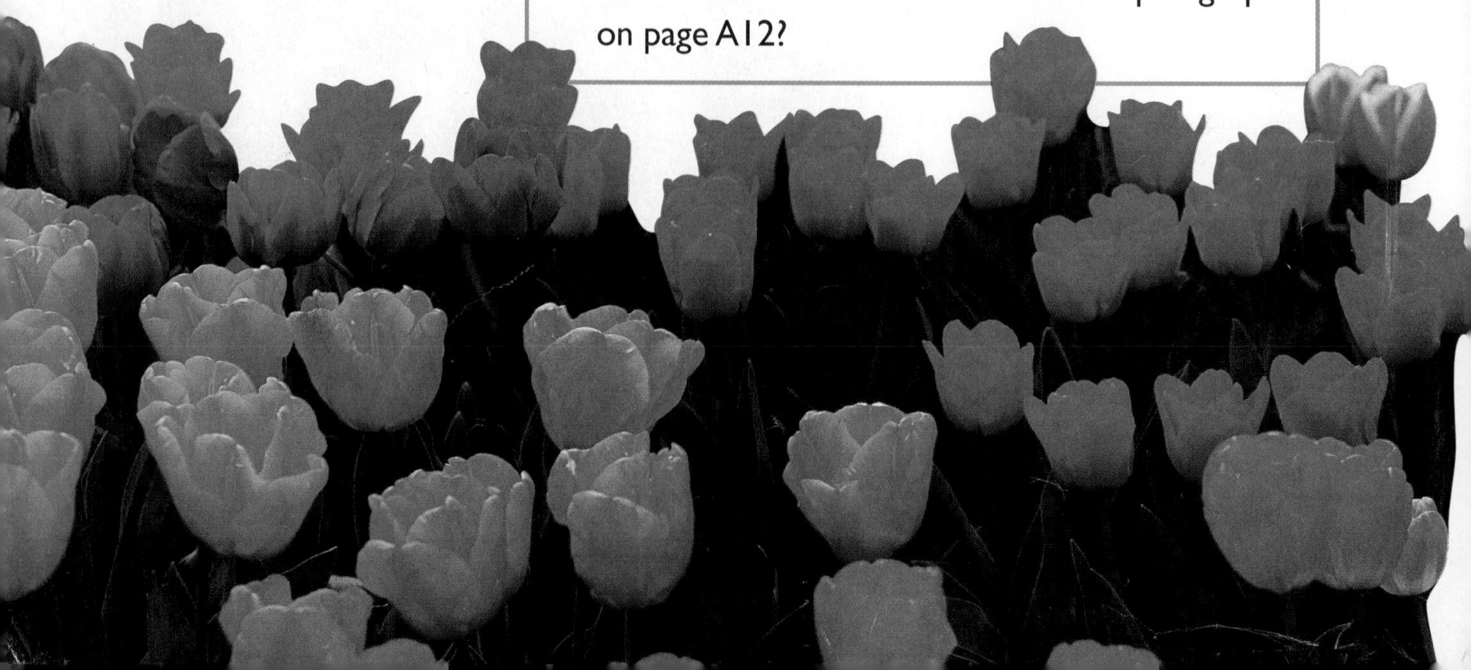

Lesson 2

What Are the Parts of a Flower?

Ooooohh! Bright yellow tulips, tiny blue violets, white daisies, sweet-smelling lilacs, or fields of wildflowers! Flowers can be found in all sizes, shapes, and colors. When you hear the word *flower*, what do you think about?

What's the Big Idea?

You will learn:
• what the four parts of a flower do.
• how flowers with fewer than four parts produce seeds.

Flowers with Four Parts

What kinds of flowers have you seen? You may have seen small flowers or big flowers. They might have been snow white—or red like the ones in the picture. You know that flowers can be very colorful, but flowers don't just make plants pretty. Flowering plants need flowers to make seeds that grow into new plants.

Red, orange, yellow! The bright colors of flowers attract many insects and birds that help the flowers make seeds. ▶

A 15

Glossary

sepal (sē′pəl), one of the leaflike parts that protects a flower bud and that is usually green

pistil (pis′tl), part of a flower that makes the eggs that grow into seeds

stamen (stā′mən), part of a flower that makes pollen

pollen (pol′ən), tiny grains that make seeds when combined with a flower's egg

Most flowers, like the ones in the pictures on this page and the next page, have four parts. Notice the flower buds. The green parts of a flower bud are the **sepals.** They cover and protect the flower growing inside. As the flower grows, it forces the sepals apart. The bud opens into a beautiful flower.

When you look at a flower, you probably notice the petals first. The petals are the colorful parts of the flower. The petals attract bees, butterflies, birds, and other living things.

Notice the five small, knoblike structures in the center of the ring of petals. These structures make up the pistil. The **pistil** is the part of the flower that makes eggs. The eggs will grow into seeds when they are combined with sperm in pollen.

Now look just below the pistil. You can see the cluster of stamens with rounded tips. The **stamens** make tiny grains of **pollen** at their tips. A flower needs sperm in pollen to combine with the flower's egg to make seeds.

Find the buds between the two flowers. ▼

The Four Parts of a Flower

Pistil
The five knobs make up the pistil that makes eggs.

Stamens with Pollen
Each stamen is covered with grains of pollen.

Petals
The petals surround and protect the parts of the flower that make seeds.

Sepals
The sepals are the leaflike parts of the flower buds. They are usually green but may be other colors.

Sperm in pollen grains from the stamens of the corn tassel combine with eggs in the pistils to form an ear of corn. ▼

Flowers with Fewer than Four Parts

As you know, most flowers have sepals, petals, stamens, and at least one pistil. However, not all flowers have all these parts. The flowers of the corn plant in the picture do not have all these parts.

The corn plant is one of the plants that has two kinds of flowers. One kind of flower has one or more pistils, but no stamens. The other kind of flower has stamens, but no pistil. The sperm in the pollen from the stamens on one flower combine with the eggs in the pistil of the other flower to make seeds.

The corn plant has two kinds of flowers on the same plant. Notice the top part of the corn plant in the picture. This is the corn flower called a tassel. This flower has stamens. Notice the ear of corn near the bottom of the picture. Corn forms from a flower with pistils. Plants such as squash plants, maple trees, and oak trees also have two kinds of flowers on the same plant.

Other plants have two kinds of flowers, but not on the same plant. Cottonwood trees have one kind of flower on one tree. The other kind of flower grows on another cottonwood tree.

Lesson 2 Review

1. In what part of a flower are seeds made?

2. How do plants with two kinds of flowers make seeds?

3. **Main Idea**
   What is the main idea of the second paragraph on this page?

How Do Flowers Make Seeds and Fruits?

CRUNCH! You take a bite out of a crisp apple. You know that pollen is needed to make seeds. But did you know that without tiny grains of pollen, there wouldn't be any apples? Amazing, isn't it?

Pollination and Fertilization

Before an apple tree can make an apple, something else must happen. Pollen grains from a stamen of an apple flower must be moved to the sticky tip of a pistil. The movement of pollen from the tips of stamens to the sticky tips of pistils is **pollination.**

Wind carries pollen from the tassels to the pistils of corn plants. Wind also helps pollinate the flowers of grasses and many trees. Small animals, such as insects, pollinate the flowers on an apple tree.

You have probably watched bees and butterflies flit from flower to flower. These insects gather nectar from the flowers. Insects use the liquid for food. As the insects gather nectar, they are also helping the flowers they visit.

When bees and butterflies gather nectar, pollen sticks to their bodies. As they move from flower to flower, they may brush against pistils. The pollen on their bodies can stick to the pistils. Other animals, such as birds and bats, also pollinate flowers. The colors and smells of flowers attract the animals.

What's the Big Idea?

You will learn:
- how pollination and fertilization occur.
- how seeds and fruits form.

Glossary

Glossary

pollination
(pol′ ə nā′ shən), the movement of pollen from a stamen to a pistil

Can't you almost taste the juicy, red apple? An apple is a fruit that forms from an apple flower. ▼

Glossary

ovary (ō′vər ē), the bottom part of the pistil in which seeds form

ovule (ō′vyül), the inner part of an ovary that contains an egg

fertilization √ (fèr′tl ə zā′shən), the combination of sperm from a pollen grain with an egg to form a seed

Notice the pictures of the flower and butterfly below. Pollen from the flower sticks to the body of the butterfly. The butterfly carries the pollen to the sticky pistil of the flower. Then each pollen grain grows a thin tube from the tip of the pistil to its thick bottom, or **ovary.** Find the ovary and the ovules in the picture on the next page. Each **ovule** contains an egg. The sperm from a pollen grain moves through the pollen tube to the ovary. When the sperm reaches an ovule, it combines with an egg. This combining of a sperm and an egg to make a seed is **fertilization.**

How Pollination Occurs

The butterfly below may carry pollen from the stamen of one flower to the pistil of the same flower. Sometimes the butterfly may carry pollen from the stamen of one flower to the pistil of another flower of the same kind.

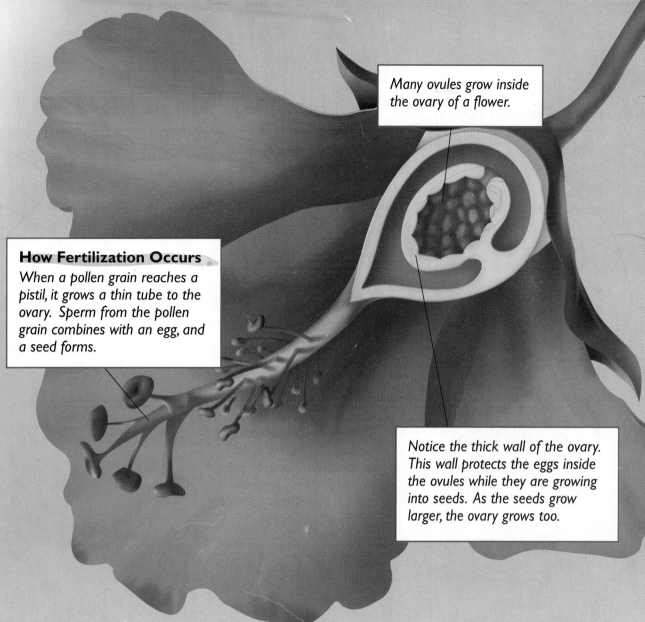

Many ovules grow inside the ovary of a flower.

How Fertilization Occurs

When a pollen grain reaches a pistil, it grows a thin tube to the ovary. Sperm from the pollen grain combines with an egg, and a seed forms.

Notice the thick wall of the ovary. This wall protects the eggs inside the ovules while they are growing into seeds. As the seeds grow larger, the ovary grows too.

How Seeds Form

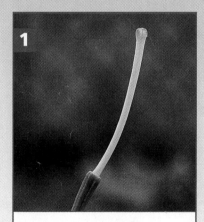

1

These pictures show how seeds form in a different flower. After fertilization, the flower dries up and the petals fall off, leaving just the pistil and its ovary.

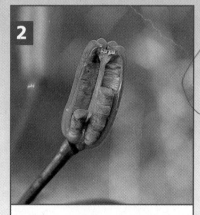

2

The top of the pistil falls off and the ovary gets larger as one or more seeds form inside it. This ovary is cut open to show the growing seeds.

3

When the seeds are formed, the ovary dries up and the seeds fall out.

Glossary

embryo (em′brē ō), tiny part of a seed that can grow into a new plant

monocot (mon′ə kot) **seed,** a seed that has one seed leaf and stored food outside the seed leaf

dicot (dī′kot) **seed,** a seed that has two seed leaves that contain stored food

Seeds and Fruits

When you think about seeds, you probably think of seeds that you plant. However, many of the foods you eat are seeds. Corn, peas, and beans are some seeds you may have eaten.

Look at the pictures of seeds. You can see a tiny **embryo** inside each seed. This is the part of the seed that can grow into a new plant. Each seed is covered by a seed coat that protects the seed.

Some flowering plants are monocots and some are dicots. The seeds of these two kinds of flowers are shown here. Find the differences between these seeds.

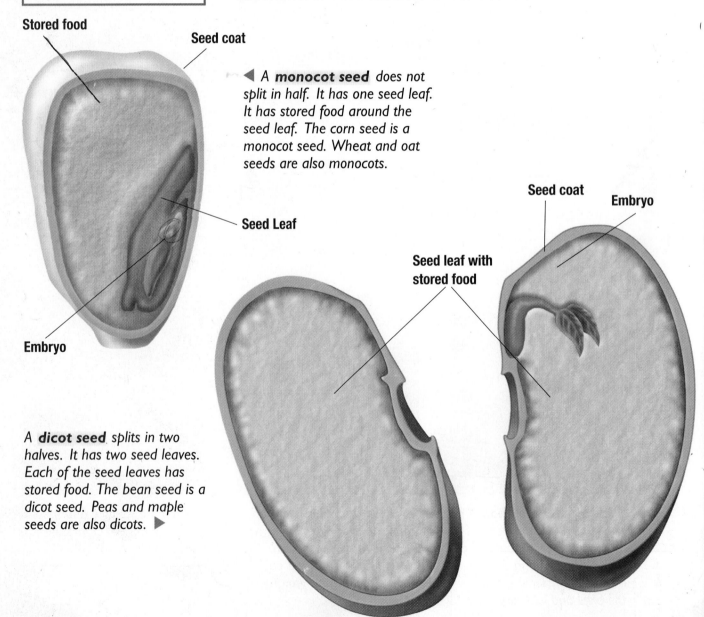

Stored food

Seed coat

◀ A **monocot seed** does not split in half. It has one seed leaf. It has stored food around the seed leaf. The corn seed is a monocot seed. Wheat and oat seeds are also monocots.

Seed Leaf

Embryo

Seed coat

Embryo

Seed leaf with stored food

A **dicot seed** splits in two halves. It has two seed leaves. Each of the seed leaves has stored food. The bean seed is a dicot seed. Peas and maple seeds are also dicots. ▶

A22

The ovary that surrounds the seed or seeds grows larger and forms the fruit. The fruit covers and protects the seeds. Notice the different kinds of fruits in the picture.

Some fruits, such as apples, tomatoes, and grapes, have a large amount of water. Other fruits, such as the shells of nuts, are dry. The part of the nut you eat is the seed.

Don't these fruits make you hungry? Some fruits have only one seed. Others have many seeds. ▶

Lesson 3 Review

1. How are flowers pollinated?

2. How is a monocot seed different from a dicot seed?

3. **Main Idea**
   What is the main idea of the first paragraph on this page?

A23

Observing the Parts of Flowers

Process Skills

- observing
- collecting and interpreting data
- communicating
- inferring

Materials

- safety goggles
- newspapers
- 2 different flowers
- hand lens
- plastic knife

Getting Ready

In this activity you can find out how the flowers of different plants are similar and different.

Follow This Procedure

❶ Make a chart like the one shown. Use your chart to record your observations.

	Flower 1	Flower 2
Number of sepals		
Color of sepals		
Number of petals		
Color of petals		
Number of stamens		
Number of pistils		
Drawing of stamen		
Drawing of pistil		

❷ Put on your safety goggles. Spread newspapers on your desk. **Observe** the sepals of the flowers (Photo A). **Collect data** by recording the number of sepals and their color.

❸ Observe the petals, stamens, and pistils. Record the information listed in the chart.

Photo A

4 Use the hand lens to observe the stamens of each flower. What do you notice on the ends of the stamens? Make a drawing to record your observations.

5 Use the plastic knife to carefully cut open the bottom of the pistil. Use the hand lens to observe the inside of the pistil (Photo B). Make a drawing of your observations.

Self-Monitoring
Have I carefully observed all four parts of the flowers?

Interpret Your Results

1. Communicate. Explain how the parts of the two flowers are similar and different.

2. What might you **infer** about the parts of other flowers with four parts? How might they be similar to these flower parts? How might they be different?

Inquire Further

How might you test your inference about the parts of other flowers with four parts? Develop a plan to answer this or other questions you may have.

Self-Assessment

- I followed directions to **observe** the parts of two different flowers.
- I **collected** and **interpreted data** about the flowers.
- I made drawings of the stamens and pistils.
- I **communicated** by explaining how the two flowers are similar and different.
- I made an **inference** about the parts of other flowers with four parts.

Photo B

You will learn:

- how plants grow from seeds.
- about the mature stage of a flowering plant's life cycle.

Lesson 4

What Is the Life Cycle of a Flowering Plant?

All living things have a life cycle. Yes, even you! When you were born, you were a baby. In a few years, you will be a teenager! **Wow!** Your parents are adults. These are some of the stages in your life cycle.

Plants Grow from Seeds

The bean seeds in the picture are hard and dry. These seeds are in the resting stage, or are **dormant**. Seeds that are dormant will not begin to grow. Seeds can be dormant for a few days or a few weeks. Some seeds are dormant for years.

A dormant seed will begin to grow if it has water, oxygen, and the right temperature. The pictures on the next page show how a bean seed begins to sprout, or germinate. The first three pictures show stages of growth from a dormant seed to a sprouting seed. Find the new leaves and the root. The fourth picture on the page shows a young seedling—with leaves, stem, and roots.

◄ *These beans can grow into bean plants. Some black beans are eaten in foods, such as black bean soup.*

Life Cycle of the Bean Plant

1

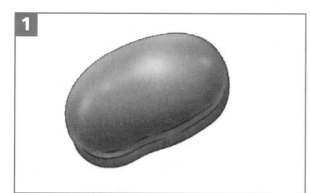

Dormant Seed

The dormant seed takes in water and the seed coat gets soft. If the seed has enough oxygen and the right temperature, it will begin to germinate.

2

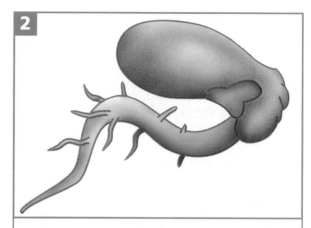

Germinating Seed

First a root pushes through the seed coat and grows downward.

3

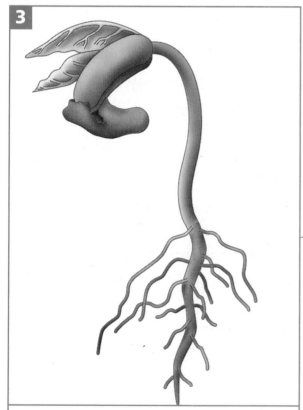

Germinating Seed

The top part of the root grows upward and becomes the stem. The stem carries the seed coat and the seed leaves with it. The seed coat falls off. The seed leaves provide food for the plant. Two small leaves begin to grow from between the seed leaves.

4   Seedling

When the stored food in the seed leaves is used up, they dry up and drop off. More leaves grow from buds on the stem as the plant grows taller. The new leaves can trap energy from sunlight and make sugar. Plants use the energy in the sugar to grow.

Mature Stage of a Plant Life Cycle

With time, young seedlings can grow into mature plants like the one in the picture. To become mature plants, the seedlings need water, air, and the right temperature. They also need sunlight for energy. Many plants also need to grow in soil.

When you eat green beans, you are eating the fruits of the bean plant. ▼

After a few weeks, the bean plant is full grown. Then the plant blooms. The flowers are pollinated and grow into bean pods, or fruits. Inside the bean pods, new bean seeds grow.

When the seeds are full grown, the fruits dry up. Farmers then remove the seeds from the dry fruits. These beans are dormant and will remain so until they have what they need to grow. The bean plant also dries up and dies. When the new bean seeds are planted, they will continue the life cycle of the bean plant.

Lesson 4 Review

1. How does a bean plant grow from a bean seed?
2. What do seedlings need to grow into mature plants?
3. **Main Idea**
   What is the main idea of the first paragraph on this page?

Experimenting with Seed Germination

Materials

- masking tape
- 3 resealable plastic bags
- marker
- measuring cup
- seed starter mix
- plastic spoon
- 3 plastic cups
- radish seeds
- water
- grid paper

Process Skills

- formulating questions and hypotheses
- identifying and controlling variables
- experimenting
- collecting and interpreting data
- communicating

State the Problem

How does the amount of water affect the germination of radish seeds?

Formulate Your Hypothesis

Will more radish seeds germinate when they are dry, moist, or very wet? Write your hypothesis.

Identify and Control the Variables

The amount of water is the variable you can change. You will set up three test bags. Place no water in bag 1, 50 mL of water in bag 2, and 150 mL of water in bag 3. Keep the temperature the same for each group of seeds.

Test Your Hypothesis

Follow these steps to perform an experiment.

❶ Make a chart like the one on the next page. Use your chart to record your data.

❷ Use a marker and masking tape to label the three plastic bags with the numbers 1, 2, and 3.

❸ Use the spoon to fill the measuring cup to 150 mL with seed starter mix. Do not pack the mix. Pour the mix into a plastic cup. Place five radish seeds in the cup and cover them with a thin layer of seed starter mix. Place the cup in bag 1 and seal it as shown.

Continued ➔

4 Repeat step 3, but this time add 50 mL of water to the cup before planting the seeds. Use the spoon to completely mix the water through the seed starter mix. Then plant the seeds. Place the cup in bag 2 and seal it.

5 Repeat step 3 once more, but this time add 150 mL of water to the cup before planting the seeds. Place the cup in bag 3 and seal it.

6 Place the bags in the same place in your classroom. Do not put the bags in direct sunlight.

7 Observe the bags each day for 10 days to see how many seeds have sprouted. **Collect** and **record** your data in your chart.

Collect Your Data

Day	Observations		
	Bag 1	Bag 2	Bag 3
1			
2			
3			
4			
5			
6			
7			
8			
9			
10			

Interpret Your Data

1. Label a piece of grid paper as shown. Use the data from Day 10 on your chart to make a bar graph on your grid paper.

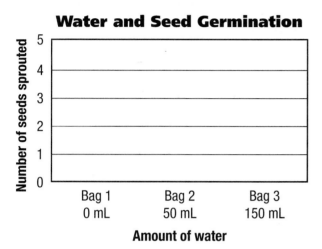

2. Study your graph. Describe how the amount of water affected the number of radish seeds that sprouted.

State Your Conclusion

How do your results compare with your hypothesis? **Communicate** your results. Explain how the amount of water affected the number of radish seeds that germinated. How would you change your experiment if you were going to repeat it?

Inquire Further

If you use a different kind of seed, will you get the same results? Make a plan to answer this or other questions you may have.

Self-Assessment

- I made a **hypothesis** about how many radish seeds would germinate with different amounts of water.
- I **identified** and **controlled** variables.
- I followed instructions to perform an **experiment** with radish seeds and different amounts of water.
- I **collected data** in a chart and **interpreted data** by making a graph.
- I **communicated** by stating my conclusion.

Chapter 1 Review

Chapter Main Ideas

Lesson 1

• Plants can be classified into two large groups—plants that make seeds and plants that do not make seeds.

• Flowering plants and conifers make seeds.

• Plants that do not make seeds reproduce by making spores. Ferns and mosses do not make seeds.

Lesson 2

• The four parts of a flower are the sepals, petals, pistil, and stamens. Each part has a role in helping the flower make seeds.

• Some flowers have fewer than four parts but can still make seeds.

Lesson 3

• Pollination occurs when pollen from a stamen is moved to a pistil. Sperm in the pollen combines with an egg during fertilization to form a seed.

• Fruits grow from the ovary of the pistil, and seeds form inside the fruit.

Lesson 4

• Seeds grow into plants when they have enough water, oxygen, and the right temperature.

• The full-grown plant that produces seeds is the mature stage of a flowering plant's life cycle.

Reviewing Words and Concepts

Write the letter of the word or phrase that best completes each sentence.

a. classify   i. ovule
b. conifer   j. pistil
c. dicot seed   k. pollen
d. dormant   l. pollination
e. embryo   m. reproduce
f. fertilization   n. sepal
g. monocot seed   o. spore
h. ovary   p. stamen

1. To _____ means to make more plants of the same kind.

2. Scientists _____ plants into two groups.

3. A _____ has one seed leaf.

4. A pine tree is a _____ because it makes seeds inside a cone.

5. A bean seed is a _____ because it has two seed leaves.

6. A _____ is a tiny cell that can grow into a new plant.

7. One of the leaflike parts that protect a flower bud is a _____.

8. A _____ is a part of a flower that makes pollen.

9. Seeds are made when sperm in tiny grains of _____ combine with a flower's eggs.

10. The part of the flower that makes eggs is the _____.

11. The movement of pollen from a stamen to a pistil is _____.

12. The _____ is the part of the pistil that grows when seeds form.

13. An _____ is the inner part of the ovary that contains eggs.

14. Combining sperm and an egg to make seeds is _____.

15. The part of a seed that can grow into a new plant is an _____.

16. A seed can be in a resting stage, or _____, for years.

Explaining Science

Draw a picture or write a paragraph to answer these questions.

1. How can plants be classified?

2. Describe what each of the four parts of a flower does.

3. What is a fruit and how does it form?

4. Draw and describe the stages of the life cycle of a bean plant.

Using Skills

1. What is the **main idea** of the last paragraph on page A26?

2. Write a paragraph to **communicate** what you know about how butterflies and bees pollinate flowers.

3. **Observe** the plants in your classroom, near your school, or in and around your home. **Collect data** about whether or not these plants produce flowers. **Interpret the data** by **classifying** the plants into two groups: flowering plants and nonflowering plants.

Critical Thinking

1. List the following in **sequence** starting from the word *flower* to *new plant*: germinate, fertilization, pollination, seeds, flower, new plant.

2. You plant some flower seeds. You observe that the seeds did not germinate. What would you **infer** may have caused the seeds not to germinate?

3. You have a plant that has one or more pistils, but no stamens. You have another plant with stamens and no pistils. **Draw a conclusion** about how your plant will make seeds. Write a paragraph to explain.

It's an Animal World!

Did you know that animals are found almost everywhere in the world? From the dry deserts to the humid rain forests to the frozen Antarctic, some kind of animal makes its home there!

Chapter 2

Animal Structure and Function

Inquiring about Animal Structure and Function

**Lesson 1
How Are Animals Alike and Different?**

In what ways are animals similar and different?

How do animals without backbones vary?

How do insects compare to other animals with jointed legs?

**Lesson 2
How Do Animals with Backbones Vary?**

What characteristics of fish and amphibians are the same?

How are the characteristics and life cycles of reptiles alike and different?

How are birds alike and different?

How are the characteristics and life cycles of mammals alike?

**Lesson 3
What Characteristics Do Animals Get from Their Parents?**

How are young animals similar to and different from their parents?

What behaviors do animals get from their parents?

What animal behaviors are learned?

Copy the chapter graphic organizer onto your own paper. This organizer shows you what the whole chapter is all about. As you read the lessons and do the activities, look for answers to the questions and write them on your organizer.

Exploring Animal Characteristics

Process Skills

- observing
- inferring
- communicating

Materials

- paper towel
- plastic cup with water
- dropper
- earthworm
- hand lens

Explore

1 Place a paper towel on your desk. Put several droppers of water on the paper towel so that it is damp.

2 Place the earthworm on the damp paper towel. Be sure to keep the worm and the towel moist throughout this activity.

3 Watch the earthworm as it moves on the paper. Record your **observations.**

4 Use a hand lens to observe the earthworm. Make a drawing to record your observations.

5 Gently feel along the back, or topside, of the earthworm. Do you think the earthworm has bones?

Reflect

1. From your observations, why can you **infer** that an earthworm is an animal? What inference can you make about whether an earthworm has bones?

2. Communicate. Discuss your ideas with the class. Make a list of reasons for your inferences.

? Inquire Further

How is an earthworm like other small animals? How is it different? Develop a plan to answer these or other questions you may have.

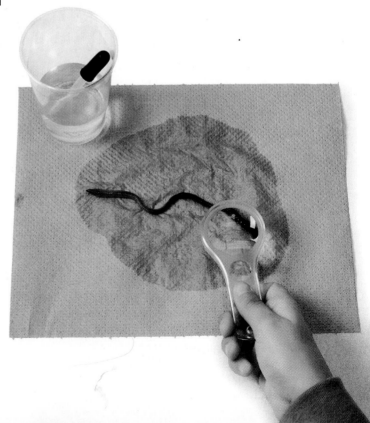

Making Bar Graphs

You can learn a lot from teeth! The number of teeth can help classify an animal.

Materials
- grid paper

Math Vocabulary

bar graph, a graph that uses bars to show data

Work Together

A **bar graph** can help you compare the number of teeth for different animals. Use the data in the table.

Animal	Teeth
Dog	42
Chimp	32
Hyena	34
Walrus	18

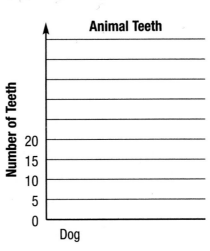

Animal Teeth

Number of Teeth

20
15
10
5
0

Dog

1. Copy and complete the bar graph. Use grid paper.
   a. Write a title across the top of your graph.
   b. Write a label on the left side of the graph. Write a label at the bottom for each bar.
   c. Complete the scale. Count by fives.
   d. Draw a bar for each animal. Use the scale to make each bar the correct height. Color the bars.

2. Which animal shown on the graph has the most teeth?

Problem Solving Hint

When you make a number scale for a bar graph, look at the greatest number in the data.

Talk About It!

1. How did you decide on the height for each bar?

2. Crocodiles have 100 teeth. If you wanted to add crocodiles to your bar graph, how would you change your graph?

You will learn:

- ways that animals are similar and different.
- how animals without backbones vary.
- how insects compare to other animals with jointed legs.

Lesson 1

How Are Animals Alike and Different?

Insects, snakes, birds, cats, fish! You have probably seen many of these animals. You also know that some of these animals have feathers, some have scales, and others have hair. But they are all animals!

How Animals Are Similar and Different

Look at the pictures of the different animals on these two pages. A snake, a spider, and a cat—they certainly don't look much alike! Why are they all called animals? You might be surprised to find out that all of these and other animals are alike in some ways.

Most animals are able to move from place to place on their own. Most animals also find their own food. The snake, the spider, and the cat are alike in yet another way. They all produce young—either by laying eggs or giving birth to live babies. So even though animals may look very different from one another, they are all alike in these ways.

Because a rattlesnake has a backbone, it can hold part of its body straight up. ▼

Groups of animals are also different. In fact, scientists group all animals into two large groups—animals without a backbone and animals with a backbone. What's a backbone? If you pet the back of a dog or cat, you can feel a number of small bones. These small bones are connected all the way down the middle of the animal's back. They make up the **backbone.** Find the backbone in the picture of the cat. A backbone helps support an animal's body.

Animals without backbones can be found in the water, on land, and in the air. They range in size from tiny mites to the giant squid, which is larger than some whales. Look at the pie chart. Notice how many of the animals in the world do not have backbones.

The snake and the cat are animals with backbones. Animals with backbones can be found in many places—oceans, rivers, forests, deserts, and mountains. The great variety of animals with backbones includes horses, birds, fish, and whales.

Glossary

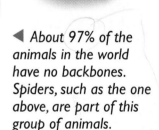

Animals with no backbones

Animals with backbones

◀ About 97% of the animals in the world have no backbones. Spiders, such as the one above, are part of this group of animals.

▲ The cat's backbone runs all the way along its back—from its head to its tail. Of course, you don't see the cat's backbone! It's inside the cat's body.

How Animals Without Backbones Vary

Animals without backbones make up most of the animals in the world. Thousands of different kinds of animals without backbones live almost everywhere. So when you think about it, you may not be surprised that many of these animals are more different from each other than alike. Find the differences among the animals in the pictures.

Jellyfish

Jellyfish are part of a large group of animals that includes the corals. Jellyfish vary greatly in size—from 12 millimeters to more than 2 meters across. They have no head and only one body opening—the mouth. Jellyfish have a soft body with no hard covering. Large, armlike tentacles with stinging cells protect them and help them get food. Poison from the stinging cells stuns or kills animals that brush against them. The tentacles then bring the food to the mouth. ▶

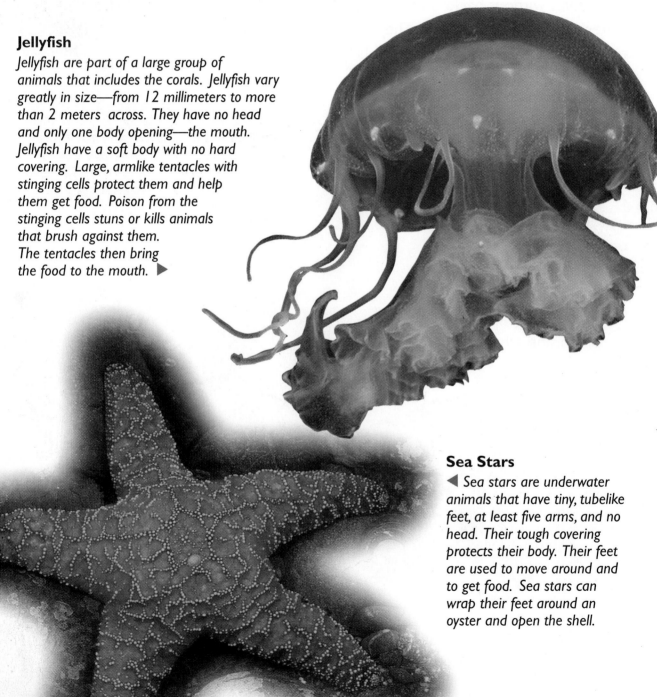

Sea Stars

◀ *Sea stars are underwater animals that have tiny, tubelike feet, at least five arms, and no head. Their tough covering protects their body. Their feet are used to move around and to get food. Sea stars can wrap their feet around an oyster and open the shell.*

Worms

Worms have soft, tube-shaped bodies and are found on land and in water. Some worms even live inside other animals. Worms are classified by their body shapes and structures—flatworms, roundworms, and segmented worms. ▶

Snails

◀ *Snails are covered by a single hard shell that protects their soft body. A snail can pull its body back into the shell. Then the snail can shut the hard trapdoor that covers the opening in the shell. A snail has a head and one large, strong foot. Its mouth is in its foot! Can you imagine eating with your feet?*

Sponges

Unlike most other animals, sponges stay fixed in one place—attached to a rock or other hard surface. Sponges vary in size from microscopic to more than 2 meters across. The body of a sponge is full of holes. As water flows into the holes, it carries in food and the food then becomes trapped in the sponge. A sponge the size of a hot dog can filter about 115 liters of water daily! Many sponges smell or taste so bad that other animals won't eat them. ▶

Insects and Other Animals with Jointed Legs

You have probably seen an army of ants, such as the ones in the picture, marching along a sidewalk. Ants are one of the nearly one million kinds of animals known as insects. In fact, insects form the largest group of animals in the world.

Insects, such as butterflies, bees, flies, and beetles, can be very different from one another. However, all insects have three body parts—a head, a thorax, and an abdomen. Insects also have three pairs of jointed legs and an **exoskeleton,** or hard outer covering. The exoskeleton does not grow. For an insect to grow, it must **molt,** or shed its outer covering. Once insects are full grown, they do not molt.

Insects are the only animals without backbones that can fly. Some insects have two pairs of wings; others have only one pair. Still other insects have no wings.

Like insects, spiders have jointed legs. However, spiders have only two body parts. Also, they have four pairs of legs—one more pair than insects. Look at the pictures on the next page, and read to find out about other animals with jointed legs.

Ants are social insects and belong to the same group of insects that bees and wasps do. ▼

Lobsters

Lobsters are animals that have jointed legs and only two body parts. They have two pairs of antenna and a tail shaped like a fan. The female lobster lays thousands of eggs about once every two years. Lobsters grow by molting. They live their entire life in water. They eat mostly dead animals and waste matter. ▶

Scorpions

▲ Scorpions are related to spiders, but they have flat, narrow bodies with eight legs. Like lobsters, they have two claws. The tail of the scorpion is long and segmented. At the end of the tail, the scorpion has a poisonous stinger. Scorpions eat mostly spiders and insects. Their young are born alive.

Spider Crabs

Spider crabs have long, thin legs similar to those of spiders. Both spiders and spider crabs have fangs—long, pointed structures for capturing food. The young of both spiders and spider crabs hatch from eggs. Spiders live mostly on dry land, but spider crabs live in water. ▼

Lesson 1 Review

1. What is one difference among animals that is used to classify them into two large groups?

2. What are two ways in which animals without backbones differ from one another?

3. How are insects and spiders different?

4. **Main Idea**
   What is the main idea of the second paragraph on page A42?

Classifying Animals Without Backbones

Process Skills

Process Skills

- observing
- classifying
- communicating

Materials

- animal photographs
- paper
- pencil

Getting Ready

In this activity you will observe characteristics to classify some animals without backbones.

Follow This Procedure

❶ Make a chart like the one shown. Use your chart to record your classification.

Characteristics

Number of legs	Number of body parts	Other features	Names of animals
6	3	Jointed legs, may have wings	
8	2	Jointed legs, no claws	
8 (not including claws)	2	Jointed legs, claws	

❷ Look at the characteristics listed in your chart.

❸ Carefully **observe** the pictures of the animals shown on the next page. Compare the characteristics of each animal pictured to the characteristics in the chart.

❹ **Classify** each animal in the pictures by writing its name in the last column of your chart following the characteristics that it matches.

Self-Monitoring

Have I carefully observed and compared each animal picture to the characteristics in my chart?

Interpret Your Results

1. Communicate. Compare your finished chart with your classmates' charts. Discuss any differences.

2. Explain why you classified each animal as you did.

Spider

Crayfish

Honeybee

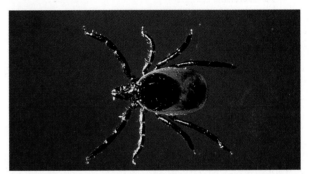

Deer tick

Lobster

Butterfly

 ## Inquire Further

Observe other kinds of animals without backbones or find pictures of animals without backbones. How can you classify these animals? Develop a plan to answer this or other questions you may have.

What's the Big Idea?

You will learn:

- what characteristics of fish and amphibians are the same.

- how the characteristics and life cycles of reptiles are alike and different.

- how birds are alike and different.

- how the characteristics and life cycles of mammals are alike.

Goldfish belong to the minnow family, also known as carp. ▼

Lesson 2

How Do Animals with Backbones Vary?

How is a frog like a goldfish and an elephant? You will probably answer, **"In no way!"** But a frog, a goldfish, and an elephant are alike in one way. They all have a backbone.

Fish and Amphibians

Fish are the largest group of animals with backbones. The goldfish in the picture is just one of more than 30,000 kinds of fish known. All fish live in water. They can be found in every water habitat on the earth. The killifish lives in the world's highest large lake—Lake Titicaca in South America. Fish are even found in the deepest trenches in the ocean. Many fish live in the warm waters of lakes and rivers all over the world. Others live in the icy waters of mountain lakes and even in the Antarctic!

The body temperature of fish is about the same as the temperature of the water they live in. If the temperature of the water changes, the fish's body temperature changes. Animals whose body temperature changes with the temperature of the water or air around them are called cold-blooded animals.

Most fish have fins that help keep them upright in the water. Fins also help fish steer their way through the water. Most fish are covered with a layer of scales that help protect their bodies. Scales are bony plates in overlapping rows. The scales grow as the fish grows. Some kinds of fish, such as the eel, have only tiny scales. Other fish, such as the catfish, have almost no scales.

Fish breathe through **gills**, or feathery structures on the sides of their heads. As water flows over the gills, the fish take in oxygen from the water. The gills also give off carbon dioxide into the water.

Another large group of animals with backbones is formed by **amphibians.** The salamander in the picture belongs to this group of animals. Frogs and toads are also among the over four thousand kinds of amphibians.

Amphibians usually live in water after hatching from an egg, but the adults can live on land. However, amphibians usually live in wet places. Like fish, an amphibian's body temperature changes with the temperature of its environment.

The frog in the picture, like other amphibians, begins its life in the water. Young frogs, or tadpoles, have gills and breathe like fish. Tadpoles use their tails to help them swim. As the young amphibians get older, they grow legs and lose their gills. Adult frogs get air through their skin but also breathe air through their lungs. Frogs lose their tails as they grow, but salamanders do not. Some amphibians, such as mud puppies, live most of their life underwater.

Glossary

gills, organs for breathing found in fish and amphibians

amphibian
(am fib/ē ən), one of a large group of animals with backbones that live part of their lives in water and part on land

Most salamanders are long and thin and have four legs. They look somewhat like a lizard. ▼

If you ever tried to catch a frog, you probably know that frogs can see in almost any direction. ▼

Glossary

reptile (rep'tĭl), an animal with a backbone that has a dry, scaly skin

Reptiles

Snakes, such as the one in the picture, are one kind of reptile. You may have seen other reptiles, such as turtles and lizards. A **reptile** is an animal with a backbone and a dry, scaly skin. Reptiles live in many places. They are found in hot, dry deserts; in warm, wet, tropical rain forests; and in many other environments. Reptiles are cold-blooded. Some warm their bodies by lying in the sun.

The alligator in the picture is still another kind of reptile. Alligators, like most other reptiles, lay their eggs on land. Their eggs have a leathery shell. An alligator lays between 20 to 50 eggs, covers them with mud, and then stands guard while the sun keeps the eggs warm. In about 60 days the eggs hatch. The female cares for the young for about a year—sometimes carrying them in her mouth. Alligators, like most reptiles, breathe air their entire life. Look at the pictures on the next page, and read to find out about the life cycles of two other reptiles.

▲ You might be surprised to see a snake hanging from a tree limb!

Alligators eat almost anything, but they mainly feed on fish, turtles, and snails. ▼

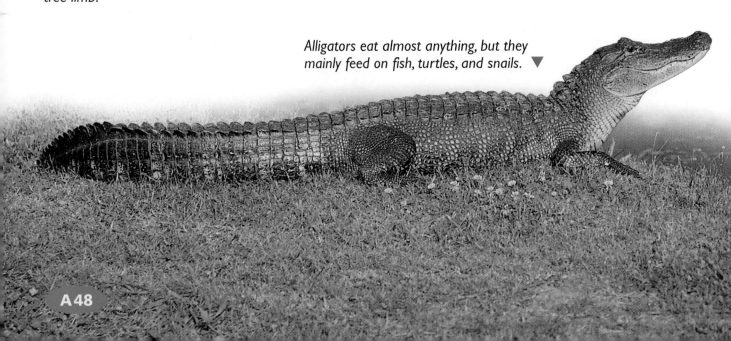

A 48

Sea Turtles

The sea turtle shown here, like other turtles, comes out of the water to lay its eggs. A female sea turtle digs a hole in the sand with her hind feet and lays the eggs into it. She then covers the eggs with sand, packs down the sand, and returns to the sea. A female turtle cares for neither her eggs nor the young. A sea turtle may lay more than 150 eggs at a time. ▶

▲ When the young sea turtles hatch, they find their way to the ocean at once. Most turtles become adults in about 6 to 15 years. Some kinds of turtles have been known to live more than 50 years.

▲ Turtle eggs hatch in about 45 to 78 days, depending on the kind of turtle.

Garter Snakes

The garter snake is one reptile that does not lay eggs. The eggs of a garter snake are hatched inside the body of the female snake. In late summer, a female garter snake gives birth to live baby snakes. The number of babies may vary from 12 to 70 at one time. Luckily for the female snake, young snakes do not have to be fed! They can find their own food. ▶

A 49

Birds

Have you seen birds like the ones in the pictures? What other kinds of birds have you seen? Although the birds you saw may have been of different sizes and colors, all birds are alike in some ways.

All birds are animals with backbones, but they are different from other animals with backbones. Unlike fish, amphibians, and reptiles, birds have the same body temperature all the time. Their body temperature does not change with the temperature of the air around them. Birds are warm-blooded. Birds also have feathers that cover their bodies. They have a pair of wings and a pair of legs.

As you probably know, birds vary greatly in size. The smallest bird, a kind of hummingbird, is about the size of your finger. On the other hand, an ostrich can be taller than an adult human. The ostrich is one bird that cannot fly, but it can run very fast. The penguins in the picture are another kind of bird that cannot fly.

All birds hatch from eggs. Most birds lay from two to six eggs at one time. Birds build nests to lay their eggs in. The nests are made from many kinds of materials—twigs, string, leaves, feathers, mud, and many other things. Some birds make their nests in holes in wood or dead trees. Unlike turtles, birds care for their eggs until they hatch. One or both parents may sit on the eggs to keep them warm.

Unlike the ostrich and penguin, most birds can fly. A bird's entire body is well adapted for flying. Its wings, large breastbone, wishbone, and large chest muscles all make flying possible. The pictures on the next page show other adaptations that help birds.

▲ *A cardinal is a North American songbird that belongs to the finch family.*

Penguins are sea birds that live mostly in Antarctica and other cold places in the Southern Hemisphere. ▼

Wings

▲ The owl's wing is somewhat like your arm. It has the same three parts—the hand, the lower arm, and the upper arm. The owl can bend its upper arm the way you can bend your upper arm. The owl flaps its large wings to lift itself into the air.

Hollow Bones

▲ Your bones are much heavier than those of a bird. Unlike your bones, a bird's bones are hollow, like the one shown. Its skeleton is very lightweight. Some bird bones have spaces filled with air throughout the bone. A bird's lightweight skeleton helps make the bird able to fly.

Feathers

▲ Birds have two kinds of feathers. The feathers near the body are small and fluffy. These small feathers, called down, trap heat. During cold weather, a bird can fluff up the down feathers to keep warm. These feathers help the bird maintain its body temperature. A bird's large, stiff feathers, especially those on the wings, help a bird fly.

Glossary

mammal (mam′əl), an animal with a backbone that usually has hair on its body and feeds milk to its young

Mammals

If you have a cat or a dog for a pet, you have a mammal. Other mammals that you might know include horses, cows, and rabbits, as well as many other such animals. A **mammal** is an animal with a backbone that usually has hair and feeds milk to its young. Most mammals have furry coats that trap a layer of air near the body. This helps the animals stay warm. However, some mammals have very little hair. Elephants, like the dolphins in the picture, are mammals with little hair.

Mammals live in many different places. Dolphins and whales are mammals that live in the water. Even though they spend their whole life in the water, these animals have lungs and breathe air. Most mammals, such as bats, mountain lions, bison, and caribou, live on land. Bats are the only mammals that can fly.

Can you imagine an animal that weighs more than twenty elephants? It's the blue whale—the largest living mammal! It's probably a good thing that the blue whale lives in the water. What kind of feet could carry all that weight? The smallest mammal is a shrew. The body of this tiniest mammal is smaller than your finger. However, it has a tail that makes it seem longer.

The young of most mammals are born alive. However, two kinds of mammals, the duck-billed platypus and the spiny anteater, lay eggs. The babies that hatch are fed milk from their mothers—just like other mammals. The pictures on the next page show the life cycle of a mammal that is born alive.

Dolphins breathe air through a blowhole at the top of the head. They can stay underwater for long periods of time, but they must come to the surface to breathe. ▶

Adult

Gerbils are similar to other rodents, such as rats and mice. The body of an adult gerbil measures about 10–15 centimeters. Gerbils are found in the wild in deserts or desertlike places in Africa and Asia. They are kept as pets in the United States. ▶

Baby

▲ Like other mammals, young gerbils are born alive. The female gerbil may have from 1 to 12 babies—usually 4 to 7—at one time. The tiny, hairless babies are pink in color. They first open their eyes after about 2 or 3 weeks.

Young

After about 3 weeks, mother gerbils no longer nurse their young. The young then begin to eat green plants, seeds, roots, bulbs, cereals, fruits, and insects. Young gerbils take about 7–12 weeks to become adults. ▼

Lesson 2 Review

1. What characteristics do fish and amphibians both have?

2. How does the life cycle of a turtle differ from the life cycle of a garter snake?

3. What characteristics do all birds have?

4. How are mammals alike?

5. **Bar Graphs**
   Make a bar graph comparing the number of legs that each of these animals has: bird, 2; spider, 8; insect, 6; dog, 4.

What's the Big Idea?

You will learn:

- how young animals are similar to and different from their parents.
- what behaviors animals get from their parents.
- what animal behaviors are learned.

Lesson 3

What Characteristics Do Animals Get from Their Parents?

What if you saw a dog followed by a group of kittens? Or saw a robin feeding worms to a duckling? You would probably laugh and say, " Wow! Something's wrong here!" Why doesn't this happen?

Young Animals and Their Parents

You know that baby animals look somewhat like their parents. Cats give birth to kittens and lions give birth to lion cubs. Also, if you find a robin's nest with eggs in it, you know that baby robins will hatch from the eggs.

Have you ever seen a family of guinea pigs? If so, you know that all the babies do not look alike. Some of the babies, such as the one in the picture, may be different colors—white, black, or tan. Others may be white with streaks or patches of darker colors. Some guinea pigs may have long hair. Others may have short hair. Another difference may be smooth or rough hair.

The other baby guinea pigs in this family may look different from this baby. ▼

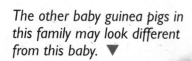

However, all the babies look somewhat like each of their parents. Notice that the baby guinea pig on page A54 has some of the characteristics of its parent.

Now look at the picture of the ground squirrels below. What do you notice? That's right! All the baby squirrels look the same and they all look like their parents. The babies of most other wild animals, such as rabbits and deer, also look the same as their parents.

Baby ground squirrels look like tiny adult squirrels. ▼

Glossary

behavior (bi hā′vyər), the way a living thing acts

instinct (in′stingkt), a behavior that an animal is born with and does not need to learn

Behaviors from Parents

What are some things you have done today? You got up, dressed yourself, and came to school. In school, you read, write, and speak. You might play a musical instrument or play basketball. Each of these things you do is a behavior. The way a living thing acts is its **behavior.** Dogs, cats, and other animals have behaviors. Dogs bark, cats meow, and birds build nests. Some behaviors are learned. Others are inborn— behaviors that animals have without being taught. Some inborn behaviors are **instincts.** Which of the animal behaviors shown in the pictures have you seen?

Instincts

◀ The squirrel in the picture gathers nuts and other food and stores it away for winter. For a squirrel, this behavior is an instinct. Remember the baby sea turtles. When they hatched, they found their way to the ocean. Their parents were not there to teach them where to go. Crawling to the ocean is an instinct for baby sea turtles.

The fox kits do not have to learn to play. Pawing and pouncing on one another are instincts. However, as the kits grow, they will learn to use these behaviors to hunt and capture food. ▼

The caterpillar does not have to learn how to spin a cocoon. It can spin a cocoon by instinct. Some hairy caterpillars line the cocoon with hairs from their body. Different kinds of caterpillars spin different kinds of cocoons. Amazing! ▶

Glossary

reflex (rē′fleks), a simple, automatic behavior

stimulus (stim′yə ləs), the cause of a behavior

response (ri spons′), a behavior caused by a stimulus

Reflexes

◀ *The dog is wagging its tail as the child pets it. Wagging its tail is another example of an inborn behavior called a reflex. A* **reflex** *is a simple, automatic behavior that an animal does not have to think about. A reflex is controlled by nerves. A* **stimulus** *brings about a reflex. The child petting the dog is a stimulus. How the dog acts—wagging its tail—is a* **response** *to the stimulus. However, it is a learned response.*

Reflexes also help keep animals safe. You may have seen animals move away quickly when you got too close. When animals hear a noise, they also move away quickly. These behaviors help animals protect themselves from enemies.

Learned Behaviors

When you were a baby, you did not behave in the same way that you do now. As a baby, you could not talk. You cried when you were hungry. Then you learned how to talk and you could ask for food. When did you learn to read or ride a bicycle? What other behaviors have you learned?

Sometimes a learned behavior is a response to a stimulus. If you hold up food for your dog and say "speak," your dog may bark. Then you give the dog the food. In this way the dog may learn to bark when you hold up food and say "speak." After much practice, the dog may bark without your saying anything. The dog has learned the response of barking to the stimulus of food.

Certain kinds of dogs may even be taught to help people who are blind. Dogs, such as the one in the picture, can learn to help people cross streets. The dog will stop at a street corner and wait for the traffic light to change. They can also be taught to lead the person around a hole in the street or other danger.

Guide dogs help people who are blind to walk safely along streets. ▼

Young animals learn many behaviors by watching their mothers or other animals. The otter in the picture learned how to use a rock to break open a shell. Many animals learn how to hunt for food. They also learn behaviors such as hiding to keep safe.

▲ Sea otters learn how to open shells by watching other animals.

Lesson 3 Review

1. How may baby guinea pigs differ from their parents?

2. What is an instinct?

3. How do animals learn behaviors?

4. **Main Idea**
   What is the main idea of the paragraph above?

Observing How Animals Respond to Stimuli

Process Skills

- predicting
- observing
- communicating
- inferring

Materials

- earthworm
- paper towel
- water
- dropper
- cotton swab
- plastic cup of moist soil

Getting Ready

In this activity you can find out how earthworms respond to some stimuli. Remember that earthworms are living organisms and need to be handled carefully.

Follow This Procedure

1 Make a chart like the one shown. Use your chart to record your predictions and observations.

Stimulus	Predicted response	Response
Vibration from slap on desk		
Touched while on paper towel		
Touched while on soil		

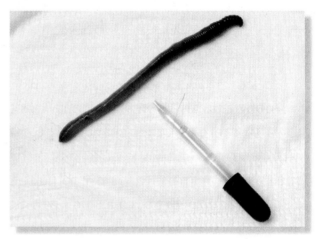

Photo A

2 Put a few drops of water on the paper towel so that it is damp. Place the earthworm on the moist paper towel (Photo A). Be sure to keep the worm and towel moist throughout this activity.

3 How will an earthworm respond to a vibration? Record and explain your **prediction.**

4 Slap your desktop near the worm. **Observe** the worm's response. Record your observation.

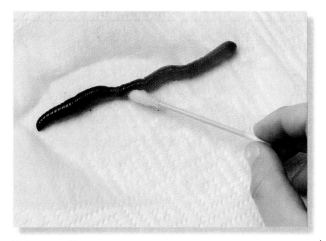

Photo B

Photo C

5 How will an earthworm respond to being touched? Record and explain your prediction.

6 Gently touch a cotton swab to the front, middle, and tail end of the earthworm (Photo B). Observe the worm. Record your observations.

7 How will an earthworm respond if it is touched while on top of soil? Record and explain your prediction.

8 Place the earthworm on top of a cup of soil. Touch it gently with the cotton swab (Photo C). Record the worm's response.

Interpret Your Results

1. How did your predictions compare with your observations?

2. Communicate. Describe the response of the earthworm to each of the stimuli used.

3. Make an inference. How do you think the earthworm's responses might protect it from danger?

 **Inquire Further**

How will an earthworm respond to other kinds of stimuli, such as light and dark? Develop a plan to answer this or other questions you may have.

Self-Assessment

- I followed instructions to **predict** and **observe** the responses of an earthworm to stimuli.
- I recorded my predictions and observations.
- I compared my predictions with my observations.
- I **communicated** by describing the responses of the earthworm to the stimuli.
- I made an **inference** about how the earthworm's responses protect it from danger.

Chapter 2 Review

Chapter Main Ideas

Lesson 1
• Scientists group animals into two large groups—animals without backbones and animals with backbones.
• Animals without backbones have many different sizes, shapes, and body parts.
• Insects and other animals with jointed legs have different numbers of legs and body parts.

Lesson 2
• Fish and amphibians are animals that have backbones and spend all or part of their lives in water.
• Reptiles are animals with backbones that have dry, scaly skin and reproduce by laying eggs or giving birth to live young.
• Birds are warm-blooded animals that have backbones and feathers covering their bodies.
• Mammals are animals with backbones that have hair and feed milk to their young. Most mammals give birth to live young and care for their young.

Lesson 3
• Baby animals inherit certain traits from their parents but can differ in color, kind of hair, and other characteristics.
• Instincts are inborn behaviors that animals get from their parents.
• Some behaviors that animals learn are responses to stimuli, hunting, and hiding to keep safe.

Reviewing Science Words and Concepts

Write the letter of the word or phrase that best completes each sentence.

a. amphibian   g. mammal

b. backbone   h. molt

c. behavior   i. reflex

d. exoskeleton   j. reptile

e. gills   k. response

f. instinct   l. stimulus

1. Bones that connect down the middle of your back make up your ____.

2. An ____ is the hard outer covering that supports the body of an insect.

3. A ____, such as petting a dog, is something that causes a behavior.

4. An inborn behavior, such as spinning a cocoon, is called an ____.

5. The way a living thing acts is called a ____.

6. An animal with dry, scaly skin, such as a lizard, is a ____.

7. A ____ is a behavior caused by a stimulus.

8. A ____ has a backbone, has hair, and feeds milk to its young.

9. An ____ lives part of its life in water and part on land.

10. Fish and amphibians have ___ that help them breathe.

11. A simple, automatic behavior is called a ___.

12. To ___ is to shed an outer covering.

Explaining Science

Write a sentence or paragraph to answer these questions.

1. What is the main difference between an earthworm and a snake?

2. Some animals, such as fish, are cold-blooded. Explain what is meant by cold-blooded.

3. What is an instinct? Describe one instinct of a caterpillar.

Using Skills

1. Use the following information to **make a bar graph** comparing the number of eggs that some animals lay.

The average number of eggs laid by these animals is: turtle, 50; frog, 60; python, 25; salamander, 15.

2. You discover some animals that you have never seen before. You **observe** that the young animals have gills and live in water, but the adult animals live on land. What might you **infer** from your observations?

3. A friend is watching television and sees a dolphin jumping through a hoop. **Communicate** to your friend what type of behavior he or she is observing.

Critical Thinking

1. You and your classmates visit a zoo. You see a monkey feeding milk to its young. Your classmates wonder if the monkey is a mammal. Apply what you know about mammals to **make a decision** about whether the monkey is a mammal. Explain your answer.

2. **Classify** the following animals as amphibians, mammals, or reptiles: frog, lizard, whale, salamander, alligator, elephant, snake, bat.

3. **Draw a conclusion** about how crying is both an instinct and a learned behavior in people.

It's Really Dry Here!

Do you ever wonder how plants and animals can live in a desert? Where do plants and animals get the water they need to survive?

Chapter 3
Energy in Ecosystems

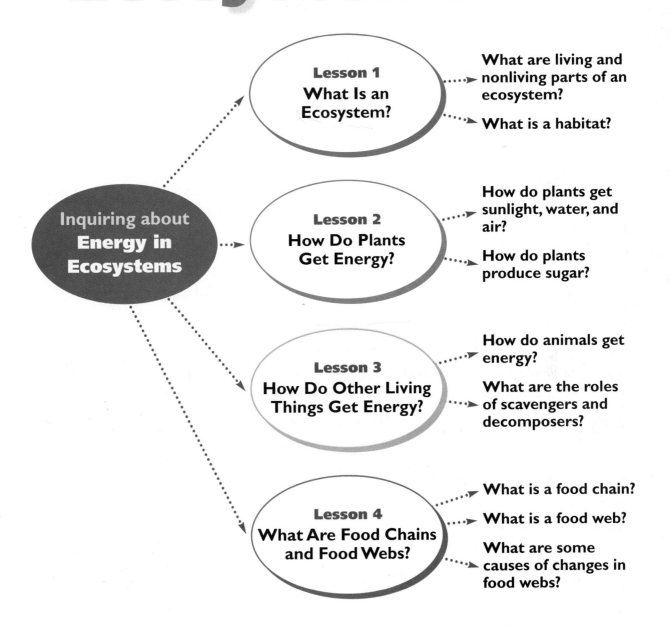

Inquiring about Energy in Ecosystems

Lesson 1
What Is an Ecosystem?

What are living and nonliving parts of an ecosystem?

What is a habitat?

Lesson 2
How Do Plants Get Energy?

How do plants get sunlight, water, and air?

How do plants produce sugar?

Lesson 3
How Do Other Living Things Get Energy?

How do animals get energy?

What are the roles of scavengers and decomposers?

Lesson 4
What Are Food Chains and Food Webs?

What is a food chain?

What is a food web?

What are some causes of changes in food webs?

Copy the chapter graphic organizer onto your own paper. This organizer shows you what the whole chapter is all about. As you read the lessons and do the activities, look for answers to the questions and write them on your organizer.

Making a Woodland Habitat Model

Process Skills

Process Skills

- making and using models
- observing

Materials

- 2 plastic bottles with tops removed
- gravel or pebbles
- metric ruler
- potting soil
- large spoon
- small houseplant
- rocks
- wood chips
- plastic cup of water
- scissors
- masking tape

Explore

① Spread 2 cm of gravel in the bottom of one of the bottles. Use a spoon to add 6-8 cm of potting soil on top of the gravel.

② Gently place the plant in the bottle. Cover the roots with soil. Arrange some rocks and wood chips on the soil. Sprinkle about half a cupful of water on the soil.

③ Cut a slit in the open end of the second bottle. Place it over the first bottle and tape them together as shown. You have made a **model** of a woodland habitat. Keep your model out of direct sunlight. **Observe** the model for two weeks to see how it changes.

Reflect

1. Describe any changes you saw in your model over two weeks.

2. Did you need to add water to your woodland model? Explain why or why not.

3. Compare and contrast your woodland model with a real forest.

? Inquire Further

What items could you use to make a desert habitat model? Develop a plan to answer this or other questions you may have.

Using Context Clues

Have you ever come across a new word while you were reading and wondered what it meant? If you see a word in dark print, you often will find the definition of that word in the same sentence. You will also find clues about the word you don't know in the words or sentences before or after the unfamiliar word. You can often tell the meaning of the word from its **context**.

Reading Vocabulary

context (kon′tekst), the parts directly before or after a word or sentence that influence its meaning

Example

In Lesson 1, *What Is an Ecosystem?*, there are two words that you may not know. Make a chart like the one below to help you understand what these words mean. When you get to these words, carefully read the sentence in which they appear. Write down the definition. Then read the words and sentences before and after the word for context clues that might give you more information. The first word, *ecosystem*, is done for you.

New Words	Definition	Clues
ecosystem	all the living and nonliving things in an environment and how they interact	backyard is a home to plants and animals, large as a forest, small as a drop of water
habitat		

In Lesson 2, *How Do Plants Get Energy?*, make a chart like the one above for these four words — *chlorophyll, carbon dioxide, photosynthesis, producer.* Fill in the chart as you read Lesson 2.

Talk About It!

1. What is the definition of an ecosystem?

2. Name an ecosystem near where you live.

What Is an Ecosystem?

Chirp! Chirp! You look up into a tree and see a bird building a nest. You look behind the tree and see a squirrel eating an acorn. Down on the soil, you see a worm. These organisms are living together in an ecosystem.

What's the Big Idea?

You will learn:

- what living and nonliving parts make up an ecosystem.
- what a habitat is.

Glossary

ecosystem
(ē′kō sis′təm), all the living and nonliving things in an environment and how they interact

Squirrels depend on trees for shelter. ▼

Living and Nonliving Parts of an Ecosystem

Do you know that even a tiny backyard is an ecosystem? Whether a backyard is large or small, many plants and animals make their homes there. An **ecosystem** is all the living and nonliving things in an environment and how they interact. Ecosystems can be as large as a forest or as small as a drop of water.

Animals and plants are living parts of an ecosystem. The plants and animals interact in many ways. Plants, such as trees, provide shelter for birds, squirrels, and other living things. The activities of squirrels and birds, such as those in the pictures, help spread the seeds of plants. Nonliving things, such as the wind, also help spread seeds.

Blue jays build their nests in trees. ▶

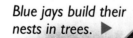

▲ *An ecosystem contains both living and nonliving things.*

Rocks, soil, water, and sunlight are examples of nonliving parts of an ecosystem. Notice the children planting flowers in the picture. These flowers will depend on the soil, water, and sunlight to grow. Have you ever planted flowers? Did you find insects and worms in the soil? As the insects and worms move through the soil, they make tunnels. The tunnels help air and water get into the soil.

Do you know that you are also a part of the ecosystem where you live? The air you breathe and the water you drink are parts of your ecosystem. Plants and animals in your ecosystem provide food for you. What you do also affects the plants and animals that live in your ecosystem. What do you think you might do to help plants and animals where you live?

Habitats

All plants and animals live in a **habitat.** For example, a whale's habitat is an ocean. Habitats provide food, water, and shelter that animals need for survival. The ocean provides for all of the needs of a whale. Look at the woodland habitat in the picture. How do you think this habitat meets the needs of the plants and animals that live there?

Glossary

habitat (hab′ə tat), a place where an animal or a plant lives

Red squirrels depend on trees for nuts, seeds, and buds. Using twigs and leaves, squirrels build nests high up in trees where their young will be safe.

Foxes make homes underground. During the day, they come out to search for food.

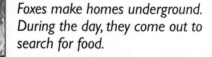

Hummingbirds build tiny nests held together with spiderwebs! They gather nectar from flowers and also eat insects and spiders.

Grass and soil are home to many tiny animals, such as grasshoppers, spiders, and earthworms. Grasshoppers eat grasses, and earthworms eat dead plants and animals.

Lesson 1 Review

1. What makes up an ecosystem?

2. How are habitats important?

3. **Context Clues**
   Use context clues from the paragraph on page A70 to write a definition for *habitat*.

Investigating a Habitat

Process Skills

- estimating and measuring
- classifying
- observing
- communicating

Materials

- plot area in schoolyard
- 3 pieces of string
- thermometer
- hand lens
- 4 sheets of paper
- 4 plastic bags
- masking tape

Getting Ready

In this activity you can discover what makes up a habitat.

Be sure to leave enough space in your chart for recording all descriptions.

Follow This Procedure

❶ Make a chart like the one shown. Use the chart to record your observations.

Square	Plant life	Animal life	Other observations
A			
B			
C			
D			

Temperature at plot surface_____

Photo A

❷ Go to your assigned plot area. Tie the two ends of the long string together. Lay the string on the ground in the shape of a square. Then cross the other two pieces of string within the square so you have four equal squares (Photo A). Decide which squares will be assigned the letters A, B, C, and D.

❸ Place the thermometer on the surface of the ground in square A. After three minutes, **measure** and record the temperature.

Photo B

④ Have each member of your group choose a square in the plot. Use the hand lens to examine your square for living things. **Classify** organisms as plant or animal and record their descriptions. Record other **observations,** such as signs of living things, the amount of light and moisture, rocks, or litter (Photo B).

⑤ On a sheet of paper, draw the organisms as they appear in your square. Have the members of your group do the same for their squares. Make sure your group's papers are all turned in the same direction as you draw. Write the letter of your square in the lower left corner of your paper.

⑥ In the plastic bags, collect items such as feathers and leaves from the squares. Use masking tape to label each bag with the letter of the square and the date. If you are unsure about taking something, ask your teacher. Wash your hands after this activity.

Interpret Your Results

1. Put the drawings of the four squares together and study them. Look at any items you may have collected from the plot. What are the most common living things or signs of living things you could see in your plot?

2. Describe some possible sources of food and water for the organisms in your plot.

3. Communicate. Compare and contrast your observations with those of other groups.

Inquire Further

How can changes in weather or seasons change your plot? Develop a plan to answer this or other questions you may have.

Self-Assessment

- I followed instructions to study a habitat plot.
- I **measured** and recorded the temperature in my plot.
- I **classified** the organisms I found in my square.
- I recorded my **observations** and drew a picture of my square.
- I **communicated** by comparing and contrasting my observations with those of other groups.

You will learn:

- how plants get sunlight, water, and air.
- how plants produce sugar.

Lesson 2

How Do Plants Get Energy?

When you get hungry and you hear your stomach growl, you know it is time to get some food. You know that food has energy that your body needs. Do you know that plants need energy too?

Glossary

chlorophyll (klôr′ə fil), the green substance found in plants that traps energy from the sun and gives plants their green color

Getting Sunlight, Water, and Air

Plants get the energy they need from the sun. Plant leaves change light energy into energy the plant can use.

Notice the long green cells in the leaf in the picture. These cells and other plant cells contain **chlorophyll**. Chlorophyll is a green substance in plants that traps light energy from the sun. Chlorophyll also gives plants their green color.

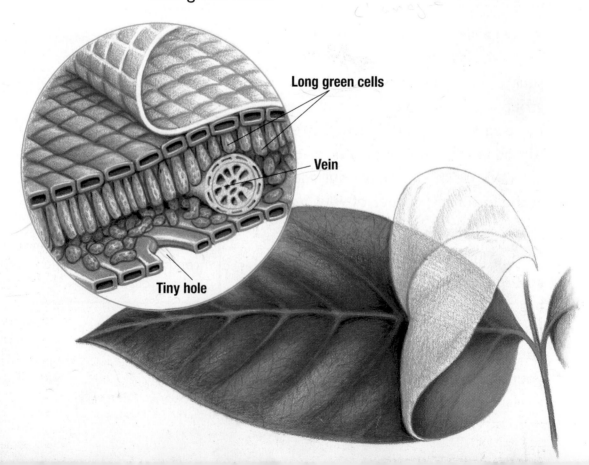

Long green cells

Vein

Tiny hole

Plants need water and air to change light energy into food energy. Look again at the leaf on page A74. Find the cells that form a circle. These cells form a pipe called a vein that runs through the leaf. The veins of a leaf bring water and minerals to the leaf from the stems and roots. Roots get water and minerals directly from the soil.

Now find the air space in the leaf. Plants use a gas, called **carbon dioxide,** from the air. Tiny holes on the bottom of the leaf let air in and out.

How Plants Produce Sugar

Plants use light energy from the sun, carbon dioxide, and water to make sugar. Plants produce sugar during a process called **photosynthesis.** As the plant makes sugar, oxygen is released. When the plant uses the sugar, water and carbon dioxide are given off. Plants get rid of these wastes through holes in their leaves.

Glossary

carbon dioxide
(kär′bən dī ok′sīd), a gas found in air

photosynthesis
(fō′tō sin′thə sis), a process by which plants change light energy from the sun and use it to make sugar

Orange trees, like other plants, use the sun, carbon dioxide, and water to make sugar. ▼

Glossary

producer (prə dü′sər), a living thing that uses sunlight to make sugar

Plants are different from most other living things. As you know, plants can use light energy to make sugar. Because plants can make sugar, they are **producers**. Plants can use the sugar along with minerals from the soil to make plant parts such as leaves, stems, and roots. Some of the sugar is stored in the plants' parts, such as the oranges in the picture on page A75. Some sugar is changed to starch and then stored—mostly in roots.

Look at the foods below. They are all parts of plants. Each one has stored energy.

Foods that are parts of plants ▼

Lesson 2 Review

1. What is the main source of energy for plants?

2. What do plants need to make sugar?

3. **Context Clues**
   Using the context clues in the first paragraph on this page, what would you add to the definition given for *producer* in the glossary?

How Do Other Living Things Get Energy?

Have you ever been to a zoo? Did you see the elephants eat with their trunks? Maybe you saw the ducks dive into the water for food. Animals need energy to survive.

You will learn:

- how animals get energy.
- the roles of scavengers and decomposers.

How Animals Get Energy

All living things need energy to survive. Plants get the energy they need from trapping light. Animals are different from plants because animals cannot use light energy to make sugar. Animals depend on plants for food.

When an animal eats a part of a plant, it is eating energy stored as sugar or starch. The animal also gets other materials, such as minerals, that are stored in the plant. The animal uses the materials from the plant to grow. When you eat fruits and vegetables, you are eating parts of a plant that have stored energy.

Animals are called **consumers** because they get the energy they need by eating plants and other animals. The deer in the picture gets the energy it needs to live by eating plants.

Glossary

consumer
(kən sü′mər), a living thing that gets energy by eating plants and other animals

This deer is getting the energy it needs from eating leaves. Leaves get their energy from the sun. ▼

A77

Glossary

herbivore
(hėr′bə vôr), a
consumer that eats plants

carnivore
(kär′nə vôr), a
consumer that eats
other consumers

omnivore
(om′nə vôr′), a
consumer that eats
both plants and other
consumers

Not all animals eat the same kinds of foods. Animals, like the deer, that eat only plants are called **herbivores.** Another group of animals, **carnivores,** eats only other animals. **Omnivores** are those animals that eat both plants and other animals. Look at the pictures on these two pages to see some animals that are herbivores, carnivores, and omnivores.

Flying Squirrel
A flying squirrel is an omnivore. Flying squirrels search for food at night. They eat nuts, seeds, insects, and spiders. ▶

◀ **Spider**
A spider is a carnivore. Spiders spin their webs and use them to catch flies, mosquitoes, and grasshoppers.

◀ Great Horned Owl

An owl is a carnivore. At night, owls swoop down from trees to capture mice, rats, and rabbits.

Crow

A crow is an omnivore. Crows hunt for spiders, small birds, and dead animals. They also eat corn and wheat. ▶

Rabbit

A rabbit is a herbivore. Rabbits get the energy they need by eating green leafy plants like clover and grass. ▼

Chipmunk

A chipmunk is a herbivore. Chipmunks come out of their burrow to search for seeds and nuts. ▼

A79

Glossary

scavenger
(skav′ən jər), an animal that eats dead animals

decomposer
(dē′kəm pō′zər), a consumer that puts materials from dead plants and animals back into the soil, air, and water

Scavengers and Decomposers

When plants and animals die, what happens to the energy that was stored in them? Some of that energy will be used by other living things. For example, some animals find and eat other animals that are already dead. Animals that eat other dead animals are called **scavengers.** A vulture, such as the one in the picture, is a scavenger. It feeds on dead animals, such as fish. By eating the dead fish, the vulture gets some of the energy that was stored in the fish.

Other living things that get energy from dead plants and animals are some worms and fungi. Find the worm and fungi in the pictures. This worm and the fungi are decomposers.

A vulture is a scavenger. ▼

▲ *The fungi are growing on dead wood and leaves.*

◀ *The earthworm the boy is holding is a decomposer.*

Decomposers break down the bodies of dead plants and animals into minerals and nutrients. Because of the work of decomposers, minerals and nutrients are put back into the soil, air, and water. Living plants can use these minerals and nutrients to grow. When animals eat the plants, the minerals and nutrients are passed on to the animals.

Decomposers are helpful to farmers and gardeners. Decomposers break down piles of leaves, grass, and other garden clippings into compost. Look at the compost in the picture. Compost is a natural fertilizer made of dead plant parts. Farmers and gardeners mix compost into soil. Compost is rich in minerals. These minerals are recycled into the soil.

This man used plant parts from his garden to make a compost pile. ▼

Lesson 3 Review

1. How do animals—herbivores, carnivores, and omnivores—get the energy they need to survive?

2. How are decomposers important?

3. **Context Clues**
   Use context clues from the last paragraph on this page to write a definition of *compost*.

A81

You will learn:

- what a food chain is.
- what a food web is.
- what some causes of changes in food webs are.

A grassland food chain ▼

Lesson 4

What Are Food Chains and Food Webs?

You drink a glass of milk to get energy. How does energy get into the milk? It's like this: sun ➡ grass ➡ cow (milk) ➡ you. The energy is all in a chain—a food chain!

Food Chains

Energy is important to the survival of every organism. You've learned that sunlight is a source of energy for plants. This energy, stored in the form of sugar or starch, is passed from plants to other organisms through a **food chain.** Look at the example of a food chain below. The grasses are the producers that store energy from the sun. The grasshopper is a consumer that gets energy by eating plants. How do organisms that do not eat plants get energy?

Carnivores, such as lions and wolves, are **predators.** Predators get the energy they need to survive by hunting and killing **prey.**

In the food-chain example on these two pages, the meadow frog is a predator. The grasshopper is prey for the meadow frog. This means that the meadow frog will get the energy it needs for survival by eating the grasshopper. The garter snake is also a predator. The garter snake will get the energy it needs from the meadow frog. This is the way energy is passed from one organism to another.

Glossary

predator (pred′ə tər), an animal that hunts and kills other animals for food

prey (prā), the animals that predators hunt

A83

Glossary

food web, all the food chains in a community

Glossary

Food Webs

An ecosystem has many food chains. All the food chains that are connected in an ecosystem make up a **food web**. Some organisms are part of more than one food chain. Look at the part of the food web shown on these two pages. Find an organism that is part of more than one food chain. Use your finger to trace the flow of energy from the sun to the grasshopper, meadow frog, and the garter snake. What consumers might eat the prairie vole?

A grassland food web ▶

Grass

Grasshopper

Pocket gopher

Ground squirrel

A 84

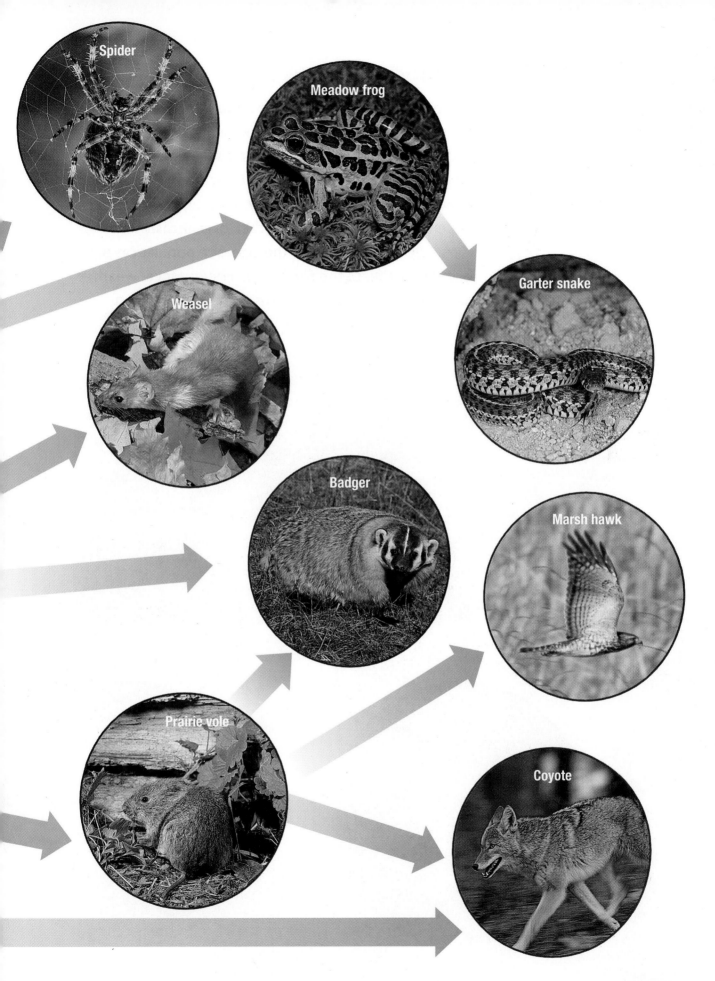

Spider

Meadow frog

Weasel

Garter snake

Badger

Marsh hawk

Prairie vole

Coyote

Changes in Food Webs

Animals within a food web depend on each other for survival. In the food web example on pages A 84 and A 85, grasshoppers need grass for energy. Meadow frogs need grasshoppers for energy. Garter snakes need meadow frogs for energy. Each animal's survival depends on the survival of other organisms.

Anything that changes the size of a population of organisms affects the food web. For instance, weather can affect a food web. Storms damage plants and sometimes cause fires.

A food chain affected by a pesticide spray ▼

When plants are destroyed by storms, herbivores cannot find food as easily as before. They must move to other areas to find food or they will die. If the plant-eating animals of an area move to other areas to find food, the carnivores that depend on them must follow.

Storms and population size are not the only things that change ecosystems and food webs. Some changes are caused by people.

Look at the food chain on these two pages. Imagine that the area where these animals live was sprayed with pesticides. Pesticides are chemicals that are used to kill harmful insects. But sometimes other animals are also affected. The grasshopper in this food chain has been killed by the pesticide spray. What effect does this have on the meadow frog? What effect does this have on the garter snake?

Oceans and rivers also contain food webs that can be affected by people. Dumping waste in oceans and rivers is harmful to the animals that live there. Animals that drink and eat from polluted water are harmed. Fish that swim in polluted water may die.

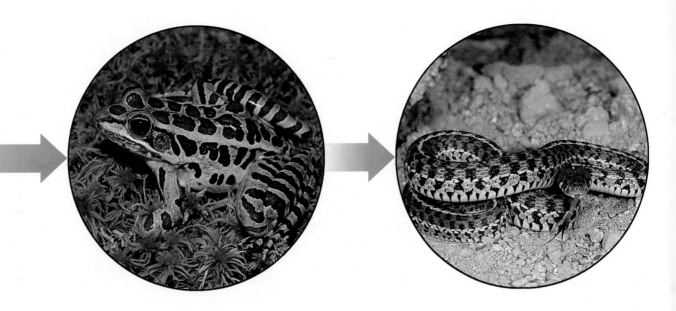

▲ Overfishing decreases the population of fish.

People can change ocean food webs by overfishing. Look at the picture on the left. The fish caught in this net were prey for larger fish. With fewer small fish, larger fish will have a harder time finding prey. Their populations may get smaller and then affect other ocean populations that depend on them for food.

Deforestation, shown in the picture, is another example of how people can change food webs. Deforestation is the clearing of a large area of trees. Insects, birds, and monkeys rely on trees for food and shelter. Monkeys, like the one in the picture, live in the trees of some forests. When trees are cut down, monkeys and other animals lose their habitats.

▲ Deforestation has changed this community.

A monkey in its natural habitat ▶

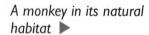

People are trying to help animals that are affected by loss of their habitats. The monarch butterfly in the picture is one animal that people are trying to help.

On a monarch butterfly farm, shown in the pictures, children learn how to attract butterflies with their favorite foods. The children also learn how to find the butterflies' eggs and keep them safe. Once the eggs turn into caterpillars, the children feed them milkweed leaves. When the caterpillars become butterflies, they are released. The goal is to increase the monarch population. The children hope to replace monarchs that were destroyed by habitat loss.

▲ The monarch is a large butterfly.

▲ These children are working on a butterfly farm where they raise monarch butterflies.

▲ When the monarch caterpillars eat all of the leaves on one milkweed plant, students move them to a new plant.

Lesson 4 Review

1. What is a food chain?

2. What is a food web?

3. List four ways people can affect a food web.

4. **Context Clues**
   Use context clues from the paragraph above to write a definition of *caterpillar*.

Investigating Decomposition

Process Skills

- making and using models
- predicting
- observing
- inferring

Materials

- safety goggles
- newspaper
- spoon
- potting soil
- 1-liter plastic bottle with top removed
- metric ruler
- piece of paper
- fruit peel
- lettuce leaves
- 2 pieces of plastic wrap
- piece of aluminum foil
- piece of bread
- piece of popped popcorn
- water
- masking tape

Getting Ready

In this activity you will compare decomposition of different objects.

Follow This Procedure

❶ Make a chart like the one shown. Use your chart to record your predictions and observations.

	Predictions	Observations
Paper		
Fruit peel		
Lettuce leaves		
Plastic wrap		
Aluminum foil		
Bread		
Popcorn		

❷ Put on your safety goggles. Place several pieces of newspaper on your desk. To make a model landfill, first use the spoon to scoop about 5 cm of soil into the bottom of the bottle.

❸ Place the piece of paper in the bottle, near the side. You should be able to see the paper from outside of the bottle. Cover the paper with soil (Photo A).

❹ Repeat step 3 with the other objects listed in your chart (Photo B). Use only one of the pieces of plastic wrap. The last layer in the bottle should be soil.

Photo A

5 Add water to moisten the soil and cover the container with plastic wrap. Use masking tape to hold the plastic wrap in place. Draw a picture of your bottle and the buried objects. Label the objects to keep track of them.

6 Which objects do you think will decompose easily? Which objects will not decompose easily? Record your **predictions** in your chart. Explain why you predicted as you did.

7 Place the bottle in a warm place, but out of direct sunlight. Observe the bottle for two or more weeks. Record the date and your **observations.**

Self-Monitoring
Have I correctly completed all of the steps?

Interpret Your Results

1. Which object or objects changed the most? Which object or objects changed the least? Were your predictions correct?

Photo B

2. The aluminum foil and the plastic wrap do not come from plant sources. The other products do. What can you **infer** about the decomposition of these products from plant sources?

Inquire Further

A compost pile contains items that can be broken down in soil. What kinds of items would you include in a compost pile at your home? Develop a plan to answer this or other questions you may have.

Self-Assessment

- I followed instructions to make a **model** landfill.
- I drew a complete picture of my model.
- I recorded my **predictions** and **observations** of which materials would decompose easily.
- I compared my predictions and observations.
- I made an **inference** about decomposition of products from plant sources.

Chapter 3 Review

Chapter Main Ideas

Lesson 1

• Plants and animals are living parts of an ecosystem. Rocks, soil, water, and sunlight are nonliving parts of an ecosystem.

• Habitats provide food, water, and shelter for survival.

Lesson 2

• Plants use their leaves to trap sunlight and to let air in and out. Plants get water from the soil through their roots.

• Plants use carbon dioxide, water, and light energy from the sun to produce sugar.

Lesson 3

• Consumers get the energy they need by eating plants and animals.

• Scavengers are animals that eat dead animals. Decomposers break down dead plants and animals and put minerals and nutrients back into the soil, air, and water.

Lesson 4

• Energy is passed from one organism to another through a food chain.

• Many food chains make up a food web.

• Changes in the environment, such as flooding, storms, fires, using pesticides, overfishing, deforestation, or pollution, can affect food webs.

Reviewing Science Words and Concepts

Write the letter of the word or phrase that best completes each sentence.

a. carbon dioxide
b. carnivore
c. chlorophyll
d. consumer
e. decomposer
f. ecosystem
g. food chain
h. food web
i. habitat
j. herbivore
k. omnivore
l. photo-synthesis
m. predator
n. prey
o. producer
p. scavenger

1. A _____ eats only plants.

2. A vulture is a _____ because it eats dead or decaying animals.

3. A plant is a _____ because it can make sugar.

4. An organism that hunts other organisms is called a _____.

5. A _____ puts minerals and nutrients back into the soil, air, and water.

6. The process by which plants use sunlight to make energy is called _____.

7. Living and nonliving things interact in an _____.

8. The flow of energy from a plant to a grasshopper to a frog is _____.

9. A _____ gets energy from other plants and animals.

10. A consumer that eats nuts, seeds, and insects is an _____.

11. The _____ of a whale is the ocean.

12. A gas found in the air that is used by plants is called _____.

13. Because it eats only other animals, a lion is a _____.

14. The green substance in plants is called _____.

15. Food chains in a community make up a _____.

16. A rabbit is _____ to a wolf.

Explaining Science

Draw a picture or write a paragraph to answer these questions.

1. You win a goldfish at a school festival. You know that all organisms have needs for survival. Apply what you know about an organism's needs and write a paragraph telling what things you must provide for the goldfish.

2. How do a plant's leaves help the plant get sunlight and air?

3. Not all living things eat plants, but all living things depend on plants for their energy. Explain why this is true.

4. How can an animal be both a predator and prey?

Using Skills

1. Use **context clues** from the first paragraph on page A88 to write a definition for overfishing.

2. Suppose there is a severe shortage of rain in an area of mostly farmland. **Predict** how this change will affect the food chains in this area. Write a paragraph to explain.

3. Suppose there is a vacant lot near your home. What could your community do to attract organisms to this area? **Communicate** your ideas to your class.

Critical Thinking

1. Write a paragraph to **communicate** ways in which people in your community have changed habitats.

2. Put each of the following food chains in the correct **sequence**:

a. rabbit, wolf, lettuce

b. grass, bird, grasshopper

c. grass, lion, zebra

3. **Apply** what you have learned to answer these questions:
What are two food chains of which you are a part? Are you at the beginning, the middle, or the end?

That's My Shell!

Did you know that hermit crabs don't grow shells? They "borrow" the empty shells of other animals. Their bodies are especially adapted to fit into the borrowed shells and keep the shells supported on the body.

Chapter 4
Surviving in the Environment

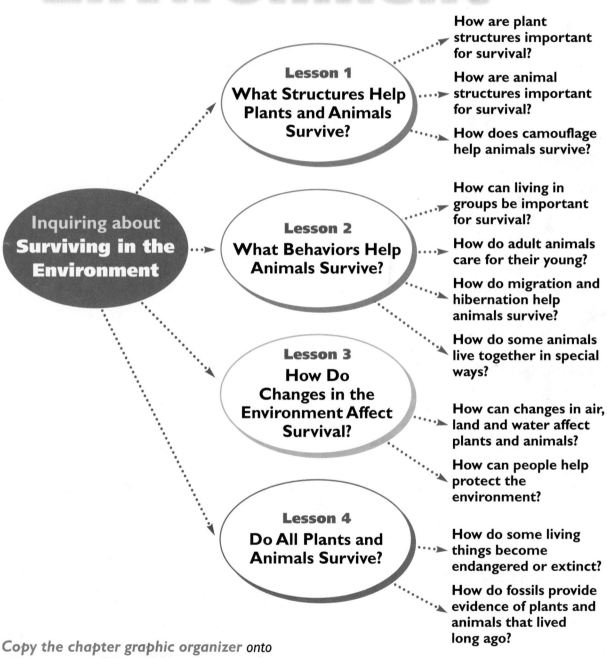

Inquiring about Surviving in the Environment

Lesson 1
What Structures Help Plants and Animals Survive?

How are plant structures important for survival?

How are animal structures important for survival?

How does camouflage help animals survive?

Lesson 2
What Behaviors Help Animals Survive?

How can living in groups be important for survival?

How do adult animals care for their young?

How do migration and hibernation help animals survive?

How do some animals live together in special ways?

Lesson 3
How Do Changes in the Environment Affect Survival?

How can changes in air, land and water affect plants and animals?

How can people help protect the environment?

Lesson 4
Do All Plants and Animals Survive?

How do some living things become endangered or extinct?

How do fossils provide evidence of plants and animals that lived long ago?

Copy the chapter graphic organizer onto your own paper. This organizer shows you what the whole chapter is all about. As you read the lessons and do the activities, look for answers to the questions and write them on your organizer.

Exploring How Animals Hide

Process Skills

- making and using models
- observing

Materials

- 4 index cards
- scissors
- crayons
- clear tape
- clock

Explore

1 **Observe** colors and patterns of objects in the classroom. Think about how you could design and hide an insect **model.** The insect must be placed out in the open, not hidden behind an object. The place must be easy to reach without standing up on anything.

2 Have each student in your group use an index card, scissors, and tape to design an insect. Color your insect so that it will be hard for your partners to see.

3 Ask your partners to close their eyes. Hide your insect and tape it to its hiding place.

4 Have your partners open their eyes. Record how long it takes for them to find the hidden model. Stop after three minutes if they haven't found it. Repeat, with each of your partners hiding his or her own insect.

Reflect

1. How did your group design your insects to make them hard to find?

2. How could you change the insects to make them even more difficult to find?

? Inquire Further

What will happen to the time it takes to find the insects if you put them where they do not blend in? Develop a plan to answer this or other questions you may have.

Solving Word Problems

Be a problem solver! Using a guide can help you solve any problem. Were there more new listings of endangered species and threatened species in 1991 than in 1990?

Math Vocabulary

line graph, a graph that connects points to show how data change over time

Work Together

Understand	What do you know?	There were 53 new listings in 1990 and 86 new listings in 1991.
	What do you need to find?	Were there more new listings in 1991 than in 1990?
Plan	Decide how you will find the answer.	You need to compare 86 to 53.
Solve	Find the answer. Write your answer.	86 is greater than 53, so there were more new listings in 1991 than in 1990.
Look Back	Check to see if your answer makes sense.	Look at the **line graph**. The point for 1991 is higher than the one for 1990.

Did You Know?

The American bald eagle was taken off the endangered species list in 1994.

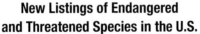

New Listings of Endangered and Threatened Species in the U.S.

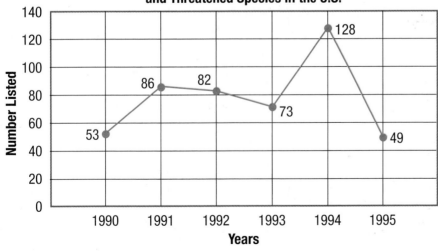

Talk About It!

How did the steps in the guide help you solve the problem?

What's the Big Idea?

You will learn:

• how plant structures are important for survival.

• how animal structures are important for survival.

• how camouflage helps animals survive.

Vines climb toward the sunlight. ▼

The pads of this giant water lily are adapted to get sunlight. ▶

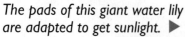

Lesson 1

What Structures Help Plants and Animals Survive?

Have you ever looked at something far away through binoculars? Just think—a hawk can see things far away all the time! The hawk's excellent eyesight helps it spot small animals from high in the sky.

Plant Structures for Survival

Plants and animals live in many different environments—hot, cold, wet, dry. But no matter where they live, all living things have basic needs that must be met. An **adaptation** is any structure or behavior that helps a living thing meet those needs and survive in its environment.

Plants need sunlight to live and grow. Many plants have special adaptations for getting sunlight. Vines, like the ones in the picture, climb up the sides of taller plants or objects where there is more sunlight.

Water lilies have large, round leaves called pads that float on the water. These large leaves capture sunlight for the plant. The giant water lily pads in the picture are so big that you could stand on them without sinking!

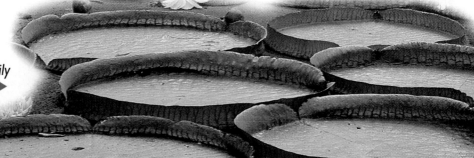

Plants also need water. In cold climates, water is frozen in ice and snow for part of the year. Plants that live in these areas have adaptations to help them conserve water. Because trees and other plants lose water through their leaves, some trees lose their leaves before the weather gets cold. Pine trees, like the ones in the picture, do not lose their leaves. However, their leaves are very thin and have a waxy covering that helps keep the trees from losing water. This adaptation helps pine trees survive during the cold winter months.

Plants that grow in very dry places have special adaptations for getting and storing water. The cactus plant in the picture lives in the desert, where it doesn't rain very often. A cactus has long, shallow roots that cover a large area. When it rains, the roots can absorb a great deal of water very quickly. The cactus stores the extra water. Its thick, waxy covering is an adaptation that helps keep moisture inside the plant. The spines of the cactus, which are actually very thin leaves, also help keep the plant from losing water.

▲ *Pine trees grow well in cold places.*

A cactus has grooves that allow the plant to get bigger as it takes in water. ▶

Animal Structures for Survival

Animals need food, water, and protection from predators and from their environments to stay alive. Like plants, animals have structures that help them meet these needs. Some adaptations help animals get food or water. Other adaptations help animals survive in very cold or very warm weather. Adaptations also help keep them from becoming some other animal's food. Find the different adaptations in the pictures on these two pages.

Adaptations for Protection

Having eyes on long stalks makes it easier for this fiddler crab to watch for predators. It scares off predators with its large claw. ▼

Adaptations for Living on Water

Ducks have adaptations that help them survive on rivers, ponds, and lakes. Their feathers are covered with oil, which keeps the ducks dry and protects them from the cold. Ducks also have webbed feet that make it easier to paddle through water. ▶

An Adaptation for Getting Food and Protection

Many kinds of spiders make silk. This garden spider spins a web and uses it to catch insects for food. It can also use its silk as protection from predators. When a predator is near, the spider can escape by sliding down the web. ▶

Adaptations for Keeping Warm and Getting Food

◀ *Walruses live in the Arctic, where the temperature can get very cold. They have layers of fat, or blubber, that help keep them warm. Walruses use their tusks to dig up shellfish and open clams.*

Adaptations for Protection and Getting Water

This thorny devil lizard's spikes protect it from snakes and other predators. It also has thousands of tiny grooves on its body that help it get water. When the desert cools off at night, dew forms on its skin. The water runs down the grooves and into its mouth! ▼

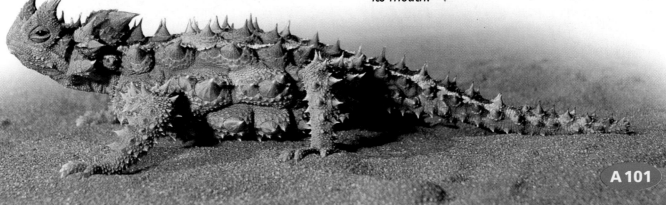

Glossary

camouflage

(kam/ə fläzh), any coloring, shape, or pattern that allows a living thing to blend into its surroundings

Camouflage

Some animals have adaptations that make it hard for predators or prey to see them. **Camouflage** is any coloring, shape, or pattern that allows a living thing to blend into its environment. The colors, shapes, and patterns of the animals in the pictures on pages A102–A104 keep them hidden in their surroundings. Find each animal as you read about it.

Walking Stick

This walking stick looks almost exactly like the object it is clinging to. In a quiet forest, you can hear the eggs of female walking sticks falling on the forest floor, but you can't see the insects. ▶

Leafy Sea Dragon

The leafy sea dragon looks just like floating seaweed, which keeps it hidden from predators. These animals live off the coast of Australia. ▼

Nightjar on a Nest

If you look closely, you can see this bird's eyes. This animal is protected by blending into the leaves around it. ▶

Horned Frog

◀ *These animals have colors and markings that help them blend into their surroundings. Horned frogs have such big mouths that they are sometimes called "mouths with legs"!*

Timber Wolf

Find the pattern on this animal's body that helps it hide among trees and sneak up on prey. The timber wolf is at the very top of the food chain. ▶

Bark Mantis

◀ This insect is barely visible against the tree it clings to. Bark mantises can stay still for long periods, making it even harder for predators to see them.

Allied Cowry

This animal's colors match those of the coral it lives on, keeping it hidden from predators. Cowries are known around the world for their beautiful shells. ▶

Lesson 1 Review

1. How can plant structures help plants survive in their environments?

2. How can animal structures help animals survive in their environments?

3. List three examples of camouflage.

4. **Main Idea**

   What is the main idea of the paragraph at the top of page A102?

What Behaviors Help Animals Survive?

Teamwork! Have you ever been part of a school team? Teams are successful when all the players work together. Animals have teams, or groups, that work together too!

Living in Groups for Survival

As you know, animals have special structures that help them survive in their environments. Behaviors that help animals survive are also adaptations. Getting food, water, and protection is hard work. Some animals make this work easier by living in groups. Living in groups is an adaptation in behavior that helps animals meet their basic needs.

Just as a sports team has a name, scientists give names to groups of animals. You may have heard of a flock of seagulls, a herd of buffalo, or a school of fish. The picture shows another animal group, a hive of bees.

What's the Big Idea?

You will learn:
- how living in groups can be important for survival.
- how adult animals care for their young.
- how migration and hibernation help animals survive.
- how some animals live together in special ways.

Honeybees live in groups called hives. Each hive has one queen bee and many workers. The workers build combs where the queen bee will lay her eggs. The workers also gather nectar for the queen. ▶

The group of lions in the picture is called a pride. Each pride may have one or two male lions and up to five lionesses. In a pride, the lionesses work together to hunt for food. While one group of lionesses chases the prey, another group hides behind a tree or in tall grass and waits for the right moment to join in. The male lion stays behind to protect the pride's territory. When the pride can no longer find resources to meet its needs, it will move to another area. Living in groups makes it easier for animals to hunt for food.

Living and working as a group makes it easier for lions to get food. ▼

The meerkats in the picture below live in groups called colonies. Each adult member of the colony has a special job. Hunters search for food, sentries watch for predators, teachers show the young how to hunt, and baby-sitters take care of the young. Working as a group makes it easier for meerkats to find food and to protect themselves.

Like meerkats, ants live in groups called colonies. The ants in a colony have different jobs. The queen lays all the eggs. Workers take care of the colony. Most workers gather food. Others take care of the eggs and feed the young. Some colonies have soldier ants that defend them. What other animals can you name that live in groups?

These meerkats are watching out for predators. ▶

Caring for Young

When a baby sea turtle hatches from its shell, it is ready to go out into the world. It can walk, swim, and catch its own food. But many animals are helpless at birth and need to be taken care of. They need to be fed, protected, and kept warm. Usually, the mother takes care of her young, but sometimes the father helps too.

This adult monkey is grooming a baby monkey. ▼

After laying her eggs, the mother bird sits on them to keep them warm. Once her eggs hatch, she will search for food to feed the young birds. In some bird families, both the mother and the father keep the eggs warm. They both also search for food after the babies hatch.

Birds and many other adult animals also protect their young from predators. The red fox in the picture protects her kits from predators by digging a hole for her family to live in. A young kangaroo is kept safe by riding in its mother's pouch. Baby opossums cling tightly to their mother's back for protection.

Some adult animals also groom their young. Notice how the mother monkey in the picture above is picking fleas out of a young monkey's hair.

The mother fox is watching for predators while her kits stay hidden. ▶

Glossary

migration
(mī grā′shən), the movement of an animal from one location to another as the seasons change

Migration and Hibernation

Some behaviors help animals survive the winter. Many animals travel to warmer locations for the winter months and then go back when spring arrives. **Migration** is the movement of an animal from one location to another as the seasons change. For example, before winter some birds fly to warmer places in search of food. Animals that live in the mountains may migrate down to the valleys. Food is easier to find in valleys, where there is less snow.

Each animal on the map below migrates. Gray whales swim from the cold North Pacific down to Mexico. Their journey takes two to three months. In the springtime, the whales migrate back to the North Pacific to find food.

Green sea turtles migrate south from the North Atlantic coast to Brazil, where they find their favorite sea grasses and algae to eat.

Millions of monarch butterflies migrate from the Northern United States and Canada to areas in California and Mexico each year. The monarchs spend the winter hanging from trees. In the spring, they fly back north.

Monarch butterflies, sea turtles, and gray whales all migrate long distances each year. ▼

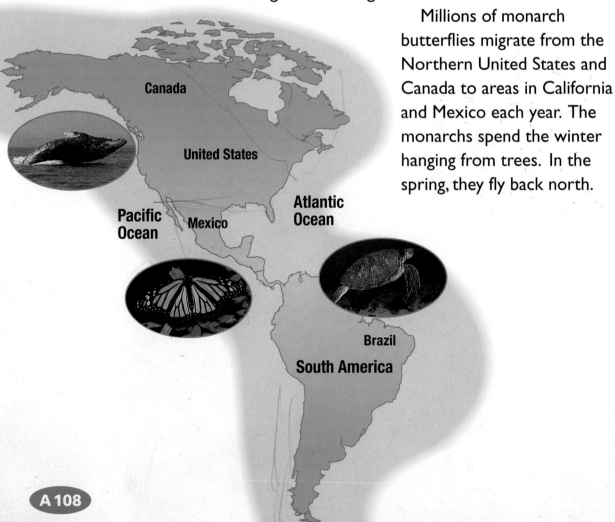

Canada

United States

Pacific Ocean

Mexico

Atlantic Ocean

Brazil

South America

You have just read how some animals migrate to warmer areas for the winter. Other animals go into a deep sleep called **hibernation.** During hibernation, the body of an animal slows down so that it uses hardly any energy. When animals are hibernating, they appear almost dead. They don't eat or even move, and their heart rate and breathing are much slower than normal.

There are two kinds of hibernating animals. True hibernators, like the ground squirrel in the picture, stay in a deep sleep for the whole winter. Before hibernating, ground squirrels eat as much as possible. They build up body fat, which they will use for energy during the long winter.

The other kind of hibernators don't sleep through the whole winter. The brown bear below hibernates for weeks or months at a time. But on warmer winter days, it may wake up and leave its den in search of food.

Brown bears hibernate for most of the winter, but they may wake up on warmer days and search for food. ▼

Glossary

hibernation
(hī′bər nā′shən), a long, deep sleep in which an animal's heart rate and breathing are much slower than normal

▲ *Ground squirrels are true hibernators. This ground squirrel may sleep the entire winter without waking up.*

Glossary

symbiosis
(sim′bē ō′sis), a special way in which two different kinds of living things live together

parasite (par′ə sīt), a plant or animal that feeds off another living thing and harms it

host (hōst), a plant or animal that is harmed by a parasite

Special Ways That Animals Live Together

Sometimes, two different kinds of living things live together in a special way. This relationship is called **symbiosis**. The pictures below show some of the ways that an animal can have a special relationship with another kind of animal.

Dog and Flea

*Fleas live on the skin of some dogs. The flea is a **parasite**. A parasite gets its food from a **host**. The flea draws blood from the skin of the dog. Fleas can carry disease and make dogs itch.* ▶

Sea Anemone and Clown Fish

The tentacles on the sea anemone are used to sting and capture small sea animals for food. The clown fish has a coating that keeps the anemone from stinging it. The clown fish swims among the tentacles to keep safe from predators. It attracts other fish to the anemone and keeps the anemone clean. ▼

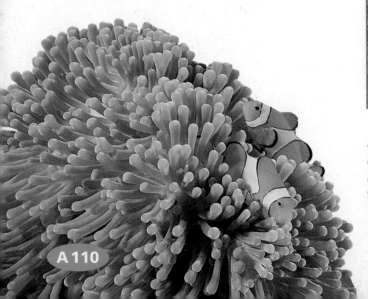

▲ Whale and Barnacles

Barnacles filter food directly from the water. By attaching themselves to the skin of this whale, they can filter more water as the whale swims. They do not seem to help or harm the whale.

Giraffe and Oxpeckers

◄ *Oxpeckers land on the backs of giraffes in search of ticks and fleas to eat. They help the giraffe by getting rid of these parasites.*

Cleaner Shrimp and Blueface Angelfish

The cleaner shrimp eats small living things that it picks off the fish. In this way, the shrimp is helped by getting food, and the fish is helped by being clean. ▶

Lesson 2 Review

1. How does living in groups help animals?

2. What are some ways adult animals care for their young?

3. How do migration and hibernation help animals?

4. How do some animals live together in special ways?

5. **Main Idea**
   What is the main idea of the paragraph at the top of page A110?

Investigating Migration

Process Skills

- making and using models
- collecting and interpreting data

Materials

- two sheets of paper
- scissors
- 24 chips
- paper bag containing paper slips numbered 1-8

Getting Ready

This activity is a simulation, or model, of how changing environments can affect migrating birds.

Follow This Procedure

❶ Make a chart like the one shown. Use your chart to record your data. Your chart should begin with Migration 1 and end with Migration 8.

Migration	Environmental change	Number of chips
1		
2		
3		

❷ Work in two teams to **model** bird migration. One team represents the spring habitat of migrating birds. The other team represents the birds' winter habitat.

Photo A

❸ Cut each sheet of paper into twelve equal pieces. Arrange six pieces in front of each team. The paper pieces represent spring and winter habitats of migrating birds (Photo A). Each team also has extra habitats.

❹ To begin the simulation, place two chips on each spring habitat. Each chip represents thousands of birds. In this simulation a habitat can have no more than two chips on it.

5 A winter student now draws a number from the bag and reads the corresponding environmental change statement. The student follows the instructions, then says, "Migrate."

6 Spring students move as many chips as possible to the winter habitats. Any chip left without a habitat must be set aside. These birds do not survive. **Collect data** by recording the environmental change and the number of chips moved to the winter habitats.

7 Reverse the roles in steps 5 and 6, moving the chips from winter to spring habitats. If there are enough spring habitats available, chips that have been set aside can be placed on the habitats. These represent new hatchlings.

8 Continue to draw numbers and migrate between winter and spring habitats until all of the numbers have been used. Record the environmental change and the number of chips moved for each migration.

Interpret Your Results

1. Which environmental changes caused the population of birds to increase? Which changes caused the population of birds to decrease?

2. What other environmental changes could affect populations of migrating animals?

Environmental Change Statements

1. No change in habitat or habitat number.

2. A drought reduced the food and water supply. Take away two habitats.

3. Weather conditions were excellent this season. Add two habitats.

4. An airport, business offices, and shopping areas were added. Take away two habitats.

5. Many acres were designated a wildlife preserve. Add two habitats.

6. Wetlands were drained for a housing development. Take away one habitat.

7. Toxic waste was illegally dumped in the area. Take away two habitats.

8. A major source of water pollution was stopped. Add two habitats.

Inquire Further

How could you graph the population changes in this activity? Develop a plan to answer this or other questions you may have.

You will learn:

- how changes in air, land, and water can affect plants and animals.
- how people can help protect the environment.

Glossary

pollution (pə lü′shən), anything harmful added to the air, land, or water

Lesson 3

How Do Changes in the Environment Affect Survival?

Have you ever walked along a lake and noticed wrappers or other garbage floating in the water? Have you ever seen thick, brown smog hanging over a city? These are forms of pollution!

Changes in Air, Land, and Water

Adaptations help plants and animals survive in their environments. However, objects or substances that make it harder for living things to stay alive sometimes end up in the air, land, or water. **Pollution** is any harmful material that is added to the environment.

Most air pollution is caused by volcanoes and forest fires, which add ash and dust to the air. But more and more often, air pollution results from the actions of people. Automobiles and coal-burning power plants release harmful chemicals into the air. These can be unhealthy to breathe. Chemicals in the air can also harm plants. Animals that depend on the plants may lose their source of food or shelter.

▲ Smog is a kind of pollution that results from the burning of coal and oil.

Land becomes polluted by garbage, litter, and other solid waste. Garbage from people's homes used to be put into open dumps. Dumps created many problems. Rain that fell on a dump washed harmful chemicals into the soil. Disease germs could grow and spread in the dirty garbage. Today, most garbage is buried under the ground in landfills. Trees and grass can then be planted on top of the ground, and people can use the land again.

Sometimes people throw bottles, cans, wrappers, and other garbage onto the ground. This kind of land pollution is called litter. You have probably seen litter on the side of the road. Litter can be harmful to many animals. The bird in the picture has become caught in plastic. Animals can be cut by broken glass. Litter can also spread germs.

Water is sometimes polluted by factories that dump harmful chemicals into rivers, lakes, and oceans. Some of these chemicals can harm or kill fish and other plants and animals that live in the water.

Oil is sometimes moved from one place to another in special ships called tankers. If a tanker leaks, oil gets into the water and can wash up onto shore. Oil spills can harm or kill animals and plants that live in the water and on the coast. An oil spill has polluted the beach in the picture.

▲ *This bird is caught in plastic that holds a six-pack of cans together. You can help by cutting the rings before they leave your home.*

This oil spill is washing up on the beach, where it can harm plants and animals that live there. ▼

Protecting the Environment

There are many ways to keep air, land, and water from becoming polluted. One way to keep the air clean is to reduce the amount of harmful substances released into it. Perhaps your family is part of a car pool. When people car pool, there are fewer cars on the road, and less pollution is added to the air. Riding in a school bus is a form of car pooling.

You might have ridden your bike to school. Riding a bike is another way to help keep the air clean, because bikes don't release harmful chemicals. Millions of people around the world ride their bikes each day. This helps to reduce the amount of pollution added to the air.

These are ways to help keep the air clean. ▼

Glossary

recycle (rē sī′kəl), to use the same materials over and over again

◄ *These people are working together to clean up a beach.*

Recycling is one way to reduce pollution. To **recycle** means to use the same materials over and over again. Glass, paper, metals, and many plastics can be separated from other garbage and used to make new items. When people recycle, less garbage goes into landfills.

Another way that people can keep the land and water clean is to avoid littering. Many people even volunteer their time to pick up garbage that other people leave in parks and on beaches. The people in the picture are removing litter from a beach.

There are other ways to repair the damage done by pollution. Some people rescue animals that have been caught in oil spills. Once the bird in the picture has been cleaned, it will be released back into the wild.

These people are cleaning oil off a bird. After it is cleaned, the bird will be released. ▼

Lesson 3 Review

1. How do air, land, and water pollution affect living things?

2. What are some things that people can do to keep the air, land, and water clean?

3. **Main Idea**
   What is the main idea of the first paragraph above?

You will learn:

- how some living things become endangered or extinct.
- how fossils provide evidence of plants and animals that lived long ago.

Glossary

endangered
(en dān′jərd), having a population that is falling low in number and that is in danger of becoming extinct

extinct (ek stingkt′), no longer existing

Lesson 4

Do All Plants and Animals Survive?

You turn the TV to your favorite sci-fi movie channel. There you see a dinosaur. **YIKES!** You wonder, "How do scientists know that dinosaurs once roamed the earth?"

Endangered and Extinct

Every living thing is adapted to its habitat. If a habitat changes, the plants and animals that live there may not be able to survive. Living things are called **endangered** when fewer of them survive each year. If a kind of plant or animal disappears completely, it has become **extinct**.

Extinction happens naturally as habitats change over time. But sometimes, people cause plants and animals to become endangered or extinct. Habitats are destroyed to make room for people to live. Some animals have been hunted until there were none left. Pollution also affects habitats. Find what caused the plants and animals in the pictures to become endangered or extinct.

Giant Panda
◀ The giant panda has become endangered because of the loss of habitat. Now the Chinese government has set aside wild areas for pandas to live. About a hundred pandas are kept in zoos in China and other countries.

California Condor

As their habitat changed, California condors nearly became extinct. Thanks to the efforts of many people, the condors are making a comeback. In 1985 there were only 9 left in the world. Today, there are more than 120.

Tasmanian Wolf

Also called the Tasmanian tiger because of the dark stripes on its back, this animal was killed by ranchers trying to protect their sheep. Most scientists think it is now extinct. ▶

Silene Perlmanii

This flowering plant was discovered in 1987 on the cliffs in Oahu, Hawaii. Another kind of plant brought in from outside the island overgrew the area and destroyed the Silene perlmanii. The last known plant died in 1997. ▶

Glossary

fossil (fos′əl), any mark or remains of a plant or animal that lived a long time ago

The boy is using a hand lens to help him draw a trilobite fossil. ▼

Fossils

Scientists learn about some plants and animals that are extinct by studying fossils. A **fossil** is any remains or mark left behind by a plant or animal that was once alive. There are many kinds of fossils. You may have seen fossils of shells, bones, or even whole trees. A fossil can also be an imprint, such as a footprint or the mark left by a leaf.

Scientists study fossils to learn about plants and animals that lived long ago. For example, scientists can guess what kinds of food an animal ate by studying its teeth. Scientists have also learned that most of the plants and animals that existed long ago are now extinct.

The fossil that the boy is drawing is a trilobite. Scientists know that certain kinds of trilobites lived only at certain times in the past.

◀ *Dinosaur skull*

One kind of fossil forms when a living thing dies and gets covered by mud. As the years go by, more and more layers of mud and dirt pile on top of the plant or animal. The pressure from these layers turns the mud around the plant or animal into rock. The shape of the living thing is pressed into the rock, creating a fossil.

Fossils can form in other ways too. The amber in the picture on the right looks like yellow glass, but it is actually a clear gum from a tree. Sometimes, insects get trapped in tree gum. After many years the gum hardens, creating a fossil of the insect. Leaves and flowers can also be covered in amber and become fossils.

▼ *Insects in amber*

Dinosaurs have been extinct for a very long time. Everything scientists know about dinosaurs they have learned from fossils. Scientists dig up the bones of these animals and put them together to form skeletons. The picture above shows what the skull of one type of dinosaur looked like. Footprints of dinosaurs and tracks left by their tails are also fossil evidence that help people learn about dinosaurs.

Lesson 4 Review

1. What does it mean for an animal to become endangered or extinct?

2. What can scientists learn from fossils?

3. **Word Problems**
   In 1985 there were only 9 California condors left in the world. By 1998 there were about 120 condors in the world. How many more condors were there in 1998 than in 1985?

Chapter 4 Review

Chapter Main Ideas

Lesson 1

• Plants have structures that help them get water and sunlight.
• Animals have structures that help them get food, water, and protection.
• Camouflage helps protect animals from predators.

Lesson 2

• Living in groups makes it easier for animals to get food, water, and protection.
• Adult animals care for their young by providing food, protection, and grooming.
• Migration and hibernation are ways that animals survive during winter weather.
• Different kinds of animals live together in special ways that may help, harm, or not affect one another.

Lesson 3

• Changes in air, land, and water can be harmful to plants and animals.
• People can help protect the environment by keeping air, land, and water clean.

Lesson 4

• Changes in habitat, hunting, and pollution can make some living things become endangered or extinct.
• Fossils, such as shells, bones, and footprints, provide information about organisms that lived long ago.

Reviewing Science Words and Concepts

Write the letter of the word or phrase that best completes each sentence.

a. adaptation	**g.** host
b. camouflage	**h.** migration
c. endangered	**i.** parasite
d. extinct	**j.** pollution
e. fossil	**k.** recycle
f. hibernation	**l.** symbiosis

1. A ___ is any remains or mark of a plant or animal that once lived.
2. The deep sleep that some animals go into during the cold winter months is ___.
3. To ___ means to use materials over again.
4. A structure or behavior that helps an organism meet its needs for survival is an ___.
5. An example of ___ is the color and shape of a leafy sea dragon.
6. A special way in which two different kinds of animals live together is ___.
7. A ___ gets its food from a host.
8. An example of ___ is when geese fly south for the winter.

9. Organisms that are ___ no longer exist.

10. A ___ is an organism that is harmed by a parasite.

11. An organism that is ___ may become extinct unless something happens to help it survive.

12. Any harmful material added to air, water, or land is ___.

Explaining Science

Write a paragraph to answer these questions.

1. What adaptations does a cactus have that help it survive in a dry climate?

2. How does living in groups help animals survive?

3. How does water become polluted?

4. How do fossils form?

Using Skills

1. Analyze the **word problem** below and then solve it.

In 1996, the following numbers of animals were endangered: 741 mammals, 971 birds, 316 reptiles, 169 amphibians, and 977 fish. How many more birds were endangered than amphibians?

2. Think about an animal you have **observed** in your neighborhood. What adaptation does it have that helps it survive?

3. Suppose you are a scientist digging for fossils. You find one animal's fossil skull that has sharp teeth like those of a wolf. What might you **infer** about what this animal ate?

Critical Thinking

1. The fur of one kind of rabbit is gray during the summer, but it changes to white during the winter. **Infer** how this adaptation might help the rabbit survive.

2. Compare and contrast three types of symbiosis and give one example of each.

3. Your class wants to do something to help protect the environment. **Make a decision** about what you can do to help keep the land clean.

Unit A Review

Reviewing Words and Concepts

Choose at least three words from the **Chapter 1** list below. Use the words to write a paragraph about how these concepts are related. Do the same for each of the other chapters.

Chapter 1
classify
conifer
fertilization
ovary
pistil
reproduce

Chapter 2
amphibian
backbone
mammal
reflex
response
stimulus

Chapter 3
carbon dioxide
chlorophyll
ecosystem
food chain
photosynthesis
producer

Chapter 4
adaptation
camouflage
endangered
extinct
hibernation
pollution

Reviewing Main Ideas

Each of the statements below is false. Change the underlined word or words to make each statement true.

1. Flowering plants reproduce by making <u>spores</u>.
2. Ferns and <u>conifers</u> make spores.
3. The four parts of a flower are sepals, petals, stamens, and <u>leaves</u>.
4. Amphibians and <u>worms</u> are animals with backbones that spend all or part of their lives in water.
5. <u>Birds</u> are animals that have dry, scaly skin covering their bodies.
6. Instincts are behaviors that animals <u>must learn</u>.
7. <u>Scavengers</u> provide food, water, and shelter for plants and animals to survive.
8. Many food chains make up a <u>decomposer</u>.
9. Some changes in the environment can cause plants and animals to become <u>pollution</u> or extinct.
10. A <u>habitat</u> provides evidence of organisms that lived long ago.

Interpreting Data

The following diagram shows the parts of a flower. Use the diagram to answer the questions below.

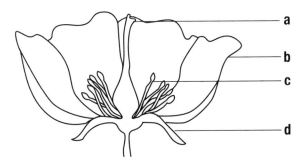

1. Write the letter and the name of the flower part that makes pollen.

2. Write the name of the flower part labeled *d*. How does this part help the flower?

3. How do the bright colors of flower petals help flowers produce seeds?

Communicating Science

1. Draw and label a picture to show how a flower is pollinated.

2. Make a chart to show some characteristics of five groups of animals with backbones and some animals that belong to each group.

3. Draw and label a food chain that includes plants, animals, and you.

4. Write a paragraph explaining how some plants and animals survive during winter weather.

Applying Science

1. Imagine that you have discovered a new plant. Explain how you would use the appearance of the plant to decide if your plant is a flowering plant, a moss, a fern, or a conifer.

2. Many scientists think that dinosaurs became extinct because an asteroid struck the earth. The asteroid caused dust to fill the air around the earth and blocked out the rays of the sun. How might the blocking of the sun's rays cause dinosaurs to become extinct?

Unit A
Performance Review

Environmental Fair

Using what you learned in this unit, create exhibits for an Environmental Fair. The exhibits will help visitors learn about plants and animals and how environmental changes affect them. Complete one or more of the following activities. You may work by yourself or with a group.

Photography

Use a camera to take pictures of some plant and animal habitats near your home or school. Display your pictures in a photo album and write a paragraph telling about each plant or animal and its habitat.

Art

Make a model of an ecosystem. Include models of plants and animals that might live in the ecosystem. Make a tape recording that visitors can listen to while viewing the models. On the tape, explain the importance of the sun and how each plant and animal is a part of the food web of the ecosystem.

Drama

Write a skit about plant and animal adaptations. Have each plant and animal tell about an adaptation that helps it survive. Make costumes for each character and perform the skit for your classmates. Choose background music to play during the performance.

Technology

Display examples of kinds of research and technology that scientists use to study the environment. Write a paragraph for each example telling how the research or technology affects the environment. Evaluate how the research or technology has affected society.

Geography

Make and label a large map of the United States. On the map, locate places in the United States where the habitats and ecosystems that are displayed at your fair might be found. Label bodies of water near the habitats and ecosystems that might affect the ecosystem. Write a paragraph to explain how the locations of the habitats and ecosystems might affect the kinds of plants and animals that live there.

Researching a Topic

You can use many types of resources to research a topic. Books, encyclopedias, and magazines are common reference sources found in libraries. You can also obtain information about many topics by using on-line resources such as Web sites or encyclopedias. On-line information is available on almost every topic.

Use On-Line Reference Sources

In Chapter 4, you learned why some plants and animals become endangered or extinct. Use the internet to gather information about five plants and animals from your state that are endangered. Try to find out why they are endangered and what efforts are being made to protect these living things. To find this information, try contacting your state wildlife agency or the U.S. Fish and Wildlife Service. When you find an agency you want to use, try to obtain information by e-mail from a representative of that agency.

Write an Article

Use the information you find to write an article for your school or local newspaper. Your article should inform people about what they can do to help save some of the endangered plants and animals in your area.

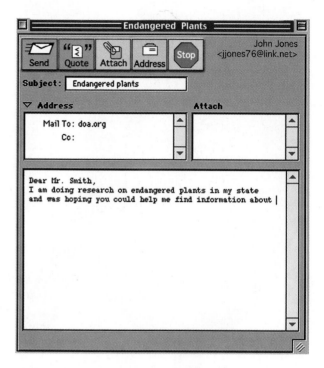

Remember to:

1. **Prewrite** Organize your thoughts before you write.

2. **Draft** Write your article.

3. **Revise** Share your work and then make changes.

4. **Edit** Proofread for mistakes and fix them.

5. **Publish** Share your article with your class.

Unit B
Physical Science

B 1

Science and Technology
In Your World!

Tiny Chips Power Amazing Games!

Did you know that dozens of computer chips can fit on the head of a pin? Video games use these chips to power games so real you think you are there! Years of studying matter came before the invention of computer chips. You will learn about matter in **Chapter 1 Measuring Matter.**

Get in Gear!

In the late 1800s, bicycle pedals were attached directly to the front wheel. Tires were steel or solid rubber! Inventors and engineers use their knowledge of forces, work, and machines to make bicycles better and better. You will learn about forces, work, and machines in **Chapter 2 Force and Motion.**

Cellular Phones Revolutionize the Communication Industry!

Alexander Graham Bell wouldn't believe his eyes today! His invention, the telephone, has changed how people communicate with one another. Now phones are so small that they can fit in the palm of your hand. And they don't even have to be connected to the wall! You will learn more about what powers these tiny devices in **Chapter 3 Electricity and Magnetism.**

Pinpoint Laser Beams Make Big Sound!

The audio CDs (compact discs) you now listen to have great sound. A tiny laser beam scans a fast-moving disc. The changes in the amount of light reflected off the disc are changed into an electric signal. The result is great music you hear! Scientists needed to understand the basic science of light and sound before they could begin to invent CDs. You will learn some of this basic science in **Chapter 4 Light and Sound.**

What's the Matter?

Everything around you is made of matter that can be measured. How much matter do you think there is in an apple?

Chapter 1
Measuring Matter

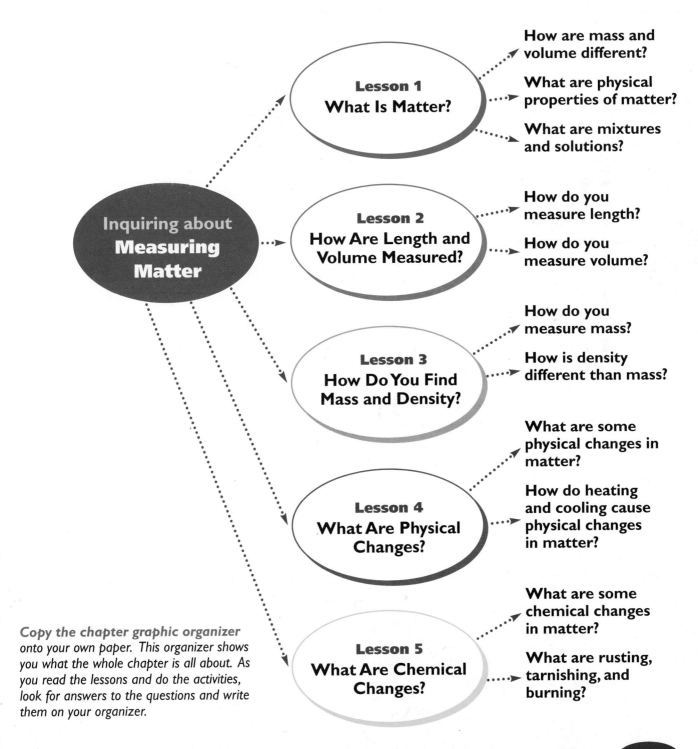

Inquiring about Measuring Matter

Lesson 1
What Is Matter?

How are mass and volume different?

What are physical properties of matter?

What are mixtures and solutions?

Lesson 2
How Are Length and Volume Measured?

How do you measure length?

How do you measure volume?

Lesson 3
How Do You Find Mass and Density?

How do you measure mass?

How is density different than mass?

Lesson 4
What Are Physical Changes?

What are some physical changes in matter?

How do heating and cooling cause physical changes in matter?

Lesson 5
What Are Chemical Changes?

What are some chemical changes in matter?

What are rusting, tarnishing, and burning?

Copy the chapter graphic organizer onto your own paper. This organizer shows you what the whole chapter is all about. As you read the lessons and do the activities, look for answers to the questions and write them on your organizer.

Exploring Matter

Process Skills

Process Skills

- observing
- communicating
- inferring

Materials

- water in plastic cup
- syrup in plastic cup
- vegetable oil in plastic cup
- celery
- modeling clay
- raisin
- aluminum foil

Explore

1 In this activity you will explore some properties of liquids and solids. Make a list of the materials. Leave room by each item to record observations.

2 **Observe** each item and write three words to describe each one.

3 Slowly pour the water into the cup of syrup as shown. Then pour the vegetable oil into the cup. Record your observations of the syrup, water, and vegetable oil.

4 Carefully drop the celery, the modeling clay, and the raisin into the cup. Record your observations for each item.

5 Tear the aluminum foil into two pieces. Squeeze one piece into a tight ball. Put both foil pieces in the cup. Record your observations.

Reflect

1. **Communicate.** Compare and contrast your observations with those of other groups.

2. Think about the layers of liquids. Make an **inference.** Which do you think has greater mass, 30 mL of syrup or 30 mL of vegetable oil? Explain.

? Inquire Further

What common liquids or solids might float in vegetable oil? Develop a plan to answer this or other questions you may have.

Exploring Mass

Kim Brownfield's wheelchair doesn't keep him from setting world records. His record lift of 237 kilograms earned him a gold medal at the Paralympic Games in 1996. A **kilogram** is a metric unit of mass. Below you will learn about another metric unit of mass, the **gram**.

Working Together

Use a **balance**, gram cubes, a nickel, and small classroom objects to explore mass.

1. Use the balance and gram cubes to find the mass of the nickel.

2. Choose a small object, such as a piece of chalk. Hold it in one hand. Hold the nickel in the other hand. Do you think the mass of the object is greater or less than the mass of the nickel? Use the balance to check.

3. Is the mass of a penny greater or less than 5 grams? How could you find out without using the balance?

4. Choose 5 small objects. Estimate which have a mass greater than 5 grams and which have a mass less than 5 grams. Use the nickel and the balance scale to check.

Materials
- balance
- gram cubes
- a penny
- a nickel
- small classroom objects

Math Vocabulary
balance, an instrument used to measure an object's mass

gram (g), a metric unit of mass

kilogram (kg), a metric unit of mass equal to 1,000 grams

Talk About It!

1. Which is greater, a gram or a kilogram?

2. A cotton ball and a marble are about the same size. The mass of the cotton ball is less than 1 gram, but the mass of the marble is about 10 grams. How can you explain their difference in mass?

You will learn:

- how mass and volume are different.
- what physical properties of matter are.
- what mixtures and solutions are.

Glossary

matter (mat′ər), anything that has mass and takes up space

mass (mas), the amount of material that an object has in it

volume (vol′yəm), the amount of space that matter takes up

Lesson 1

What Is Matter?

Big, twisted pretzels and small, twisted pretzels. Long, thick pretzels and short, skinny pretzels. These pretzels all have one thing in common. They are all made of matter—the same kind of matter!

Mass and Volume

Just like the pretzels, you, a car, and a dog all are made of matter. In fact, all living and nonliving things, even your socks, are made of matter. **Matter** is anything that has mass and takes up space. **Mass** is the amount of material that an object has in it.

The two pretzels shown below are made up of matter. Both of the pretzels have mass and take up space. However, one of the pretzels is thicker than the other. The pretzels are made of the same material. The thinner pretzel has less mass because it is made of less material.

The thinner pretzel also takes up less space. It has less volume than the thicker pretzel. **Volume** is the amount of space that matter takes up.

Both of these pretzels have volume. Which pretzel has more volume? ▶

Physical Properties of Matter

Think about the last time you described a new toy to a friend. You probably described it by its color, shape, and size. You described the properties of the toy. A property is something about matter that can be observed and tells you what the matter is like. Color, shape, size, and mass are some physical properties of matter. These properties can be used to describe or sort matter.

One important property of matter is the state, or form, that matter has. Matter has three states—solid, liquid, and gas. A solid has a shape and a volume of its own. Your desk and books are solids.

A liquid has a certain volume, but it has no shape of its own. A liquid takes the shape of its container. Milk and water are liquids. The boy below is pouring soapy water into a bowl. What shape do you think the water will take?

The air you breathe is made up of gases. Notice the girl blowing air into the soapy water to make bubbles. The air in the soap bubbles takes the shape of the bubbles. A gas, like a liquid, does not have a shape of its own. Unlike a liquid, a gas does not have a volume of its own. When the bubbles break, the gases spread out and take up more space.

States of matter include solid, liquid, and gas. Find a solid, a liquid, and a gas in the picture. ▼

Some materials have the ability to float and others do not. ▶

Another property of matter is the ability of some matter to float in a gas or liquid. An onion and a piece of celery are floating in the water in one of the bowls in the picture. The potato and carrot in the other bowl are not floating. They sank to the bottom of the water.

Mixtures and Solutions

You can mix matter together in different ways. For example, you can cut up lettuce, cucumbers, and carrots and mix them with tomatoes to make a vegetable salad. Notice the vegetable salad in the picture. You can see that the pieces of vegetables have the same colors and other properties that they had before being mixed together. The pieces of vegetables can also be easily separated. They have not joined together to make a new substance.

A salad is one kind of mixture. ▼

The vegetable salad is one kind of mixture. A **mixture** is two or more substances that are mixed together but can easily be separated. Mixtures can have different kinds and amounts of substances. The salad could have different amounts of each vegetable or different kinds of vegetables.

Another kind of mixture forms when you mix salt and water together. The salt dissolves in the water. Notice the glass of salt water in the picture. You cannot see the salt. When it dissolves, the salt breaks into tiny bits that are too small to see. These bits spread out evenly through the water. The water and salt become a kind of mixture called a solution. A **solution** is a mixture in which one substance spreads evenly throughout another substance. However, the salt and water can be separated. Let the glass sit in a warm place until the water evaporates. The salt will be left in the glass.

Glossary

mixture (miks′chər), two or more substances that are mixed together but can be easily separated

solution (sə lü′shən), a mixture in which one substance spreads evenly throughout another substance

Glossary

▲ *Now you see it, now you don't! Salt disappears as it dissolves in water.*

Lesson 1 Review

1. How are the mass and volume of an object different?

2. What are two physical properties of matter?

3. How is a solution different from other mixtures?

4. **Mass**
   Which would you estimate has the greater mass—a 6 cm piece of celery or a 6 cm carrot? How can you check your estimate?

You will learn:

- how to measure length.
- how to measure volume.

Lesson 2

How Are Length and Volume Measured?

How tall are you? How long is your arm? What length is your foot? What volume of matter can you hold in your hands? To find the answers, you need to measure length and volume!

Measuring Length

Length is a property of matter. Length measures the distance between one point and another, or how far apart the two points are. People use measurements, such as length, to help describe matter in exact ways. For example, the boy in the picture is measuring the length of his lower arm and hand.

A meter stick is a measuring tool that can be used to accurately measure length. ▼

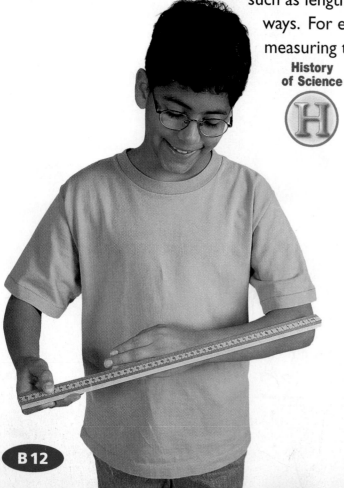

History of Science 🅗

In ancient times, people used their body parts or things in nature to measure. Fingers, hands, and arms were measuring tools. For example, people measured a horse by how many hands high it was.

Scientists found that using body parts to measure was not very accurate. When different people measured the same object, their measurements were not always the same. Can you think of reasons why using body parts such as your arms to measure might not be accurate?

Prefixes for Meter

centi- means $\frac{1}{100}$	centimeter (cm) = $\frac{1}{100}$ of a meter
milli- means $\frac{1}{1,000}$	millimeter (mm) = $\frac{1}{1,000}$ of a meter
kilo- means 1,000	kilometer (km) = 1,000 meters

Glossary

meter (mē′tər), a unit for measuring length

Glossary

In 1790, France passed a law making the metric system of measurement its standard. Today, this system is used in most countries. In the metric system, a unit for measuring length is the **meter**. The symbol for meter is m. To measure the width of a desk, you would use a meter stick as the boy in the picture is. A meter stick is divided into 100 equal parts called centimeters. Find the centimeter marks on the meter stick to the right. The symbol for centimeter is cm. The prefix *centi-* means $\frac{1}{100}$.

A meter stick is also divided into 1,000 tiny, equal parts called millimeters. The prefix *milli-* means $\frac{1}{1,000}$. The symbol for millimeter is mm. Find the millimeter marks on the meter stick shown.

A kilometer is 1,000 meters. The prefix *kilo-* means 1,000. The symbol for kilometer is km. Kilometers are used to measure long distances, such as the distance between two cities or how tall a mountain is.

How long is this paper clip in millimeters? in centimeters? ▼

This boy is using a meter stick to measure the width of a desk. ▶

Measuring Volume

Like length, volume is a property of matter that can be measured. Suppose you want to know how much a box will hold. Like people in ancient times, you might use things around you to measure volume. You might fill the box with smaller boxes. But if other people measure using different-sized boxes, they might get a different volume than you do.

To measure something accurately, it's best to use the same tools scientists use. One way to measure the volume of a solid is by using a meter stick, as the children in the picture are doing. To find out the volume of a box, first measure the length, width, and height of the box. Then multiply the length times the width times the height. If the box measures 2 meters long, 2 meters wide, and 1 meter high, multiply 2 meters $\times$ 2 meters $\times$ 1 meter. The volume of the box is 4 cubic meters. A **cubic meter** is a unit for measuring volume. A cube 1 meter long, 1 meter wide, and 1 meter high is a cubic meter. If the box is 4 cubic meters, it means that the box can hold four cubes that are 1 meter $\times$ 1 meter $\times$ 1 meter.

Volume also is often measured in liters. Liquids like juices are sold in liters. A **liter** is another unit for measuring volume. The symbol for liter is L. A milliliter is equal to $\frac{1}{1,000}$ of a liter. The symbol for milliliter is mL. Medicines are sometimes measured in milliliters.

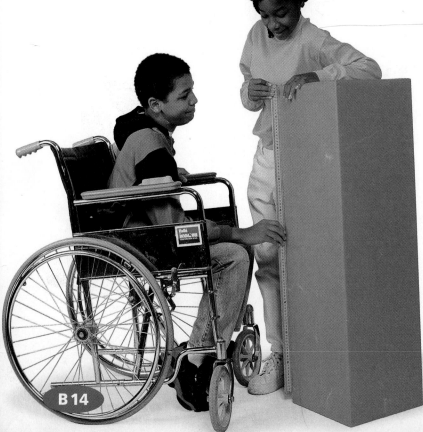

To measure the volume of a box, first measure its length, width, and height. Then multiply length X width X height. ▼

Scientists use a special kind of measuring tool called a graduated cylinder to measure the volume of liquids. A **graduated cylinder** is marked with lines that are equal distances apart.

A graduated cylinder can be used to measure the volume of an object that has an irregular length, width, or height. To measure the volume of a hard solid, like a small rock, fill a graduated cylinder with water. Record the height of the water in the graduated cylinder. Place the rock inside the graduated cylinder and record the height of the water. Subtract the first measurement from the second measurement. The difference is the volume of the rock, or the space the rock takes up. What is the volume of the rock in the picture?

Glossary

graduated cylinder
(graj′ü ā′tid sil′ən dər),
a tool used to measure
the volume of liquids

Glossary

When the rock is dropped into the water, it takes up space. The space the rock takes up is its volume. ▶

Lesson 2 Review

1. What unit would you use to measure the length of your classroom?

2. What are two different units scientists use to measure volume?

3. **Mass**
   Which would you estimate has the greater mass—a rock with a volume of 1 mL or a rock with a volume of 4 mL? How can you check your estimate?

You will learn:
- how to measure the mass of an object.
- what the difference between mass and density is.

Lesson 3

How Do You Find Mass and Density?

Here's a riddle for you: Which has more mass—a kilogram of gold or a kilogram of feathers? **Right!** They both have the same mass.

Measuring Mass

Like length and volume, mass is a property of matter that can be measured. Mass is closely related to how heavy something is, but weight and mass are not the same thing.

Sometimes you can tell that one object has more mass than another. It just feels heavier. The child in the picture is trying to compare the mass of two objects by lifting them. However, for things that are about the same mass, a balance like the one on the next page can help you find out which object has the most mass.

◄ *The box of chalk and the box of crayons are the same size, but they have different masses.*

Some metric units used to measure mass are gram, milligram, and kilogram. The **gram** is the basic unit for measuring mass. A small paper clip has about 1 gram of mass. A milligram is $\frac{1}{1,000}$ of a gram. Substances that are used in small amounts, such as vitamins and medicines, are usually measured in milligrams. A kilogram is equal to 1,000 grams. Kilograms are useful in measuring the mass of large objects. The mass of a person is measured in kilograms.

The girl in the picture below is balancing a box of crayons with objects of a known mass. First the girl placed the crayons on the balance. The pan with the crayons in it moved down. Now the girl is placing the known objects on the balance. When the two pans on the balance are even, she will stop adding objects. By adding together the masses of the known objects, the girl knows the mass of the crayons.

Now look at the balance on the right. A box of crayons is on one side and a box of chalk is on the other side of the balance. Which has more mass—the crayons or the chalk? How do you know?

Glossary

gram, the basic unit for measuring mass

Glossary

A balance can help you find the mass of an object, or which of two objects has the most mass. ▼

Glossary

density (den′sə tē), how much mass is in a certain volume of matter

The red vinegar and oil have the same volume but a different density. ▼

Density

Density is another property of matter. Have you ever helped an adult mix vinegar and oil to make salad dressing? Watching what happens to the vinegar and oil in the salad dressing can help you find out about density. The salad dressing is a great example of the density of different liquids.

The girl in the picture below is mixing vinegar and oil to make salad dressing. The particles in the vinegar are mixed with the particles in the oil. The bottle contains the same volume of vinegar and oil—100 mL of red vinegar, 100 mL of oil, and some seasonings. Then the girl sets the bottle down for a few minutes.

The two liquids do not have the same mass. After sitting still in the bottle, what happened to the mixture? Yes! It separated! Why do you think the vinegar is on the bottom? The vinegar is denser. It has more matter in it than the same volume of oil does.

Density is how much mass is in a certain volume of matter. The 100 mL of vinegar has a greater mass than the 100 mL of oil does. Therefore, the vinegar sinks to the bottom of the bottle. The oil floats on top of the vinegar. The density of the vinegar is greater than the density of the oil.

Look at the balance. The cork and the wood each have a mass of about 1 gram. That is why they balance. However, notice the size of the piece of cork on the right and the size of the piece of wood on the left. It is easy to see that the volume of the cork is larger than the volume of the wood. Which object do you think is denser? The wood is denser because the small piece of wood has the same mass as the larger piece of cork. If the pieces of wood and cork were the same size, the mass of the cork would be less than the mass of the wood. Therefore, the wood has the greater density.

Now think about the riddle at the beginning of the lesson. A kilogram of gold has the same mass as a kilogram of feathers, but which has the greater density? Think about how light a feather is. Imagine how many feathers it would take to have a kilogram of mass. So which has the greater density—gold or feathers?

▲ The wood and the cork have the same mass, but they have different volumes.

Lesson 3 Review

1. What metric units are used to measure mass?

2. How is density different than mass?

3. **Mass**
   Is the mass of a cup of water greater or less than the mass of a cup of rocks? How can you check your answer?

Describing and Measuring Matter

Process Skills

- observing
- estimating and measuring
- classifying

Materials

- rubber stopper
- 2 plastic cups
- balance
- masking tape
- gram cubes
- water
- graduated cylinder
- measuring cup
- paper towels
- steel bearing
- cork
- pencil

Getting Ready

In this activity you will practice describing and measuring properties of matter.

Follow This Procedure

1 Make a chart like the one shown. Use your chart to record your observations and measurements.

	Properties of matter		
Object			
Description			
Mass			
Volume of water in cylinder			
Volume after adding object			
Volume of object (mL)			

2 Place one plastic cup at each end of the balance. Use masking tape to attach each cup to the balance. Be sure the two cups are in balance.

3 **Observe** and describe the shape, color or colors, hardness, and any other properties of the rubber stopper. Record your observations.

Photo A

Photo B

4 **Measure** the mass of the rubber stopper. Place the rubber stopper in one of the cups. Observe what happens. Add gram cubes to the other cup until both cups are balanced (Photo A). Record your measurements in the chart.

5 Measure the volume of the rubber stopper. Pour water into a graduated cylinder until it is about half full. Record the volume of water in the cylinder.

6 Put the rubber stopper in the water. Record the new water level (Photo B).

7 Subtract the first water level from the second to find the volume of the rubber stopper. Record the volume. Carefully pour the rubber stopper and water into the measuring cup and remove the rubber stopper. Dry it with a paper towel and set it aside.

8 Repeat steps 2–7 using the steel bearing.

9 Repeat steps 2–7 using the cork. When you put the cork in water, use a pencil to hold it just under the surface of the water.

Interpret Your Results

Classify the objects by mass and volume. Rank the objects from least mass to greatest mass. Then rank the objects from least volume to greatest volume. Does the object with the greatest mass have the greatest volume?

Inquire Further

How can you find the volume of an object bigger than the graduated cylinder? Develop a plan to answer this or other questions you may have.

Self-Assessment

- I followed instructions to describe and measure properties of matter.
- I **observed** and described shape, color, hardness, and other properties of three objects.
- I **measured** the mass and volume of each object.
- I recorded my observations and measurements.
- I **classified** the objects and ranked them by mass and volume.

You will learn:

- about some physical changes in matter.
- how heating and cooling cause physical changes in matter.

What Are Physical Changes?

DRIP! Water melts from an ice cube. **SNIP!** Scissors cut paper into bits. **SPLAT!** Clay smashes flat or crumbles into bits. **BOING!** A rubber band breaks. In these and other ways, physical changes can happen to matter.

Glossary

physical (fiz′ə kəl) **change,** a change in matter that changes physical properties, but does not produce a different kind of matter

Physical Changes in Matter

Matter goes through changes. Sometimes the changes are rather slow, as when a puddle of water dries up. Sometimes the changes are rather fast, as when a glass slips from your hand and you see it break.

Changes in the shape, size, color, or state of matter are some examples of physical changes. A **physical change** does not change matter into a different kind of matter. For example, the paper the child in the picture is painting is being changed. However, the paper is still paper. It is just a different color. Also, the cut paper, the clay, and the play dough can change shape, but they are still the same kind of matter. Only the physical properties of the matter are changed.

Heating and Cooling Matter

Another way to change matter is by heating or cooling it. Heating or cooling matter to certain temperatures causes matter to change state. A solid can become a liquid, and a liquid can become a solid or a gas.

When the temperature of a solid rises enough, it melts. Steel, rock, glass, plastic, butter, and ice—all these things melt when they reach a certain temperature. Steel, rock, and glass must reach very high temperatures before they start to melt. On the other hand, plastic, butter, and ice melt at lower temperatures.

Look at the picture of the ice. Notice the temperature on the thermometer. A temperature of 0°C isn't very high, but it is high enough for ice to melt. As the temperature of the ice rises, the ice changes state. It changes from a solid to a liquid. The **melting point** of a material is the temperature at which it melts and becomes a liquid.

Notice that the temperature of the water is 100°C. This is the boiling point of water. The **boiling point** of a material is the temperature at which it boils. It is also the temperature at which a material changes from a liquid to a gas. The bubbles you see rising in boiling water are gases. The gas bubbles form in water as it begins to boil. The gas escapes into the air.

Glossary

melting (mel′ting) **point,** the temperature at which matter changes from a solid to a liquid

boiling (boi′ling) **point,** the temperature at which matter changes from a liquid to a gas

Glossary

The melting point and the boiling point of water are some of its physical properties. ▼

Glossary

freezing (frē′zing)
point, the temperature
at which matter changes
from a liquid to a solid

Energy must be added to matter for the matter to melt or boil. Adding energy causes the temperature of the matter to rise. When the temperature of the matter reaches the melting point or the boiling point, the matter changes state.

Matter is cooled when energy is lost. When the temperature of water drops to 0°C, the water changes from a liquid to a solid—ice. This is called the freezing point of water.

The **freezing point** of a substance is the temperature at which the substance changes from a liquid to a solid. However, the freezing point of many substances is not very cold. For example, many substances, such as butter, are solids at room temperature. Their freezing point is much higher than 0°C.

The pictures on the next page show how heating and cooling are used to make crayons. When crayons are made, energy is added to solid wax. As the bits of matter that make up the wax gain energy, they move faster. As the particles move farther apart, the wax becomes a liquid. The liquid wax can be stirred and mixed with other materials. Dyes are added to the wax to give the crayons their colors.

The melted wax is placed in forms that give the crayons their shape. The cold water causes the wax to lose energy and cool. When the wax reaches its freezing point, it becomes a solid.

1 First, paraffin wax or beeswax gets heated until it melts.

2 The melted wax is mixed with pigments, or colored materials.

3 The hot, liquid crayon material is poured into crayon-shaped holes in a large mold. Cold water chills the mold until the crayons harden.

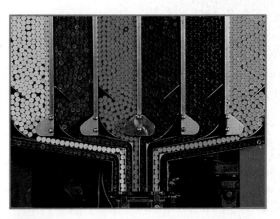

4 Each cooled, solid crayon is wrapped in a label. Finished crayons are placed into boxes and sent to stores.

Now you can use the crayons! ▼

Lesson 4 Review

1. Name four physical changes that can happen to material.

2. How does heating and cooling cause changes in matter?

3. **Main Idea**
   What is the main idea of the last paragraph on page B24?

You will learn:
- about chemical changes in matter.
- how rusting, tarnishing, and burning are chemical changes.

Lesson 5

What Are Chemical Changes?

WHIRRR! **SIZZLE!** You mix pancake batter and pour some on a hot griddle. The batter puffs up as bubbles form inside it. You flip the pancakes over. Chemical changes have changed the batter into pancakes.

Glossary

chemical change (kem′ə kəl chānj), a change in matter that produces a different kind of matter

Chemical Changes in Matter

Unlike a physical change, a **chemical change** produces a completely different kind of matter. In a chemical change, the matter produced by the change may have very different properties from the original matter.

Chemical Changes in Pancakes
Pancake batter is a liquid mixture of eggs, oil, milk, baking powder, salt, and flour. ▶

The pictures on these two pages show an example of a chemical change—making pancakes. To make pancakes, you mix some ingredients together as a liquid batter. As the batter cooks, a change takes place. The batter on the griddle browns and hardens as it cooks.

As the liquid batter on the griddle changes, another change also takes place. A gas is formed by the ingredients in the batter. The gas bubbles form inside the batter, rise to the top, and escape into the air. The rising bubbles fluff up the pancake and leave tiny air pockets. The liquid batter changes into a browned, spongy, solid pancake.

▲ During cooking, bubbles of gas form and rise to the top of the batter. The batter browns and hardens into a spongy, solid, cakelike material.

Human Body

When you eat the pancakes or any food, many chemical changes take place. Chemical changes even take place in your mouth.

As you chew, your saliva starts to break down the food into different substances. Inside your body, food goes through more chemical changes. Your body uses some of the substances produced for energy. Some of these materials are used to grow and repair your body parts.

◄ When you eat pancakes, more chemical changes take place as your body digests the food.

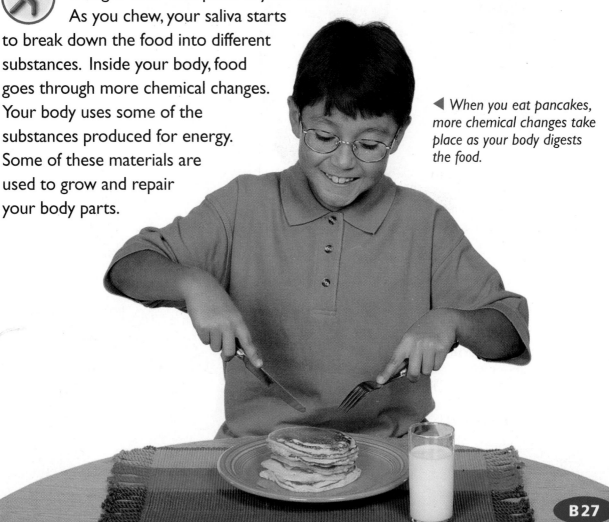

Rusting, Tarnishing, and Burning

Some other examples of chemical changes are rusting, tarnishing, and burning. Each of these chemical changes produces different matter. Find out what matter is produced in the examples on these pages.

Rusting

◀ *Rust forms slowly as oxygen from the air joins with iron on the surface of a bicycle or other object that contains iron. Iron is hard and dark gray or black. Rust is orange-red and powdery or flaky. Rust has different properties from both air and iron. It is a different material formed by a chemical change.*

Tarnishing

Have you ever wondered why some coins look shiny and others look dull? Tarnish, like rust, forms slowly when air mixes with certain metals. On copper, tarnish looks dark brown or green. On silver, tarnish is black. On any metal, tarnish causes the metal to lose its shiny look. ▶

Burning

◀ *Exploding is the fastest kind of burning. The rocket boosters that lift the space shuttle into orbit contain liquid oxygen and liquid hydrogen fuel. When the oxygen and the hydrogen combine, they explode instantly and powerfully. The explosion releases energy whose force lifts the rocket from the surface of the earth. As the oxygen and hydrogen combine to form water, steam is given off.*

Lesson 5 Review

1. How does baking pancakes produce a different kind of matter?

2. Name three examples of chemical changes other than cooking.

3. **Main Idea**
   What is the main idea of the paragraph on the bottom of page B28?

Chapter 1 Review

Chapter Main Ideas

Lesson 1
• Mass is the amount of material in matter, and volume is the amount of space that matter takes up.
• A property is something about matter that can be observed and tells you what the matter is like.
• Matter can be mixed together in solutions and other mixtures.

Lesson 2
• Length is measured in meters.
• Volume is measured in cubic meters or liters.

Lesson 3
• The metric system uses gram, milligram, and kilogram to measure mass.
• Density is how much mass is in a certain volume of matter.

Lesson 4
• A physical change is a change in size, shape, color, or state of matter.
• Heating and cooling cause physical changes in matter.

Lesson 5
• A chemical change produces a completely different kind of matter.
• Rusting, tarnishing, and burning are chemical changes of matter.

Reviewing Science Words and Concepts

Write the letter of the word or phrase that best completes each sentence.

a. boiling point
b. chemical change
c. cubic meter
d. density
e. freezing point
f. graduated cylinder
g. gram
h. liter
i. mass
j. matter
k. melting point
l. meter
m. mixture
n. physical change
o. solution
p. volume

1. Anything that has mass and takes up space is ___.
2. The amount of material that an object has in it is its ___.
3. The amount of space that a box takes up is its ___.
4. A salad is an example of a ___ because the vegetables can be easily separated.
5. A ___ is a kind of mixture in which a substance spreads evenly throughout another substance.
6. The unit you would use to measure the length of your classroom is a ___.

7. The unit for measuring the volume of a large box is a ___.

8. The unit used to measure the volume of a liquid is a ___.

9. To measure the volume of a liquid, scientists use a tool called a ___.

10. A ___ is the basic unit for measuring mass.

11. The amount of mass in a certain volume of matter is called ___.

12. A ___ does not produce a different kind of matter.

13. Water changes from ice to liquid water at its ___.

14. The temperature at which a liquid changes to a gas is its ___.

15. The ___ of water, or the temperature at which it changes from a liquid to a solid, is 0°C.

16. A change in matter, as in baking a cake, is an example of a ___.

Explaining Science

Draw and label a diagram or write a paragraph to explain each of the following.

1. What are physical properties of matter? Give three examples.

2. How would you measure the volume of a small piece of iron that has an irregular shape?

3. What are three metric units used to measure mass, and how is each unit used?

4. Ice cream melts at room temperature, but butter is a solid at room temperature. Explain how this is true.

5. How is a chemical change different from a physical change?

Using Skills

1. **Estimate** which has more **mass**— an apple or a lemon. How can you check your estimate?

2. A balloon filled with helium gas rises in the air. What might you **infer** about the density of helium as compared to the density of air?

3. Suppose you mix a substance in water and stir it well. Then you **observe** that tiny bits of the substance are floating in the water. From your observation, do you think this mixture is a solution? Why or why not?

Critical Thinking

1. Write a paragraph to **communicate** how heating and cooling causes matter to change from one state to another.

2. You fill a sink about three-fourths full of water. You turn a clear, plastic cup upside-down and push it into the water. The cup does not fill up with water, and it is hard to push into the water. **Draw a conclusion** about why the cup does not fill up with water.

Put Your Energy into Motion!

On your bike you slowly climb a hill. You use energy to pedal as hard as you can. You reach the top and apply the brakes to stop! Hey, that's friction!

Chapter 2
Force and Motion

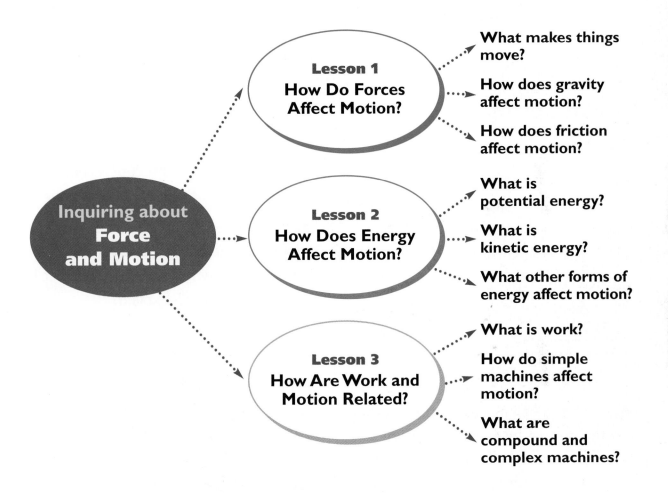

Inquiring about Force and Motion

Lesson 1
How Do Forces Affect Motion?

What makes things move?

How does gravity affect motion?

How does friction affect motion?

Lesson 2
How Does Energy Affect Motion?

What is potential energy?

What is kinetic energy?

What other forms of energy affect motion?

Lesson 3
How Are Work and Motion Related?

What is work?

How do simple machines affect motion?

What are compound and complex machines?

Copy the chapter graphic organizer onto your own paper. This organizer shows you what the whole chapter is all about. As you read the lessons and do the activities, look for answers to the questions and write them on your organizer.

Exploring Changes in Motion

Process Skills

- observing
- inferring

Materials

- safety goggles
- plastic cup
- index card
- quarter
- ball

Explore

1 Put on your safety goggles. Set the plastic cup on a flat surface and put an index card on top of the cup. Place a quarter in the center of the card.

2 Hold on to the cup. With your other hand, use your thumb and index finger to flick the card off the cup as shown. **Observe** and record what happens to the card and the coin.

3 Place the ball in the plastic cup, then put the cup on its side on the floor. Hold on to the cup as you rapidly slide it, open end forward, across the floor. Stop the cup suddenly and observe what happens to the ball. Record your observations.

Reflect

1. What caused the card to move sideways? What caused the quarter to move down?

2. Why did the ball continue to move when you stopped the cup? What finally caused the ball to stop moving?

3. Make an **inference.** What would happen to the ball if there was no friction to slow it down or no object in the way to stop it? Explain.

Inquire Further

What could you do to make the quarter stay on the card when you flick the card off the cup? How could you keep the ball in the cup when you stop the cup? Develop a plan to answer these or other questions you may have.

Exploring Weight

The mass of an object is the amount of matter it contains. An object's mass is the same anywhere in the universe. However, an object's weight depends on gravity. The force of gravity is different on the moon than it is on the earth, and so is an object's weight. In this chapter, you will learn about weight. How can you find out whether one object weighs more than another?

Work Together

Pick 5 small objects in your classroom (such as a box of crayons, a stapler, a large marker) and compare their weights.

1. Pick up the objects and estimate which is the heaviest, which is the next heaviest, and so on.

2. Arrange the objects in order from heaviest to lightest.

3. Now use a balance. Compare the weights of the objects you chose. Did you arrange the objects in the correct order?

Talk About It!

1. Which weighs more, a dollar bill or a quarter? Does the larger object always weigh more? Explain.

2. Did any of your objects weigh the same? How could you tell?

Materials
- balance
- small classroom objects

> **Did You Know?**
> An object weighs $\frac{1}{6}$ as much on the moon as on the earth, but its mass stays the same.

▼ *Which of these two objects is heavier?*

What's the Big Idea?

You will learn:

- what makes things move.
- how gravity affects motion.
- how friction affects motion.

Glossary

Glossary

force (fôrs), a push or a pull on an object that can cause it to change motion

---

How Do Forces Affect Motion?

VROOM! Up, down, and around you go on a roller coaster. **EEEE!** You scream as you feel yourself being pushed and pulled from side to side. You're in motion!

Moving Objects

The dog in the picture is using force, a pull, to move the child. A **force** is a push or a pull on an object that can cause it to change motion. Forces also make roller coasters go up and down.

Forces can cause objects to start moving, speed up, slow down, stop, or change direction. For example, your friend kicks a soccer ball to you. You kick it back. You've just used a force to change the direction of the soccer ball. The harder you kick the soccer ball, the farther it will go. Heavier objects, such as bowling balls, need more force to move them.

When the dog pulls the girl, it is using force. ▼

Force of Gravity

Have you ever gone down the slope of a roller coaster and felt as if you were falling? You felt the effects of gravity. **Gravity** is the force that pulls two objects toward one another because of their mass. Gravity pulls you toward the center of the earth. The roller coaster cars in the picture are being pulled down toward the earth by the force of gravity.

You can see the force of gravity at work. Think about the last time you tossed a ball up in the air. What happened? The ball came down because the force of gravity pulled it toward the earth. No matter how high or how hard you toss the ball, it will always come back down.

Gravity is a force that can be measured. How much do you weigh? When you step on a scale to find out, the scale measures the force of gravity between you and the earth. Your weight is a measure of the pull of the earth's gravity on your body. How much you weigh depends on the mass of your body. The greater the mass of your body, the greater the pull of gravity on your body and the more you weigh.

Glossary

gravity (grav/ə tē), a force that pulls any two objects toward one another, such as you toward the center of the earth

Gravity is the force pulling the roller coaster cars toward the earth. ▶

Glossary

inertia (in ėr′shə), the tendency of a moving object to stay in motion or a resting object to stay at rest

Force of Friction

History of Science

Many years ago, the scientist Isaac Newton made a discovery about moving objects. He learned that a moving object will continue moving in a straight line until a force causes it to slow down or stop. Newton also discovered that an object not moving, or at rest, will stay at rest until a force, such as a push or pull, moves it. The tendency of an object to keep moving in a straight line or to stay at rest is called **inertia**. All objects have inertia.

The children in the picture are in motion on in-line skates. The children used a pushing force to overcome inertia and begin moving. They will continue to move until another force slows them down or stops them. When the children stop, they will stay at rest until a force moves them.

These children will stay in motion until a force slows them down or stops them. ▼

Imagine that you find a soccer ball on the ground. The soccer ball is at rest and will stay at rest until a force acts on it to move it. You kick the soccer ball. You have applied a force and the soccer ball begins to move. The soccer ball will keep moving until another force stops it.

As the soccer ball moves over the ground, the ground rubs against the ball. The rubbing of the ground slows the ball down. The ball continues to slow down until it stops.

The ground rubbing against the soccer ball caused friction. **Friction** is a force that slows down or stops moving objects such as a soccer ball in motion. Friction occurs when two objects rub against each other. Rub your hands together. Do your hands get warm? You are causing friction. Friction changes the energy of rubbing your hands into heat energy.

As the children move on their in-line skates, such as the one in the picture, the wheels rub against the ground. The rubbing causes friction. If the children stop pushing the skates, the friction slows them down. Using the brake causes more friction. The friction will slow them down or stop them.

Glossary

friction (frik′shən), a force that slows the motion of moving objects

When two things rub together, they cause friction. The brakes on this in-line skate rub on the ground, causing friction. ▼

Lesson 1 Review

1. What are two effects that forces can have on motion?

2. How is a ball tossed in the air like a roller coaster car rolling down a track?

3. Describe how friction affects the motion of an object.

4. **Weight**
   Arrange the following objects in order from lightest to heaviest: bowling ball, roller coaster, soccer ball, astronaut.

Reducing Friction

Process Skills

- observing
- estimating and measuring
- inferring

Materials

- safety goggles
- glue
- spool
- cardboard circle with hole
- smooth, level surface
- masking tape
- half-meter stick
- balloon
- sinker

Getting Ready

You can find out how air can reduce friction by making a hovercraft.

Follow This Procedure

❶ Make a chart like the one shown. Use your chart to record your measurements.

	Distance of movement		
	Trial 1	Trial 2	Trial 3
No balloon			
With balloon			
With balloon and sinker			

❷ Put on your safety goggles. Glue the spool to the cardboard on top of the hole. Make sure the holes line up. Use enough glue to assure that no air can escape from between the spool and cardboard (Photo A). Allow the glue to dry. This is your hovercraft.

❸ Place the hovercraft, spool side up, on a smooth, level surface. This could be a desk, table, or the floor. Mark a starting point with tape. Give the hovercraft a small push with your hand. **Observe** its motion and **measure** how far it goes. Record your measurement. Repeat two more times.

❹ Blow up the balloon and twist the end to keep the air from escaping.

 Safety Note *Do not overinflate the balloon. Never inhale from a balloon while inflating it.*

Photo A

Photo B

5 Keep the end twisted closed. Have a partner hold the balloon while you stretch the opening of the balloon over the top of the spool. Be sure to center the balloon opening over the hole in the spool (Photo B).

6 Repeat step 3 but untwist the balloon before you push the hovercraft.

7 Test to see how far the hovercraft travels with a sinker taped near to the spool. Repeat two more times. Try to push the hovercraft with the same force each time.

Interpret Your Results

1. Friction causes the hovercraft to slow down and stop. What can you **infer** about the friction between the hovercraft and the surface when air from the balloon was forced between them?

2. What can you infer about the friction between the hovercraft and the surface when you added the sinker?

 **Inquire Further**

How would the hovercraft work on other surfaces? Develop a plan to answer this or other questions you may have.

Self-Assessment

- I followed instructions to make a hovercraft.
- I **observed** and **measured** the distance the hovercraft moved.
- I recorded my observations and measurements.
- I made an **inference** about friction when air was forced between the hovercraft and the surface.
- I made an inference about friction when the sinker was added to the hovercraft.

What's the Big Idea?

You will learn:

• what potential energy is.

• what kinetic energy is.

• about other forms of energy that affect motion.

Glossary

energy (en′ər jē), the ability to do work

potential (pə ten′shəl) **energy,** energy that an object has because of position

How Does Energy Affect Motion?

YIPPIE! Back and forth you swing. Higher and higher you go as you lean forward and tilt back. **WHEE!** Did you know that swinging uses energy?

Potential Energy

You have probably heard people talk about energy many times, but what is energy? In science, **energy** is the ability to do work. You use energy every time you do work—or move an object. Energy has many forms and can change from one form to another.

Did you ever sit at the top of a slide, such as the one in the picture, waiting to go down? While you sat at the top of the slide, you had potential energy.

Potential energy is energy that an object has because of position. Find the child in the picture on the next page who is at the highest point on the swing set. The swing has the most potential energy at this point. The higher the swing goes up, the faster it will come down and the farther it will move forward.

◀ The boy has potential energy because he is at the top of the slide.

Kinetic Energy

When anything moves, it has a form of energy called kinetic energy. **Kinetic energy** is the energy of motion. Look again at the children on the swings. The swing moving downward has kinetic energy. As it goes back up, the kinetic energy becomes potential energy, or energy of position. Potential energy changes to kinetic energy and back to potential energy with each swing.

Glossary

kinetic (ki net′ik) **energy,** energy of motion

Glossary

Potential energy changes to kinetic energy as the swing moves down. Kinetic energy changes to potential energy as the swing moves up. ▼

Glossary

mechanical
(mə kan′ə kəl) **energy,**
the kind of energy an
object has because it
can move or because it
is moving

chemical (kem′ə kəl)
energy, energy that
comes from chemical
changes

electrical (i lek′trə kəl)
energy, energy that
comes from the flow of
electricity

Other Forms of Energy

Kinetic and potential energy may take different forms. Mechanical, chemical, and electrical energy are forms of energy. Light, heat, and sound are other forms of energy. Think about the last time you plugged in your radio, turned the propeller of a model airplane, or put a battery into a game. Each of these objects uses energy. Look at the pictures to see how energy affects motion.

◀ **Mechanical energy** *is the energy an object has because it can move or because it is moving. Mechanical energy can be potential energy or kinetic energy. When the bicycle moves, potential mechanical energy is changed to kinetic mechanical energy.*

Chemical energy is a kind of potential energy you find in things like gasoline and other fuels. The battery that runs the toy in the picture has potential chemical energy. All matter has potential chemical energy. Some matter, such as the foods you eat, can release their chemical energy. Your body uses the chemical energy from the food to grow and move. ▶

Lesson 2 Review

1. What is potential energy? Give an example.

2. When does an object have kinetic energy? Give an example.

3. List three other forms of energy. Describe how each one affects motion.

4. **Main Idea**
   What is the main idea of the caption for chemical energy on page B44?

Changing Forms of Energy

Process Skills

- observing
- measuring

Materials

- safety goggles
- scissors
- 2 rubber bands
- sinker
- cylindrical cardboard box
- half-meter stick
- masking tape

Getting Ready

In this activity you will observe changes in potential and kinetic energy.

Follow This Procedure

① Make a chart like the one shown. Use your chart to record your measurements.

	Distance box rolls
First roll	
Second roll	
Third roll	

② Put on your safety goggles. Use scissors to cut each rubber band into one long piece.

③ Thread one end of each rubber band through the hole at the top of the sinker (Photo A).

Photo A

④ Remove the lid from the box. Thread the ends of one rubber band through the holes in the inside bottom of the box. Pull the ends of the rubber band through the holes until the sinker is in the center of the box. Tie the ends of the rubber band together on the outside of the bottom of the box (Photo B).

Photo B

Photo C

⑤ Have a partner hold the bottom of the box. Thread the ends of the other rubber band through the lid of the box. Place the lid back onto the box. Pull the ends of the rubber band tight so that the sinker does not touch the side of the box. Tie the ends of the rubber band together. Photo C shows the completed device with the top removed so you can see how it is assembled.

⑥ Attach 1 m of masking tape to a table or the floor. Place the box on its side at one end of the tape.

⑦ Push the box gently so that it rolls along the tape strip. **Observe** the movement of the box. Ask a partner to mark how far the box rolls before it stops and begins to roll back to you. **Measure** how far it rolled. Record your measurement.

⑧ Repeat step 7 two more times, pushing the box a little harder each time.

Interpret Your Results

1. Describe how the potential and kinetic energy changed as you pushed the box and as it rolled back to you.
2. How did the force of the push affect the box's potential and kinetic energy?

? Inquire Further

What would happen if you did not stop the box when it rolled back to you? Develop a plan to answer this or other questions you may have.

Self-Assessment

- I followed instructions to make a device showing changes in potential and kinetic energy.
- I **observed** the movement of the box.
- I **measured** how far the box rolled when pushed with different amounts of force.
- I recorded my measurements.
- I described how the potential and kinetic energy of the box changed.

You will learn:
- what work is.
- how simple machines affect motion.
- what compound and complex machines are.

Glossary

work (werk), the result of a force moving an object

Lesson 3

How Are Work and Motion Related?

Homework! Housework! Yard work! **WHEW!** Do you ever wonder what the word *work* means? How do you know you are doing work?

Work

You use energy to work every day. When you lift a glass of milk or pull open a door, you have done work.

Two things must happen for work to be done. A force must act on an object and the force must have enough energy to make the object move. **Work** is done when a force moves an object. You learned that pushes and pulls are forces. When pushes and pulls move objects, work is done.

The woman in the picture is using a force, a push, to move the swing. When the swing moves in the direction of the force, work is done.

The amount of work you do depends on how much force you use and how far the object moves. The woman does more work if she pushes harder and the swing moves higher. The woman would do even more work if the child were heavier. She would need to use more force to move the swing.

◀ *The woman is using a force to move the swing. Work is being done.*

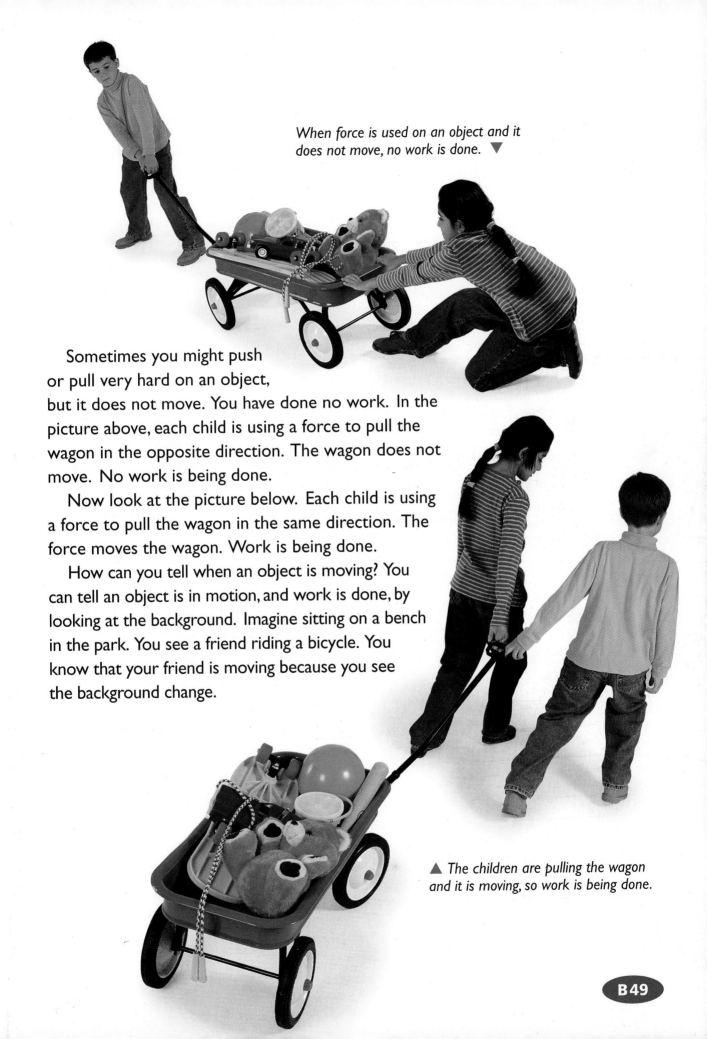

When force is used on an object and it does not move, no work is done. ▼

Sometimes you might push or pull very hard on an object, but it does not move. You have done no work. In the picture above, each child is using a force to pull the wagon in the opposite direction. The wagon does not move. No work is being done.

Now look at the picture below. Each child is using a force to pull the wagon in the same direction. The force moves the wagon. Work is being done.

How can you tell when an object is moving? You can tell an object is in motion, and work is done, by looking at the background. Imagine sitting on a bench in the park. You see a friend riding a bicycle. You know that your friend is moving because you see the background change.

▲ *The children are pulling the wagon and it is moving, so work is being done.*

Glossary

simple machine
(sim′pəl mə shēn′),
a machine made of one
or two parts

Simple Machines

Suppose you want to help build a tree house for your community. What things will you need? You will definitely need tools. A tool is a machine that makes work easier. A **simple machine** is a machine made of one or two parts. Notice that everyone in the picture is using a simple machine to help build the tree house. Read to find out about each of the simple machines.

Inclined Plane

The child below is easily moving heavy materials in a wheelbarrow by using an inclined plane. An inclined plane is a simple machine with a flat surface and one end higher than the other. A ramp is an inclined plane. It makes moving heavy items easier.

Wheel and Axle

The wheelbarrow is rolling on a wheel and axle. A wheel and axle is a simple machine made of a wheel attached to a rod. As the wheel turns, it turns the rod.

Wedge

A wedge is a simple machine that has slanted sides. A nail is a wedge. The slanted sides of the nail make it easier to pound the nail into the wood. The adult is about to use a nail to hold wood together.

Pulley

This child is using a pulley to raise materials up to the tree house. A pulley is a simple machine that uses a rope and a wheel. As the child pulls down on one end of the rope, the other end of the rope pulls the materials up.

Screw

This child is using a screw to put up the sign. A screw is a simple machine that holds materials together. A screw is an inclined plane wrapped around a rod. The inclined plane makes the screw easier to put into the wood. The grooves also help hold the screw in the wood.

Lever

The screwdriver is an example of a simple machine called a lever. The edge of the paint can is part of this lever too. Notice that the child puts one end of the screwdriver under the lid of the can. The edge of the can supports this lever. Therefore, the edge of the can is the fulcrum for this lever. To open the can, the child pushes down on one end of the screwdriver. The fulcrum changes the direction of the force, and the other end of the screwdriver pushes up on the lid.

B51

Glossary

Glossary

compound machine
(kom′pound mə shēn′),
a machine made of two
or more simple machines

▲ *Garden shears*

Compound and Complex Machines

A **compound machine** is made up of two or more simple machines. The simple machines that make up the garden shears shown in the picture are a lever and two wedges. The cutting edges of the blades are wedges. The pin is the fulcrum that changes the direction of the force on the garden shears. When the handles of the shears are pulled in one direction, the blades of the shears move in the opposite direction.

The hand mower below is also a compound machine. Notice the simple machines that make up the hand mower. The handle is a lever. Each blade is a wedge that cuts grass. The mower rolls on two wheels and an axle. All these simple machines together make up a compound machine—the hand mower.

On the next page, notice the picture of another compound machine—a bicycle. Look at the pictures to see what kinds of simple machines make up a bicycle.

◀ *Hand mower*

Parts of a Compound Machine

Wheel and Axle
The pedals are connected by cranks to the big sprocket. The big sprocket is the big-toothed wheel that is turned by the pedals and cranks.

Screws
A bicycle has many screws that hold the parts of the bicycle together.

Levers
The hand brakes on the bicycle are levers.

Wheel and Axle
The small sprocket, or small-toothed wheel, and the rear wheel on the bicycle are another wheel and axle. When the sprocket turns, the rear wheel turns. When the back wheel turns, it makes the front wheel turn, and the bicycle moves.

Wheel and Axle
Together, the pedals, cranks, and big sprocket make up a wheel and axle.

Glossary

complex machine
(kom′pleks mə shēn′),
a machine made of many
simple and compound
machines

*A car engine is made up of
many moving parts.* ▶

Motorcycles, cars, and robots are complex machines. A **complex machine** is a machine made up of many simple and compound machines. The car engine in the picture is a complex machine. Most complex machines are run by electricity or fuels.

Lesson 3 Review

1. When is work done? Give an example.

2. How many parts does a simple machine have? Describe a situation in which a simple machine can be used to do work.

3. How is a compound machine similar to a simple machine? How are complex machines different from compound machines?

4. **Main Idea**
   What is the main idea of the paragraph at the top of this page?

Experimenting with Pulleys

Materials

- dowel
- 2 desks
- masking tape
- metric ruler
- lump of clay
- measuring cup
- water
- plastic bottle with handle
- string
- spring scale

Process Skills

- formulating questions and hypotheses
- identifying and controlling variables
- experimenting
- estimating and measuring
- collecting and interpreting data
- communicating

State the Problem

How does the number of pulleys used affect the effort needed to lift an object?

Formulate Your Hypothesis

If you increase the number of pulleys used, will you need to use more, less, or the same effort to lift an object? Write your **hypothesis.**

Identify and Control the Variables

The number of pulleys used is the **variable** you can change. In Trial 1 you will lift an object with a single pulley system. In Trial 2 you will lift the object with a double pulley system. In Trial 3 you will use a triple pulley system. The mass lifted must remain the same for each trial.

Test Your Hypothesis

Follow these steps to perform an **experiment.**

1 Make a chart like the one on the next page. Use your chart to record your observations.

2 Place the dowel between two desks and tape the ends down to the desk. Stick a ruler in clay on the floor to stand it up. Place the ruler under the dowel (Photo A).

Photo A

Continued →

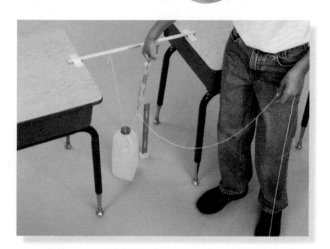

Photo B

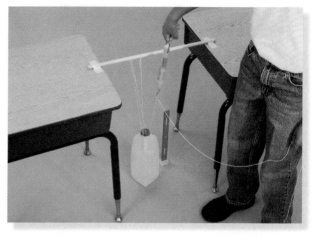

Photo C

3 Pour about 200 mL of water into the bottle. Put the cap on the bottle. Tie one end of the string to the dowel. Make a single pulley system by passing the string behind and through to the front of the handle of the bottle. Tie the end of the string to the spring scale.

4 Pull up on the spring scale to raise the bottle 10 cm from the floor (Photo B). Notice the effort shown on the spring scale. **Collect data** by recording the **measurement** in your chart.

5 Untie the spring scale. Pass the end of the string over the top of the dowel from the front. Then pass the string behind and through to the front of the bottle handle. Tie the end of the string to the spring scale. Now you have a double pulley system.

6 Repeat step 4 (Photo C).

7 Repeat step 5 to make a triple pulley system. Then repeat step 4 one more time (Photo D).

Collect Your Data

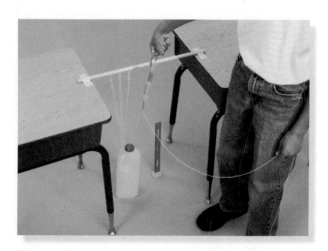

Photo D

Pulley system	Effort to raise bottle 10 cm
Single	
Double	
Triple	

Interpret Your Data

1. Label a piece of grid paper as shown. Use the data from your chart to make a graph on your grid paper.

2. Study your graph. Describe what happened to the effort required to lift the bottle as you added pulleys. Did the effort increase, decrease, or remain the same?

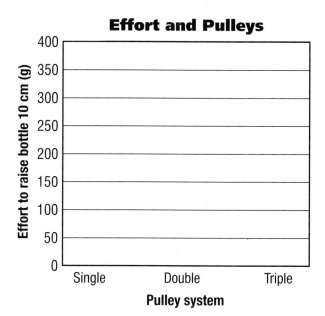

Effort and Pulleys

State Your Conclusion

How do your results compare with your hypothesis? **Communicate** your results. How does the number of pulleys used affect the effort needed to lift an object?

Inquire Further

Would adding another pulley system make lifting the load easier? Develop a plan to answer this or other questions you may have.

Self-Assessment

- I made a **hypothesis** about the effects of pulleys on the effort needed to lift an object.
- I **identified** and **controlled variables** and I followed instructions to perform an **experiment** with pulleys.
- I **measured** the effort needed to lift a bottle with pulleys.
- I **collected** and **interpreted data** by recording measurements and making a graph.
- I **communicated** by stating my conclusion.

Chapter 2 Review

Chapter Main Ideas

Lesson 1

• A force is a push or a pull that can make an object move.

• Gravity is the force that pulls two objects together and pulls you toward the center of the earth.

• Friction slows down or stops objects that are in motion.

Lesson 2

• Potential energy is energy that an object has because of its position.

• Kinetic energy is the energy an object has because of its motion.

• Mechanical, electrical, and chemical energy are forms of energy that can affect motion.

Lesson 3

• When a force moves an object, work is done.

• Simple machines are tools with one or two parts that are used to make work easier.

   • Compound machines are made up of two or more simple machines; complex machines are made of many simple and compound machines.

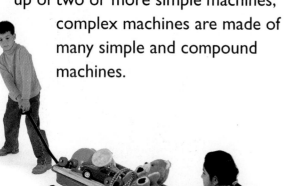

Reviewing Science Words and Concepts

Write the letter of the word or phrase that best completes each sentence.

a. chemical energy

b. complex machine

c. compound machine

d. electrical energy

e. energy

f. force

g. friction

h. gravity

i. inertia

j. kinetic energy

k. mechanical energy

l. potential energy

m. simple machine

n. work

1. A roller coaster car goes up and down because it is moved by a ____.

2. The force of ____ is what pulls a roller coaster car to the earth.

3. The tendency for an object to stay in motion until a force stops it is called ____.

4. When you apply the brakes on your bike, the brakes rub against the wheel and cause ____.

5. You can do work because you have potential ____.

6. As a child moves down a slide, ____ becomes energy of motion.

7. When you throw a ball, potential energy becomes ___.

8. A bicycle in motion has kinetic energy in the form of ___.

9. A battery has a kind of potential energy called ___.

10. A merry-go-round can be moved by the flow of electricity, or ___.

11. If you kick a soccer ball and it moves, you know that you have done ___.

12. A wheel and axle is a ___ that has two parts.

13. A bicycle is a ___ that is made up of several simple machines.

14. The engine of a car is a ___.

Explaining Science

Write a sentence or sentences to answer these questions.

1. What did Isaac Newton discover about moving objects?

2. What is the difference between kinetic energy and potential energy?

3. How do you know when work is done?

Using Skills

1. Use what you learned about **weight** to arrange the following objects in order from heaviest to lightest: pencil, bicycle, soccer ball, feather.

2. Suppose a small child and an adult are climbing a hill at the same speed. **Apply** what you have learned to decide who is doing more work. Explain your answer.

3. **Observe** your arms and legs. Decide which simple machine your arms and legs are similar to.

Critical Thinking

1. A child has a box of comic books she got from a garage sale. She brought the books home in a wagon, but she can't carry the box up the steps into the house. **Make a decision** about which simple machine she can construct that will help her get the box of comics up the steps.

2. A boy hits a ball as hard as he can. The ball bounces along the field and comes to a stop without anyone touching it. **Make** an **inference** about what forces caused the ball to slow down and stop.

3. What changes in forms of energy take place when you walk to school? **Communicate** your explanation.

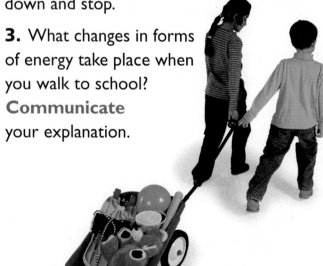

It's For You!

Imagine what life would be like without electricity and magnetism. No phone calls, CD players, or headphones. What would you miss the most?

Chapter 3
Electricity and Magnetism

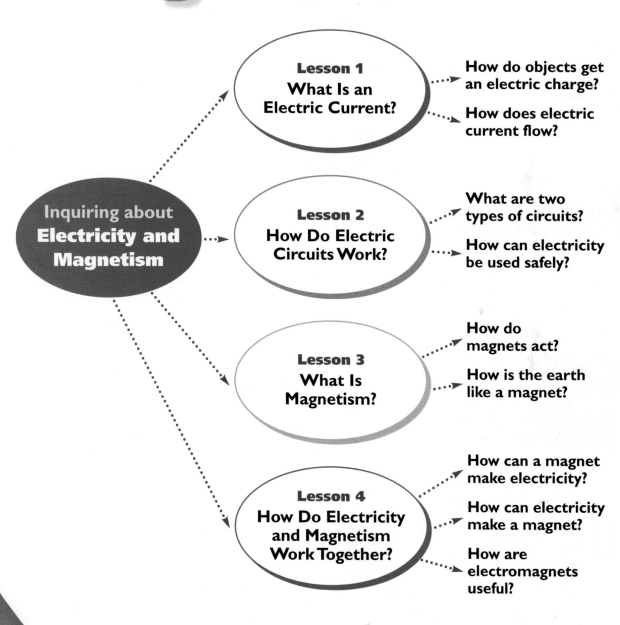

Inquiring about **Electricity and Magnetism**

Lesson 1
What Is an Electric Current?

How do objects get an electric charge?

How does electric current flow?

Lesson 2
How Do Electric Circuits Work?

What are two types of circuits?

How can electricity be used safely?

Lesson 3
What Is Magnetism?

How do magnets act?

How is the earth like a magnet?

Lesson 4
How Do Electricity and Magnetism Work Together?

How can a magnet make electricity?

How can electricity make a magnet?

How are electromagnets useful?

Copy the chapter graphic organizer onto your own paper. This organizer shows you what the whole chapter is all about. As you read the lessons and do the activities, look for answers to the questions and write them on your organizer.

Exploring Electric Charge

Process Skills

- observing
- inferring
- communicating

Materials

- safety goggles
- balloon
- string
- unflavored gelatin powder
- dark construction paper
- wool cloth

Explore

1 Put on your safety goggles. Inflate a balloon. Hold the opening closed while another student ties a string tightly around the neck of the balloon so no air can escape.

2 Pour some of the gelatin powder onto the center of the construction paper.

3 Bring the balloon very close to the gelatin powder, as shown in the photo. Record and draw your observations.

4 Give the balloon an electric charge by rubbing it on the wool cloth for about 30 seconds. Then repeat step 3.

5 Now rub the powder back onto the construction paper. Rub your hand over the entire surface of the balloon. Then repeat step 3.

Reflect

1. What cause and effect did you observe?

2. Make an inference. How can a balloon become charged and uncharged? Explain your answer. Communicate. Discuss your ideas with the class.

? Inquire Further

What happens when a charged balloon is brought near other materials? Develop a plan to answer this or other questions you may have.

Identifying Cause and Effect

In the first lesson, *What Is an Electric Current?*, you will find examples of cause and effect. A cause makes something happen. An effect is the outcome or result. As you read the lesson, look for effects. Then ask yourself what caused the effects to happen.

Example

One way to better understand the activity and the lesson is to make a chart like this one. Then look for the causes of each of the effects listed in the chart. Write the causes in your chart.

Causes	Effects
? →	A balloon gains a negative charge.
? →	Two charged balloons repel each other.
? →	Two charged balloons attract each other.

Talk About It!

1. What is the difference between a cause and an effect?

2. What caused the gelatin powder to jump to the balloon in the activity *Exploring Electric Charge?*

Reading Vocabulary

cause (kȯz), a person, thing, or event that makes something happen

effect (ə fekt′), whatever is produced by a cause; a result

B 63

What's the Big Idea?

You will learn:
- how objects get an electric charge.
- how electric current flows.

What Is an Electric Current?

ZAP! Your friend shuffles her feet and walks toward you across the rug. She touches you. **OUCH!** You get an electric shock. What caused this to happen?

Electric Charge

If you rub two objects together, negative electric charges can move from one object to the other. Objects, such as balloons, people, and rugs, are all made up of matter. Matter is made up of tiny particles, and each of these particles is made of even smaller bits of matter. Some of the smaller bits have a negative (−) electric charge. Other bits have a positive (+) charge, and some have no charge.

Usually, objects have a balance of negative and positive charges. But this can change. Your friend rubbed the rug with her feet. The rubbing caused some bits of matter with negative charges to rub off from the rug onto her.

Before she rubbed the rug, your friend's body and clothing had an equal, or balanced, number of positive and negative charges. The more she rubbed her feet on the rug, the greater the number of negative charges she picked up.

When one person or object has more negative charges than positive charges, the extra negative charges move toward the positive charges in the other person or object. ▼

▲ These balloons have different charges. The positive and negative charges attract each other.

▲ These two balloons each have a negative charge. Like charges repel, or push apart.

Meanwhile, you sat there. Your body had a balanced number of negative and positive charges. Notice the different numbers of negative and positive charges on each child in the picture on page B64. When your friend reached toward you, the extra negative charges on her flowed toward the positive charges on you. Zap! You felt an electric shock. She felt the shock too.

What else can happen when an electric charge builds up in things? The electric charges in two objects can cause either a pulling or a pushing force. Look at the pictures on this page to see what happens when objects have like and different charges.

When two objects have different charges, they pull together. When two objects have the same charge, they repel each other, or push apart. If you rub two balloons on your sleeve, negative charges rub onto the balloons. If you hold them each up by a string, the like charges will push the balloons apart.

▲ Suppose you held up these two balloons. Would their charges push them apart or pull them together? Explain why.

Glossary

resistance

(ri zis′təns), a measure of how much a material opposes the flow of electric current and changes electric current into heat energy

conductor

(kən duk′tər), a material through which electric current passes easily

insulator

(in′sə lā′tər), a material through which electric current does not pass easily

Electric Current

Electric current is the flow of negative charges through matter. You make small electric charges when you drag your feet on the rug, touch someone, and cause a spark to jump. However, these charges only last a moment. To run a VCR, light bulb, or computer, you need an electric current that continues to flow. In the case of the spark, the charges flow through the air or the person or thing you touch. In the case of a VCR or a light bulb, the electric current flows through metal wires to these appliances.

At home, you plug machines into an outlet or turn on a switch. A strong electric current flows. This current travels to your house through wires from an electric power generator. A battery, such as the ones in the picture, can also provide an electric current to light a bulb or run a radio. However, electric current can only flow when it has a closed path, or a closed circuit, to flow through.

The diagram on the next page shows how electric current flows in a closed circuit. Trace the path of the electric current beginning at the battery.

Battery

Have you noticed the "+" and "–" marks on batteries? The "+" end of the battery has a positive charge. The "–" end has a negative electric charge. When the battery is in a closed circuit, the negative charges flow out from the negative end of the battery, through the wires, and back to the battery's positive end. Follow the path of the closed circuit on the next page. ▶

A Closed Circuit

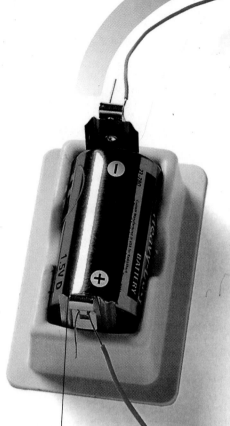

Switch
A switch can be used to open or close a circuit.

Light Bulb
*There is a coiled wire inside the light bulb. This wire has a high **resistance** to electric current—it does not allow current to flow easily through it. Resistance to the flow causes the wire to get white hot and give off a bright glow. The bulb lights up.*

Wire
*The wire is made of a copper metal that is a good **conductor** of electric current. Electric current passes easily through a conductor. The metal wire is usually covered with plastic or rubber. Plastic and rubber are good **insulators** because electric current does not pass easily through them. The insulation keeps the electric current in its path in case the wires touch other metal objects.*

Battery
See Battery caption on page B66.

Lesson 1 Review

1. How does an object get an electric charge?

2. What happens to an electric current when a circuit is closed?

3. Cause and Effect
What causes the bulb to light in a closed circuit?

You will learn:
- about two types of circuits.
- how electricity can be used safely.

How Do Electric Circuits Work?

Light! Color! **Sound!** Flip a switch, and your computer comes alive. Because electric current flows through wires in circuits in your home or school, you can learn by computer or surf the internet. Visit the website at www.sfscience.com.

Electric Circuits

You know that electric current flows only through a closed circuit. As long as the path is unbroken, the current flows. To break a closed circuit, you turn off a switch or remove a part of the path. When electric current does not travel through a circuit, the circuit is open. Just think! Every time you turn off a light, you open a closed circuit.

◀ **Series Circuit**
The bulbs and wires make one single path. Use your finger to trace the path of the current through the circuit.

A series circuit is one way to build a closed electric circuit. In a **series circuit**, several light bulbs or other appliances are connected in one path. Find the series circuit in the picture on page B68. Notice that there is only one possible path for the electric current to follow.

In a series circuit, all the parts must be "on" to complete the circuit. If even one light bulb is missing or burned out, the whole circuit won't work. If your classroom had a series circuit, the computer would shut off every time someone turned off the lights!

Another way to build a closed electric circuit is a parallel circuit. In a **parallel circuit**, each bulb has its own path. Find the parallel circuit in the picture.

The circuits in your home and school are parallel circuits. You plug in your desk lamp. This puts the desk lamp on one parallel circuit. Your radio might run on the same parallel circuit. With a parallel circuit, you can turn off the desk lamp and the radio can stay on. Parallel circuits allow electric items to be turned on and off separately.

Glossary

series circuit
(sir′ēz ser′kit), a circuit that connects several objects one after another so that the current flows in a single path

parallel circuit
(par′ə lel ser′kit), a circuit that connects several objects in a way that the current for each object has its own path

Glossary

Parallel Circuit ▶
If a bulb is burned out, the circuit is still closed. The current can still flow. Use your finger to trace two ways to make a closed circuit.

Using Electricity Safely

⚠ Electricity must always be used with great care. A strong electric current traveling into your body can be very dangerous. The shock can cause bad burns to your body, or even stop your heart! Electric current also produces heat and can start fires. To use electricity safely, follow the guidelines on these pages.

◀ Unload That Outlet!

Don't plug too many appliances into one outlet. Too much current traveling through one circuit can cause an overload. The wires inside a wall can get too hot and start a fire. Using a special safety power strip can help prevent overloading a circuit.

Replace That Cord!

Frayed, cut, or broken electric cords cannot protect you from electric current. Electricity can travel to your body through the break. Worn wires can also overheat and cause a fire. ▶

▲ Unplug Those Appliances!

Be sure to unplug your hair dryer or curling iron when you finish using it. It could cause a fire.

Move Those Papers!

Make sure that papers and other objects that can burn are moved away from an electric heater before it is turned on. Papers, curtains, and other objects that can burn might catch fire from the heater. ▶

▲ Keep It Dry!

Water conducts electricity. So can your body. Never touch electric appliances or cords when you are wet. Never use electric appliances around water. Make sure counters, sinks, and floors are dry.

Lesson 2 Review

1. How is a series circuit different from a parallel circuit?

2. Name three ways to use electricity safely.

3. Cause and Effect
Write about how the unsafe use of electricity can cause harm.

Comparing Series and Parallel Circuits

Process Skills

Process Skills

- predicting
- observing
- inferring

Materials

- safety goggles
- D-cell battery
- battery holder
- 2 flashlight bulbs and holders
- 4 pieces of insulated wire with ends stripped

Getting Ready

You can safely investigate circuits using electricity from a D-cell battery.

Look at the pictures of circuits on the next page. You will need to study these carefully to complete the activity.

Follow This Procedure

❶ Make a chart like the one shown. Use your chart to record your predictions and observations.

	Predictions	Observations
One bulb removed from series circuit		
One bulb removed from parallel circuit		

❷ Put on your safety goggles. Look at the picture of the series circuit (Photo A). With your finger, trace the path that electricity takes through the circuit. Make a drawing of the circuit. Build the series circuit as shown.

❸ Both bulbs should now be lit. What will happen if you remove one of the bulbs? Record your **prediction.**

❹ Remove one of the bulbs and record your **observation.** Replace the bulb, then disconnect the circuit.

❺ Look at the picture of the parallel circuit (Photo B). With your finger, trace the different paths that electricity can take through the circuit. Make a drawing of the circuit. Build the parallel circuit as shown.

❻ Repeat steps 3 and 4.

Self-Monitoring

Do I have questions to ask before I continue?

Photo A
Series circuit

Photo B
Parallel circuit

Interpret Your Results

1. Look at your drawings of the series circuit and the parallel circuit. Draw arrows to show the paths electricity can take through each circuit.

2. Were your predictions about removing a bulb from each circuit correct? Explain how series circuits and parallel circuits are alike and different.

3. You may have noticed that the bulbs were dim in the series circuit and bright in the parallel circuit. Make an **inference.** What would happen to the brightness of the bulbs if you added another bulb to the series circuit? Explain.

Inquire Further

Does the number of bulbs in a series circuit or a parallel circuit affect the brightness of the bulbs? Develop a plan to answer this or other questions you may have.

Self-Assessment

- I followed instructions and used pictures to draw and construct a series circuit and a parallel circuit.
- I recorded my **predictions** and **observations.**
- I drew arrows to show the path of electricity through each circuit.
- I explained how parallel and series circuits are alike and different.
- I made an **inference** about the brightness of bulbs connected in a series circuit.

You will learn:
• how magnets act.
• how the earth is like a magnet.

Lesson 3

What Is Magnetism?

You notice a note on the refrigerator door. Then you pull open the door. **Guess what?** You just found two magnets. One magnet holds the note on the metal door. Another magnet, hidden inside the door, holds the door closed.

Glossary

magnet (mag′nit), anything that pulls iron, steel, and certain other metals to it

magnetism (mag′nə tiz′əm), the force around a magnet

magnetic field (mag net′ik fēld), the space around a magnet where magnetism acts

How Magnets Act

A **magnet** is anything that will attract, or pull, iron, steel, and certain other metals to it. **Magnetism** is the pulling or pushing force that exists around a magnet. When you place a magnet near iron or steel, the two objects pull toward each other with a strong force. Because a refrigerator door is made partly of steel, a magnet will easily stick to it.

A **magnetic field** is the space around a magnet where magnetism acts. Magnetic force is invisible, but you can use tiny pieces of iron to see the magnetic field formed by magnetic force. Find the magnetic field in the picture below.

The tiny pieces of iron line up along the lines of magnetic force. The iron pieces cluster around the poles, where the magnetic force is the greatest. ▶

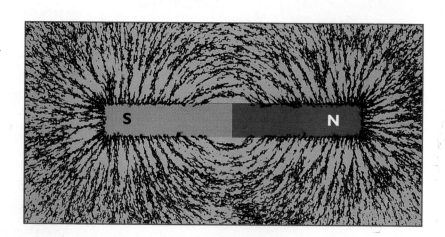

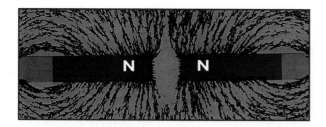

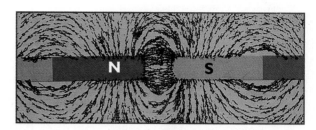

▲ Like poles push apart. Here the like ends of two magnets are near each other. The magnetic forces repel, or push away from, each other. The magnets push apart.

▲ Unlike poles pull together. Here the unlike ends of two magnets are near each other. The magnetic forces attract, or pull strongly together. The magnets may snap together.

The magnets shown here have two ends called **poles.** If these magnets are allowed to swing freely, one pole, the north-seeking pole, points north. Sometimes it is marked N. The south-seeking pole points south. Sometimes it is marked S.

How else do a magnet's poles act? You know that like electric charges push away from each other and that unlike charges pull strongly toward each other. Magnets act the same way. The pictures above show what happens when like and unlike poles are placed near each other.

A magnet's poles also act in another way. Look at the picture below. Which parts of the magnet pick up the most paper clips? You can see that the magnetic force is strongest at a magnet's poles.

Glossary

pole (pōl), a place on a magnet where magnetism is strongest

Glossary

More paper clips stick to the ends, or poles, of the magnet. ▶

Glossary

compass (kum′pəs), a small magnet that can turn freely

▲ *The lodestone attracts the metal nails.*

The Earth: A Giant Magnet

In ancient times, people noticed certain rocks that pulled together or pushed apart. These rocks, such as the one in the picture, are called lodestones. The early Greeks had legends, or stories, about magnetic rocks. One story was about a shepherd. The legend claimed that the iron tacks in his sandals stuck to a rock when he stepped on it. Another legend claimed that a magnetic mountain could pull nails out of wooden ships.

History of Science The Chinese used lodestones thousands of years ago. They discovered that if a lodestone swings freely, one end points north. A Chinese general used this method to lead his army through heavy fog.

In about 1600, an English doctor named William Gilbert made a compass needle that acted the same toward the earth as it did toward a lodestone. This showed that the earth itself is a magnet. Now scientists know that the earth, like all magnets, has a south magnetic pole, a north magnetic pole, and a magnetic field.

Notice the compass in the picture. A **compass** is a small magnet that can turn freely. Its north-seeking pole points toward north. Today people use a compass to find directions.

The earth's north magnetic pole is about 1,600 kilometers from its north geographic pole. The compass is pointing toward the north magnetic pole. ▼

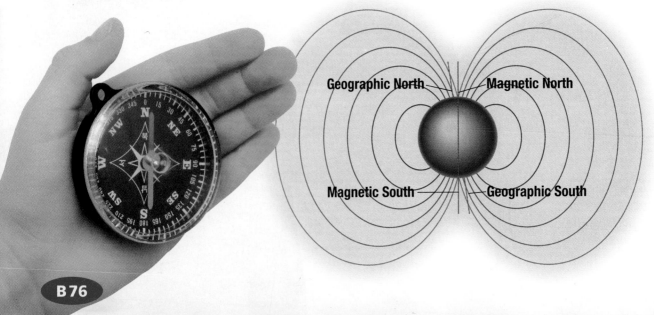

Geographic North — — Magnetic North

Magnetic South — — Geographic South

Earth Science

If you live in the far northern parts of the United States or Canada, you can sometimes see the northern lights. The lights, as shown in the picture, are caused by the earth's magnetic field. You remember how bits of iron are pulled and pushed into a pattern around a magnet's poles. Charged particles from the sun are pulled and pushed into patterns in the sky near the earth's magnetic poles. The particles react with gases in the air, making the brightly colored lights.

▲ *The northern lights, seen near the earth's magnetic north pole, are also called the aurora borealis. Lights seen near the earth's magnetic south pole are called the southern lights, or aurora australis.*

Lesson 3 Review

1. What is magnetism?

2. How is the earth's magnetism useful?

3. Cause and Effect
What causes the northern and southern lights to occur?

Making an Electromagnet

Process Skills

- observing
- making operational definitions

Materials

- safety goggles
- metric ruler
- insulated wire with ends stripped
- bolt
- paper clip
- directional compass
- D-cell battery
- battery holder

Getting Ready

You can find out how electricity is related to magnetism by making an electromagnet. You will learn more about electromagnets in the next lesson.

Look at the self-assessment section at the end of the activity. This tells you what your teacher will expect of you.

Follow This Procedure

❶ Make a chart like the one shown. Use your chart to record your observations.

	Bolt held near	
	Paper clip	**Compass**
Circuit disconnected		
Circuit connected		

❷ Put on your safety goggles. Measure about 25 cm from one end of the wire. Start near the head of the bolt. Wind the wire tightly around the bolt 20 times (Photo A).

❸ Hold the head of the bolt near a paper clip. Record your observations.

❹ Hold the head of the bolt near the needle of a compass. Record your observations.

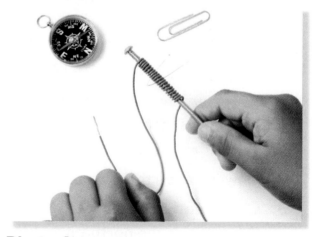

Photo A

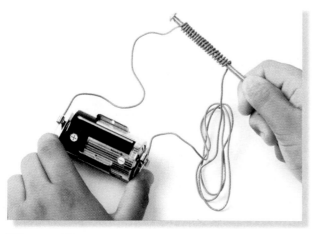

Photo B

5 Place the battery in the battery holder. Attach the ends of the wire to the clips on the battery holder (Photo B). Electricity is now flowing.

 Safety Note *If the bolt and battery begin to feel warm, disconnect the battery and allow them to cool.*

6 Repeat steps 3 and 4. Record your observations. Disconnect the circuit.

Self-Monitoring
Have I correctly completed all the steps?

Interpret Your Results

1. Write an **operational definition** of an electromagnet. Remember: An operational definition describes what the object does, or what you can observe about the object.

2. Write the definition of an electromagnet found on page B82.

3. How are the two definitions alike? How are they different?

Inquire Further

What other objects can be attracted by an electromagnet? Develop a plan to answer this or other questions you may have.

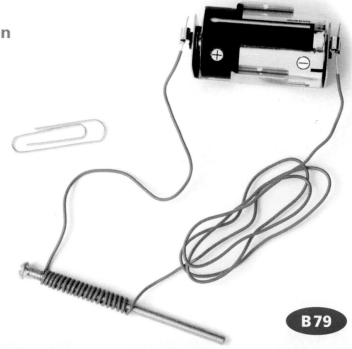

What's the Big Idea?

You will learn:

- how a magnet can make electricity.
- how electricity can make a magnet.
- how electromagnets are useful.

Lesson 4

How Do Electricity and Magnetism Work Together?

Brrring! A telephone rings. **Beeeeep!** An alarm clock beeps. **Ding-Dong!** A doorbell chimes. All of these things work because electricity and magnetism work together.

Electricity from Magnets

Magnets and electricity are closely linked. You already know that they act in some similar ways. However, you may not know that you can make electricity using magnets. The electric current that lights the lamp in the picture is made from a magnet.

Find the magnets in the pictures on the next page. Wires are wound in loops or coils around the magnets. The wires are attached to meters that measure electric current.

◀ *The electricity used to light lamps in your home is made by powerful magnets in a power plant.*

▲ When no electric current flows, the pointer points straight up, at 0.

▲ The pointer moves or jumps when electric current flows. As a student moves the magnet back and forth inside the wire coil, the pointer moves. Electricity is flowing through the wire.

The picture shows how electric current can be made, or generated, by moving a magnet through coils of wire. Electricity can be made from a magnet in several ways. You can slide a magnet back and forth inside a coiled wire or spin a magnet inside a coiled wire. You might also slide a coiled wire back and forth along a magnet or spin a coiled wire around a magnet.

The coiled wire and magnet make just a small model, but it shows how electricity is generated for your home. Most electric power is made by large machines called **generators.** Generators have huge magnets and huge coils of wire. Of course, they are too heavy to move or turn by hand. Some electric generators are powered by wind or rushing water. Others are powered by steam produced by nuclear power or by the burning of coal, gas, or oil.

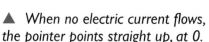

Glossary

generator
(jen′ə rā′tər), a machine that uses an energy source and a magnet to make electricity

Glossary

Glossary

electromagnet
(i lek/trō mag/nit), a magnet made when an electric current flows through a wire

Magnets from Electricity

History of Science

About 180 years ago, a scientist named Hans Christian Oersted was experimenting with electricity. Oersted connected some wire to a large battery so that electricity would flow through the wire. To his surprise, he noticed that when the electric current flowed through the wire something else happened. The needle on a nearby compass moved and pointed toward the wire. Oersted then realized that electricity and magnetism are linked. He concluded that electric current causes a wire to become magnetic.

An **electromagnet** is a temporary magnet made when electric current flows through a wire coil. The picture on this page shows one way to make an electromagnet. If you pass electricity through a coiled wire, the wire becomes magnetic. When the electric current stops flowing, the wire loses its magnetism.

Electric current makes any wire magnetic. Notice the direction that each compass needle is pointing. ▶

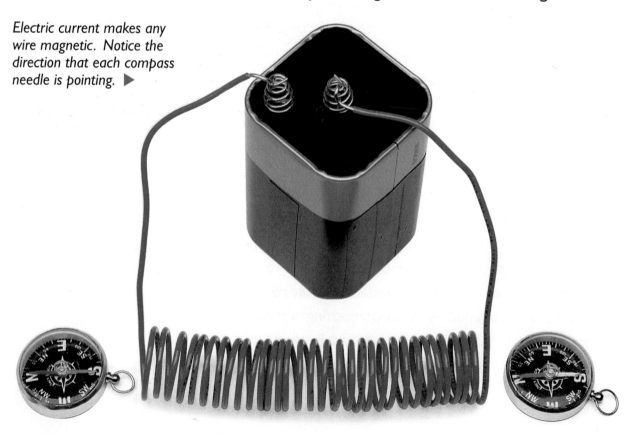

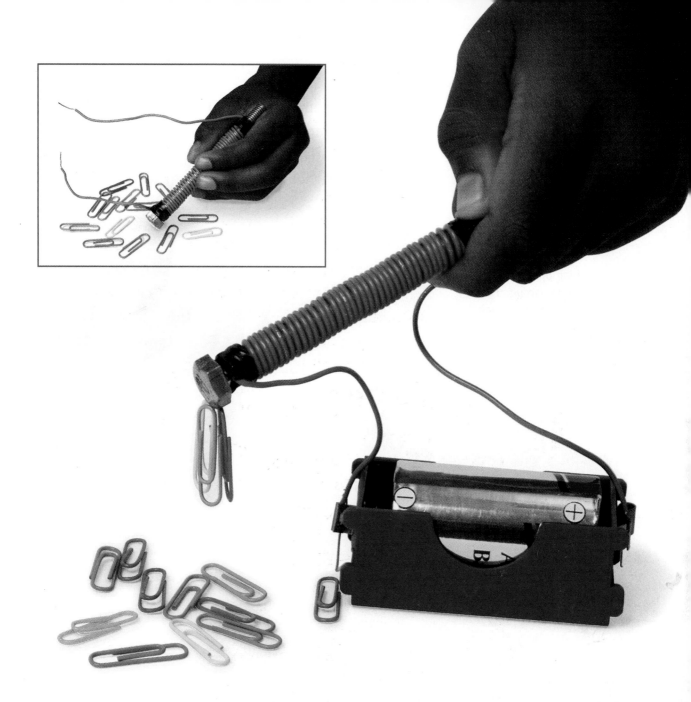

Now look at the picture above showing a wire wrapped around a bolt. This is another way to make an electromagnet. The wire is wrapped about 40 times around a bolt. When the ends of the wire are connected to a battery, electric current flows through the wire. The bolt and the coiled wire together make an electromagnet that is stronger than the electromagnet made with the coiled wire alone.

▲ *The magnetic field of the wire joins the magnetic field of the bolt. This makes an electromagnet strong enough to pick up paper clips.*

Many Uses for Electromagnets

Electromagnets have many uses because they can be turned on and off by closing and opening an electric circuit. The appliances shown on this page all have electromagnets that make them work.

▲ *The pushing of the doorbell closes an electric circuit. Then electric current flows through an electromagnet, and the doorbell rings.*

▲ *When the switch on a fan is turned on, electric current creates an electromagnet that runs the motor in the fan.*

▲ *When electricity flows through an electromagnet in a telephone, the telephone rings.*

Lesson 4 Review

1. How can a coil of wire and a magnet be used to make electricity?

2. How can electricity be used to make a magnet?

3. Why are electromagnets sometimes more useful than ordinary magnets?

4. **Cause and Effect**
   In your own words, write in the correct order the steps that describe how an electric fan runs.

Experimenting with Electromagnets

Materials

- safety goggles
- 25 large paper clips
- metric ruler
- insulated wire with ends stripped
- bolt
- D-cell battery
- battery holder

Process Skills

- formulating questions and hypotheses
- identifying and controlling variables
- experimenting
- estimating and measuring
- collecting and interpreting data
- communicating

Process Skills

State the Problem

How does the number of coils in an electromagnet affect its strength?

Formulate Your Hypothesis

If you increase the number of coils in an electromagnet, will its strength increase, decrease, or remain the same? Write your hypothesis.

Identify and Control the Variables

The number of coils is the variable you can change. You will perform three trials. Use 20 coils of wire in Trial 1 and 30 coils of wire in Trial 2. You may choose the number of coils for Trial 3. Use the same bolt, wire, and battery for each trial.

Test Your Hypothesis

Follow these steps to perform an experiment.

❶ Make a chart like the one on the next page. Use your chart to record your data.

❷ Put on your safety goggles. Bend a paper clip to form a hook (Photo A).

Continued →

Photo A

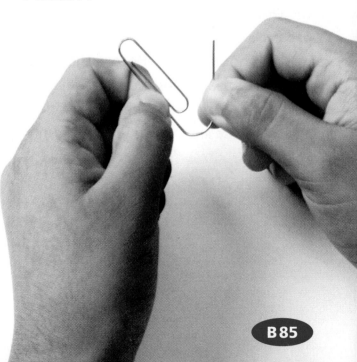

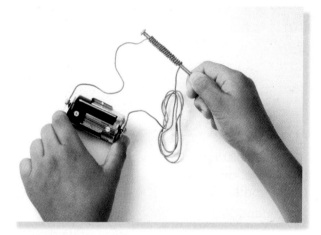

Photo B

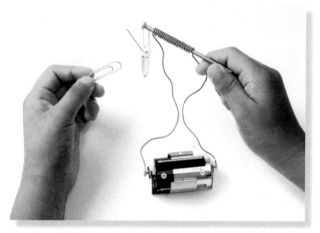

Photo C

3 Construct an electromagnet as you did in the activity on page B78. Place the battery in the battery holder.

4 Attach the ends of the wire to the clips on the battery holder. Electricity is now flowing in the wire (Photo B).

 Safety Note *If the bolt and battery begin to feel warm, disconnect the battery and allow them to cool.*

5 Now you will **measure** the strength of the electromagnet. Pick up the hook-shaped clip with the head of the electromagnet (Photo C). Place paper clips, one at a time, on the hook until the hook falls off. Record the number of paper clips the electromagnet held. Be sure to count the hook-shaped clip. **Collect** and record your **data** in your chart.

6 Disconnect the battery and change the number of coils around the bolt for Trial 2. Repeat steps 4 and 5.

7 Disconnect the battery, and change the number of coils around the bolt for Trial 3. Repeat steps 4 and 5. Then disconnect the battery.

Collect Your Data

Trial	Coils of wire on the electromagnet	Number of clips held
1	20	
2	30	
3		

Interpret Your Data

1. Label a piece of grid paper as shown. Use the data from your chart to make a bar graph on your grid paper.

2. Study your graph. Describe what happened to the number of paper clips held as the number of coils increased or decreased.

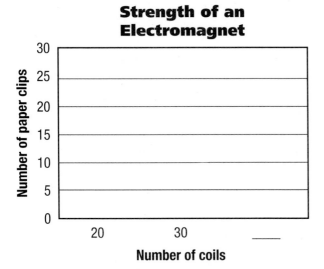

Strength of an Electromagnet

Number of paper clips (y-axis: 0, 5, 10, 15, 20, 25, 30)

Number of coils (x-axis: 20, 30, ____)

State Your Conclusion

How do your results compare with your hypothesis? Explain how the number of coils affects the strength of an electromagnet. **Communicate.** Discuss your conclusion with the class.

Inquire Further

If you add another battery to the electromagnet, will its strength increase? Develop a plan to answer this or other questions you may have.

Self-Assessment

- I made a **hypothesis** about the strength of an electromagnet.
- I **identified** and **controlled variables.**
- I followed instructions to perform an **experiment** with an electromagnet.
- I **collected** and **interpreted** data by recording **measurements** and making a graph.
- I **communicated** by stating my conclusion about the number of coils and strength of an electromagnet.

Chapter 3 Review

Chapter Main Ideas

Lesson 1
• An object gets an electric charge when it gains or loses negative charges.
• An electric current will not flow unless it has a closed pathway, or circuit, to flow through.

Lesson 2
• Series circuits and parallel circuits are two types of electric circuits.
• You need to use electricity safely because it can be dangerous.

Lesson 3
• Magnets have a magnetic field that is strongest at its poles.
• A compass works because of the earth's magnetism.

Lesson 4
• A magnet moving inside a coil of wire makes electricity.
• An electric current flowing through a wire causes the wire to become magnetic.
• Electromagnets are useful in the home because they can be turned on and off.

Reviewing Science Words and Concepts

Write the letter of the word or phrase that best completes each sentence.

a. compass   g. magnetic field

b. conductor   h. magnetism

c. electromagnet   i. parallel circuit

d. generator   j. poles

e. insulator   k. resistance

f. magnet   l. series circuit

1. An electric current passes easily through a wire that is a ___.

2. A material's ___ measures how much the material opposes the flow of electric current.

3. A circuit that connects several objects in a single path is a ___.

4. An object that attracts iron and steel is a ___.

5. An electric current does not pass easily through an ___.

6. The force around a magnet is ___.

7. When electric current runs through a loop of wire, it makes an ___.

8. A small magnet that can turn freely is a ___.

9. The current for each appliance has its own path in a ___.

10. A machine that uses an energy source and a magnet to make electricity is a ___.

11. The space around a magnet where magnetism acts is a ___.

12. Magnetism is strongest at the ___ of a magnet.

Explaining Science

Draw and label a diagram or write a paragraph to answer these questions:

1. How does an object get a positive or negative charge?

2. How are a series circuit and a parallel circuit different?

3. Where is the magnetic field around a magnet strongest?

4. How does an electromagnet work?

Using Skills

1. Use **cause** and **effect** to explain how an electromagnet is useful.

2. How does the use of electricity make your life different than it would be without electricity? **Communicate** your thoughts by writing a paragraph.

3. Suppose you saw a bunch of balloons tied together, but none of the balloons were touching one another. What might you **infer** about the electric charges on the balloons?

Critical Thinking

1. You construct a circuit, but electricity will not flow through it. **Draw a conclusion** about what kind of circuit you think you constructed. Explain your reasoning.

2. Imagine you have just combed your hair with a plastic comb. You hold the comb near a small stream of water running from a faucet. You are amazed that the water stream bends toward the comb. What would you **infer** caused the stream of water to be attracted to the comb?

3. A friend is going to wire a model house. He is not sure if he should wire the lights in a series or parallel circuit. **Make a decision** about the best kind of circuit to use. Write him a note telling him what you think he should do and why it would be best.

Turn on the Music!

Did you know that without light you could not play your CDs? The great music you hear from your CDs is the result of reflected light!

Chapter 4
Light and Sound

Inquiring about Light and Sound

**Lesson 1
What Is Light?**

What is visible light and what are some of its sources?

How do light waves act?

**Lesson 2
What Happens When Light Hits an Object?**

How does light act when it hits different materials?

How do flat and curved mirrors reflect light?

How does light bend?

**Lesson 3
How Does Sound Travel?**

How is sound made?

What are some properties of sound?

How do sound waves travel?

**Lesson 4
How Do You Hear Sound?**

How does your ear work?

How can sounds be made louder?

Copy the chapter graphic organizer onto your own paper. This organizer shows you what the whole chapter is all about. As you read the lessons and do the activities, look for answers to the questions and write them on your organizer.

Exploring Colors in Light

<table>
<tr><td rowspan="2">**Process Skills**</td><td>**Process Skills**
• observing
• communicating</td><td>**Materials**
• direct sunlight
• white sheet of paper
• prism
• colored pencils</td></tr>
</table>

Explore

❶ Hold a piece of white paper so the sunlight shines on it. The sun should be behind you. What color does the sunlight appear to be on the paper?

❷ Hold the prism so that the sunlight shines through it. Move the prism around until the sunlight strikes the white piece of paper. You should move the prism until you see different colors.

❸ What colors do you see? What is the order of the colors you see? Record your **observations.** Make a drawing of the colors.

Reflect

1. When the sunlight passes through a prism, colors that are in sunlight become visible. Describe how the prism changed the appearance of the sunlight.

2. Where have you seen colors like this before? **Communicate.** Discuss your observations with the class. Compare and contrast your observations and your drawing with others in the class.

? Inquire Further

What happens if you shine light from a lamp through the prism? Develop a plan to answer this or other questions you may have.

Using Graphic Sources

In the Explore Activity, *Exploring Colors in Light*, you studied some of the properties of light. The drawing you made in the activity helped you to understand that sunlight is made up of all the colors of the rainbow and the colors in between. Drawings and photographs are examples of graphic sources. Tables, charts, and diagrams are some other examples. Because **graphic sources** show information visually, they can help make facts and ideas clearer.

Reading Vocabulary

graphic source (graf′ik sôrs), drawing, photograph, table, chart, or diagram that shows information visually

Example

In Lesson 1, *What Is Light?*, you discover that light is a form of energy. You also learn that different colors of light have different wavelengths. The diagram below provides information about a rainbow. The parts of the diagram include a drawing, labels, and a caption. Use the diagram to answer the questions below.

Colors of Light in a Rainbow						
Violet	Indigo	Blue	Green	Yellow	Orange	Red

Short wavelength ←——————————————→ Long wavelength

▲ *Each color of light in a rainbow has a different wavelength.*

▲ *Have you ever wondered what causes a rainbow?*

Talk About It!

1. What are the colors of the rainbow?

2. Which color has the longest wavelength? the shortest?

You will learn:
- what visible light is and what some of its sources are.
- how light waves act.

Glossary

visible spectrum (viz′ə bəl spek′trəm), light energy that can be seen and can be broken into the colors of the rainbow

Lesson 1

What Is Light?

WOW! That may be what you thought when you last saw a rainbow. Was it in the sky after a rainstorm? Or was the rainbow made by the sun shining through water? What causes a rainbow to appear?

Visible Light and Its Sources

Can you imagine what the world would be like without light? You would not be able to see the world around you. Plants could not grow, and you would not have any food to eat.

Light is all around you, but you probably don't think about it very often. Do you know that light is really energy? Unlike most energy, light is a form of energy that you can see. The light energy that you can see is the **visible spectrum.**

Notice the rainbow in the picture. You might have seen a rainbow in the sky after a rain shower. When the sun shines through the clouds during or after a rain shower, the sunlight passes through water droplets in the air. The droplets break up the light into all the colors of the visible spectrum, making a rainbow.

◀ Water droplets in the air act like prisms and break white light into the colors of the visible spectrum.

Look at the rainbow again. You can see the colors—red, orange, yellow, green, blue, indigo, and violet—in the rainbow. All of these colors, and the colors in between them, make up white light. Light from the sun is white light.

Most of our light comes from the sun. Even moonlight is light from the sun bouncing off the moon. However, some other objects are sources of light. Which objects in the pictures give off light? The sun, fire, and electric lights are all sources of light. Candles, matches, and flashlights also make light.

The burning wood, the electric lights, and the sun all produce light. ▶

Glossary

Glossary

wavelength
(wāv′lengkth′), the distance from a point on a wave to the same point on the next wave

How Light Waves Act

You may have used a flashlight to see in a dark place. If so, you know that the flashlight shines brightly on an object nearby. If you shine the flashlight on an object farther away, the light isn't as bright because it spreads out.

Light energy moves in a straight line away from its source in waves. If you have thrown a stone into water, you have seen how waves move out away from the stone. Light waves move somewhat like waves in water. Unlike the waves in water, light waves can move through empty space.

The picture shows a light wave that might come from the flashlight. The distance from a point on a wave to the same point on the next wave is the light's **wavelength.** Different colors of light have different wavelengths. Other kinds of energy also have waves like light waves. Microwaves, X rays, and radio waves are like light waves. However, they have wavelengths that are different from light wavelengths, and you can't see them.

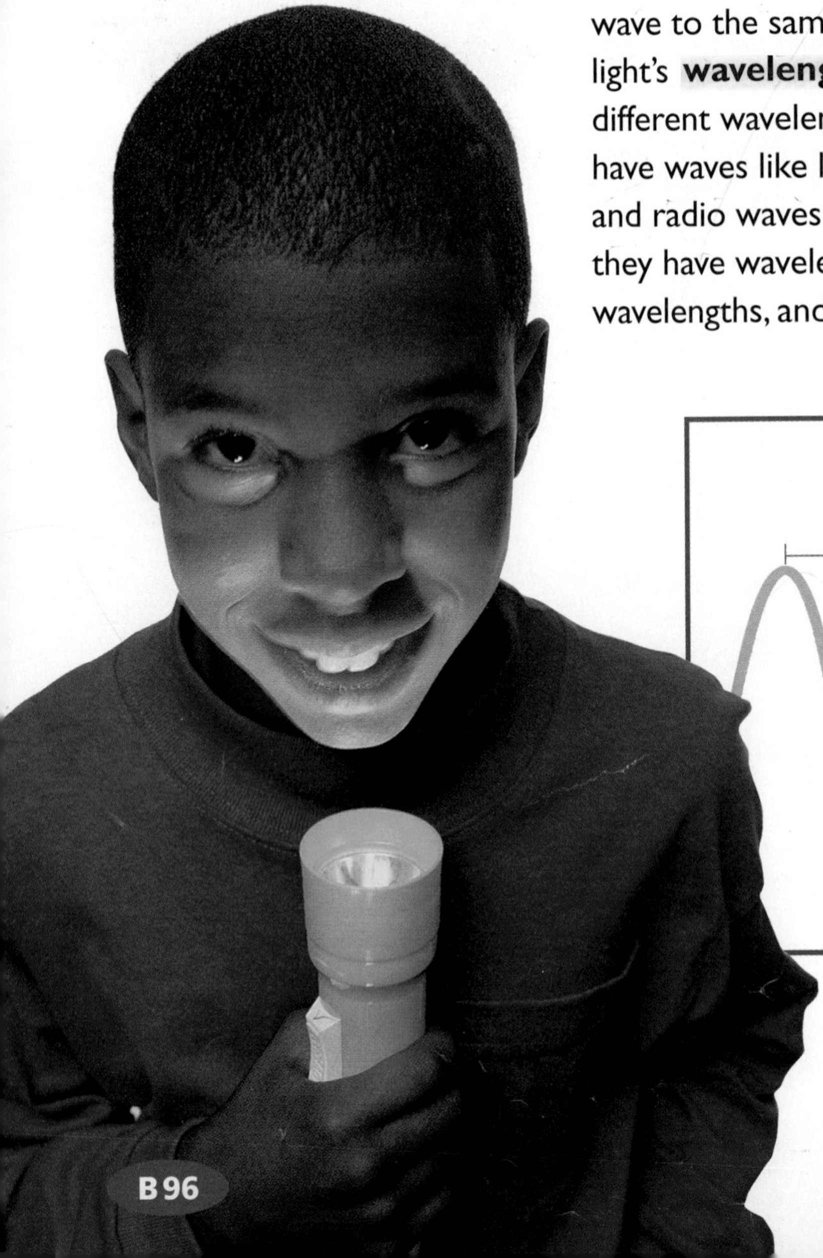

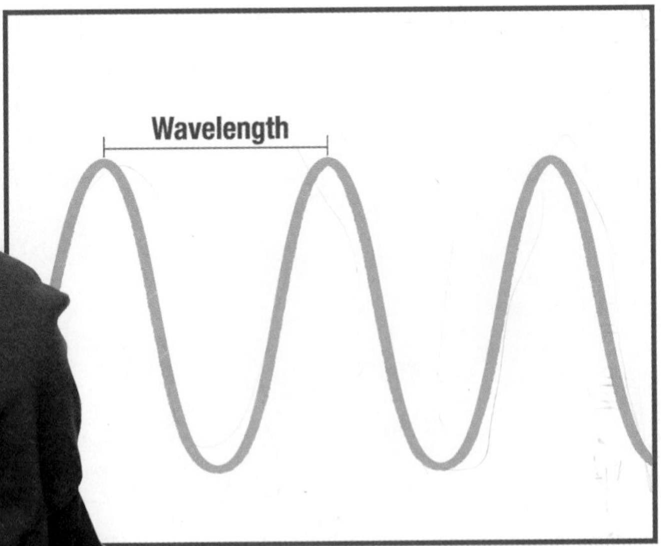

Wavelength

◀ *Light from the flashlight moves in a straight line away from the flashlight in waves.*

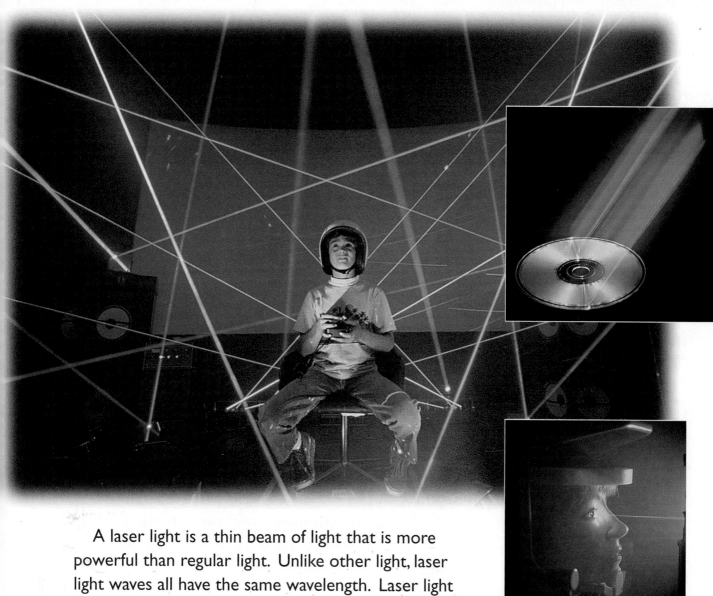

A laser light is a thin beam of light that is more powerful than regular light. Unlike other light, laser light waves all have the same wavelength. Laser light can travel long distances without spreading out very much and is therefore useful in communications and medicine. The pictures show some uses of laser light—a light show, a CD scanner, and eye surgery.

▲ Laser light beams can be fun, as well as useful.

Lesson 1 Review

1. What is light, and where does it come from?

2. How are light waves different from waves in water?

3. **Graphic Sources**
   Describe what happens to the light as it moves away from the flashlight on page B96.

You will learn:

- how light acts when it hits different materials.
- how flat and curved mirrors reflect light.
- how light bends.

Glossary

transparent
(tran spâr′ənt), allows light to pass through so that whatever is behind can be seen

translucent
(tran slü′snt), allows light to pass through but scatters it so that whatever is behind it cannot be clearly seen

Lesson 2

What Happens When Light Hits an Object?

Have you ever watched sunlight shining through a stained glass window? If the sunlight hits a wall, you can see the beautiful colors. **AMAZING!** Why do you think this happens?

Different Materials and Light

Notice the pictures below. In the first picture, you can see the picture behind the glass. You can see the picture because glass is **transparent.** Light passes through a transparent object, and you can see what is behind it. Clear glass, clean water, and clear plastic are transparent.

Now look at the second picture. You can see the picture, but it is not as clear as in the first picture. Light passes through the thin paper, but the paper spreads the light around in different directions. The thin paper is **translucent.** Tissue paper, wax paper, and some kinds of glass and plastic are translucent.

▲ Transparent

▲ Translucent

▲ Opaque

In the third picture, you cannot see the picture behind the paper at all. Light cannot pass through the paper covering the picture. The paper is **opaque**. You cannot see through opaque material. Bricks, wood, and your book are opaque.

Have you ever wondered why you can see colors? You see colors because of what happens to light when it hits different materials. You also see colors because white light is made up of all the colors. Look at the pictures below and read to find out what happens.

Glossary

opaque (ō pāk´), does not allow light to pass through

transmit (tran smit´), to allow to pass through

absorb (ab sôrb´), to take in

reflect (ri flekt´), to bounce back

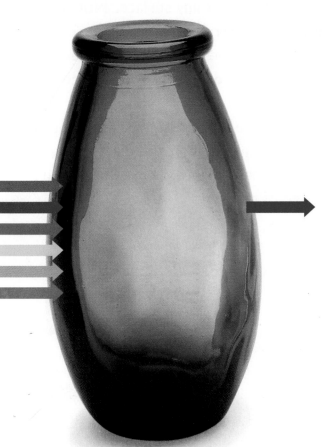

Seeing Color of Transparent and Translucent Objects

◀ *The blue glass looks blue because it absorbs all the colors in light except blue. Blue glass lets blue light pass through it. Therefore, it looks blue. Transparent and translucent objects are the color of the light they **transmit**, or let pass through.*

Seeing Color of Opaque Objects

*When light hits the chili pepper in the picture, the pepper **absorbs**, or takes in, all the colors in the light except red. The pepper looks red because it **reflects**, or bounces back, the red light. Then why do some objects look white? That's right! A white object reflects all the colors in white light. However, black objects absorb almost all of the light that hits them. They do not reflect any colors of light.* ▼

Mirrors and Light

When you look at some objects, you see your image. When you look at other objects, you do not see your image. Why does this happen?

To answer this question, first you must think about how you see objects. You know that if you are in a totally dark room, you cannot see anything. You see objects because the objects reflect light to your eyes.

If you place objects in front of a flat mirror, you see an image of the objects. The flat mirror in the picture, like all mirrors, has a smooth, shiny surface. Notice that the light rays hit the mirror at a certain angle or direction. Also notice that the rays reflect off the mirror at the same angle or direction. You can see a good image of the toys.

In the other picture, the toys are in front of a rough wall. Notice that when light rays hit the rough surface, they reflect in many different directions. You cannot see an image of the toys.

The picture shows how light rays reflect off the flat mirror. ▼

The picture shows how light rays reflect off the rough surface. ▼

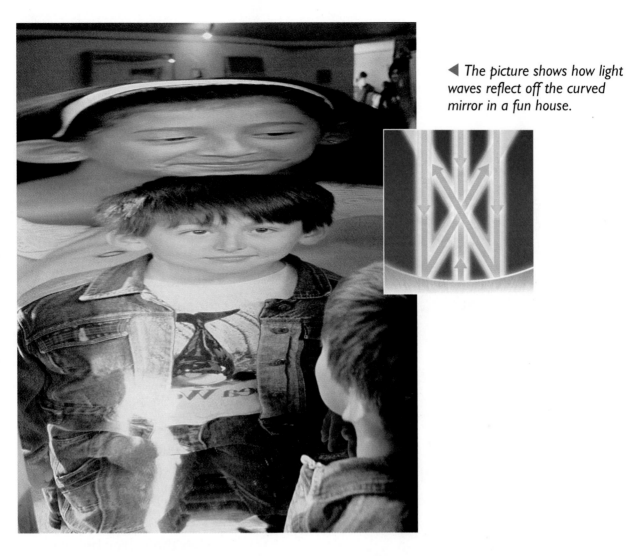

◀ The picture shows how light waves reflect off the curved mirror in a fun house.

Notice the picture of the fun house mirror. Why do you think the image looks so strange? Each light ray that hits the surface of the curved mirror is reflected back at the same angle that it hits. Because the surface is curved, the light rays that hit the mirror in different places bounce off in different directions. Therefore, you do not see a good image. The image may be larger or smaller—or even upside down.

Curved mirrors can be fun, but they can also be useful. Curved mirrors are used in stores so that clerks can see people all over the stores. The mirrors in some cars are curved to help drivers see a larger area of traffic behind them.

How Light Bends

Why do you think the stems of the flowers in the picture seem to be broken? The stems look broken because light sometimes bends or changes direction.

Have you ever tried to run through sand or deep snow? If so, you know that you can't run as fast as on solid ground. Light also travels at different speeds through different materials. However, when light changes speed, it also changes direction. Light bends when it moves from one material to another.

The light rays that reflect from the top of the flowers in the vase move through air. These rays do not bend. The light rays that reflect from the stems in the water travel back through the water before they reach the air. Light travels faster through air than it does through water. When these rays move into the air, they change speed and bend. The stems look broken.

Notice the lenses in the pictures on the next page. A lens is a transparent object that has at least one curved surface. When light moves from air into a lens, the light bends. Lenses bend light in a way that makes an image.

◀ *When light bends, it makes objects look different than they really are.*

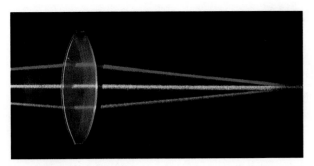

▲ Convex lens

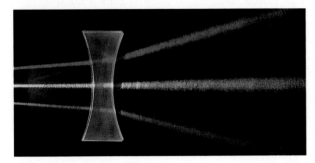

▲ Concave lens

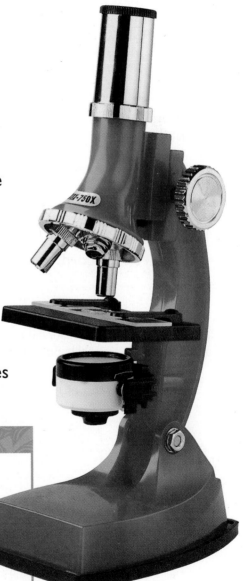

Glossary

convex lens
(kon veks′ lenz), a lens that is thicker in the middle than at the edges

concave lens
(kon kāv′ lenz), a lens that is thinner in the middle than at the edges

The lens in the first picture bulges in the middle like a football. This kind of lens is a **convex lens**. Notice how the convex lens bends light. Each of your eyes has a convex lens. The microscope in the picture also uses convex lenses.

The lens in the second picture is thinner in the middle than at the edges. This kind of lens is a **concave lens**. Notice that the concave lens spreads light rays apart. A concave lens makes objects look smaller.

Lesson 2 Review

1. Why do some objects look white?

2. How does a curved mirror help a car driver?

3. What happens to light rays when they move from water into air?

4. **Graphic Sources**
   Use the pictures above to help you describe what happens to light rays as they pass through lenses.

▲ Convex lenses in a microscope make small objects look much larger.

B 103

Observing Light Through Different Materials

Process Skills

- observing
- inferring

Materials

- textbook
- small object to cast shadow
- sheet of white construction paper
- flashlight
- sheet of clear plastic
- sheet of wax paper
- sheet of aluminum foil

Getting Ready

In this activity you will observe how different materials transmit light.

Follow This Procedure

❶ Make a chart like the one shown. Use your chart to record your observations.

Material held in front of flashlight	Observations of shadow of object
No material	
Clear plastic	
Wax paper	
Aluminum foil	

❷ Darken the room. Place the textbook on a desk. Place the object on the textbook. Have a partner hold the sheet of white construction paper behind the textbook and object.

❸ Shine a flashlight on the object so that a shadow appears on the construction paper (Photo A). How does the shadow appear? Are the edges of the shadow clear and sharp? Record your **observations.**

❹ Continue shining the flashlight on the object while holding a sheet of clear plastic in front of the flashlight (Photo B). Look at the shadow of the object. Record your observations.

❺ Repeat step 4 using wax paper.

❻ Repeat step 4 using aluminum foil.

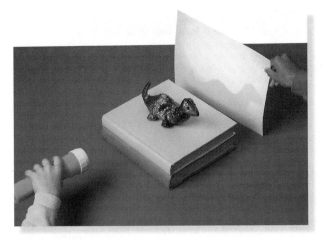

Photo A

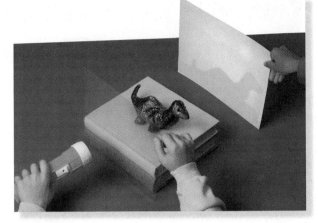

Photo B

Self-Monitoring

Did I notice differences in steps 4, 5, and 6? Do I need to repeat any of my observations to make sure?

Interpret Your Results

1. Compare and contrast the shadows you observed. Which material formed the sharpest shadow? Which material formed a shadow that was not sharp?

2. Describe what you observed when the aluminum foil was placed in front of the flashlight. Make an **inference.** Which material transmits the most light? Which material transmits the least light?

Inquire Further

What do you think will happen to the shadow of the object if you move the object closer to or farther away from the white construction paper? Develop a plan to answer this or other questions you may have.

Self-Assessment

- I followed instructions to investigate how different materials transmit light.
- I **observed** what happened to the shadows when different materials were placed between the flashlight and the object.
- I recorded my observations.
- I compared and contrasted the shadows produced.
- I made an **inference** about the light transmitted through the different materials.

You will learn:

- how sound is made.
- what some properties of sound are.
- how sound waves travel.

Lesson 3

How Does Sound Travel?

SCREECH! Sounds are all around you. Stop and listen a minute. What sounds do you hear? You might hear doors closing, people talking, or dogs barking. What makes these sounds?

How Sound Is Made

You know that light is a kind of energy that you can see. Sound is also a kind of energy, but you can't see sound. However, you can hear sound. Sometimes you might even feel sound.

Each of the instruments that the children in the picture are playing makes a different sound. The sound of music is different from a door banging or the crack of a bat against a baseball. However, all of these sounds are alike in some ways.

The sounds of doors, bats, and music are made in the same way. All these sounds are made when matter **vibrates,** or moves quickly back and forth.

Anything that takes up space is matter. Even though you cannot see it, air is matter. The instruments in the picture, the air, and the children are all made of matter.

If you pluck the strings of a guitar, you make the strings vibrate. Each string makes a different sound, and you make music. If you hit a drum, you make the drum vibrate. Then the drum makes a booming sound. Even though these sounds are very different, each of the sounds is made when something makes matter vibrate.

The children cause each of the instruments to vibrate, and music is made. ▼

Properties of Sound

Now you know how the drum makes sound, but how can you hear the sound? The booming of the drum must reach your ear. When the drum begins to vibrate, sound waves move out from the drum. As the sound waves move through the air, they make the air vibrate. Look at the picture on the left and read to find out more about sound waves.

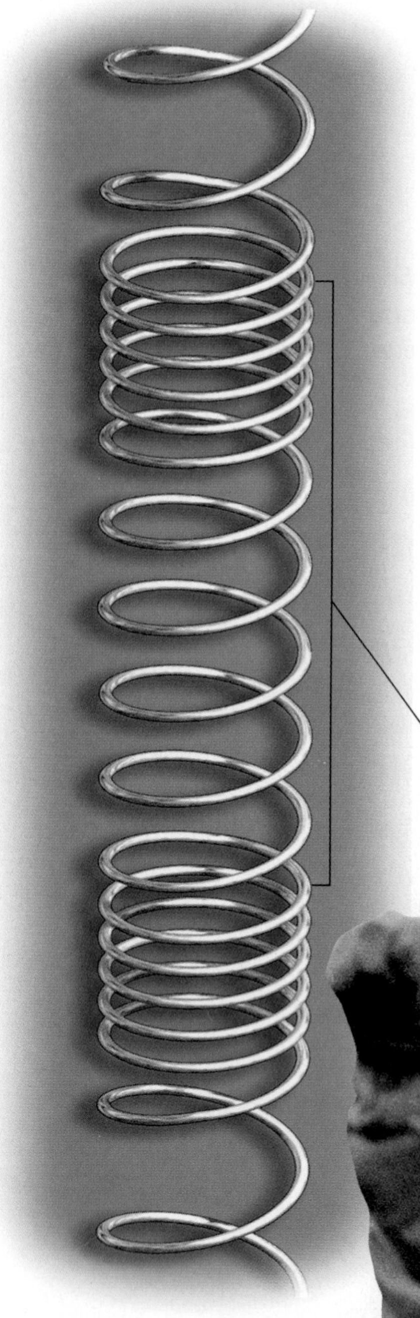

◀ **Sound Waves**
Sound waves are different from light waves. Sound waves are more like the waves that move through the spring shown here. Notice that in some places the parts of the spring are close together. When sound vibrations move through matter, they push the particles of matter closer together. As the sound vibrations pass, the particles move apart again.

Wavelength
The wavelength of a sound wave is the distance from a point on one part of a wave to the same point on the next wave.

The boy uses a lot of energy to shout and makes a loud sound. A person can hear him at a long distance. ▼

You have seen how sounds are alike. Now look at some ways that sounds are different. Notice the picture on page B108 of the boy shouting. A shout is a loud sound. It has more **volume** than a whisper. The girls in the picture on this page are whispering. A whisper is a soft sound. Now look at the graph. Find another soft sound on the graph.

What makes some sounds louder than others? You know that when you shout you put a lot of energy into it. You use much less energy to whisper. Also, if you have ever hit a drum, you know that you can make the drum sound loud or soft. If you hit the drum lightly, the drum makes a soft sound. If you hit the drum hard, the drum makes a loud sound. It takes more energy for you to hit the drum hard, so the sound waves have more energy, and the sound is louder.

A lion's roar or the sound of an airplane's engine are some other loud sounds. A bird singing and a gentle breeze blowing through leaves make soft sounds. What other loud sounds and soft sounds can you think of?

Volume of Sound

People whispering

Bird singing

Jet landing

Soft ➤ Loud

◀ *The girl uses only a little energy to whisper. To hear a whisper, a person must be nearby.*

Glossary

pitch (pich), the highness or lowness of a sound

Sounds can also be different in other ways. If you have ever heard the music from a trombone, you know that it sounds very low. What makes a trombone sound so low? Notice how large the trombone in the picture is. When the child blows air into the large trombone, the air vibrates slowly. Because the air vibrates slowly, the sound waves from the trombone are very long. Sound waves that have long wavelengths make a sound with a low pitch. The **pitch** of a sound is how high or how low the sound is.

Look at the flute in the picture. Would you expect the flute to play a sound with a low pitch or a high pitch? If you said "high," you're right. The flute has a smaller opening through it than a trombone does. When the child blows air into the flute, the air vibrates quickly. The sound waves have short wavelengths, and the sound has a high pitch.

Think about the strings on a guitar. Some of the strings are thin and some of the strings are thick. If you pluck the thin strings of the guitar, they vibrate quickly. The thin strings make sounds with a high pitch. If you pluck the thick strings, they vibrate slowly. The thick strings make sounds with a low pitch.

The larger column of air in the trombone does not vibrate as quickly as the smaller column of air in the flute. ▼

You probably enjoy listening to music. What kinds of music do you like? Your family or friends may not like the same music that you do. Rock music may sound pleasant to you, but some friends may think that rock is too noisy. However, most people enjoy listening to some kind of music. Music is usually thought to be a pleasant sound.

The world around you is filled with sounds. Some of the sounds are pleasant, but some of the sounds are not so pleasant. Sounds made by the leaves in the picture below are pleasant sounds. Birds singing or a gentle rainfall are also pleasant sounds.

Other sounds, such as a jet plane taking off, are unpleasant sounds, or noise. Brakes screeching and car horns blowing are also noisy sounds. Too much noise can be harmful to your health. Notice that the airport worker in the picture above is wearing ear protectors. They keep the noise from harming her ears.

Beside being harmful to your ears, noise can affect you in other ways. Being in a noisy place for a long time can make people feel upset. Noise can also affect the way people sleep or digest food.

Even listening to pleasant sounds, such as music, can be harmful. Listening to loud music or other loud sounds for long periods of time can cause hearing loss. If you use earphones to listen to music, be sure to keep the volume low.

▲ *This airport worker is wearing ear protectors. Without them, she could suffer hearing loss because of the loud noises.*

When leaves fall, they make a very soft sound. ▼

How Sound Travels Through Different Materials

As you know, sound waves, unlike light waves, cannot travel through empty space. Since sound waves travel by making matter vibrate, they must travel through matter. However, sound waves travel faster in some materials than they do in other materials. Look at the pictures and read to find out why this happens.

◄ How Sound Travels Through Air

When the bird in the picture chirps, the sound waves make the particles in the air vibrate. When the particles vibrate, they bump into other particles. The sound waves move from one particle of air to the next. Notice how far apart the air particles are. The sound waves move slowly from one particle of air to the next.

How Sound Travels Through Water

When the whale in the picture sings, the sound waves make the particles in water vibrate. The sound waves move from one particle of water to the next. Notice that the particles in the water are closer than the particles in the air. The particles of water bump into one another faster than the air particles do. Therefore, sound waves move faster in water than they do in air. ▼

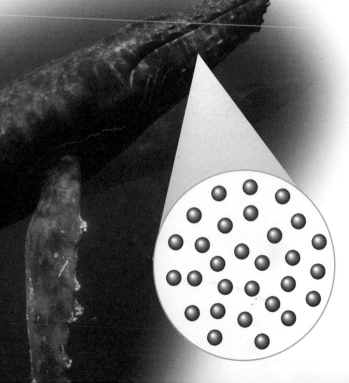

How Sound Travels Through Wood

When the child in the picture taps on the door, the sound waves make the particles in the wood vibrate. Notice how close together the wood particles are. They are almost touching one another. The particles of wood bump into one another very quickly. The sound waves move quickly from one particle of wood to the next. Sound waves travel faster in a material such as wood than they do in air or water. ▶

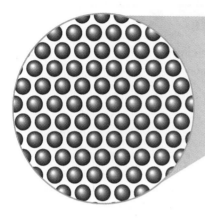

Lesson 3 Review

1. How does hitting a drum cause the drum to make a sound?

2. When does an object make sound with a high pitch?

3. Why does sound travel faster through wood than it does through water?

4. **Graphic Sources**
   How does the picture of the particles in wood above help to explain why sound travels faster through wood than other materials?

Classifying Sounds

Process Skills

- observing
- classifying
- collecting and interpreting data
- inferring

Materials

- small paper clip
- metric ruler
- large paper clip
- small coin
- large coin
- small rubber band
- large rubber band
- small plastic cup
- large plastic cup
- small ball of aluminum foil
- large ball of aluminum foil

Getting Ready

In this activity you will compare the pitch and volume of sounds.

You will have to listen and concentrate carefully to hear differences in the sounds. You may have to repeat some of the tests until you are sure of your answers.

Follow This Procedure

① Make a chart like the one shown. Use your chart to record your observations.

② Drop a paper clip from a height of 10 cm onto a desk (Photo A). **Observe** its pitch.

③ Drop another object from a height of 10 cm. If the pitch is lower than the paper clip, place it on your desk below the clip. If the pitch is higher than that produced by the paper clip, place it on your desk above the paper clip.

Pitch Highest to lowest	Volume Highest to lowest

④ Repeat step 3 with each of the other objects (Photo B). When you are done you will have **classified** the items. They will be placed in order of the pitch they produce, from highest to lowest. **Collect** your **data** by recording the ranked items in your chart.

Photo A

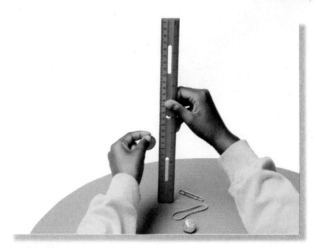

Photo B

⑤ Repeat steps 3 and 4 with all of the objects, but this time rank them by the volume of sound they produce when dropped.

Self-Monitoring
Do I need to repeat any of the steps to be sure of my answers?

Interpret Your Results

1. Interpret your data. Which of the objects made the sound highest in pitch? lowest in pitch? Make an inference. What are some properties of objects that produce sounds high in pitch? What are some properties of objects that produce sounds low in pitch?

2. Which of the objects made the sound highest in volume? lowest in volume? Make an inference. What are some properties of objects that produce sounds high in volume? What are some properties of objects that produce sounds low in volume?

Inquire Further

What would happen to the sounds if you dropped the items on different surfaces? Develop a plan to answer this or other questions you may have.

Self-Assessment

- I followed instructions to compare the pitch and volume of sounds produced by different objects.
- I observed the sounds produced by dropping different objects.
- I classified the sounds of the objects by ranking their pitch and volume.
- I collected data by recording the ranking of the objects in a chart.
- I made inferences about the properties of objects that produce sounds of different pitch and volume.

You will learn:

- how your ear works.
- how sounds can be made louder.

Music to sing along with or music to dream by! You can play music for any mood on a CD player. ▼

Lesson 4

How Do You Hear Sound?

Sound plays an important part in your life. **BRRING!** Alarm clocks ring, doorbells ring, school bells ring, and railroad crossing bells ring! How are you able to hear all of these and other sounds?

How Your Ear Works

Human Body

Imagine that you are the child in the picture listening to a CD. You turn on the CD player. How does the music reach your ear so that you can hear it? Sound waves move out from the speakers of the CD player and make the air around them vibrate. The shape of your outer ear directs the sound waves to the part of the ear inside your head. Look at the picture on the next page. Notice how sound waves move through your ear so that you can hear the music.

When the messages get to your brain, it helps you understand the sound that is received. Then you hear the music from the CD player. You know that when you start a CD, you hear the music right away. That's how fast the sound waves travel from the speakers, to your ear, and through your ear to your brain.

Hearing music is fun, but many of the other sounds you hear help to keep you safe. Hearing some sounds, such as a fire alarm at your school or a smoke alarm in your home, can warn you of danger. Hearing a tornado siren or other storm warning gives you time to move to a safe place.

Life Science Many animals have ears somewhat like your ears. Each of their ears catches sound and directs it to the eardrum. Then the sound waves move through their ears to their brain, and they hear the sound.

However, many animals can hear sounds that you cannot hear. For example, dogs can hear high-pitched sounds that you can't hear. Some animals, such as rabbits, can also hear sounds that are too soft for you to hear. Being able to hear sounds helps keep animals safe.

Three Tiny Bones
As the eardrum vibrates, it causes the three tiny bones to vibrate.

Eardrum
Sound waves hit a thin skin called the eardrum. The sound waves cause the eardrum to vibrate.

Liquid in the Ear
The part of the ear that is shaped like a snail's shell is filled with liquid. When the tiny bones vibrate, they cause the liquid to vibrate. The liquid carries the sound waves to nerve endings.

Nerve
The nerve is the part of the ear that carries messages to the brain.

Making Sounds Louder

Sometimes sounds must be made louder to be heard at a distance. Sounds that warn people of danger must be loud enough to get people's attention. Also, doctors and nurses often must listen to the sound of people's body organs to know if they are healthy. Some of these sounds must be made louder to be heard. Look at the pictures and read the text on pages B118–B121 to find out some ways to make sound louder.

Glossary

stethoscope
(steth′ə skōp), an instrument used to hear the sounds of body organs

microphone
(mī′krə fōn), an instrument used to amplify voices, music, and other sounds

electric signal
(i lek′trik sig′nəl), a form of energy

amplify (am′plə fī), to make stronger

bullhorn (bul′hôrn′), an instrument with a built-in microphone that makes sound louder

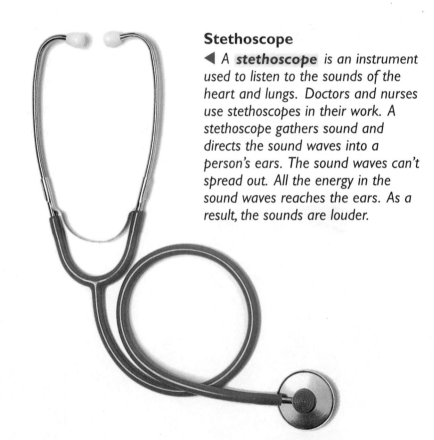

Stethoscope

◀ A **stethoscope** is an instrument used to listen to the sounds of the heart and lungs. Doctors and nurses use stethoscopes in their work. A stethoscope gathers sound and directs the sound waves into a person's ears. The sound waves can't spread out. All the energy in the sound waves reaches the ears. As a result, the sounds are louder.

The doctor in the picture is using a stethoscope to listen to the child's lungs. The lung sounds are louder because the sound waves are directed to his ears by the stethoscope. ▼

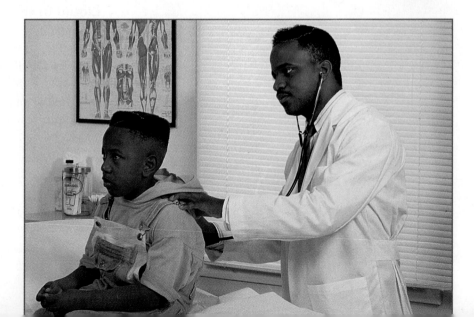

Microphone

A **microphone** can be used to amplify the sound of your voice. The woman in the picture is using a microphone. Sound waves from the woman's voice hit the microphone and make a part inside the microphone vibrate. ▼

The microphone collects the sound waves and changes the sound energy into electric energy, or **electric signals**. The electric energy moves through a wire in the microphone to an amplifier. The amplifier makes the electric energy stronger, or amplifies it. **Amplify** means to make stronger. The stronger electric energy moves to a speaker. The speaker changes the signals back into sound waves. The woman's voice comes out of the speaker with more volume than the sound that entered the microphone. ▶

Bullhorn

◀ A **bullhorn** has a built-in microphone. A bullhorn can increase the energy of the sound waves made by your voice. Sound waves from a bullhorn can be heard much farther away than the unaided voice.

▲ You speak into the mouthpiece of the bullhorn. The microphone changes the sound energy into electric energy. These signals travel to another part of the bullhorn that amplifies them. The amplified signals then move into the speaker of the bullhorn. The speaker changes the signals back into sound waves that have more energy than those that entered the mouthpiece. Having more energy makes the sound louder.

▲ The firefighter in the picture is using a bullhorn to direct people to safety during a fire. The bullhorn allows people who are far away to hear the firefighter.

Glossary

hearing aid, an instrument used to help people with a hearing problem hear better

History of Science

A **hearing aid** is an instrument used to help people with a hearing loss. Hearing aids of different kinds have been used for many years. Look at the pictures and read to find out how hearing aids have changed through the years.

How Hearing Aids Have Changed

One of the early hearing aids was the hearing tube. As you can see, people had to sit close to one another to use this hearing aid. The tube acted somewhat like a stethoscope. It directed the sound of a person's voice to another person's ear. ▶

The first hearing aids with microphones in them were usually large and bulky. They needed electricity to work. The person who wore them had to wear a battery pack. ▶

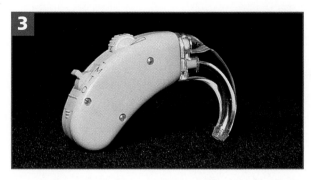

During the 1950s and early 1960s, a tiny battery was made that helped make hearing aids smaller. Some hearing aids were worn behind the ear or on a person's eyeglasses.

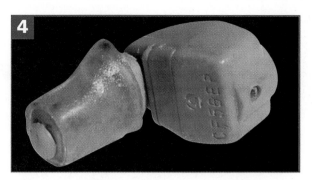

During the 1970s, a hearing aid could fit in a person's outer ear. However, people still had problems with hearing aids. The hearing aid amplified background noises as well as voices. The loud noises made it hard for people to understand voices.

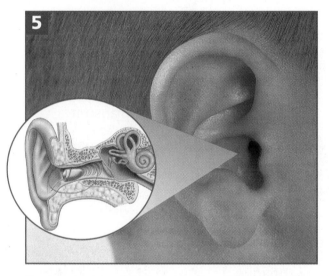

During the late 1970s, a hearing aid was made that could fit entirely in the ear canal.

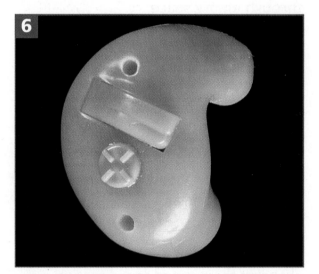

During the 1980s and 1990s, hearing aids have been made with digital controls. A person can program the hearing aid to make hearing better. The batteries in the newer hearing aids also last longer.

Lesson 4 Review

1. Draw a picture to show how sounds travel through the ear.

2. How does a stethoscope make sounds louder?

3. **Graphic Sources**
   Use the pictures and captions on these two pages to make a time line showing the changes in hearing aids.

Chapter 4 Review

Chapter Main Ideas

Lesson 1

• The visible spectrum is light energy that can be seen. The sun, fire, electric lights, candles, matches, and flashlights are all sources of light.

• Light waves move in a straight line away from their source and can move through empty space.

Lesson 2

• Light can be reflected, absorbed, or transmitted when it hits different materials, and the color of light that is reflected or transmitted gives objects their color.

• Flat mirrors reflect good images, while curved mirrors reflect somewhat changed images.

• Lenses cause light rays to bend by changing their speed and direction.

Lesson 3

• Sound is made when matter is caused to vibrate.

• Volume and pitch are properties of sound.

• Sound waves travel through different materials at different speeds; they cannot travel through empty space.

Lesson 4

• You hear sounds when sound waves cause vibrations to move through your ear to a nerve and the nerve then sends messages to the brain.

• Stethoscopes, microphones, bullhorns, and hearing aids can be used to make sounds louder.

Reviewing Words and Concepts

Write the letter of the word or phrase that best completes each sentence.

a. absorb
b. amplify
c. bullhorn
d. concave lens
e. convex lens
f. electric signal
g. hearing aid
h. microphone
i. opaque
j. pitch
k. reflect
l. stethoscope
m. translucent
n. transmit
o. transparent
p. vibrate
q. visible spectrum
r. volume
s. wavelength

1. The _____ is made up of all the colors of the rainbow.

2. People with a hearing loss may use a _____ to help them hear better.

3. The distance from a point on one wave to the same point on the next wave is the _____.

4. A loud sound has more _____ than a soft sound.

5. Light cannot pass through an object that is _____.

6. An opaque object can _____ some colors and reflect others.

7. A _____ is an instrument with a built-in microphone.

8. The color of transparent objects depends on the color they _____.

9. A _____ makes small objects look larger than they are.

10. People may use a _____ to amplify their voices when giving a speech.

11. Wax paper is _____ because it lets light pass through but scatters it.

12. Sound is made when an object is caused to _____.

13. Yellow flowers look yellow because they _____ yellow light.

14. The thin strings on a guitar make sounds with a higher _____ than the sounds made by the thick strings.

15. Doctors and nurses use a _____ to hear the sounds of the heart and lungs.

16. A _____ spreads light rays apart because it is thinner in the middle than at the edges.

17. Microphones change sound waves into an _____.

18. Glass is _____ because you can see through it clearly.

19. If you make a sound stronger, you _____ it.

Explaining Science

Draw and label a picture or write a paragraph to answer these questions.

1. How does light act when it hits different materials?

2. Why do green apples look green?

3. Why do sound waves travel faster in wood than in air?

4. How do you hear a person's voice?

Using Skills

1. How can you **use a graphic source** to help you understand a difficult concept?

2. Suppose you are in a dark room and you have a white ball. You put the white ball under a red light. **Predict** what color the ball will appear. **Communicate** your reason for the prediction by writing a short paragraph.

3. Suppose you **observe** a rainbow in the sky, but it hasn't rained where you are. What might you **infer**?

Critical Thinking

1. Classify these sounds as having a high pitch or low pitch: flute, trombone, a singing bird, a roaring lion.

2. Compare and contrast light waves and sound waves.

3. Infer why an opaque object will make a shadow when light hits it.

Unit B Review

Reviewing Words and Concepts

Choose at least three words from the Chapter 1 list below.
Use the words to write a paragraph about how these concepts
are related. Do the same for each of the other chapters.

Chapter 1
density
graduated cylinder
gram
mass
matter
volume

Chapter 2
force
friction
gravity
inertia
kinetic energy
potential energy

Chapter 3
conductor
electromagnet
insulator
magnet
magnetism
resistance

Chapter 4
opaque
pitch
reflect
vibrate
visible spectrum
volume

Reviewing Main Ideas

Each of the statements below is false. Change the
underlined word or words to make each statement true.

1. A <u>solution</u> is anything that can be observed or measured about matter.
2. Matter can occur in three <u>mixtures</u>: solid, liquid, or gas.
3. The <u>boiling point</u> of a material is the temperature at which it changes from a solid to a liquid.
4. <u>Inertia</u> can cause objects to move, slow down, or stop.
5. Levers, inclined planes, and pulleys are examples of <u>closed circuits</u>.
6. A <u>series circuit</u> uses an energy source and a magnet to make electricity.
7. The magnetic field of a magnet is strongest at the <u>center</u> of the magnet.
8. A <u>transparent</u> object spreads light in different directions as the light passes through it.
9. When sound waves reach your ear, they make your <u>brain</u> vibrate.
10. A <u>bullhorn</u> is an instrument used to help people with a loss of hearing hear better.

Interpreting Data

The following graph shows the speed of sound through different materials. Use the graph to answer the questions below.

Speed of Sound

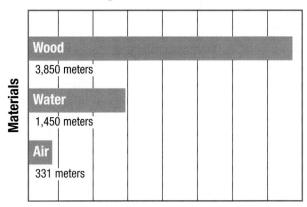

Materials

Wood — 3,850 meters
Water — 1,450 meters
Air — 331 meters

0   500   1,000 1,500 2,000 2,500 3,000 3,500
Distance traveled in 1 second

1. Does sound travel faster through air or through wood?

2. How much faster does sound travel through water than through air?

3. If you wanted to soundproof a room, would you use wood, water, or air as insulation?

Communicating Science

1. Draw and label a diagram to show a chemical change.

2. Draw a picture of work being done and label it to explain the work. List five other examples of work being done.

3. Draw a series circuit and a parallel circuit. Describe how they are different from each other.

4. Draw and label a diagram that shows how sound travels through your ear. Explain what parts of the ear vibrate as the sound waves move through the ear.

Applying Science

1. Write a paragraph or draw a diagram to explain the physical changes and the chemical changes that happened to the food you ate for breakfast—before you ate it and afterward.

2. Write an advertisement from an electric company advising customers how to use electricity safely.

Unit B
Performance Review

Matter and Energy Museum

Using what you learned in this unit, complete one or more of the following activities to be included in a Matter and Energy Museum. These exhibits will help the visitors learn more about matter and energy. You may work by yourself or in a group.

New Invention

Think of a new way to combine two or more simple machines to do work. Draw a diagram and make a model of your machine. Then write an advertisement that tells what your machine can do to help make work easier. Display your machine in the museum.

Art

As part of a museum display, make a poster to show examples that explain the difference between physical changes and chemical changes. You may draw pictures or cut pictures from magazines.

Music and Dance

Plan a musical revue for the museum. Make up a song or a dance to show how sound travels through different kinds of materials. Plan to use instruments that you make—such as drums made from coffee cans—to accompany the song or dance.

Graphs

For the math room of the museum, make a graph to show some data you have collected about matter and energy. Display your graph and write a brief summary of what data the graph shows.

Electromagnets

Collect pictures or items that use electromagnets. Arrange them for display in your museum. Write tags to describe each item and tell how an electromagnet is used in the item.

Outlining and Writing a Report

An outline can help you organize your thoughts before you write. An outline lists the main ideas and the supporting details for the different sections or paragraphs of a report.

Each main idea on an outline is listed next to a Roman numeral, such as I, II, and III. All of the supporting details listed below a main idea are listed next to a letter, such as A, B, and C.

The sample outline below shows an outline for Chapter 3 of this unit.

Chapter 3: Electricity and Magnetism

I. **Electric Current**
    A. How objects get a charge
    B. How electric current flows

II. **Electric Circuits**
    A. How two types of circuits are different
    B. How electricity can be used safely

III. **Magnetism**
    A. How magnets act
    B. How the earth is like a magnet

IV. **How Electricity and Magnetism Work Together**
    A. How a magnet can make electricity
    B. How electricity can make a magnet
    C. How electromagnets are useful

Make an Outline

Use this model to write an outline for Chapter 4 of this unit. Use the lesson titles and the main ideas from each lesson to complete your outline.

Write a Report

Use the information from your Chapter 4 outline to write one sentence about what you learned for each of your main ideas. Then write one sentence about what you learned for each of your supporting details. Use transition words such as *first, next, then, because,* and *however* to shape groups of words into four paragraphs. Add a brief introduction and closing. Remember to give your report a title.

Remember to:

1. **Prewrite** Organize your thoughts before you write.

2. **Draft** Make an outline and write your report.

3. **Revise** Share your work and then make changes.

4. **Edit** Proofread for mistakes and fix them.

5. **Publish** Share your report with your class.

Unit C
Earth Science

Science and Technology
In Your World!

Seeing the Invisible Wind!

How can you see something that is invisible? Thanks to satellites, radios on weather balloons, high-flying aircraft, and computers, weather scientists can "see" the path, strength, and direction of winds. You'll learn more about how meteorologists track and predict weather in **Chapter 1 Measuring Weather.**

Building Blocks that Rock and Roll!

When the earth starts shaking, buildings start breaking—but not when they rest on roller-bearing blocks! Made of rubber and metal, such as lead or steel, these bearings slip and slide, allowing a building to roll with the punches and survive an earthquake without major damage. You'll learn more about the action of earthquakes in **Chapter 2 The Makeup of the Earth.**

Live from Under Two Oceans!

How'd they do that? In 1998, the ninth annual JASON expedition brought live video broadcasts of ocean divers underwater—one in the Pacific Ocean and one in the Atlantic—to each other as well as to students and classrooms in several countries. You'll read more about how scientists explore the oceans in **Chapter 3 Exploring the Oceans.**

Close Encounters with Cosmic Dust

Wow! Bristling with high-tech equipment like dust detectors, telescopes, heat shields, radios, and atom counters, the *Galileo* spacecraft observes, measures, and communicates to Earth some of the mysteries of the solar system. You'll learn more about *Galileo* and how scientists study the planets in **Chapter 4 Movements in the Solar System.**

How's the Weather?

Thick, dark clouds build up. Flash! Lightning streaks across the sky. Crash! Thunder rolls and crackles in the air. The TV weather reporters predict more rain for tomorrow. How do they do that?

Chapter 1
Measuring Weather

Inquiring about Measuring Weather

Lesson 1
How Does Sunlight Affect Air Temperature?

What causes changes in air temperature?

How do different surfaces on the earth affect air temperature?

How is air temperature measured?

Lesson 2
How Does Temperature Affect Air Movement?

How does air temperature affect air pressure and wind?

How is air pressure measured?

How are wind direction and speed measured?

Lesson 3
What Causes Clouds and Precipitation?

How do clouds form?

How are clouds different?

What are different kinds of precipitation?

How are precipitation and humidity measured?

How does water move through a cycle?

Lesson 4
How Do Meteorologists Predict Weather?

What are air masses and fronts?

How do meteorologists track and predict weather?

How does the National Weather Service help keep people safe?

Copy the chapter graphic organizer onto your own paper. This organizer shows you what the whole chapter is all about. As you read the lessons and do the activities, look for answers to the questions and write them on your organizer.

Exploring Surface Temperatures

Process Skills

- collecting and interpreting data
- estimating and measuring
- predicting
- inferring

Materials

- thermometer
- white construction paper
- clock with second hand
- black construction paper
- concrete surface
- blacktop surface

Explore

1 Place a thermometer on a piece of white construction paper that has been in sunlight for at least 20 minutes. After three minutes, read the thermometer. **Collect data** by recording your measurement.

2 Repeat step 1 with a piece of black construction paper.

3 Study your data and make a **prediction.** Which outdoor surface will be warmer in sunlight, concrete or blacktop? Record your prediction.

4 Place the thermometer on a concrete surface that has been in full sunlight for at least 20 minutes. After three minutes, read the temperature. Record your measurement.

5 Repeat step 4 on a blacktop surface.

Reflect

1. How close was your prediction?

2. What **inferences** can you make from your data about light and dark surfaces, sunlight, and temperature?

? Inquire Further

If the surfaces were in the shade, how would their temperatures change? Develop a plan to answer this or other questions you may have.

Exploring Range, Median, and Mode

Records are kept of the highest air temperatures recorded in each state in the United States. How much do you think the high temperatures vary?

Work Together

These are the high temperatures recorded for eleven states in the United States. Organize the data to compare the temperatures.

Alaska 38°C	Arkansas 49°C	Florida 43°C
Illinois 47°C	Maryland 43°C	Montana 47°C
Nevada 52°C	Ohio 45°C	Oregon 48°C
Texas 49°C	Utah 47°C	

Materials
- 3 x 5 cards
- markers

Math Vocabulary

median, the middle number when the data are put in order

mode, the number that occurs most often in the data

range, the difference between the highest and lowest numbers in the data

1. Make a card for each of the temperatures. Write the temperature and the name of the state on the card.

2. Arrange them in order. Start with the lowest temperature.

3. Find the **range**. What is the difference between the highest and the lowest temperatures?

4. Look for the **mode**. What temperature or temperatures occur most often?

5. Find the **median**. When the temperatures are in order from lowest to highest, what temperature is in the middle?

Talk About It!

Why would the questions be difficult to answer if you had not put the cards in order?

You will learn:

- **what causes changes in air temperature.**
- **how different surfaces on the earth affect air temperature.**
- **how to measure air temperature.**

When the sun is low in the sky, sunlight hits the earth less directly. ▼

Lesson 1

How Does Sunlight Affect Air Temperature?

It's summer. You wake up and bright sunlight streams in your window. It makes you squint. As the sun rises in the sky, the day gets warmer and warmer. **YES!** It's a beautiful, warm, sunny day!

Changes in Air Temperature

Most days are warmest in the afternoon and cooler in the morning and evening. Why is the air temperature different at different times of day? The temperature of the air has to do with how much sunlight, or light energy from the sun, reaches the earth. Sunlight passes through the air but does not heat it. Rather, light energy from the sun hits liquids and solids on the surface of the earth. The liquids and solids get warm, and they warm the air above them.

However, the earth's surface does not heat evenly. The uneven heating is caused by sunlight hitting the earth at different angles. Direct sunlight hitting the earth's surface causes higher temperatures than indirect sunlight.

Notice the shadows in the pictures below. You can see by the shadows that sunlight hits the earth at different angles during the day. Sunlight hits the earth most directly around noon. It hits the earth less directly early in the morning and in the evening. You can infer the rotation of the earth by watching shadows on the ground.

The temperature of the air is usually lowest just before sunrise. Then, as the sun rises and the surface of the earth is heated, the air temperature rises. The earth's surface is usually warmest around midday, when the sunlight is most direct. However, the surface of the earth takes time to heat the air. Therefore, air temperatures are often highest in the middle of the afternoon.

The number of hours of daylight also affects air temperature. During the summer, there are more daylight hours than during the winter. The earth's surface has more time to heat up on summer days. Therefore, air temperatures are usually warmer.

How Shadows Change During a Day

In the morning, the sun shines from the east, making shadows stretch toward the west. Angled light rays are more spread out and less bright.

At midday, the sun's rays shine from almost directly overhead, and the shadow is almost directly under the umbrella. Light rays are strongest and brightest when the sun is highest in the sky.

In the late afternoon, the sun is low in the west, and shadows stretch eastward.

Different Surfaces and Temperature

It's one of those really hot days. You decide to go swimming. In your bare feet, you walk across the pavement toward the lake. Yikes! The pavement is hot! You run to the beach. Yow! The sand is almost as hot! Quickly, you head for some grass. Ahh, that's better. The grass is much cooler than the sand or the pavement.

Why do some surfaces stay cool while other surfaces get hot? The sunlight falls equally on all of them. However, different surfaces absorb different amounts of light energy. Some surfaces get hot faster than others. Blacktop, cement, and buildings warm quickly. Large bodies of water warm slowly. Warmer surfaces heat the air above them more than cooler surfaces do.

During a summer day, the ocean in the picture heats up more slowly than the land around it. The air above the ocean will stay cooler than the air above the land. The cool air above the ocean may move over the land. Then the air temperature above the land becomes cooler, but the land farther from the ocean stays warmer.

The pavement heats the air above it more than the grass or the water does. ▼

Measuring Air Temperature

Air temperature is measured using a tool called a thermometer. Some thermometers are a tube with liquid inside. When the air around the liquid gets warmer, the liquid gets warmer. Then the liquid expands, or spreads out, and moves up the thermometer. When the air around the liquid is cooled, the liquid contracts, or pulls together, and moves down the thermometer.

Find the letter C on the thermometer on the right. The C stands for Celsius—a metric scale for measuring temperature. The tube is marked in a scale of degrees. Each mark on the thermometer is for 5 degrees Celsius. A higher number means warmer temperatures. A lower number means cooler temperatures. What temperature does the thermometer in the picture show in degrees Celsius?

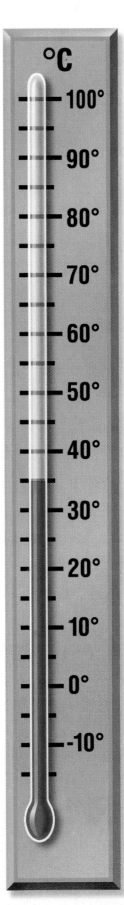

The temperature shown on this thermometer is in degrees Celsius. ▶

Lesson 1 Review

1. Why are air temperatures usually higher in the late afternoon than in the morning?

2. Why is the air above warm surfaces warmer than the air above cooler surfaces?

3. What causes the liquid in a thermometer to rise in the tube?

4. **Range, Median, and Mode**
   The high temperatures recorded in one place for a week are: 35°C, 20°C, 30°C, 32°C, 30°C, 25°C, and 30°C. Find the range, median, and mode of the temperatures.

What's the Big Idea?

You will learn:

- how air temperature causes changes in air pressure and wind.
- how air pressure is measured.
- how to measure wind direction and speed.

Glossary

air pressure
(âr presh′ər), the amount that air presses or pushes on anything

Air becomes colder as you go higher above the earth. ▼

Colder

Cooler

Warmer

Lesson 2

How Does Temperature Affect Air Movement?

You're riding in an elevator and suddenly you can hardly hear. You swallow. **POP!** Oh, much better. What caused your ears to pop? It's called air pressure.

Air Pressure and Wind

The earth is surrounded by a layer of air. Air is made of matter and has mass. Air presses down on the surface of the earth and on you too! This pressing down of air is called **air pressure**. Usually, you don't notice the pressure of the air, but you do notice its effects. If you have ever flown in an airplane, you may have felt the effects of air pressure. The change in air pressure pushes on your eardrum. Then when you swallow, the eardrum makes a popping sound.

As you go higher above the earth, the air pressure changes. When you are high above the surface of the earth, there is less air above you than when you are on the earth. Less air is pressing down on you. Therefore, the air pressure is lower.

Air temperature also changes as you go higher above the earth. Since the surface of the earth heats the air above it, the air is warmer near the ground. Notice the changes in air temperature in the picture on the left. As you go higher above the earth, the air gets colder.

Air pressure on the earth's surface also changes. Changes in temperature cause changes in air pressure. As the air near the surface of the earth becomes warmer, the particles of air move farther apart. The air becomes lighter and rises. The lighter air pushes down on the surface of the earth with less pressure. A **low-pressure area** forms.

Cold air is heavier than warm air. Its matter is more closely packed together. It pushes down harder on the earth's surface than warm air does. Therefore, a cold air mass is called a **high-pressure area**.

As you can see in the picture, air moves from a place with high pressure to a place with low pressure. The moving air is called wind. When the cooler air from a high-pressure area sinks toward the earth, it causes wind. Then you feel a nice, cool breeze.

Glossary

low-pressure area
(lō′presh′ər âr′ē ə), a place where warm air rises and pushes down on the earth's surface with less pressure

high-pressure area
(hī′presh′ər âr′ē ə), a place where cool air sinks and pushes down on the earth's surface with more pressure

Wind blows from an area of high pressure to an area of low pressure. ▼

Cool air sinking

Warm air rising

Wind

Glossary

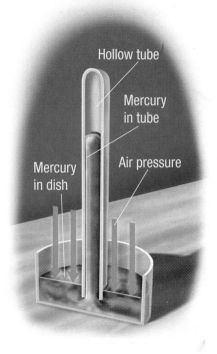

Glossary

barometer
(bə rom′ə tər),
a tool that measures
air pressure

Hollow tube

Mercury
in tube

Mercury
in dish

Air pressure

▲ *The drawing shows how a*
mercury barometer works.

Measuring Air Pressure

Air pressure can be measured using a tool called a
barometer. One type of barometer is made of a
hollow tube that is closed at one end and open at the
other end. The tube is filled with mercury. Then the
tube is turned upside down in a dish of mercury.
Notice in the picture that the mercury in the tube has
moved down. It no longer fills the tube. Air pressure
on the mercury in the dish affects the level of mercury
in the tube. When air pressure gets higher, it causes
the mercury to rise in the tube. When air pressure
gets lower, some of the mercury in the tube falls back
down into the dish.

Another type of barometer is a circular dial in a
sealed box, as shown below. The outside of the box
moves slightly as air pressure changes. It is connected
to a spring that moves a pointer on a dial. As the air
pressure gets lower, the pointer moves to a lower
number on the dial. When the air pressure gets higher,
the pointer moves to a higher number on the dial.

▲ *The scale on this barometer shows*
air pressure in millimeters (mm),
millibars (mb), and inches (in.).

Measuring Wind Direction and Speed

Even though wind is invisible, you can tell its direction by watching things move. You can see the direction that a flag moves or that trees bend in the wind. You can even get a quick idea of the wind's direction by wetting your finger and holding it up. Your finger will feel cooler on the side the wind is blowing from.

For a more exact measurement of the wind's direction, scientists use a **wind vane**. A wind vane rotates on top of a pole. It has a tail that can be pushed by the wind. The tail of the vane swings away from the wind. An arrow on the opposite end of the vane points into the wind. Some wind vanes have markers or crossbars showing the four main directions, *north, south, east,* and *west.* Wind vanes are one of the oldest tools for observing weather.

A wind sock, such as the one in the picture, shows wind direction. A wind sock also gives a good idea of how fast the wind is blowing. If the sock stands straight out, the wind is blowing fast and strong. If the wind sock barely lifts in the breeze, the wind force is quite low. Airports often have wind socks set up, so that pilots can tell the direction and strength of the wind.

The tail on this wind vane swings away from the wind, and the arrow points toward the wind. ▼

Some people have wind socks, such as this one, hanging near their homes. ▶

Glossary

Glossary

anemometer
(an′ə mom′ə tər),
a tool that measures
wind speed

However, exact wind speed is measured using a tool called an **anemometer**. Anemometers are usually placed high above a roof or atop the mast of a boat. Sometimes anemometers are connected to wind vanes.

An anemometer has three or four cups attached to the top of a pole. The cups are often shaped like small, hollow balls that are cut in half. As the wind blows, it pushes the cups and causes this part of the anemometer to spin. The number of turns per minute is changed to wind speed by gears, similar to the speedometer of an automobile. When the wind blows fast, the anemometer spins very fast. Anemometers are often hooked up electrically to a dial that shows the wind speed.

Lesson 2 Review

1. What causes wind?

2. How is air pressure measured?

3. How do scientists measure wind direction and speed?

4. **Range, Median, and Mode**
   Suppose the daily high wind speeds in a place for a week are 30 kph (kilometers per hour), 10 kph, 30 kph, 20 kph, 15 kph, 25 kph, and 40 kph. What is the range, the median, and the mode of the wind speeds?

The three cups on an anemometer spin faster as wind speed increases. ▼

What Causes Clouds and Precipitation?

You lie on your back, looking up at the blue sky. Tiny, wispy clouds drift along. Fluffy, white clouds pile up and move quickly across the sky. Amazing! Their changing shapes seem to form pictures. Where do clouds come from, anyway?

Clouds

Energy from the sun is needed for clouds to form. The sun's energy causes water in oceans, lakes, rivers, and puddles to evaporate, or change from a liquid to a gas. As you learned, warm air rises from the surface of the earth. As the warm air rises, it carries water vapor. The warm air cools as it rises. As it cools, water vapor in the air begins to condense as tiny drops of liquid water. The tiny water drops are so small that they stay in the air. These tiny water drops form clouds like the ones in the picture.

Since water vapor is needed to form a cloud, you will see many clouds in places where the air is very moist. In places where the air is dry, you will see fewer clouds. For example, you will not see many clouds over a desert.

You will learn:
- how clouds form.
- how clouds are different.
- what different kinds of precipitation are.
- how to measure precipitation and humidity.
- how water moves through a cycle.

These clouds are usually seen on a bright, sunny day. ▶

Types of Clouds

If you walk along a lake on a cool morning, you might walk through a cloud. This kind of cloud is fog. Fog is a cloud that forms close to the ground. It may surround a hillside, hide part of a bridge as in the picture, or even blanket the ground. Fog holds as much moisture as is possible without raining—and sometimes raindrops will fall from fog. Often fog forms during nights and mornings when moist air cools. Thick fog is very difficult to see through.

Clouds form in many shapes and sizes. Some clouds are tall and puffy, while others are long and thin. Some clouds are white, while others are dark. Knowing cloud shapes can give you clues about what kind of weather to expect. The clouds shown on the next page are the three basic types of clouds.

Stratus clouds are low clouds that form flat, wide layers. Sometimes they cover the whole sky like a blanket and block sunlight. Sometimes they are a dull gray. Rain or snow may fall from these clouds.

Where's the rest of the bridge? It's covered by the dense fog. ▼

C 18

Cumulus clouds form as warm, moist air moves high into the sky. They are often seen around midday or in the afternoon, when the air near the earth gets warm. Cumulus clouds are often dome shaped with flat bottoms. When you see cumulus clouds, it's a good time to plan a picnic! Cumulus clouds are often seen during fair weather.

Cirrus clouds are formed high in the sky where the temperature is very cold. They are formed mostly of ice crystals. Cirrus clouds look like thin threads or feathers arranged in bands. They often move very quickly across the sky on bright, sunny days. Cirrus clouds often mean that warm air is on the way.

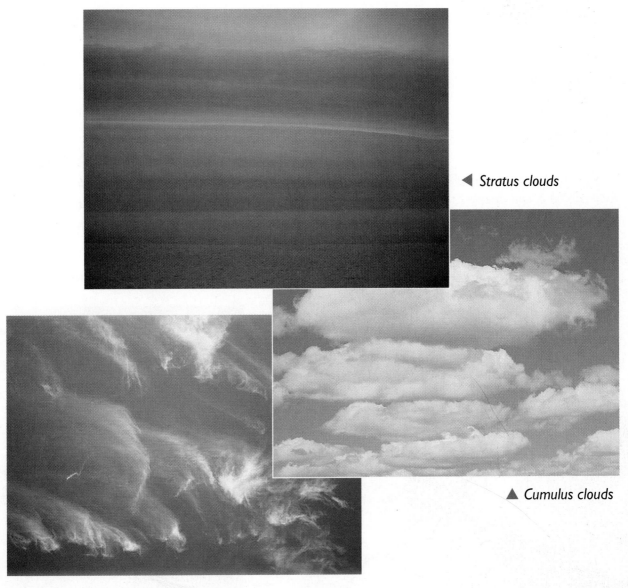

◀ Stratus clouds

▲ Cumulus clouds

▲ Cirrus clouds

Glossary

precipitation
(pri sip′ə tā′shən),
moisture that falls from
clouds to the ground

Kinds of Precipitation

You walk outdoors on a cloudy, gray day. Suddenly you feel drops of water on your face. It's raining. This moisture that falls from clouds to the ground is called **precipitation**.

Rain is one kind of precipitation. As you learned, air carries water vapor. When water vapor rises, it cools and forms tiny water drops. These tiny drops freeze into ice crystals. Then more water vapor freezes onto the ice crystals and they become larger and heavier. Then they begin to fall toward the earth. If the temperature near the earth is above freezing, these tiny ice crystals melt and fall to the earth as raindrops as in the picture on the left.

At times, the temperature on the earth is below freezing. Then the ice crystals do not melt. They fall to the earth as snow as in the picture below.

Notice the hailstones in the picture below. Hail forms when strong winds carry frozen water drops higher into the clouds. Another layer of ice is added to the hail, and it begins to fall. Again and again, the hail falls and is pushed back up through the clouds. Each time, the hail gets larger. When the hail becomes too heavy for the wind to hold up, it will fall to the earth.

▲ *Better get your umbrella! Rain can be a light drizzle or a heavy downpour.*

Hailstones that reach the ground can be as small as these or larger than golf balls. Large hailstones can do a lot of damage. ▼

If the temperature is below freezing, snow soon covers the ground with a white blanket. ▶

Measuring Precipitation and Humidity

You can measure the amount of rain that falls with a rain gauge like the one in the picture. A **rain gauge** is simply an open-topped container that collects rain. Marks on the side of the rain gauge show how much rain has fallen.

Humidity is a measure of the amount of water vapor in the air. However, the amount of water vapor in the air is not always the same. Also, the amount of water vapor that air can hold changes with air temperature. Cold air can hold less water vapor than warm air can. That's why on very cold days, the air feels dry. You may have heard a weather report say that the humidity is 100 percent and the temperature is 20°C. That means the air has all the water vapor that it can hold at 20°C.

Humidity can be measured using a **hygrometer**. A hygrometer uses a hair attached to a pointer. As the hair absorbs water vapor from the air, it gets longer. The pointer shows what the humidity is.

This rain gauge shows how much precipitation fell. ▼

C21

The Water Cycle

Do you ever wonder where the water goes after a rain? Water is always moving from the earth into the air and back to the earth again. Water from lakes, ponds, rivers, oceans, and even puddles evaporates, condenses, and falls as precipitation. Trace the movement of water through the water cycle.

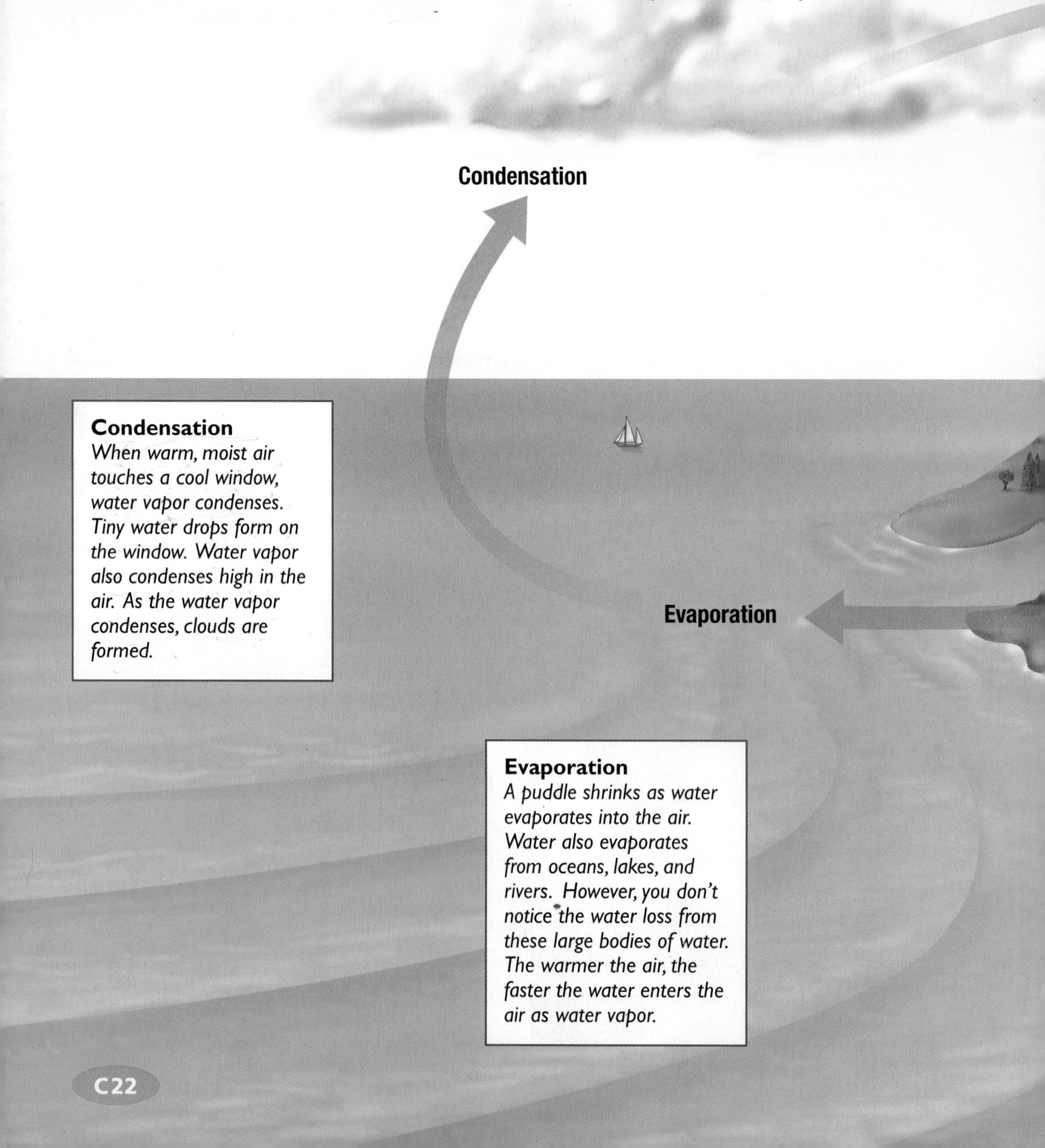

Condensation

Evaporation

Condensation
When warm, moist air touches a cool window, water vapor condenses. Tiny water drops form on the window. Water vapor also condenses high in the air. As the water vapor condenses, clouds are formed.

Evaporation
A puddle shrinks as water evaporates into the air. Water also evaporates from oceans, lakes, and rivers. However, you don't notice the water loss from these large bodies of water. The warmer the air, the faster the water enters the air as water vapor.

Precipitation

Water drops fall from the cloud. It's raining! Time to get out the umbrella and look for puddles to splash in! In freezing temperatures, the water falls as snow. Most precipitation falls over the oceans.

Precipitation

Runoff

Runoff

As water reaches the ground, some of it soaks in. What doesn't soak into the ground runs downhill into puddles, streams, rivers, or lakes. Then the whole cycle starts again!

Lesson 3 Review

1. How do clouds form?

2. Which types of clouds might you see on a bright, sunny day?

3. How does rain form?

4. What tools are used to measure precipitation and humidity?

5. How does water move through the water cycle?

6. **Range, Median, Mode**
   The following are the humidity reports for one week: 50%, 85%, 70%, 50%, 85%, 50%, and 65%. Find the range, median, and mode of the humidity.

Investigating Air Pressure and Weather

Process Skills

- estimating and measuring
- collecting and interpreting data
- observing

Materials

- safety goggles
- scissors
- balloon
- plastic jar
- rubber band
- tape
- glue
- plastic stirrer
- metric ruler
- clay

Getting Ready

In this activity you will be making a barometer, observing clouds, and monitoring changing weather.

Follow This Procedure

❶ Make a chart like the one shown. Use your chart to record your weather observations.

Date	Barometer measurement	Cloud types	Weather

Cloud type choices: cirrus, stratus, cumulus, fog, other (describe)

Weather choices: cloudy, partly cloudy, windy, rain, snow, hail, thunderstorm, other (describe)

Photo A

❷ Put on your safety goggles. Cut off the open end of the balloon. Have a partner hold the jar while you stretch the rest of the balloon over the open end of the jar. Hold the balloon in place with a rubber band. Use tape to seal the edge of the balloon around the jar (Photo A).

❸ Glue one end of the stirrer to the center of the stretched balloon. Use a small piece of tape to hold the stirrer in place until the glue dries.

④ Stand the metric ruler on end in some clay. Place the ruler next to the end of the stirrer (Photo B).

⑤ When the glue has dried, carefully remove the tape from the stirrer. You have made a barometer. Read the number of millimeters at the top edge of the stirrer. Record your **measurement** in your chart. This represents the air pressure on the balloon.

⑥ **Collect data.** Use your barometer to record changes in the air pressure over ten days. Always measure using the top edge of the stirrer. Record the data in your chart.

⑦ Each day, also **observe** and record the cloud type and weather conditions.

Photo B

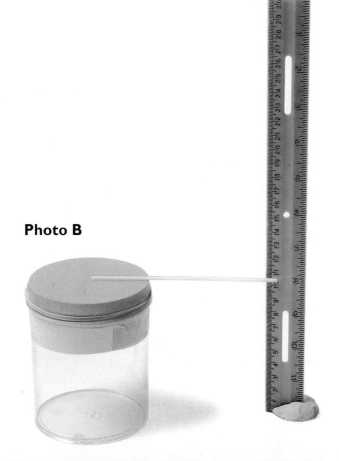

Self-Monitoring
Have I made complete recordings for each day of observation?

Interpret Your Results

1. What was the weather like when the air pressure was low or decreasing? What kind of clouds were present?

2. What was the weather like when the air pressure was high or increasing? What kind of clouds were present?

3. Draw a conclusion. How is air pressure related to changing weather conditions?

Inquire Further

How can you measure temperature, precipitation, wind, and other weather conditions? Develop a plan to answer this or other questions you may have.

Self-Assessment

* I followed instructions to make a barometer and track air pressure, cloud types, and weather conditions.
* I **measured** pressure on my barometer.
* I recorded my **observations.**
* I **interpreted** my observations relating air pressure and weather conditions.
* I drew a conclusion about how air pressure is related to changes in weather.

What's the Big Idea?

You will learn:

- what air masses and fronts are.
- how meteorologists track and predict weather.
- how the National Weather Service helps keep people safe.

Glossary

air mass (âr mas), a large body of air that has about the same temperature and humidity

front (frunt), the line where two air masses meet

Lesson 4

How Do Meteorologists Predict Weather?

Your family plans a camping trip for the weekend. You hope the weather will be fair and sunny. You turn on the TV to see the weather report. The reporter shows some maps. Sunny and fair here! Chances of showers there!

Air Masses and Fronts

Have you ever wondered what causes the weather to change? It's moving air masses. An **air mass** is a large body of air that has about the same temperature and humidity throughout. Air masses can be warm or cold and can have a little or a lot of water vapor. They take on the temperature and humidity of the area where they form. Air masses are so large that two or three can cover most of the United States. Differences in air pressure and wind often cause air masses to move.

Air masses usually move from west to east in the United States. As an air mass moves, it meets another air mass. You might think that air masses would mix together where they meet, but they don't. The air masses stay separate. The line where two air masses meet is a **front**.

Strong winds arrive just ahead of a line of clouds. Dark clouds and rain will arrive soon afterwards. ▶

The drawing of the cold front shows what happens when a cold air mass pushes into a warm air mass. The warm air rises quickly and cools rapidly, causing huge storm clouds to build up. Soon rain or snow may fall. Thunder and lightning may also occur during a rainstorm. Cold fronts move very quickly, so the storm may not last very long.

The drawing of a warm front shows how warm air slides slowly upward over a cold air mass. As the warm air rises, it cools and forms clouds. However, these clouds are feathery clouds that form high in the sky. Thicker clouds that form lower in the sky follow the high clouds. The gentle rain or snow produced by a warm front may last several days. When the front passes, warm, mild weather follows.

Cold Front

A cold air mass pushes into a warm air mass. The warm air gets pushed upward quickly. Tall storm clouds form along the cold front. They may bring heavy rain or thunderstorms—or in winter, a snow storm. ▼

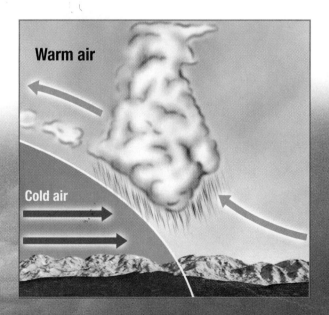

Warm Front

A warm air mass slides slowly over the top of a cold air mass. Cirrus clouds form high in the sky, followed by lower and thicker clouds. A warm front may produce light rain or snow for several days. ▼

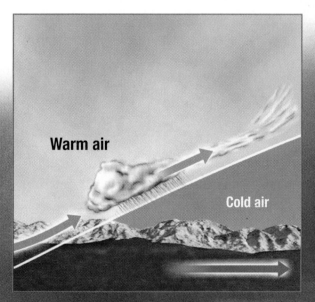

Glossary

forecast (fôr′kast′),
a prediction of what the
weather will be like

meteorologist
(mē′tē ə rol′ə jist),
a person who studies
weather

Tracking and Predicting Weather

A weather **forecast** is a prediction of what the
weather will be like for the next few days. A weather
forecast is made by a **meteorologist**—a person
who studies the weather. To make a prediction, a
meteorologist must track weather.

Meteorologists record the high and low
temperatures each day from many places. They also
keep track of humidity, air pressure, precipitation, air
masses, and fronts in these places. The speed and
direction of the wind is also important in making
weather predictions. Knowing wind speed and
direction helps predict where air masses will move.

Meteorologists use computer-generated maps to
track weather patterns and to predict what future
weather might be. One important weather map is
the radar image map shown below. The location of
precipitation shows up on a map on a computer
monitor. Weather maps are always changing.

Radar Maps

▲ Precipitation shows as bright colors on a radar
map. Find the areas that are yellow, orange, or
red. These areas are having heavy precipitation.
The blue areas show moderate precipitation.

▲ The radar picture a few hours later shows how
the storm has moved. In which direction is the
storm traveling?

Many meteorologists get their information from the **National Weather Service.** This government agency has weather stations all over the United States. The government weather stations use many advanced tools to study weather. Satellites high above the earth collect weather information from all over the world. Weather balloons are also used to collect information about temperature, air pressure, and humidity high above the earth.

Glossary

National Weather Service
(nash′ə nəl weᴛʜ′ər sėr′vis), a government agency that collects information about weather

Glossary

Weather satellites constantly send images of weather conditions on the earth to meteorologists. In this way, the movement of cold air masses and fronts can be tracked. ▶

A TV weather forecaster gives reports about the kind of weather that may be expected during the next few days. ▼

Keeping People Safe

You're watching television and you hear a long beep. You look to the bottom of the screen and notice a line moving across. It reads, "Tornado watch in effect for Orange County." A watch is issued by the National Weather Service when weather conditions are right for producing severe weather. For example, a tornado watch is issued when conditions are such that a tornado may form.

The National Weather Service also issues warnings when certain weather conditions are spotted. For example, when severe thunder, lightning, and rain are spotted, the National Weather Service might issue a thunderstorm warning. Other warnings include hurricane, tornado, flash flood, and winter storm warnings.

When a storm warning is issued, it means that people should take precautions to keep safe. For example, if a tornado, such as the one in the picture above, is sighted in your area, you should go to a basement or storm cellar. If you don't have a basement or storm cellar, go to an inside room without windows, such as a closet or hallway.

▲ A tornado

A hurricane ▼

If a hurricane warning is issued, prepare to leave the area. Listen to your local TV and radio stations. Follow your family's emergency plan. Board up doors and windows. When told to leave the area, leave early and in daylight if possible. Shut off water, gas, and electricity. Take an emergency supply kit and medicines. Drive to the nearest shelter. Hurricanes, such as the one in the picture on page C30, can cause much damage.

▲ *A winter storm*

Flash floods sometimes happen during hurricanes or heavy thunderstorms. To keep safe during a flash flood, stay away from all moving water, such as rivers and creeks. If you are near a river, try to move to higher ground, such as a hill.

Thunderstorms also may bring lightning. To keep safe from lightning, stay away from tall trees. Stay inside a car with a metal roof or go inside a building. If you are indoors, don't touch electrical appliances or use a telephone, and don't take a bath or a shower.

When a winter storm warning is issued, be sure to have food, candles, and medicines on hand. You should stay indoors during a winter storm.

Lesson 4 Review

1. How do moving air masses affect weather?

2. How do meteorologists track and predict weather?

3. How do weather forecasts help people keep safe?

4. **Inferences**
   If a meteorologist reports a cold front coming into your area, what kind of weather can you expect?

Chapter 1 Review

Chapter Main Ideas

Lesson 1
• The angle of sunlight and the number of daylight hours affect air temperature.
• Different surfaces on the earth heat the air at different rates.
• A thermometer measures air temperature.

Lesson 2
• Changes in air temperature cause changes in air pressure and wind.
• A barometer measures air pressure.
• A wind vane measures wind direction. An anemometer measures speed.

Lesson 3
• Clouds form when water vapor in the air condenses into tiny water drops.
• Clouds have different sizes, shapes, and colors, and they form at different heights.
• Rain, snow, and hail are three kinds of precipitation.
• A hygrometer measures humidity. A rain gauge measures precipitation.
• Evaporation, condensation, and precipitation move water through the water cycle.

Lesson 4
• An air mass is a large body of air. A front is where two air masses meet.

• Meteorologists use information from the National Weather Service, maps, and weather instruments to track and predict weather.
• Meteorologists' predictions provide people time to take precautions to keep safe during severe weather.

Reviewing Science Words and Concepts

Write the letter of the word or phrase that best completes each sentence.

a. air mass
b. air pressure
c. anemometer
d. barometer
e. forecast
f. front
g. high-pressure area
h. humidity
i. hygrometer
j. low-pressure area
k. meteorologist
l. National Weather Service
m. precipitation
n. rain gauge
o. wind vane

1. The amount that air presses on the earth is called ___.
2. Rain, snow, and hail are kinds of ___.
3. The amount of water vapor in the air is called ___.
4. An area where cool air is sinking is a ___.

5. A ____ is a tool that shows wind direction.

6. An ____ is a large amount of air that has a certain temperature and humidity.

7. Scientists use an ____ to measure exact wind speed.

8. The ____ has weather stations all over the United States.

9. An area where warm air is rising is a ____.

10. A tool that measures precipitation is called a ____.

11. A ____ studies weather.

12. Humidity in the air can be measured using a ____.

13. A ____ is a tool that measures air pressure.

14. Two air masses meet at a line called a ____.

15. A prediction of what the weather will be like is a ____.

Explaining Science

Draw and label a diagram or write a paragraph to answer these questions.

1. How is the air above the earth warmed?

2. Why is air pressure lower as you go high above the earth?

3. How does hail form?

Using Skills

1. The following are the amounts of rainfall for seven months: 8 cm, 7 cm, 8 cm, 8 cm, 13 cm, 12 cm, and 9 cm. Find the **range, median,** and **mode** of rainfall.

2. You walk outside and look up. You see dome-shaped cumulus clouds. What type of weather would you **predict** for this day?

3. Suppose you **collected** the following **data** about how much precipitation fell in your town: April–11 cm, May–10 cm, June–6 cm, July–4 cm, August–3.5 cm, September–6 cm. **Interpret the data** to find out which month had the most rainfall and which had the least.

Critical Thinking

1. What would you **infer** causes a kite to rise in the sky?

2. You are in your backyard and see a large, dark cloud in the distance. Then, you **observe** lightning strike the ground. What should you do?

3. You hear a TV meteorologist report that a cold front is moving over your town. The meteorologist also reports high winds and clouds forming. **Draw a conclusion** about what kind of weather you should expect.

It's Really Growing!

Did you know that tiny grains of salt are actually crystals? If you put some salt under a microscope, you can see the tiny crystals! Other minerals and rocks that are found in the earth are also made up of crystals.

Chapter 2

The Makeup of the Earth

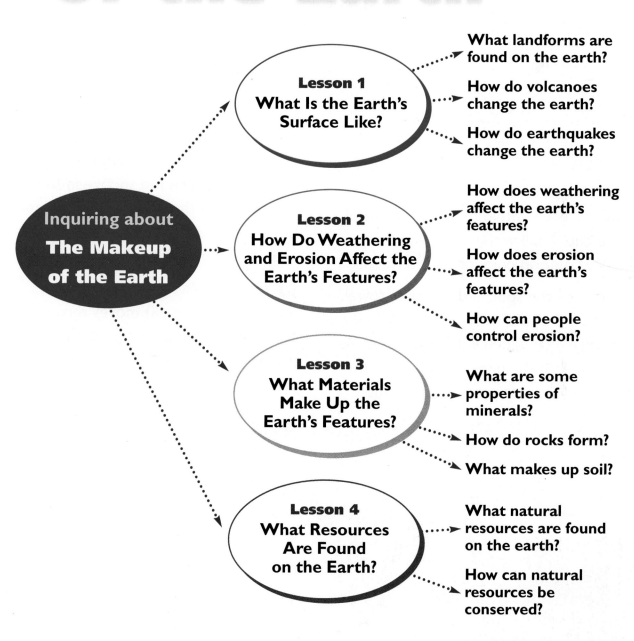

Inquiring about The Makeup of the Earth

Lesson 1
What Is the Earth's Surface Like?

What landforms are found on the earth?

How do volcanoes change the earth?

How do earthquakes change the earth?

Lesson 2
How Do Weathering and Erosion Affect the Earth's Features?

How does weathering affect the earth's features?

How does erosion affect the earth's features?

How can people control erosion?

Lesson 3
What Materials Make Up the Earth's Features?

What are some properties of minerals?

How do rocks form?

What makes up soil?

Lesson 4
What Resources Are Found on the Earth?

What natural resources are found on the earth?

How can natural resources be conserved?

Copy the chapter graphic organizer onto your own paper. This organizer shows you what the whole chapter is all about. As you read the lessons and do the activities, look for answers to the questions and write them on your organizer.

Exploring How Magma Moves

Process Skills

- making and using models
- observing

Materials

- plastic cup
- water
- red food coloring
- piece of sponge
- paper towel
- dropper
- vegetable oil
- hand lens

Explore

① Make a **model** of how molten rock moves deep within the earth. First, fill the cup $\frac{2}{3}$ full with water. Add two drops of food coloring to the water.

② Place the sponge on a paper towel. Place a dropper of vegetable oil on the sponge. **Observe** what happens as the oil touches the pores and holes in the sponge. Record your observations.

③ Place three more droppers of oil on the sponge. Place the sponge in the cup slightly below the surface of the water. Use a hand lens to observe the sponge and oil. Record your observations.

④ You have made a model of how molten rock (the oil) moves through cracks and holes deep within the earth (the sponge) toward the surface of the earth (the surface of the water).

Reflect

1. Based on your observations, describe how molten rock moves deep within the earth.

2. How is the oil in your model very different from molten rock?

? Inquire Further

What would happen if you changed the temperature of the liquids in your model? Develop a plan to answer this or other questions you may have.

Supporting Facts and Details

You group or classify objects based on properties you observe. Then you explain to others what properties you used for your classification system. In order to show why your classification system made sense, you had to describe facts and details that support the organization of your system.

Example

As you read the first part of Lesson 1, *What Is the Earth's Surface Like?*, you will discover that the earth has different landforms. Among these are mountains, plains, and plateaus. How are these landforms like or different from one another? Organizing the facts and details about these landforms can help you find out. One way to do this is to make a table like the one below. As you read the lesson, fill in the missing parts of your table.

Landforms	Facts and Details
Mountains	
Plains	
Plateaus	

Talk About It!

1. What do plateaus and mountains have in common?

2. What do plains and plateaus have in common?

▼ *Are there mountains where you live?*

You will learn:

- what landforms are found on the earth.
- how volcanoes change the earth.
- how earthquakes change the earth.

Lesson 1

What Is the Earth's Surface Like?

Would you ever live in a cave on the side of a tall cliff? Imagine looking out your door and finding that you're high above the ground. **Yikes!** But early people did build homes in high rocks.

Landforms

If you look at a picture of the earth taken from space, the earth looks mostly blue. It looks blue because about three-fourths of the earth is covered by water. The oceans are the largest bodies of water. Rivers carry water from the land to the oceans.

The surface of the earth has a great variety of features! ▼

Mountain

Plateau

On the other one-fourth of the earth, you might find mountains, plains, and plateaus, such as those in the picture on these two pages. These different shapes of the land are called **landforms.** Mountains are landforms that rise at least 600 meters above the land around them. Plains are flatland but often have small hills. Plateaus are higher than the land around them but are flat on the surface.

Life Science Some of the landforms in parts of Arizona and Colorado were used for homes by Native Americans. They built homes, like those in the picture, into the cliff walls on tall rocks. These landforms provided shade in the summer. They also allowed sunlight in during the winter. Down below the cliffs, Native Americans planted vegetable gardens. Nearby rivers and streams provided water and fish for food.

Glossary

landform, a shape of the land, such as a mountain, plain, or plateau

Native Americans used many landforms for survival. ▼

Plain

How Volcanoes Change the Earth

The surface of the earth is always changing. Some of these changes happen slowly over time. Other changes happen quickly. For example, an erupting volcano changes the earth quickly. Look at the pictures and read to find out about some of these changes. Then match the pictures on the next page with the drawings of volcanoes below.

Active Volcano

Magma forms when heat and pressure melt rocks inside the earth. Volcanoes form when heat and gases cause pressure to build up under the surface of the earth. When enough pressure builds up, the magma forces its way up through weak spots called vents. Then the magma breaks through the surface of the earth. Magma that flows onto the earth's surface is called lava. The lava cools and hardens, forming a mountain called a **volcano.** ▶

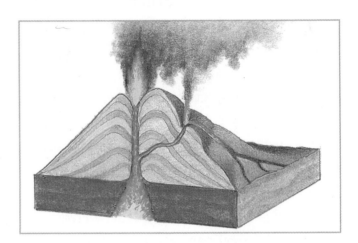

Violent Eruption

Sometimes a volcano erupts with such force that part of the volcanic mountain may be blown to pieces. Rock, volcanic ash, and lava may be spread over a wide area. ▶

Dormant Volcano

A dormant volcano is one that is "sleeping." It hasn't erupted in recent times. Inside, the mountain may be building up pressure that will some day be released. ▶

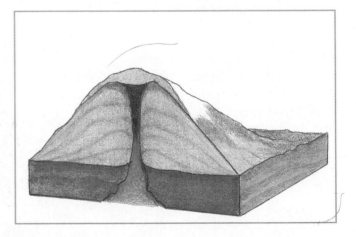

Mount Arenal

Arenal is an active volcano in Costa Rica. After being dormant for many years, Arenal erupted in 1968. Lava has been flowing ever since. The most recent eruption of Arenal took place in 1984. The volcano is 1,633 meters high. ▶

Mount St. Helens

◀ For over 100 years Mount St. Helens was dormant. However, in 1980 the volcano erupted violently. As a result, part of the mountain that had been built up by earlier volcanic activity was blown away. Mount St. Helens is now 400 meters shorter than it was before the 1980 eruption.

Mount Rainier

Mount Rainier, the highest peak of the Cascade Range in Washington, is a dormant volcano. This peak was formed by a volcano that erupted and built up the mountain. Mount Rainier is now covered by 41 glaciers that cap the peak and extend down the slopes. Some scientists think that Mount Rainier is likely to erupt again. ▶

Glossary

earthquake
(ėrth′kwāk′), the shaking of the ground caused by rock movement along a fault

fault (fôlt), a crack in the earth's crust along which rocks move

Thousands of earthquakes happen in California each year. Many of these happen along the San Andreas fault. ▼

How Earthquakes Change the Earth

Earthquakes also change the shape of the land. An **earthquake** is the shaking of a part of the ground. What causes the shaking?

The crust, or top layer of the earth, is made up of large sections of rock called plates. These plates are always moving. Sometimes the movement of the plates causes cracks in the crust. If the rock moves along the crack, the crack is called a **fault**. When the rocks along a fault move, the ground shakes. Most earthquakes do not cause enough shaking for people to feel. However, some earthquakes cause great damage to buildings, bridges, and highways.

Most faults happen deep inside the earth and are not seen on the earth's surface. The picture on the left shows one fault that can be seen. This fault extends over 1,200 kilometers along the coast of California. That's a long crack!

This Los Angeles freeway shows the kind of damage that an earthquake can cause. ▼

In 1994 the city of Los Angeles was hit by an earthquake that damaged many homes, businesses, and roads. In the picture on page C42, you can see how a freeway was damaged by the earthquake. Forty-two people lost their lives, and many were left homeless.

Scientists cannot predict exactly when an earthquake will happen. However, technology helps keep track of smaller earthquakes that may come before larger ones. Scientists use the information they collect to warn people of danger.

Wouldn't it be great to have a building that will stay up during an earthquake? Engineers thought the same thing! People have designed buildings that can survive most earthquakes. The rocket-shaped building in the picture, the Transamerica Building, is located in San Francisco, California. This building was built on a special platform. If an earthquake hits, the building should sway with the vibrations of the earth.

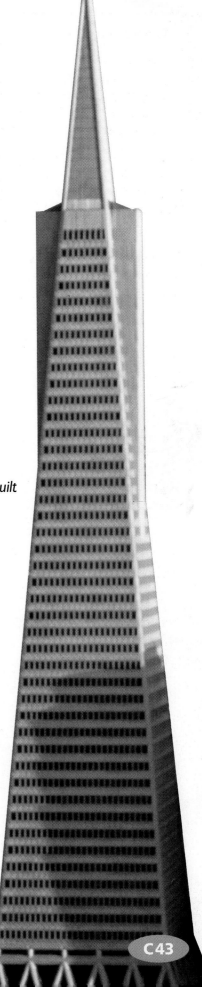

The Transamerica Building was built to withstand earthquakes. ▶

Lesson 1 Review

1. List three kinds of landforms found on the earth.

2. How do volcanoes change the surface of the earth?

3. What causes earthquakes?

4. **Facts and Details**
   In the first paragraph on this page, what facts and details are given to support the main idea?

You will learn:

- how weathering affects the earth's features.
- how erosion affects the earth's features.
- ways people can control erosion.

Glossary

weathering
(weŧH′ər ing), the breaking and changing of rocks

These rocks have been changed by weathering over many years. ▼

Lesson 2

How Do Weathering and Erosion Affect the Earth's Features?

Have you ever played in a sandbox? Would you believe that all that sand was once big rocks? Sand is made up of tiny pieces of rocks broken down by weathering.

Weathering

You have learned how volcanoes and earthquakes change the features of the earth. However, landforms are also changed in other ways. Water and ice can break rocks and wear away their surfaces. The breaking and changing of rocks is called **weathering**.

The rocks in the picture have been changed by water and ice over thousands of years. Water fills tiny cracks in the rocks and freezes when the weather gets cold. The freezing water pushes against the rocks. Then the weather gets warm and melts the ice. The rocks move back, but the cracks may be larger than they were before. The freezing and melting over and over again breaks the rocks apart.

The trees growing in cracks in the rocks in the picture on page C44 also cause weathering. As the roots grow, they push against the sides of the cracks. The pushing force helps break the rocks apart.

Bryce Canyon in the picture below shows what weathering can do over thousands of years. The cones and towers are partly a result of freezing and thawing. Water can also cause weathering when it flows over rocks. This causes a chemical change in the rocks that weathers them.

Bryce Canyon in Utah was not cut by a river's flowing water. It was hollowed out from the cliffs by weathering and erosion. ▼

Glossary

erosion (i rō′zhən), the moving of weathered rocks and soil by wind, water, or ice

dune (dün), a pile of sand formed by the wind

Erosion

The waterfall in the picture carries weathered rocks and soil as it flows downward. The flow of water at the bottom of the waterfall also moves small rocks and soil. The moving of weathered rocks and soil by water, wind, and ice is **erosion.** Years of weathering and erosion can really change what an area looks like!

Wind erosion is especially noticeable in a desert. The wind carries sediments, such as sand and other tiny particles, and deposits them in other places. Often, large piles of windblown sand, or **dunes,** build up.

Glaciers are large areas of ice formed from snow. High in the mountains and near the North and South Poles, it is cold all year. Therefore, all the snow does not melt during the summer. Layers of snow build up. The pressure of the top layers of snow causes the bottom layers of snow to become ice. As glaciers slide slowly across the land, they carry small rocks in the ice. The glaciers also push larger rocks and soil across the land. When the ice melts, the rocks and soil are left behind.

Weathered rocks are carried from the highlands by the waterfall. As the rocks fall, they may be broken into smaller pieces. At the bottom of the waterfall, sand, soil, and small pebbles are carried by water and left in new places. ▼

Controlling Erosion

Weathering can be helpful because it helps form soil, but how can erosion be helpful? In some places, such as at the mouth of a river, materials moved by erosion help build new land. This land has lots of minerals, and crops grow well.

Erosion often causes problems—especially for farmers. Erosion caused by rainwater can wash away soil from farmlands. It can also wash away roads and the ground under homes.

One way farmers control erosion is by planting a cover crop between rows of crops. Strips of grass and clover are good cover crops. Cover crops, such as the ones in the picture, help absorb rainwater. They slow or stop the movement of water over the surface. This prevents erosion of the land. Farmers also plow their fields in rows around the hills. By following the shape of the land, the rows make a kind of step where rainwater can settle. The water can then soak into the land. It doesn't flow downhill and wash away soil.

Another way to help stop erosion is by planting trees on steep hills. The roots of trees help hold soil in place. Trees also protect the soil from wind and rain, helping to slow down erosion.

▲ Notice the cover crops in between the rows of crops.

Lesson 2 Review

1. What is weathering?

2. What is erosion?

3. How can people control erosion?

4. **Facts and Details**
   In the third paragraph on this page, what facts and details are given to support the main idea?

What's the Big Idea?

You will learn:

- what some properties of minerals are.
- how rocks form.
- what makes up soil.

Luster

Luster is the way a mineral reflects light. Minerals that reflect a lot of light are shiny. Some minerals are shinier than others. Gold is an example of a mineral that reflects a lot of light. Gold is used in jewelry. It is also used in medals, such as the Olympic medal in the picture. ▶

What Materials Make Up the Earth's Features?

Diamonds, rubies, and gold! These are minerals that come from the earth. Imagine! There are places on the earth where people can dig up gems and metal!

Minerals

The rocks that make up many of the landforms on the earth may have different colors and shapes. However, all rocks are alike in one way—they are made of one or more minerals. A **mineral** is nonliving, solid matter from the earth. Minerals have physical properties such as luster, hardness, and color. Some of their properties help people identify the minerals. Read more about three properties of minerals on these two pages.

Color

▲ Minerals come in many different colors. Some minerals are found in several colors, and some may even change color. Therefore, color cannot always be used to identify minerals. Some minerals are used to make gemstones, such as those in the picture.

Hardness

▲ If you want to know how hard a mineral is, rub it against another mineral. The harder mineral will scratch the softer mineral. The hardness of a mineral helps to identify the mineral. A diamond is the hardest mineral. It will scratch any other material. Diamonds are often used in drills, such as the one in the picture above.

Rocks

You might think that all rocks are alike, but rocks form in different ways. Some rocks form deep inside the earth. Other rocks are formed at the bottom of lakes and oceans.

Rocks are used to make many things around you. For example, did you know that chalk is a rock? Look at the pictures on these two pages to find out how rocks are formed and what they are used for.

Igneous Rock

Some igneous rocks are made from magma that cools below the earth's surface. Granite is an igneous rock that forms in this way. This monument on Mt. Rushmore was carved in granite. ▼

Sedimentary Rock

▲ If you look closely at some sedimentary rocks, you might be able to see seashells. That's because sedimentary rocks are made of tiny pieces of other rocks, shells, sand, and other materials. These tiny pieces are sediments. They are carried into lakes and oceans by rivers and streams. The sediments sink to the bottom of the water and are pressed and cemented tightly together. After many years, sedimentary rocks are formed. Sandstone is a sedimentary rock. At one time, sandstone was used for buildings such as these in ruins.

Metamorphic Rock

Rocks that are deep inside the earth can change into different kinds of rocks. Heat from deep in the earth and the pressure of rocks above change rock. Over many years, this can change igneous and sedimentary rocks. Rocks that are changed in this way are called metamorphic rocks. Limestone, a sedimentary rock, is changed to a metamorphic rock called marble. Many statues are made from marble. ▶

C51

▲ Corn plants grow well in dark, rich topsoil.

Soil

Years of weathering of rocks and minerals and the decaying of dead plants and animals form soil. Soil also contains air and water.

Soil is important because plants and animals depend on soil for nutrients. Soil is also important because it holds water that plants need.

Have you ever planted a garden or dug a hole in the ground? If so, you might have noticed that soil has different colors. The color of soil helps scientists and farmers know what types of minerals are in the soil. Different soils also look and feel different. Some soils feel smooth and others have fine grains. Still other soils feel coarse and rocky.

Soils are different because they form from different kinds of rocks and minerals. The amount of humus in soil also affects the color and feel of soil. Humus is once living matter that has been broken down by decomposers. Notice the different kinds of soil in the picture below.

Have you ever built a sand castle? If you have, you know that sand is loose and has large grains. Sand does not hold water well. As the water runs through sandy soil, it washes nutrients out of the soil. Therefore, soil with too much sand is not the best for growing crops, or for living organisms. They need nutrients to live and grow.

Sand

Clay

Topsoil

Notice the clay in the picture on page C52. If you've ever held a piece of clay, you know that it is smooth and has fine, tightly packed grains. Water does not soak into clay quickly, but clay can hold a lot of water. Clay is rich in nutrients. However, plants do not grow well in clay because it is hard and roots cannot spread out well in it.

Topsoil is the dark soil you probably see in your garden or in your yard. Topsoil is dark because it has a lot of humus in it. Topsoil may also have some sand or clay in it. Topsoil is rich in nutrients and holds water well. Plants grow well in topsoil. Notice the picture of soil above. The animals help keep soil loose and help air get into the soil.

▲ The animals that live in this soil make holes that let air into the soil.

Lesson 3 Review

1. Describe some of the properties of minerals.

2. What are igneous, sedimentary, and metamorphic rocks made of?

3. Compare and contrast three types of soil.

4. **Facts and Details**
   In the last paragraph on this page, what facts and details are given to support the main idea?

Classifying Rocks

Process Skills

- observing
- classifying
- collecting and interpreting data

Materials

- scissors
- paper
- marker
- glue
- 7 rocks
- hand lens

Getting Ready

In this activity you will observe and classify rocks according to their properties.

Follow This Procedure

❶ Make a chart like the one shown. Use your chart to record your observations.

Properties	Rock numbers
Light color	
Dark color	
Visible crystals	
No visible crystals	
No visibly different minerals	
Visibly different minerals	
No visibly different minerals, visible crystals	
No visibly different minerals, no visible crystals	

❷ Carefully cut and number small pieces of paper *1–7*. Glue one number to each rock.

❸ Place all the rocks on a table. **Observe** each rock. **Classify** the rocks by separating them into two groups: those that are light in color and those that are dark in color (Photo A). Record the numbers of the rocks in each group in your chart. This is your **collected data.**

Photo A

④ Place all rocks together once again. Observe each rock with a hand lens (Photo B). Separate the rocks that have visible mineral crystals, or shiny, flat surfaces, into one group, and those that do not have visible mineral crystals into another group. Record which rocks have visible crystals and which ones do not.

⑤ Put all of the rocks together once again. Observe each rock with a hand lens. Separate the rocks into two groups: those with more than one visibly different mineral (more than one color) and those that do not have visibly different minerals (only one color). Record your data.

⑥ Take the group of rocks containing no visibly different minerals and

separate it into two groups: rocks with visible crystals and rocks without visible crystals. Record your data.

Interpret Your Results

1. Do you have any groups containing only one rock? If so, how many?

2. Which properties did you use to classify the rocks?

Inquire Further

What other properties could you use to classify rocks? Develop a plan to answer this or other questions you may have.

Self-Assessment

- I followed instructions to **classify** rocks according to their properties.
- I **observed** each of the rocks with a hand lens.
- I **collected data** by recording my observations.
- I classified rocks in different ways.
- I listed the properties I used to group the rocks.

Photo B

You will learn:

- what natural resources are found on the earth.
- how to conserve natural resources.

Lesson 4

What Resources Are Found on the Earth?

Flick! Each time you flick a light switch, you're using a natural resource. Each time you read a book, you're using a natural resource. Even the cars and buses you ride in run on natural resources.

Natural Gas

Natural gas is a natural resource. It is formed when tiny dead organisms are buried in layers of sediment. After many years of heat and pressure within these sediments, natural gas is formed. Natural gas is renewable, but it takes millions of years to form. Before natural gas is used for fuel, it is pumped to a refinery. Some products in the natural gas are removed there. ▼

Natural Resources

Natural resources are useful things the earth produces. People use natural resources every day. Air and water are natural resources. Soil and lumber are natural resources too. Some natural resources can be renewed, but others cannot. Look at the pictures and read to find out more about natural resources.

Many families use natural gas for cooking and heating their homes. ▼

Trees

▲ Trees are natural resources that are renewable. However, trees take many years to reach a large size.

Wood from trees is used to make pencils and paper. Lumber is also used to build homes and furniture. Besides providing wood products, trees give off oxygen into the air. Animals find food in trees, and they also use trees as their homes. ▼

Petroleum

Petroleum is a natural resource that is formed in ocean basins. The remains of tiny dead organisms are covered with layers of sediment. After millions of years of heat and pressure, petroleum forms. Petroleum is renewable, but the supply is being used faster than it can form. Oil wells are used to get petroleum out of the earth. ▼

▲ The car runs on gasoline, which is made from petroleum. Plastics, such as dishes and toys, are also made from petroleum.

Conserving Natural Resources

Has a family member ever told you, "Turn out that light"? Turning out lights is one way to conserve, or save, natural resources. Natural resources are important to every living thing. People try to save natural resources because they are so important. Some ways that can help conserve natural resources are shown on these two pages.

Turn Down the Heat!

Have you ever seen someone turn down the thermostat for the furnace at home? Turning down the thermostat helps reduce the amount of natural gas or other fuels you use. ▶

Ride Your Bike!

◀ Cars and buses use gasoline. Riding your bike or carpooling helps reduce the amount of gasoline that is used.

Recycle Paper!
Recycling paper reduces the number of trees that are cut down. Replanting trees that are cut down also helps conserve trees. Recycle! It's cool! ▼

Lesson 4 Review

1. What are natural resources?

2. List three ways people can help conserve natural resources.

3. **Facts and Details**
On page C57, what facts and details are given about petroleum to support the main idea of the caption?

Chapter 2 Review

Chapter Main Ideas

Lesson 1
• Mountains, plains and plateaus are landforms found on the earth's surface.
• Volcanoes change the earth's surface by forming new mountains or by destroying mountains.
• Earthquakes are caused when large sections of rocks slip past other large sections of rock. Engineers have designed buildings that can survive most earthquakes.

Lesson 2
• Weathering can affect landforms by breaking and changing rocks.
• Erosion can affect landforms by moving weathered rocks and soil.
• People can control erosion by planting a cover crop, plowing and planting crops in rows around hills, and planting trees on steep hills.

Lesson 3
• A mineral is nonliving, solid matter from the earth that has properties such as luster, color, and hardness.
• Some rocks form inside the earth, others form under lakes and oceans, and others form when the heat and pressure inside the earth change other rocks.
• Soil is made up of minerals, rocks, and dead plants and animals.

Lesson 4
• Air, water, soil, lumber, natural gas, and petroleum are some natural resources found on the earth.
• People try to conserve natural resources by reducing the amount of natural resources they use.

Reviewing Science Words and Concepts

Write the letter of the word or phrase that best completes each sentence.

a. dune   e. landform

b. earthquake   f. mineral

c. erosion   g. volcano

d. fault   h. weathering

1. A _____ is nonliving, solid matter from the earth.
2. The breaking and changing of rocks is called _____.
3. A mountain is one kind of _____.
4. The movement of rocks along a fault may cause an _____.
5. A _____ is a crack in the earth's crust along which rocks move.
6. The moving of weathered rocks and soil is called _____.

7. When windblown sand piles up, a _____ is formed.

8. A mountain formed by hardened lava is a _____.

Explaining Science

Draw a picture or write a paragraph to answer these questions.

1. How do volcanoes form?

2. How do water and ice break down rocks?

3. How is soil formed? Why is soil important?

4. What are three natural resources, and how do people use them?

Using Skills

1. In the last paragraph on page C56, what are the **supporting facts and details**?

2. You **observe** a rock closely. You notice that it has tiny pieces of seashells. What kind of rock is this? How does it form?

3. What are some of the properties used in **classifying** minerals?

Critical Thinking

1. **Contrast** how igneous and sedimentary rocks are formed.

2. Suppose you fill up a large jar with water. You place gravel in it. Then you place sand in it. You let the jar sit out for one day. What do you **predict** will happen to the contents of the jar? What kind of rock forms this way? Write a paragraph to explain.

3. You see a house on the side of a hill with no trees growing around it. **Draw a conclusion** about what might happen to the house after many heavy rainstorms.

Explore the *Titanic!*

Did you know that you can explore the *Titanic* using a computer? The JASON Project allows students to become part of a team of explorers through computers! Sometimes the students can even interact with the scientists.

Chapter 3
Exploring the Oceans

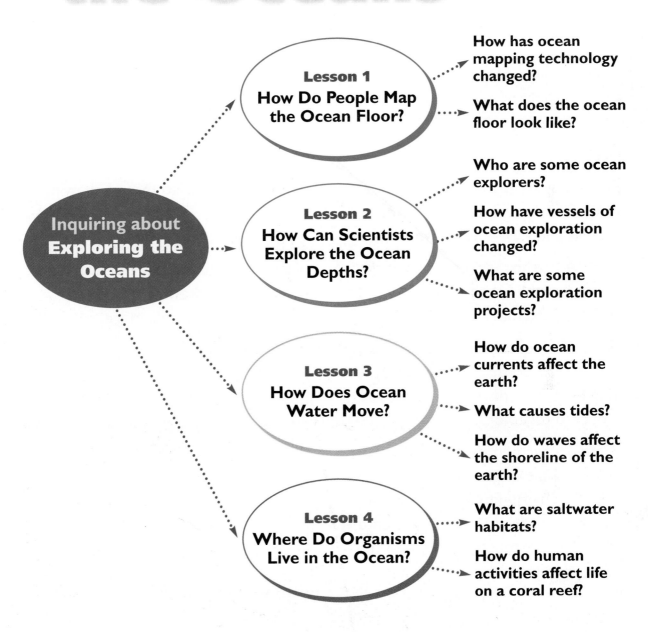

Inquiring about **Exploring the Oceans**

Lesson 1
How Do People Map the Ocean Floor?

- How has ocean mapping technology changed?
- What does the ocean floor look like?

Lesson 2
How Can Scientists Explore the Ocean Depths?

- Who are some ocean explorers?
- How have vessels of ocean exploration changed?
- What are some ocean exploration projects?

Lesson 3
How Does Ocean Water Move?

- How do ocean currents affect the earth?
- What causes tides?
- How do waves affect the shoreline of the earth?

Lesson 4
Where Do Organisms Live in the Ocean?

- What are saltwater habitats?
- How do human activities affect life on a coral reef?

Copy the chapter graphic organizer onto your own paper. This organizer shows you what the whole chapter is all about. As you read the lessons and do the activities, look for answers to the questions and write them on your organizer.

Measuring What You Can't See

Process Skills

- estimating and measuring
- collecting and interpreting data

Materials

- modeling clay
- 2 pieces of cardboard
- metric ruler
- marker
- masking tape
- straw

Explore

① Use clay to form a ridge across a piece of cardboard. Shape the ridge into hills and valleys as shown.

② Make five marks 4 cm apart at the top edge of the other piece of cardboard. Number the marks 1–5.

③ Press the second piece of cardboard over the first so that the numbers are along the top. Tape the two pieces of cardboard together.

④ Have a partner lower the straw between the two pieces of cardboard at the first mark until it hits the clay. Have your partner place a finger on the straw where it touches the top of the cardboard. Remove the straw and **measure** how many centimeters the straw was lowered. **Collect data** by recording the measurement.

⑤ Repeat step 4 at each mark.

Reflect

1. Use your data to make a drawing of the ridge.

2. Remove the tape and lift the top piece of cardboard off. Compare and contrast your drawing to the appearance of the clay ridge.

? Inquire Further

How could you increase the accuracy of your drawing? Develop a plan to answer this or other questions you may have.

Using Logical Reasoning

The fish pictured here are the blue shark, flying fish, trout, mackerel, and bluefin tuna. They are not in order. Read the clues. Then use them to identify each fish by how fast (kilometers per hour) it can swim.

a. A bluefin tuna swims fastest.

b. A flying fish swims about 23 kph faster than a mackerel.

c. A blue shark swims about twice as fast as a mackerel.

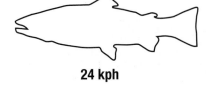

24 kph

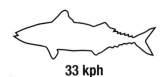

33 kph

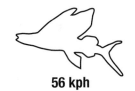

56 kph

Work Together

Understand	What do you know? What do you need to find out?	
Plan	How will you find out?	
Solve	Find the fastest speed.	A bluefin tuna swims 100 kph.
	Find two numbers that have a difference of 23 kph.	56 − 33 = 23 So, a mackerel swims 33 kph and a flying fish swims 56 kph.
	Find a speed that is about twice 33 kph.	33 x 2 = 66 69 is close to 66. So, a blue shark swims 69 kph. A trout must swim 24 kph.
Look Back	How can you check your answers?	Compare your results with the clues. Make sure all statements are true.

69 kph

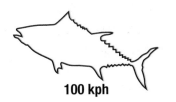

100 kph

Talk About It!

How could you change the clues to include a trout?

Problem Solving Hint

Find clues that help you narrow your choices.

What's the Big Idea?

You will learn:

- how ocean mapping technology has changed.
- what the ocean floor looks like.

How Do People Map the Ocean Floor?

Hills, valleys, and peaks! You know that these landforms are found on the earth's surface. But would you expect to find hills, trenches, and peaks on the ocean floor? **SURPRISE!**

Mapping the Ocean Floor

Did you know that most of the earth is covered by the oceans? Find the Pacific Ocean on the map. It is the largest of the four main oceans. Find the other main oceans—the Atlantic, the Indian, and the Arctic.

What do you think is under all that water? It's the ocean floor, but not the kind of floor that you probably think about. The ocean floor is not covered with carpet or tile like the floors in your home. The ocean floor looks a lot like the surface of the earth.

The Pacific Ocean is so large that all the land on the earth's surface could fit into it. Now that's a huge bathtub! ▼

Arctic Ocean
Atlantic Ocean
Pacific Ocean
Indian Ocean

History of Science

Long ago, people could not go to the bottom of the ocean. How do you think they found out what the ocean floor is like? At first, sailors used long ropes with weights tied on them to measure the depth of the water. However, this method did not work well in the deeper parts of the ocean. The sailors couldn't always tell when the weight hit the bottom of the ocean, and sometimes the rope wasn't long enough.

In the 1900s scientists began using echoes—or sounding—to map the ocean floor. You may have heard an echo of your own voice. Sometimes when you call to someone across a large room, the sound waves of your voice may hit the wall and bounce back to your ears. This also happened when sound waves were sent from a ship down into the ocean. The sound waves hit the bottom of the ocean and bounced back. Scientists measured how long it took for the sound to bounce back to the ship. Because scientists knew how fast sound travels in ocean water, they could tell how far the sound waves traveled.

Today satellites such as the one shown are used to map the ocean floor. The satellite pictures provide more detailed maps of the landforms at the bottom of the ocean than other methods did.

▲ *A satellite uses radar to map the ocean floor.*

◀ *This computer image of the ocean floor shows deep cracks in an ocean ridge.*

Structure of the Ocean Floor

Imagine taking a trip in an underwater ship that can speed across the floor of the ocean. Study the picture on these two pages and read the descriptions to find out what features you might see.

Glossary

continental (kon′tə nen′tl) **shelf**, the shallow part of the ocean at the edge of the continents

continental slope, the edge of the continental shelf that extends steeply downward to the ocean floor

ocean basin (bā′sn), the floor of the deep ocean

Continental Slope
*The **continental slope** is farther from the shore. The ocean floor drops sharply at the continental slope. The depth of the ocean water increases greatly.*

Continental Shelf
*The **continental shelf** is the part of a continent that extends under the ocean from the shoreline. The ocean averages about 135 meters deep on the continental shelf.*

Ocean Basin
*The **ocean basin** is the floor under the deep part of the ocean—about 4,000–5,000 meters deep.*

Ridge
An ocean **ridge** is the highest part of a long chain of mountains found in some parts of the ocean basin.

Trench
An ocean **trench** is a very deep, narrow valley in the bottom of the ocean. A trench is deeper than any valley on land. Some trenches are six times as deep as the Grand Canyon. That's really deep!

Lesson 1 Review

1. What is one way that scientists have used to map the ocean floor?

2. How do the mountains and valleys on the ocean floor compare to those on land?

3. **Main Idea**
   What is the main idea of the first paragraph on page C67?

What's the Big Idea?

You will learn:
- who some ocean explorers are.
- how vessels of ocean exploration have changed.
- about some ocean exploration projects.

Lesson 2

How Can Scientists Explore the Ocean Depths?

Just imagine going down into the ocean! **WOW!** At first you might see beautiful coral and many different kinds of animals. But as you go deeper, the ocean becomes pitch-black.

▲ Jacques Cousteau, seen here in scuba gear, was a pioneer in exploring the ocean.

Ocean Explorers

History of Science

In 1943 Jacques Cousteau, the French sea explorer in the picture, worked with Emile Gagnan, a French engineer. Together they developed an underwater breathing device—a tank of air attached to a face mask. By using this device, divers could stay underwater for several hours, but they could only go down into the ocean about 130 meters.

In 1960 Jacques Piccard and Don Walsh went down into the Marianas Trench with the *Trieste* shown in the picture below. It was the second bathyscaph designed by his father, Auguste Piccard. Imagine the excitement of Piccard and Walsh as they stepped into the *Trieste*. They were about to go where no human had ever gone before! They found living creatures in this deepest part of the ocean. At last people knew that living things could exist in the deep ocean!

◄ *Piccard and Walsh's journey to the deepest part of the ocean was like the astronauts' mission to the moon!*

C70

Dr. Sylvia Earle in the picture at the right is an undersea explorer. She has lived for weeks at a time on the ocean floor. Dr. Earle hopes that learning more about the ocean will make people work harder to protect it from pollution.

Dr. Robert Ballard in the picture below has explored the ocean floor in the *NR-1*. He and his research team discovered a graveyard of eight ships on the Mediterranean ocean floor. He also found the *Titanic* and the *Bismarck*, famous ships that sunk years ago.

▲ *Dr. Sylvia Earle has spent so much time in the ocean that she has been nicknamed "Her Royal Deepness." New technologies have made it possible for her to live in the ocean for long periods of time.*

Dr. Robert Ballard, shown standing here in the NR-1, a nuclear submarine, has seen more of the ocean floor than any other living person. ▼

Ocean Exploration Vessels

History of Science

Through the years technology has helped scientists design amazing vessels to study the oceans. Compare the pictures of some of these vessels shown on these two pages. Using these vessels, oceanographers have discovered more and more about the mysteries of the deep, dark ocean.

H.M.S. *Challenger*

For about four years beginning in 1872, the British ship H.M.S. Challenger carried a crew of about 200, along with 6 scientists, on the first ocean exploration. They traveled from the North Atlantic polar seas to the Antarctic. They took thousands of measurements of currents, temperatures, and depths. The crew also discovered many unknown plants and animals. The Challenger discoveries excited scientists about the mysteries of the ocean! ▶

Calypso

For over 50 years, Cousteau and his crews of divers, scientists, and photographers explored the beauty of the ocean. From the Calypso, Cousteau's crew filmed the ocean with an underwater movie camera. Cousteau's movie, The Silent World, brought the ocean into the living rooms of millions of people. Cousteau soon discovered signs of ocean pollution and waste of natural resources. He made the world aware of what people were doing to the ocean. ▼

Alvin

Alvin *carried three people down to the Mid-Atlantic Ridge. This ridge is a huge underwater mountain range in the middle of the Atlantic Ocean. The view from the* Alvin *startled the scientists. They had expected to find an empty ocean floor. Instead they found fish that light their own way as they swim in the dark waters among other strange life forms.*

In 1977, scientists used Alvin *to explore near the Galapagos Islands. They discovered giant white clams and huge tube worms that had never been seen before. These animals live in a place where warm ocean water comes up through the ocean floor.* ▶

NR-1

◀ *The NR-1 is a nuclear submarine that can stay underwater for up to a month. With its powerful sonar, this submarine can easily find sunken ships. It can even find treasures that are buried in mud. Jason was used to recover these storage jugs from one of the Roman ships found by the NR-1.*

Jason

Robots such as Jason are being used for ocean exploration because they cost less and are safer than piloted vessels. They can also stay down longer—some up to a year! Robots can be brought back to the surface by a signal from a ship. Jason was used to explore the wreckage of the Titanic, shown in the two pictures. Dr. Ballard designed Jason, Jr., a smaller robot, to explore the inside of the Titanic. ▶

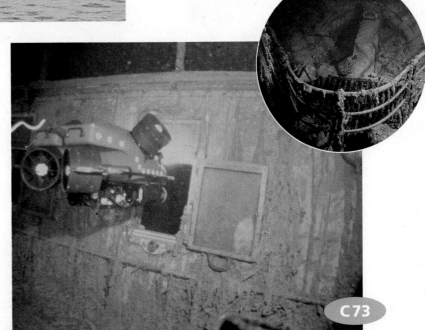

Ocean Exploration Projects

Exploring the ocean is somewhat like exploring space. Scientists must protect themselves from different temperatures, pressures, and the lack of oxygen. Two projects that are working on ocean exploration are the JASON project and the *Deep Flight* project.

Students who take part in a JASON project go to a special site that is connected to a scientific expedition. Underwater cameras, special cables, and satellite dishes allow students to be a part of the exploration. Students, such as the ones in the picture, can watch and talk to the scientists and other students who are part of the exploring team.

Robots, such as the one shown, are used to explore the inside of ship wrecks. This robot can explore in places that aren't safe or are too small for people to enter. It can be steered by remote control.

At a JASON site, students can control robots to explore on their own. ▼

The goal of the *Deep Flight* project is to explore the deepest part of the ocean. *Deep Flight* is a minisubmarine that is built of very strong materials that can withstand the water pressure of the deep ocean.

Deep Flight, shown in the picture, moves through water much like an airplane flies through the air. However, Deep Flight has upside-down wings. Instead of pulling up as an airplanes wings do, Deep Flight's wings pull it down into the ocean. It is easier to steer than other submarines. Deep Flight is faster than other underwater vehicles and can make fast turns and steep dives.

▲ Engineer Dr. Graham Hawkes and chief scientist Dr. Sylvia Earle are the main scientists working on the Deep Flight project.

Lesson 2 Review

1. Name two people who have explored the ocean.

2. What are some kinds of vessels used to explore the ocean?

3. Why is the JASON project important to students?

4. **Logical Reasoning**

   In 1872 the H.M.S. *Challenger* was exploring the polar seas. In 1977 *Alvin* was used to explore near the Galapagos Islands. Which vessel was used earlier? How many years earlier was it used?

Investigating Currents and Waves

Process Skills

- making and using models
- observing

Materials

- safety goggles
- warm water
- plastic pail
- metric ruler
- sharpened pencil
- plastic-foam cup
- small pieces of ice
- container of cold water
- red food coloring
- 6 gram cubes
- plastic straw

Getting Ready

In this activity you will make models of one type of current and waves. You will learn about another type of current in the following lesson.

Follow This Procedure

1 Make a chart like the one shown. Use your chart to record your observations.

	Observations
Motion of cold water added to warm water	
Motion of colored water when waves are produced	
Motion of gram cubes when waves are produced	

2 Put on your safety goggles. Add warm water to the pail until the water is 5 cm deep.

3 Use the pencil to punch four small holes near the bottom of the plastic-foam cup (Photo A). Fill the cup with ice.

4 Add about 15 drops of food coloring to the cold water. The water should appear to be red. Place the cup of ice in the middle of the pail.

Photo A

Photo B

5 Add colored water to the plastic-foam cup. The cold water is a model of a current in the warm water. Observe how the colored water moves. Record your observations.

6 Join six gram cubes together. Float the cubes in the pail of water. Above the water, blow air through the straw to make waves on the surface of the water (Photo B). Do not blow on the gram cubes.

7 Observe the motion of the water waves, the colored water, and the gram cubes. Record your observations.

Self-Monitoring
Have I carefully observed and recorded my observations? Do I have any questions to ask before I continue?

Interpret Your Results

1. Describe the movement of the cold water after it was added to the warm water in the pail.

2. Describe the effects the motion of the waves had on the colored water and the gram cubes.

 **Inquire Further**

What do you think would happen if fresh water and salt water were used in this activity in place of the warm water and cold water? Develop a plan to answer this or other questions you may have.

Self-Assessment

- I followed instructions to make a model of a current and waves.
- I observed the movement of water when cold water was added to warm water.
- I observed how waves affect the movement of currents and the floating gram cubes.
- I recorded my observations.
- I described the motion of cold water in warm water, and the effects of waves on the water and the gram cubes.

What's the Big Idea?

You will learn:

- how ocean currents affect the earth.
- what causes tides.
- how waves affect the shoreline of the earth.

Glossary

Glossary

current (kėr′ənt), a riverlike flow of water in the ocean

The key at the bottom of the picture gives the Celsius temperatures indicated by the different colors. ▼

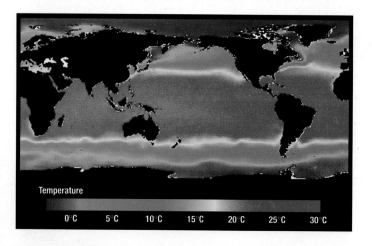

Temperature

| 0°C | 5°C | 10°C | 15°C | 20°C | 25°C | 30°C |

Lesson 3

How Does Ocean Water Move?

SPLASH! Think about a time that you jumped into a swimming pool. You may have noticed that the water around you moved. But have you ever thought about all the moving water in the ocean?

Ocean Currents

You may have seen rivers flowing on the earth's surface, but did you know that streams of water flow through the ocean? These riverlike streams of water that move at different speeds are called **currents.** Hundreds of years ago, sailors learned where these currents are and in what direction they flow. Sailors knew that if they sailed their ship with the current, they could sail faster.

Satellites that circle high above the earth take pictures with special cameras. The pictures, such as the one shown, show the different temperatures of the ocean water. Oceanographers use the pictures to trace ocean currents.

Currents have temperatures that are different from the water around them. Currents flowing from near the North Pole or the South Pole carry cold water. Currents flowing from the equator carry warm water. Find some of these currents on the map on the next page.

Notice that the arrows show in which direction the currents are flowing. The direction of the wind and the movement of the earth cause currents that flow near the surface of the ocean.

Find the Gulf Stream on the map. Notice that it flows north along the east coast of the United States. This warm current then moves east across the Atlantic Ocean to Europe. Its water warms the air that flows over Great Britain and northern Europe. Great Britain is as far north as Canada, but its winter weather is much warmer than Canada's.

Find the cold current that flows south along the western coast of the United States. This current cools the air over San Francisco in the summer. Therefore, even though San Francisco is about the same distance from the equator as Wichita, San Francisco has a cooler summer. ▼

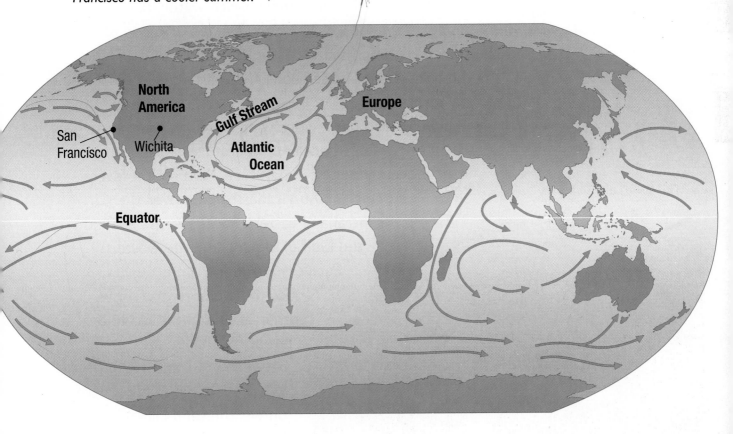

The lack of rain in Mexico and other nearby places due to El Niño caused the forests to be dry. The resulting forest fires in Mexico in the spring of 1998 spread air pollution into the United States and other countries. ▶

The warmer water around the Florida Keys caused the coral to be more likely to get diseases. Touching or breaking off pieces of coral during this time would have made their recovery harder. Scientists asked divers and people who snorkel to take extra care around the coral. ▼

Every few years an El Niño event changes weather patterns around the world. This event happens when trade winds don't blow as hard as usual. As a result, the warm-water current spreads out across the Pacific Ocean. These changes prevent the normal upward movement of the cold, nutrient-rich water that supports the food chain. Many fish die or move to colder waters in search of food. Lack of food affects the birds as well as sea lions and seals along the California coast.

El Niño also has a worldwide effect on weather. The changes in the ocean temperature cause changes in air movement and temperature. As a result, severe storms and hurricanes happen over the central and eastern Pacific. Areas around the Gulf of Mexico and the western Pacific may suffer from droughts. Notice the pictures that show other effects of the El Niño event that happened between 1997 and 1998. What effect did El Niño have on weather and climate where you live?

Tides

Notice the two pictures at the right. How is the ocean shore different? The pictures show what happens during a low tide and a high tide. A **tide** is the rise and fall of the water along the ocean shore. Most places along the ocean have tides twice each day.

Hundreds of years ago, people found out that the moon causes tides. People saw that two high tides and two low tides move onto an ocean shore each day. They also saw that the moon seems to rise and set each day.

The moon and the earth are pulled toward each other by gravity. The pull of gravity keeps the moon moving around the earth. The picture below shows how the moon's pull on the earth causes high and low tides in the oceans. Notice that one arrow shows the pull of the moon on the ocean water. The other arrow shows the moon's pull on land. The difference in the pull from one side of the earth to the other causes tides.

Glossary

Glossary

tide, the rise and fall of the surface level of the ocean

This ocean shore sure looks a lot different after the tide comes in! ▼

Low tide

High tide

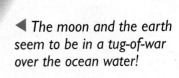

◄ *The moon and the earth seem to be in a tug-of-war over the ocean water!*

Up and down! Up and down and around! That's how the ball bobs as the waves pass by. ▼

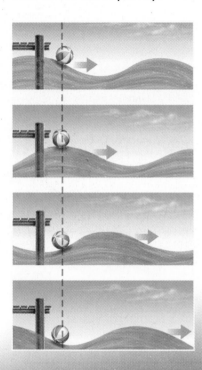

Waves

If you blow across a dish of water, you will cause the water to move. You will see the water rise and fall—making small waves. Winds that blow across the surface of the ocean do the same thing. Winds cause the water to rise and fall as the **wave** passes.

The pictures of the ball on the water show how a wave moves. The water moves up and down and around, but it comes right back to where it started. The ball stays in the same place as the waves pass by.

Look at the picture of the large wave. As a wave moves along, it picks up energy from the wind. When the wave comes near the shore, the bottom part of the wave is slowed down by the ocean floor. The water in the upper part of the wave is not slowed down. It falls forward, or breaks, against the shore. The larger the wave, the more force it carries when it breaks.

You wouldn't want to be under this large wave as it crashes against the shore. ▼

Waves, such as those shown in the picture, pound on the shoreline day after day. Over time they carry away, or erode, the rocks and sediments on the shore. During a storm, strong ocean waves crash high on the shore. Rocks and sand bump into each other and wear away surfaces. Waves can also move sand to other places and build up sandbars.

▲ *Waves can wash away parts of the shoreline of the earth.*

Lesson 3 Review

1. How do ocean currents affect the earth?

2. What causes tides?

3. How do waves affect the shoreline of the earth?

4. Main Idea
What is the main idea of the paragraph on this page?

You will learn:

- what saltwater habitats are.
- how a coral reef can be affected by human activity.

The sun warms the water in the tide pool. Some of the water evaporates and leaves the remaining water very salty. However, the animals in this pool are well adapted to shoreline changes. ▼

Lesson 4

Where Do Organisms Live in the Ocean?

You probably know where many animals live on land. You may have seen birds and squirrels in trees. You know earthworms live under the ground. But where in the ocean do the ocean animals live?

Saltwater Habitats

Life Science

You may think about the ocean as just one big place, but it really isn't. The ocean has many different habitats for plants and animals to live. One habitat is the shoreline. When the tide comes in, the plants and animals along the shore are covered with salt water. The tide waters also carry some small ocean animals onto the shore.

When the tide goes out, some of these animals are left behind. Small pools of water, like the one in the picture, are left in the sand or in the rocks.

Mussels and sea stars, shown on page C85, are animals that live along the shoreline. They have coverings that keep them from drying out during low tide. Mussels attach themselves to rocks along the shore. This keeps them from being washed into the ocean by the waves. During high tide, the mussels open their shells, and water and food flow into the shell. Then the mussels pull their shells closed. The closed shell keeps water inside the shell and they don't dry out.

If you move off the shore into the ocean water, you enter the **light zone** of the ocean. This part of the ocean receives light from the sun. Because of the sunlight, this part of the ocean is filled with living things. Tiny plantlike organisms use the sunlight to make sugar. They provide food for the animals in the ocean. Thousands of fish, along with turtles, dolphins, and jellyfish, live in this part of the ocean. You might even find some sharks, shrimps, and squids.

If you move down into the deeper ocean, the blue water will get black. You will think it's nighttime! You have entered the **dark zone** where the sunlight can't reach. Without energy from the sun, there isn't much food in the dark zone. There's not as much life in this part of the ocean.

If you look around in the darkness, you will see flashes of light. How can this be? It's because some of these fish can make light—just like fireflies! Their flashing lights attract other fish that may become a meal.

Look at the pictures on the next page to see some of the animals that live in the ocean's light zone and dark zone. People's actions have caused some of these animals to become threatened. However, steps are being taken to help protect the animals.

Look at the pictures on the next page

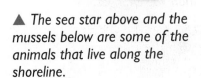

Glossary

light zone, the sunlit waters of the ocean

dark zone, the ocean water where sunlight does not reach

Glossary

▲ The sea star above and the mussels below are some of the animals that live along the shoreline.

Life in the Light Zone and Dark Zone

Dolphin

◀ Everyone enjoys watching dolphins, but people have also harmed dolphins. Some dolphins have had plastic rings from soft-drink cans caught over their snouts—causing them to starve. Others have been killed when caught in drifting tuna nets. People are now working to stop the dumping of trash into oceans. They are also trying to get tuna fishers not to use drift nets.

Sea Turtle

Sea turtles live in the ocean but go ashore to lay their eggs. Because their eggs are being eaten by people and other predators, sea turtles have become threatened. Beaches where sea turtles lay eggs are now being protected. ▶

Sea Lions

◀ Sea lions are often seen basking in the sunlight on rocks in the ocean. Oil spills from tankers and other ships are a danger to sea lions. When sea lions become covered with the oil, they die. People are working to prevent oil spills. They are also looking for ways to clean up oil spills quickly when they do happen.

Angler Fish

This fierce-looking angler fish lives in the dark zone. Even down this deep, scientists fear that poisons dumped into the ocean may harm the fish. Notice the light on the head of the angler fish. It has a chemical in its body that makes light. In the blackness of the dark zone, the light attracts other fish. Since food is scarce down there, the light helps the angler fish stay alive. ▶

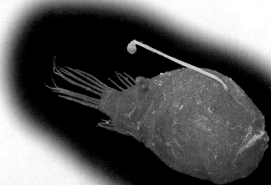

Life on a Coral Reef

Corals are small, soft-bodied animals that live in shallow waters of the ocean. These animals develop a rock skeleton that forms a hard shelter for the tiny corals. The rock, also called coral, makes up **coral reefs**.

Besides being beautiful, coral reefs are helpful to people. They protect the shoreline from tropical storms and make safe harbors for ships. The fish and lobsters that thrive on the reefs provide food for people.

Notice all the tiny fish around the coral reef in the picture. Many small fish find hiding places in reefs. They also can find food there. Of course, bigger fish also swarm to the reefs in search of food.

With sunlight reflecting off the coral towers and fish, coral reefs look like underwater cities. Coral reefs are found only in the light zone of the ocean. The tiny organisms that provide food for the corals need a lot of sunlight. ▼

Exp
Bri

Mate

- maski
- mark
- 4 clea
  cups
- tap w
  out o
- meas
- balan

Getting
In this act
brine shri
of salt.

State

Does th
affect hc
hatch?

Form
Hypo

Will mo
salt or ir
your **hy**

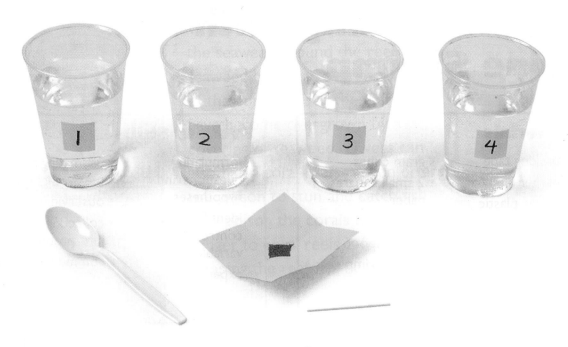

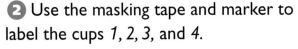

❷ Use the masking tape and marker to label the cups *1, 2, 3,* and *4.*

❸ Add 200 mL of water to each cup. Use the balance and gram cubes to **measure** the salt on a small square of paper. Place 2 g of salt in cup 2, 4 g of salt in cup 3, and 6 g of salt in cup 4. Stir each cup. Do not place salt in cup 1.

❹ Place some brine shrimp eggs on a square of paper. Use the flat end of a toothpick to place a small amount of eggs in cup 1.

❺ Place about the same amount of eggs in each of the other cups.

❻ Place the cups together in a place where they will not be disturbed.

❼ **Observe** the water in the cups each day through a hand lens. In some cups you may see brine shrimp moving. Compare the amount of movement in cups in which the eggs have hatched. Decide if there is no movement, little movement, or a lot of movement in each cup. **Collect** your **data** in your chart.

▲ *Setting up* *reefs is one w* *are trying to p*

Collect Your Data

Amount of movement in each cup				
Day	Cup 1	Cup 2	Cup 3	Cup 4
1				
2				
3				

Interpret Your Data

1. In which of the cups did you see the most movement? In which of the cups did you see the least movement?

2. How much salt was in the cups with the most and least movement?

State Your Conclusion

How do your results compare with your hypothesis? **Communicate** your results. Explain how the amount of salt in the water affected the hatching of the brine shrimp eggs.

Inquire Further

Do you think the temperature of the water would affect how fast the brine shrimp eggs hatch? Develop a plan to answer this or other questions you may have.

Self-Assessment

- I made a **hypothesis** about how the amount of salt in water would affect the hatching of brine shrimp eggs.
- I **identified** and **controlled variables.**
- I followed instructions to perform an **experiment** with brine shrimp.
- I **collected** and **interpreted data** by recording my **observations** in a chart.
- I **communicated** by stating my conclusion about how the amount of salt affected the hatching of brine shrimp eggs.

Chapter 3 Review

Chapter Main Ideas

Lesson 1
• New sounding technology and the use of satellites provide detailed maps of the ocean floor.
• The ocean floor has continental shelves, continental slopes, ocean basins, trenches, and ridges.

Lesson 2
• Many scientists have explored and are still exploring the ocean.
• New technology, such as a nuclear submarine, has allowed scientists to explore more of the ocean and live for long periods on the sea floor.
• Several ocean exploration projects are in operation, and some bring students into ocean exploration.

Lesson 3
• Ocean currents may affect the kind of weather coastal areas have, and at times a current, such as an El Niño, has worldwide effects on weather.
• The pull of the moon on ocean water causes tides.
• Waves may cause erosion of the shoreline of the earth.

Lesson 4
• Tide pools, the light zone, and the dark zone are three saltwater habitats that are sometimes harmed by human activities.

• Coral reefs protect the shoreline, provide safe harbors for ships, and provide seafood; therefore, people need to be aware of how their activities can affect a coral reef.

Reviewing Science Words and Concepts

Write the letter of the word or phrase that best completes each sentence.

a. continental shelf
b. continental slope
c. coral reef
d. current
e. dark zone
f. light zone
g. ocean basin
h. ridge
i. tide
j. trench
k. wave

1. The part of the continents near the shoreline that extends under the ocean is the ____.
2. The highest part of a chain of underwater mountains is a ____.
3. A ____ is a deep valley at the bottom of the ocean.
4. A riverlike flow of water through an ocean is called a ____.
5. A low ____ is the fall in the level of the water along the ocean shore.
6. A ____ is the up-and-down movement of ocean water.

7. The depth of ocean water increases sharply at the ___.

8. The ___ of the ocean receives the most sunlight.

9. A ___ is made up of living animals that develop rock skeletons.

10. The floor under the deep part of the ocean is called the ___.

11. Sunlight does not reach the ___ of the ocean.

Explaining Science

Draw and label a diagram or write a sentence or paragraph to answer these questions.

1. What is the difference between a continental shelf and a continental slope?

2. What is an underwater breathing device? How is it useful to explorers?

3. What causes ocean tides?

4. How are the light zone and the dark zone of the ocean different?

Using Skills

1. Use **logical reasoning** to solve the following problem: *Deep Flight, Alvin, Trieste,* and *Jason* (not in order) were vehicles used to explore the ocean. The approximate depths they reached were: 4,000 m, 5,500 m, 10,912 m, and 11,000 m. Use the following clues to identify the depth reached by each: *Deep Flight* reached the greatest depth, *Jason* reached a depth 1,500 meters greater than *Alvin*.

coral reef

2. Suppose you build a sand castle on an ocean beach. You walk away and come back later to find that your sand castle is almost underwater. Write one or more sentences to **communicate** what caused this to happen.

3. Locate Chicago, Illinois, and Boston, Massachusetts, on a map of the United States. **Predict** which city you would expect to have milder winters and explain why.

Critical Thinking

1. **Apply** what you have learned to explain why having bright colors may be a helpful adaptation for animals that live on a coral reef.

2. Suppose you visit a place near an ocean shore. Then you visit the same place a few years later. You find that the houses on the shore are nearer to the ocean than they were the first time you visited. **Draw a conclusion** about what might have happened to cause this.

3. How does the movement of water in an ocean wave **compare** to the movement of water in an ocean current?

Around and Around They Go!

Did you know that Earth is constantly moving? It spins around and around! And at the same time it moves around the sun. But Earth is so large you don't feel its movement.

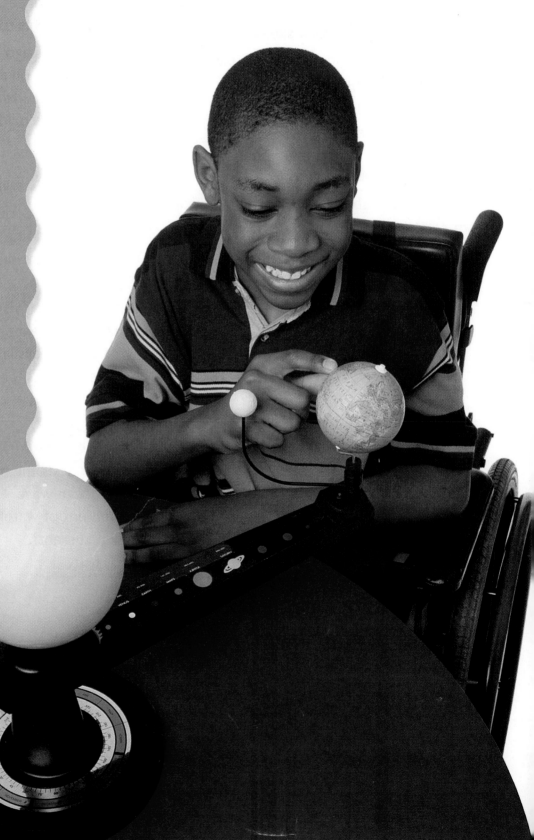

Chapter 4

Movements in the Solar System

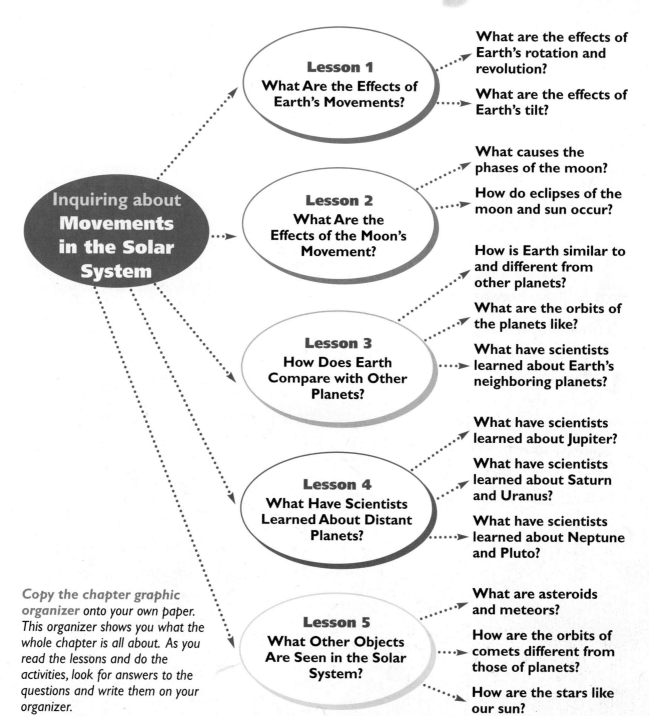

Lesson 1
What Are the Effects of Earth's Movements?

What are the effects of Earth's rotation and revolution?

What are the effects of Earth's tilt?

Inquiring about Movements in the Solar System

Lesson 2
What Are the Effects of the Moon's Movement?

What causes the phases of the moon?

How do eclipses of the moon and sun occur?

Lesson 3
How Does Earth Compare with Other Planets?

How is Earth similar to and different from other planets?

What are the orbits of the planets like?

What have scientists learned about Earth's neighboring planets?

Lesson 4
What Have Scientists Learned About Distant Planets?

What have scientists learned about Jupiter?

What have scientists learned about Saturn and Uranus?

What have scientists learned about Neptune and Pluto?

Lesson 5
What Other Objects Are Seen in the Solar System?

What are asteroids and meteors?

How are the orbits of comets different from those of planets?

How are the stars like our sun?

Copy the chapter graphic organizer onto your own paper. This organizer shows you what the whole chapter is all about. As you read the lessons and do the activities, look for answers to the questions and write them on your organizer.

Exploring Seasons

Process Skills

- observing
- making and using models
- inferring

Materials

- plastic-foam ball with pencil (model of Earth)
- marker
- flashlight

Explore

1 Observe the model of Earth. The eraser end of the pencil represents the North Pole. The point of the pencil represents the South Pole. Use the marker to draw the equator around Earth, halfway between the poles.

2 Model how sunlight strikes Earth. Have a partner hold a flashlight so it shines on the model. The flashlight represents the sun. Hold the model so that its North Pole is tilted away from the sun as shown. Which part of Earth, north or south, receives the most direct light? Record your observations.

3 Keep the model tilted in the same direction. Move Earth halfway through its orbit by moving a half circle around your partner to the right. Your partner should keep the flashlight shining on the model. Which part of Earth, north or south, receives the most direct light? Record your observations.

Reflect

Make an **inference.** In which position is it summer in the northern part of Earth? In which position is it winter?

Inquire Further

How can you model what would happen with the seasons if Earth was not tilted? Develop a plan to answer this or other questions you may have.

Making Predictions

In the Explore Activity, *Exploring Seasons*, you investigated which part of Earth receives the most direct sunlight at different places in Earth's orbit. The amount of sunlight that a place on Earth receives changes from month to month and from hour to hour. Because these changes occur regularly, you can predict when they will occur. When you **predict** something, you tell what you think will happen next based on what has already happened.

Reading Vocabulary

predict (pri dikt′), tell what will happen next based on what has already happened

Example

In Lesson 1, *What Are the Effects of Earth's Movements?*, you will learn that Earth's tilt on its axis and its movement around the sun affect the way sunlight strikes Earth. You will also learn that changes in the angle of sunlight affect how much the sunlight heats Earth. As you read Lesson 1, use the table below to help predict temperatures at different places on Earth. On your own paper, write the words *warm, cool,* or *moderate* (in between warm and cool) to describe the temperature of each place.

Place	Part of Earth	Earth's Tilt	Temperature
Canada	Northern	toward sun	
Australia	Southern	toward sun	
United States	Northern	away from sun	
Bolivia	Southern	neither toward nor away from sun	

▼ *Did you know that the position of the sun in the sky can also tell you the season?*

Talk About It!

1. Predict what season it would be in Santiago, Chile, when it is spring in Chicago, Illinois.

2. If it is nighttime in Miami, Florida, is it nighttime or daytime on the other side of Earth in Tokyo, Japan?

You will learn:
- what the effects of Earth's rotation and revolution are.
- about the effects of Earth's tilt.

Glossary

axis (ak′sis), an imaginary line through a spinning object

rotation (rō tā′shən), one full spin of an object around an axis

Lesson 1

What Are the Effects of Earth's Movements?

Sunrise! Sunset! You may have watched these events many times. But have you ever wondered what causes the sun to appear to rise and set? How would your life be different if the sun did not set?

Earth's Rotation and Revolution

Did you know that Earth is always moving? It never stands still. One way Earth moves is by spinning around its axis. It spins, or rotates, just like the ball in the picture. Imagine that you draw a line from the finger up through the ball. The ball is spinning around that line. Earth also spins around such a line, or **axis.** Each time Earth makes one full spin on its axis, it makes one **rotation.**

◀ Spin! Spin! Spin! Unlike the basketball, Earth never stops spinning. Doesn't it make you dizzy to think about that?

Notice in the picture that only the part of Earth facing the sun is lighted. This part of Earth has daytime. The part that is not lighted has nighttime. It takes Earth 24 hours, or a day, to make a rotation. So on Earth, we have both a daytime and a nighttime every 24 hours.

As Earth spins, it also moves, or revolves, around the sun. Just as you have a route, or path, that you follow to school, Earth moves in a path around the sun. The path of Earth is called its **orbit.** One full orbit around the sun is one **revolution.** Earth takes one year to make one revolution—that's about 365 days. Just think! Every time you celebrate a birthday, Earth has made another trip around the sun!

Gravity is a force of attraction that causes Earth to revolve around the sun. Without gravity, Earth would fly off into space! The force of gravity between Earth and the sun keeps Earth in its orbit.

Glossary

orbit (ôr′bit), the path of an object around another object

revolution (rev′ə lü′shən), the movement of an object around another object

When you wake up to a bright sunrise, other parts of Earth are in darkness! ▼

Effect of Earth's Tilt

Notice the pictures below. They show how the tilt of Earth affects the way different parts of Earth receive sunlight. Notice the difference between the northern part of Earth and the southern part.

June to September

The northern part of Earth gets the most direct sunlight from June to September. During this time, the northern part of Earth has summer. ▼

December to March

The southern part of Earth is tilted toward the sun from December to March. During this time, the southern part of Earth gets the most direct sunlight. The southern part of Earth now has summer. ▼

▲ *The southern part of Earth gets more indirect sunlight when the northern part gets direct sunlight. So from June to September the southern part of Earth has winter. If you lived in Argentina at this time of the year, you could have fun in the snow!*

▲ *The northern part of Earth is tilted away from the sun from December to March. During this time, the northern part of Earth gets indirect sunlight. The northern part of Earth now has winter.*

Look at the picture on page C100 again. Notice how Earth is tilted when the northern part of Earth has summer. At this time the northern part of Earth gets more direct sunlight than the southern part.

Sunlight, as shown in the picture, is a form of the sun's energy. The more energy from the sun that reaches Earth, the more the sunlight heats Earth. Direct rays of sunlight are not spread out as much as indirect rays. Therefore, the energy of direct rays is not spread out as much and they heat Earth more.

Think about this. Suppose Earth's axis was straight up and down—not tilted. Then the direct sunlight would hit the same part of Earth all the time. The part of Earth near the equator would always have summer. The northern and southern parts of Earth would have milder weather all year long. So you can see, it is the tilt of Earth that causes the seasons to change.

▲ The picture shows the sun shining on the surface of Earth. Without the energy of sunlight, Earth would be very cold.

Lesson 1 Review

1. How does Earth's rotation cause days?

2. Why does the southern part of Earth have winter when the northern part has summer?

3. **Predictions**
   How do you predict that days and nights on Earth would be different if Earth did not rotate on its axis?

You will learn:

- what causes the phases of the moon.
- how eclipses of the moon and sun occur.

Glossary

satellite (sat′l it), an object that revolves around another object

▲ *For years people could only wonder about what the moon is like, but since astronauts traveled to the moon, many of the questions have been answered.*

Lesson 2

What Are the Effects of the Moon's Movement?

You have probably seen the moon many times. But it didn't always look the same! Why does the shape of the moon change? Does it really **shrink**—to a new moon? And grow to a full moon?

Phases of the Moon

Walk outside on a night when a full moon is shining and you will see how bright the moon seems. You would never guess that the moon does not make light. The moon only reflects light from the sun.

Look at the picture of Earth and the moon on the next page. You can see that the moon revolves around Earth. Since a **satellite** is an object that revolves around another object, the moon is a satellite of Earth.

If you look at a basketball or any other ball, you only see half of the ball. The moon is shaped like a ball. When you look at the moon, you only see half of the moon. As the moon revolves around Earth, only half of the moon is lighted. You can only see the moon when at least part of the half facing Earth is lighted.

Even though the moon is shaped like a ball, it appears to change shape. Look at the picture at the top of the next page. It shows some of the different shapes, or phases, of the moon. The changes in the moon's phases take $29\frac{1}{2}$ days—the time it takes the moon to revolve once around Earth.

▲ *Each night more and more of the part of the moon facing Earth is lighted until you see a full moon! Then more and more of the part of the moon facing Earth is dark, until you don't see the moon—the new-moon phase.*

How the Moon's Phases Occur

Full Moon

During the full-moon phase, the entire half of the moon facing Earth is lighted. You see the moon as a full circle. Since the same side of the moon always faces Earth, you always see the same half of the moon.

Half Moon

During the half-moon phase, half of the part of the moon facing Earth is lighted. Half of the moon facing Earth is dark. You see the moon as a half circle. This phase is sometimes called the first quarter because you are really seeing one-half of the lighted half, or one-quarter of the whole moon.

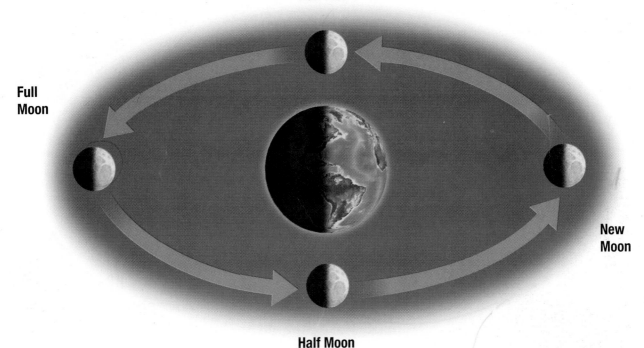

Half Moon

As less and less of the half of the moon facing Earth is lighted, you again see a half moon. This phase of the moon is sometimes called the last quarter. You are seeing half of the lighted half, or one-quarter of the whole moon.

New Moon

The entire half of the moon facing Earth is dark during the new-moon phase. You cannot see the moon in the sky. This phase occurs about two weeks after a full moon. The moon is now beginning a new set of phases.

Eclipses of the Moon and Sun

What happens if you hold a ball in front of a flashlight that is shining on a wall? You will see a shadow of all or part of the ball on the wall. Look at the pictures on these two pages to see what happens when Earth comes between the moon and the sun. Also, see what happens when the moon comes between the sun and Earth.

Lunar Eclipse

*When the moon moves through the shadow of Earth, a **lunar eclipse** happens. Sometimes the moon is fully covered by Earth's shadow. This causes a total lunar eclipse. At other times only part of the moon is covered—a partial eclipse.* ▼

Sun

Moon

Earth shadow

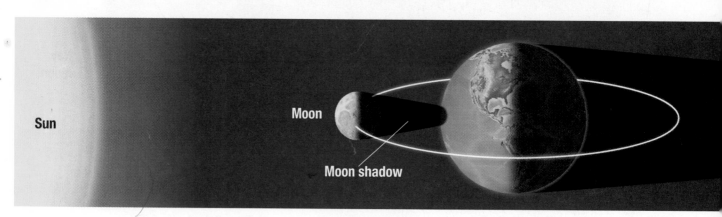

Sun

Moon

Moon shadow

Solar Eclipse

▲ *When the moon makes a shadow on Earth, a **solar eclipse** happens. Sometimes the moon blocks all the sunlight from certain places on Earth. People in these places see a total solar eclipse. Other places see a partial eclipse.*

▲ These pictures were taken at different times during a lunar eclipse. They show the moon moving out of Earth's shadow.

◄ A solar eclipse is always a tempting view, but you should never look directly at the sun. Use a pin-point camera to make a shadow of the eclipse on a sheet of paper. It's the only safe way to view an eclipse of the sun.

Lesson 2 Review

1. What causes the phases of the moon?

2. What causes a lunar eclipse and a solar eclipse?

3. **Main Idea**
   What is the main idea of the caption about a solar eclipse on this page?

Modeling the Phases of the Moon

Process Skills

Process Skills

- making and using models
- observing
- predicting

Materials

- lamp
- plastic-foam ball

Getting Ready

In this activity you will model how the moon's appearance changes as it orbits Earth.

Follow This Procedure

1 Make a chart like the one shown. Use your chart to record your predictions and drawings of the moon.

Position	Predictions	Observations
A	X	
B	X	
C	X	
D		
E		
F		
G		
H		

2 The lamp represents the sun, you represent Earth, and the ball represents the moon.

3 **Model** how sunlight strikes the moon. Face toward the lamp. Hold the ball up so it is slightly above your head as shown (Photo A). This is position A. **Observe** the ball. How much of the surface appears lit by the lamp? Draw your observation at position A.

⚠️ **Safety Note** Do not look directly into the light.

4 Slowly make a $\frac{1}{8}$ turn to your left. This is position B. Observe what happens to the light on the ball. Draw the ball and shade in the part that is in the shadow.

5 Make another $\frac{1}{8}$ turn to the left. This is position C. How much of the ball appears to be in the shadow? Draw your observation.

6 Now make a **prediction.** How much of the moon model will be in the shadow if you make another $\frac{1}{8}$ turn to the left? Draw your prediction for position D, then draw your observation.

7 Repeat step 6 four more times until you have recorded observations for positions E–H.

Interpret Your Results

1. Look at the drawings of your observations. How did your predictions compare to your observations?

2. Describe how the shadow on the moon model changed as you turned away from the light. Describe how the shadow changed as you turned to face the light.

3. Compare and contrast your sun-Earth-moon model with the real sun, Earth, and moon.

**Inquire Further**

How could you model a lunar eclipse? Develop a plan to answer this or other questions you may have.

Self-Assessment

- I followed instructions to **make a model** of the moon and its phases.
- I made drawings of my **predictions** and **observations** of the shadows on the moon in my chart.
- I compared my predictions with my results.
- I described how the shadow on the moon model changed as I turned away from the light and turned to face the light.
- I compared and contrasted my sun-Earth-moon model with the real sun, Earth, and moon.

You will learn:

- how Earth is similar to and different from other planets.
- what the orbits of the planets are like.
- what scientists have learned about Earth's neighboring planets.

Glossary

solar system
(sō′lər sis′təm), the sun, the nine planets and their moons, and other objects that orbit the sun

Earth

Earth takes one year to revolve around the sun. It takes one day to rotate once on its axis. Earth is the middle planet in size. Four of the nine planets are larger and four are smaller. Earth has one moon. ▼

Lesson 3

How Does Earth Compare with Other Planets?

Ooohh! Earth, the beautiful blue planet! Do you know why it is so blue? Water makes it blue. And water is what makes Earth so different from all the other planets. Water gives life to Earth!

Comparing Earth to Other Planets

Life Science

Earth is the only known planet that has air for you to breathe! Earth also has water for you to drink. Earth has all the resources that you and other living things need. From what we know today, Earth is the only planet in our solar system that can support the kind of life found on Earth!

Earth and the other planets are alike in one way. They are all satellites of the sun. The nine planets, their moons, and the sun make up most of our **solar system**. The planets can be seen in the sky as points of light that move among the stars. The planets seem to rise and set the way our moon does. Like Earth and its moon, the other planets do not make light. They reflect light from the sun.

Compare the pictures of the planets on the next page to the picture of Earth. Also, compare the length of days and years to those on Earth. The length of days and years are given in Earth time. A planet's day is the time it takes to rotate once on its axis. A planet's year is the time it takes to revolve once around the sun.

Mercury

Mercury takes 88 days to revolve around the sun. It takes 59 days to rotate once. Mercury is four-tenths the distance of Earth to the sun. Mercury is the second smallest planet. It is less than half the size of Earth. Mercury has no moons.

Venus

Venus takes 8 months to revolve around the sun. It takes 243 days to rotate once. Venus is about seven-tenths the distance of Earth to the sun. It is the fourth-smallest planet—almost the same size as Earth. Venus has no moons.

Mars

Mars takes 1.9 years to revolve around the sun. It takes 25 hours to rotate once. Mars is 1.5 times the distance of Earth to the sun. It is the third-smallest planet—about half the size of Earth. Mars has 2 moons.

Jupiter

Jupiter takes 12 years to revolve around the sun. It takes 10 hours to rotate once. Jupiter is 5.2 times the distance of Earth to the sun. It is the largest planet—more than 11 times the size of Earth. Jupiter has at least 16 moons.

Saturn

Saturn takes 29.5 years to revolve around the sun. It takes about 11 hours to rotate once. Saturn is 9.5 times the distance of Earth to the sun. It is the second-largest planet—more than 9 times the size of Earth. Saturn has at least 18 moons.

Uranus

Uranus takes 84 years to revolve around the sun. It takes 17 hours to rotate once. Uranus is 19.2 times the distance of Earth to the sun. It is the third-largest planet—more than 4 times the size of Earth. Uranus has 17 moons.

Neptune

Neptune takes 165 years to revolve around the sun. It takes a little more than 16 hours to rotate once. Neptune is 30 times the distance of Earth to the sun. It is the fourth-largest planet—almost 4 times the size of Earth. Neptune has 8 moons.

Pluto

Pluto takes 250 years to revolve around the sun. It takes 6 days to rotate once. Pluto is 40 times the distance of Earth to the sun. It is the smallest planet—smaller than Earth's moon. Earth is more than 5.5 times the size of Pluto. Pluto has 1 moon.

Glossary

ellipse (i lips′), the shape of a flattened circle

Orbits of the Planets

Look at the picture of our solar system. What do you think keeps the planets moving around the sun? It's the pull of gravity between the sun and the planets! Even planets as far away from the sun as Neptune and Pluto are affected by the pull of gravity.

Notice the orbits of the planets nearest the sun. You can see that they are almost circles. The orbits of the planets are really **ellipses,** or circles that have been flattened a little. You can see that the farther planets are from the sun, the longer their orbits are. These planets take longer to make one revolution around the sun.

The planets that are farthest from the sun have longer years than those closer to the sun. They have longer orbits and have to travel farther in one revolution. ▼

Mercury

Venus

Earth

Mars

Jupiter

The planets that orbit nearest the sun are somewhat like Earth. Mercury, Venus, and Mars are made up mostly of solid rock. Jupiter, Saturn, Uranus, and Neptune are very different from Earth. The outer parts of these planets are made up mostly of gas. These planets may be solid in the center. Unlike its neighbors, Pluto is made up of rock and ice.

You probably think that Pluto is farthest from the sun. Most of the time you are right! However, sometimes Neptune is farther from the sun than Pluto. This is because at times Pluto's orbit crosses Neptune's orbit. Between 1979 and 1999, Neptune was farthest from the sun.

Earth's Neighboring Planets

History of Science

Before the 1970s, people on Earth knew little about the planets—even those nearby. Mercury was especially hard to study because it is so close to the sun. Then in 1974, the spacecraft *Mariner 10* traveled to Mercury. It sent back pictures such as the one shown. *Mariner 10* photographed about half of the sunlit side of Mercury. The pictures showed that the surface of Mercury is similar to Earth's moon. However, we still know less about Mercury than any other planet except for Pluto.

Venus is covered by thick clouds of gas. These clouds kept scientists from seeing the surface of Venus. Then in 1978, the Venus orbiter *Pioneer* was able to take pictures of Venus, such as the one below. The pictures showed hilly plains, highlands, large volcanolike mountains, and flat lowlands. Venus was later studied by the *Magellan* spacecraft. *Magellan* was launched from the shuttle *Atlantis*. It reached Venus on August 10, 1990. *Magellan* found that the surface of Venus is mostly covered by rocks and ash from volcanoes. However, the surface did not show wind erosion.

▲ *Out of the blazing sun into a deep freeze! That's what happens when you go from daytime to nighttime on Mercury.*

Venus is sometimes thought of as Earth's twin because the two planets are about the same size. However, they certainly are not identical twins! With no water and unbearable heat, nothing but rocks can exist on Venus. ▼

▲ Pathfinder *is shown on the surface of Mars.*

Sojourner is the robot rover that explored the surface of Mars. ▶

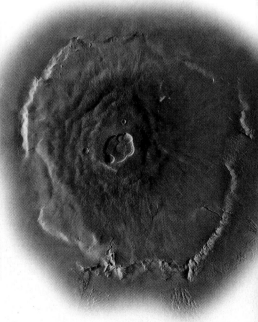

For many years, some people on Earth have expected a visit from people on Mars. In 1975, *Vikings 1* and *2* were sent to search for evidence of life on Mars. These spacecraft did not find evidence of any form of life on Mars. However, tiny amounts of water vapor were found.

Twenty-one years later, *Pathfinder* landed on Mars. *Pathfinder,* shown in the picture above, studied Martian rocks and soil. Then in 1997 the *Global Surveyor* spacecraft was launched to Mars. It sent back pictures, such as the one below. In May 1998 a report was released with new findings. The new findings gave more evidence that Mars was once a warmer, wetter planet. What scientists have thought to be old river beds may have been filled with flowing water at one time!

The Global Surveyor sent back this picture of Mars's Olympus Mons, a volcano. Radio signals that return data for pictures such as this one can reach Earth in about 14 minutes. ▼

Lesson 3 Review

1. How is Earth similar to the other planets?

2. Describe the orbits of the planets.

3. What have space probes helped scientists learn about Mars?

4. **Main Idea**
   What is the main idea of the first paragraph on this page?

You will learn:

- what scientists have learned about Jupiter.
- what scientists have learned about Saturn and Uranus.
- what scientists have learned about Neptune and Pluto.

Jupiter's Great Red Spot is really a huge storm that has lasted over 100 years—maybe as long as 300 years. That's a king-sized storm! ▼

Lesson 4

What Have Scientists Learned About Distant Planets?

"Are we there yet?" How many times have you asked that question when going somewhere? You wouldn't be a good traveler on a space probe. Some probes take up to six years to arrive at the planet they are launched to!

Jupiter

History of Science

In 1972 scientists began sending spacecraft to explore Jupiter. *Pioneers 10* and *11* sent back information about Jupiter's magnetic field and polar regions. Then in 1977 the two Voyager spacecraft were launched. *Voyager 1* sent back many pictures, such as the one of Jupiter's Great Red Spot shown here.

The most recent mission to Jupiter was *Galileo*. The *Galileo* mission was really two spacecraft—an orbiter and a probe. When *Galileo* was built it was covered with black and gold material. The material was designed to protect the spacecraft from the heat of the sun and from the cold of space. Before being launched, the *Galileo* orbiter was tested in a chamber. The chamber provided the same conditions as those *Galileo* would find in space.

In 1989 *Galileo* was launched from the shuttle Atlantis. A rocket carried *Galileo* out of Earth's orbit. It may seem strange, but *Galileo* first traveled toward the sun. *Galileo* went zooming through the inner solar system—nearest the sun. Then with a gravity assist from Venus, *Galileo* traveled back near Earth. However, *Galileo* moved past Earth, went out into the solar system, and circled back toward Venus. *Galileo* repeated this journey twice—two years apart.

▲ This is an artist's painting of Galileo.

After these two years, *Galileo* had gained enough speed to send it on its way to Jupiter. Then scientists had to wait and wait. *Galileo* still had about four years to travel! Finally, on July 13, 1995, the orbiter released the probe. About five months later, the probe entered the atmosphere of Jupiter. At last, scientists could have some questions answered. The orbiter continued to study Jupiter and send back pictures, such as the ones below of Jupiter's moons.

Scientists learned that there is far less water in Jupiter's atmosphere than they expected to find. They learned that wind speeds on Jupiter are about four times as great as most hurricanes on Earth. Lightning on Jupiter is about ten times stronger than lightning on Earth. Jupiter sure doesn't sound like a very pleasant place to be!

Jupiter's moons not only differ in size but in makeup—from fiery volcanoes to plains of ice. With 16 moons, a moonlit night on Jupiter should be very bright! ▼

Io

Europa

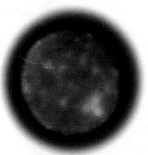

Callisto

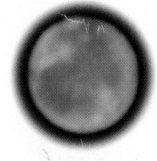

Ganymede

Saturn and Uranus

In the early 1980s, the *Voyager* missions discovered that the particles in Saturn's rings vary in size. They range from dust particles to boulders, some the size of a house. Scientists think that Saturn's rings formed from larger moons that were hit by space objects and broken up. Notice the picture of Saturn and its rings near the top of the page.

Voyager also discovered 6 new moons orbiting Saturn. Six other objects were discovered later. At least one of those is a moon—making a total of 18. The moons have irregular shapes that seem to be pieces of larger bodies. The sizes of Saturn's moons range from the tiny Phoebe to Titan—the size of some planets.

A *Voyager* mission also flew by Uranus. *Voyager* proved that Uranus has a magnetic field around it. *Voyager* also found 10 new moons orbiting Uranus, and 2 more moons were discovered later—making a total of 17. Most of the new moons are small. Unlike the rings of Jupiter and Saturn, the rings of Uranus did not form at the same time as the planet. Compare the picture of the rings of Uranus to those of Saturn.

▲ This picture was taken by Voyager. Before the Voyager missions, the only pictures we had of Saturn were artists' drawings.

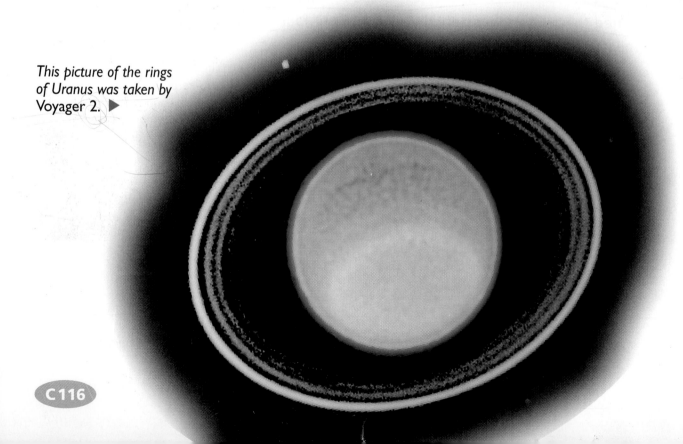

This picture of the rings of Uranus was taken by Voyager 2. ▶

Neptune and Pluto

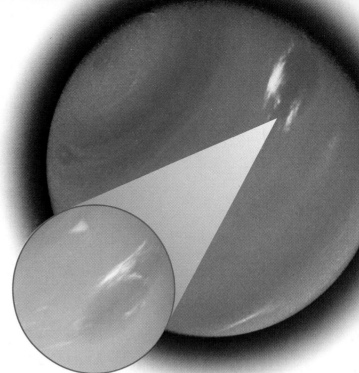

Before *Voyager*, scientists thought that Neptune had only 2 moons, but *Voyager* discovered 6 more moons. Neptune's day was believed to have been 18 hours, but *Voyager* discovered that it is just over 16 hours. Another discovery was several large, dark spots similar to Jupiter's Great Red Spot. Find these spots in the pictures of Neptune. Even though Neptune's rings seem to be incomplete, *Voyager* found that they are complete. They seem incomplete because the materials in them are so tiny.

Pluto is the only planet that has not been visited by a spacecraft. However, the Hubble Space Telescope has taken pictures of Pluto, such as the one shown. Students working on some Pluto projects have built four full-sized spacecraft models. Maybe someday one of these models will be used to build a Pluto spacecraft.

▲ The hurricanelike winds that blow around the dark spots on Neptune are stronger than the winds on any other planet. If you tried to walk on Neptune, you would be blown away!

The Hubble image of Pluto shows 12 large areas of light and dark features, but not much else. So Pluto still remains one of the mysteries of our solar system! ▼

Lesson 4 Review

1. What are two things that scientists learned about Jupiter from the *Galileo* mission?

2. What did the *Voyager* missions reveal about Saturn's rings?

3. Why do the rings of Neptune seem to be incomplete?

4. **Logical Reasoning**
   Use the information in the first paragraph on this page to solve the following problem: How many moons does Neptune have?

   6+2 = 8 moons

   Neptune has 8 moons

You will learn:
- what asteroids and meteors are.
- how the orbits of comets differ from those of planets.
- how the stars are like our sun.

Glossary

Glossary

asteroid (as′tə roid′), a rocky object orbiting the sun between the planets

meteor (mē′tē ər), piece of rock or dust from space burning up in Earth's air

meteorite (mē′tē ə rīt′), a rock from space that has passed through Earth's air and landed on the ground

This is a crater made by a meteorite that hit Earth in Arizona. ▼

C118

Lesson 5

What Other Objects Are Seen in the Solar System?

If you look at the sky during the day, you may see the sun, clouds, or the moon—an airplane or a bird. At night, the planets move among billions of twinkling stars. You may also see the moon or a comet.

Asteroids and Meteors

Thousands of objects orbit the sun, mostly between the orbits of Mars and Jupiter. These objects are made of rock and are known as **asteroids.** Some of them are shaped like planets, but others are more oval or have irregular shapes. The largest asteroid, Ceres, is about the same size across as the state of Texas. Some asteroids have satellites of their own.

Besides asteroids, other smaller pieces of dust and rock orbit the sun. Sometimes one of these small pieces comes close enough to Earth to be pulled into Earth's air. As the rock moves through the air, friction causes the rock to heat up and burn. Then the rock or dust is called a **meteor.** Have you ever seen a "shooting star" at night? These flashes of light in the sky are meteors. Sometimes a meteor is so large that all of it does not burn up before reaching Earth. A meteor or part of a meteor that reaches the ground is a **meteorite.** Some meteorites hit Earth hard enough to make deep holes, or craters, in Earth's surface. Notice the size of the meteorite crater in the picture.

Comets

In 1994 comet Shoemaker-Levy 9 broke up near Jupiter. A **comet** is a large chunk of ice and dust that orbits the sun. A piece of the comet is shown hitting the surface of Jupiter in the picture below.

In 1997 many people were excited about the comet Hale-Bopp. Hale-Bopp, shown in the picture, was one of the brightest comets to pass near the sun in history. It came closest to Earth on March 27, 1997. Scientists think that Hale-Bopp passed by the sun about 4,200 years ago. Can you imagine how long its orbit must be?

Comets have orbits that are much longer and flatter than the orbits of planets. During most of its orbit, a comet is far away from the sun. When they are far away, comets can't be seen from Earth. At that time, they also do not get much heat from the sun. As a comet moves closer to the sun, the sun's energy begins to heat the comet. Some of the ice becomes a gas. Then the gas and dust are pushed into a long tail. The tail extends from the bright part of the comet known as the head. The tail of a comet may be millions of kilometers long.

▲ *Comet Hale-Bopp was one of the brightest objects in the night sky between mid-March and early May of 1997. More people may have seen this comet than any other.*

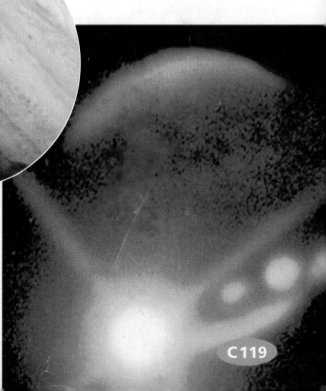

The dark spots show where pieces of Shoemaker-Levy 9 hit the surface of Jupiter. ▶

More than 20 pieces of comet Shoemaker-Levy 9 hit the surface of Jupiter in 1994. The Galileo spacecraft recorded this event. What a fiery display! ▶

Glossary

constellation
(kon′stə lā shən), a group of stars that form a pattern

▲ *The sun is the largest, brightest, and hottest object in our solar system. It has more mass than all the other objects in our solar system put together.*

Telescopes magnify distant objects in the sky. The girl can see many more stars with the telescope than with the unaided eye. ▶

Stars

The girl in the picture is using a telescope to study the stars. Just think—millions of "suns" twinkling in the sky! Yes, that's right, the stars in the picture on the next page are just like our sun in the picture on the left. They make their own light. In fact, our sun is just an average-sized star. It seems so large because it is so much closer than any of the other stars. The sun provides all the energy for life on Earth. The sun's energy heats and lights Earth.

Earth's rotation makes the sun appear to rise in the east and set in the west. The other stars also appear to rise and set slowly throughout the night. Earth's rotation makes the stars appear to circle Polaris, the North Star. However, like our sun, the other stars stay in the same place.

When you look at the stars, you may sometimes see groups of stars that seem to form a pattern. Throughout all of history, people have been watching these star patterns, or constellations. A group of stars that forms a pattern in the night sky is a **constellation**. Different cultures have named these star patterns.

You may have noticed the seven stars in the sky that make up the Big Dipper. These seven stars are part of the constellation called Ursa Major, or Big Bear. The two end stars of the dipper's bowl can help you locate Polaris—or the North Star. The North Star was important to early travelers, because it helped them find their way.

▲ We see *billions of stars, but they are not in our solar system. They are much farther away than our sun. Half of these stars may be bigger and brighter than our sun!*

Lesson 5 Review

1. How are asteroids and meteors alike?

2. How are the orbits of comets different from those of the planets?

3. How are other stars like our sun?

4. **Main Idea**
   What is the main idea of the first paragraph on page C120?

Chapter 4 Review

Chapter Main Ideas

Lesson 1

• One rotation of Earth on its axis is one day, and one revolution around the sun is one year.

• The tilt of Earth and Earth's revolving around the sun cause seasonal differences in the northern and southern parts of Earth.

Lesson 2

• As the moon revolves around Earth, different amounts of the half of the moon facing Earth are lighted.

• A lunar eclipse occurs when Earth passes between the sun and the moon, and a solar eclipse occurs when the moon passes between the sun and Earth.

Lesson 3

• All nine planets are satellites of the sun and reflect light from the sun, but Earth is the only planet that can support life such as that found on Earth.

• The orbits of the planets are ellipses.

• Scientists have learned about neighboring planets' surfaces, atmospheres, and water.

Lesson 4

• The *Galileo* missions provided information about the lack of water on Jupiter and about its strong winds and lightning.

• The *Voyager* missions provided information about the rings of Saturn and Uranus.

• Scientists have recently discovered Neptune's large, dark spots and that its rings are complete. The Hubble Telescope has taken pictures of Pluto.

Lesson 5

• Asteroids are rocky objects that orbit the sun, mostly between the orbits of Mars and Jupiter; meteors are pieces of rock or dust burning up in Earth's air.

• The orbits of comets are longer and flatter than those of planets.

• The stars, like our sun, make their own light and stay in one place.

Reviewing Science Words and Concepts

Write the letter of the word or phrase that best completes each sentence.

a. asteroid   g. meteorite

b. axis   h. orbit

c. comet   i. revolution

d. constellation   j. rotation

e. ellipse   k. satellite

f. meteor   l. solar system

1. An ____ is a rocky object that orbits the sun.

2. The nine planets, their moons, and the sun make up our ____.

3. Earth completes one full ___ around its axis every 24 hours.

4. The path of a planet around the sun is an ___.

5. A piece of rock or dust burning in the air around Earth is a ___.

6. Earth spins around an imaginary line called an ___.

7. The shape of an orbit is an ___.

8. A chunk of ice that orbits the sun is called a ___.

9. The moon is a ___ of Earth.

10. A ___ is a piece of rock that passes through Earth's air and lands on the surface of Earth.

11. A group of stars that forms a pattern in the sky is a ___.

12. It takes Earth 365 days to complete one ___.

Explaining Science

Draw and label a diagram or write a sentence or paragraph to answer these questions.

1. What causes Earth to revolve around the sun?

2. Describe what each phase of the moon looks like.

3. How is Earth different from other planets?

4. What did scientists learn about Jupiter's Great Red Spot?

5. What is the difference between a meteor and a meteorite?

Using Skills

1. What would you **predict** would happen to the seasons of the world if the axis of Earth tilted in the opposite direction?

2. Why do countries in the northern and southern parts of Earth have seasons and those near the equator do not? **Communicate** your answer by writing a paragraph to explain.

3. Make a time line to **sequence** the years that spacecraft visited Mercury, Venus, and Mars.

Critical Thinking

1. **Compare** the length of one year on Pluto to one year on Earth. How old would you be when you had your first birthday on Pluto? on Earth?

2. You go outside on a clear night and you see a half moon. A few days later on another clear night, you go outside, but you don't see a moon. **Draw** a **conclusion** about why you don't see a moon.

3. Suppose you traveled to the North Pole in June. **Apply** what you know about Earth's tilt and decide if the days would be shorter or longer near the North Pole than in the Midwest region of the United States.

Unit C Review

Reviewing Words and Concepts

Choose at least three words from the **Chapter 1** list below. Use the words to write a paragraph about how these concepts are related. Do the same for each of the other chapters.

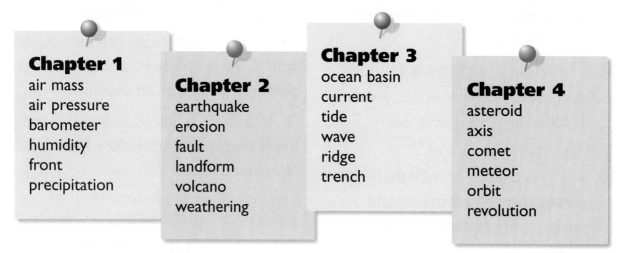

Chapter 1
air mass
air pressure
barometer
humidity
front
precipitation

Chapter 2
earthquake
erosion
fault
landform
volcano
weathering

Chapter 3
ocean basin
current
tide
wave
ridge
trench

Chapter 4
asteroid
axis
comet
meteor
orbit
revolution

Review Main Ideas

Each of the statements below is false. Change the underlined word or words to make each statement true.

1. Direct rays of sunlight heat the earth <u>less</u> than indirect rays.
2. Clouds form when water vapor in the air <u>evaporates</u> into tiny water drops.
3. Mountains and plateaus are some <u>volcanoes</u> found on the surface of the earth.
4. <u>Erosion</u> can change landforms by breaking and changing rocks.
5. The floor of the ocean <u>is smooth and flat</u>.
6. Ocean <u>waves</u> may at times have worldwide affects on weather.
7. Ocean <u>ridges</u> may cause erosion of the shoreline of the earth.
8. One <u>revolution</u> of Earth on its axis is one day.
9. A <u>solar</u> eclipse occurs when Earth passes between the sun and the moon.
10. <u>Comets</u> are rocky objects that orbit the sun, mostly between the orbits of Mars and Jupiter.

Interpreting Data

The following chart gives information about Earth and the other planets. Use the information to answer the questions below.

Planet	Length of day (in Earth time)	Length of year (in Earth time)	Number of moons
Mercury	59	88 days	0
Venus	243	8 months	0
Mars	25 hours	1.9	2
Jupiter	10 hours	12	at least 16
Saturn	11 hours	29.5	at least 18
Uranus	17 hours	84	17
Neptune	16 hours	165	8
Pluto	6	250	1

1. Which planet has the most moons?

2. How long does Venus take to revolve around the sun?

3. How old would you be if you lived on Saturn?

Communicating Science

1. Draw and label a picture to show how the tilt of Earth affects how Earth receives sunlight.

2. Draw and label a picture to show how volcanoes change the surface of the earth.

3. Draw and label a picture to show what the ocean floor looks like.

4. Write a paragraph explaining the effects of the rotation and revolution of Earth.

Applying Science

1. Write a paragraph comparing the seasons in a place in the northern part of the world and in a place in the southern part of the world on the same day. Explain the differences in the seasons in these two places.

2. Use what you have learned about the planets to explain why people cannot live on any of the planets except Earth.

Unit C
Performance Review

Earth-Space Center

Using what you learned in this unit, create exhibits for an Earth-Space Center. The exhibits will help visitors learn about Earth and other bodies in space. Complete one or more of the following activities. You may work by yourself or with a group.

Social Studies

Find information about major earthquakes around the world—include pictures and maps. Write a paragraph describing each of the earthquakes and the damage it caused. Also, report on how scientists study earthquakes.

Math

Gather mathematical information about the planets in our solar system. Make graphs and charts to report this information in the Earth-Space Center. Use your information to write some math problems for visitors to solve.

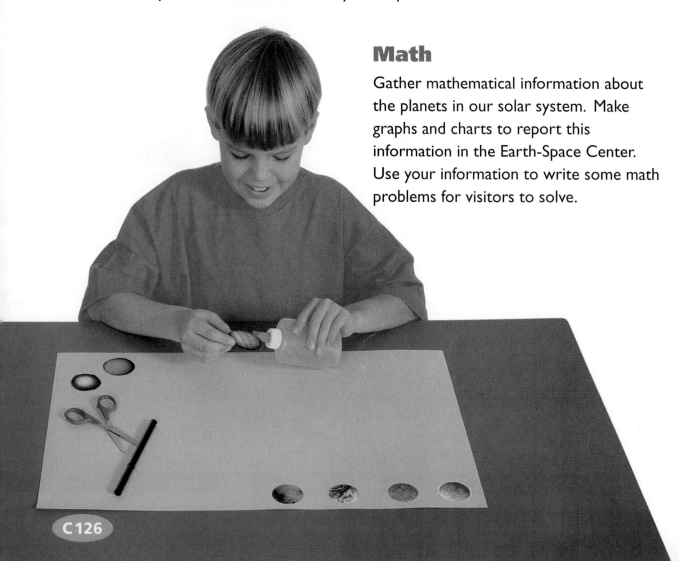

Technology

Display examples of kinds of technology that help scientists learn about Earth and space. Make drawings or models to illustrate the technology and write a brief description of what scientists have learned by using the technology.

Music

Collect tapes or CDs of music to play at the center to set a space mood. Write new words to simple melodies to tell about the planets and other space objects. Display your songs. Play the songs on musical instruments and sing the songs for visitors.

Art

Make models of the planets and other space objects. Be sure the models show the relative sizes of space objects. Display each of the models in the Earth-Space Center with a poster telling interesting facts about the object.

Using Drawings to Show Information

Drawings are useful ways to show details about an object or a group of objects. To be useful, drawings should include details such as titles, captions, and labels.

Make a Drawing

In Chapter 4, you learned about the different planets that make up the solar system. One thing you studied was the orbits of these planets. Use what you learned to make a drawing that shows all the planets in their correct orbits around the sun. Make sure that your drawing includes a title and labels.

Prepare a Presentation

Imagine that you need to teach a class of younger students about the planets of our solar system. Prepare a presentation for this class that explains where each planet is located in relationship to the sun and Earth. Be sure to include information that will help explain the orbits of the different planets. Include the drawing you made earlier as part of your presentation.

Remember to:

1. **Prewrite** Organize your thoughts before you write.

2. **Draft** Prepare your presentation.

3. **Revise** Share your work and then make changes.

4. **Edit** Proofread for mistakes and fix them.

5. **Publish** Share your presentation with your class.

Unit D
Human Body

Science and Technology
In Your World!

Computers Get Smarter and Smarter!

Today's computers can do millions—even billions—of calculations in the blink of an eye. But they can't think and learn as humans do. Some scientists want to change that, and they've made amazing progress! For example, a supercomputer named Deep Blue defeated the world's chess champion in 1997. Until then, most people believed that playing championship chess required human intelligence. You will learn about the brain in **Chapter 1 The Digestive, Circulatory, and Nervous Systems.**

Preservation Methods Keep Food from Turning Yucky!

People use many methods to keep food from spoiling, including canning, freezing, and freeze-drying. Now technology has given us aseptic packaging. In this method, solid or liquid food is heated to a high temperature to kill germs, and then put in germ-free containers. Juice and milk in foil-lined cardboard boxes are popular examples. They're easy to carry, and they can be stored outside a refrigerator for months. You will learn more about food safety in **Chapter 2 Keeping Your Body Systems Healthy.**

Your Amazing Heart!

Just think! Your heart never stops beating. It keeps on beating without your even having to think about it. When you jog, your heart speeds up to carry oxygen to your muscles so you can run.

Chapter 1
The Digestive, Circulatory, and Nervous Systems

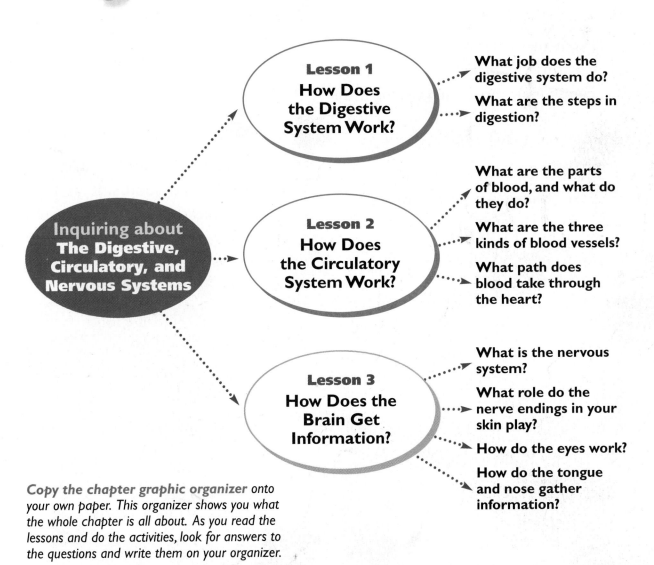

Inquiring about The Digestive, Circulatory, and Nervous Systems

Lesson 1
How Does the Digestive System Work?

What job does the digestive system do?

What are the steps in digestion?

Lesson 2
How Does the Circulatory System Work?

What are the parts of blood, and what do they do?

What are the three kinds of blood vessels?

What path does blood take through the heart?

Lesson 3
How Does the Brain Get Information?

What is the nervous system?

What role do the nerve endings in your skin play?

How do the eyes work?

How do the tongue and nose gather information?

Copy the chapter graphic organizer onto your own paper. This organizer shows you what the whole chapter is all about. As you read the lessons and do the activities, look for answers to the questions and write them on your organizer.

Exploring Teeth

Process Skills

- observing
- classifying
- communicating
- inferring

Materials

- plastic mirror

Explore

❶ Use a mirror to **observe** the fronts of all your teeth. Then observe the chewing surfaces of your lower teeth by opening your mouth and tipping the mirror until you get a good view. Then observe the chewing surfaces of your upper teeth.

❷ Make a drawing of your lower and upper teeth to record your observations.

❸ **Classify** your teeth by shape. Write a phrase describing each kind of tooth shape you observed. You should have three or four phrases.

Reflect

1. Communicate. Discuss the descriptions of your teeth with your classmates.

2. Make an **inference.** Which teeth do you think would be best to take a bite of an apple? Which teeth would be best for chewing and grinding the apple? Explain.

? Inquire Further

What do teeth with different shapes do to different kinds of food, such as a celery stick, meat, or popcorn? Develop a plan to answer this or other questions you may have.

Exploring Capacity

Liters (L) and **milliliters** (mL) are metric units of **capacity**. In math, capacity is the amount a container can hold. An Olympic-size swimming pool has a capacity of about 500,000 **liters** of water. Your heart pumps the equivalent of 7,500 liters of blood every day of your life.

Work Together

Use estimation and measurement to explore metric capacity.

1. Find the capacity of the spoon.
   a. Estimate how many milliliters of water will fit in the spoon.
   b. Fill the spoon with water and pour it into the measuring cup.
   c. Count the number of spoonfuls that will fill the measuring cup to the 25 mL mark.
   d. Divide 25 mL by the number of spoonfuls. This is the capacity of the spoon.

2. Find the capacity of the mug.
   a. Fill the measuring cup to 100 mL.
   b. Estimate how many milliliters will fit in the mug. Check.

3. Find how many milliliters are in a liter.
   a. Fill the measuring cup to 250 mL.
   b. Empty the water into the liter container. Estimate how many times it will take to fill 1 liter. Check.
   c. Multiply 250 mL by the number of times you poured. How many milliliters are in a liter?

Talk About It!

How did you find how many milliliters are in a liter?

Materials

- water
- plastic spoon
- metric measuring cup [250 mL]
- mug
- 1-liter container

Math Vocabulary

capacity, the amount a container can hold

liter, a unit for measuring capacity in the metric system

milliliter, $\frac{1}{1,000}$ of a liter

Did you know?

An average-sized man has about 4.8 to 6.6 liters of blood in his body at any one time. An average-sized woman has about 3.8 to 5.7 liters of blood.

What's the Big Idea?

You will learn:

- what job the digestive system does.
- what the steps in digestion are.

Glossary

nutrient (nü′trē ənt), a substance in food that the body uses for energy, for growth and repair, or for working well

digestion (də jes′chən), the changing of food into forms that the body can use

Lesson 1

How Does the Digestive System Work?

As you munch your favorite sandwich, your best friend comes up. "What's going on?" she asks. "Just feeding the old cells," you say. "Yum," she says. "So, how do you know that your cells like peanut butter?"

What the Digestive System Does

Of course, the cells that make up your body don't like or dislike particular foods. However, cells do need food's nourishing substances to stay alive and do their work. These substances are called **nutrients**.

Some nutrients give you the energy you need to play and do all the other things you do each day. Some nutrients help you grow, because body cells use the nutrients to make new cells. Your body also uses nutrients to make repairs, such as mending a broken bone. Certain nutrients help your body work as it should.

Any food you eat must be changed into nutrients that your cells can use. Your digestive system does this job, which is called **digestion**.

◀ Yum! Every bite of this tasty sandwich provides energy for playing and doing other activities.

Steps in Digestion

Digestion begins as soon as you bite into food. For example, as you chew a sandwich, your teeth cut and grind the bread and the filling into smaller pieces. Your tongue helps mix the chewed food with **saliva,** the liquid in your mouth. Saliva makes the food wet and easy to swallow.

Saliva also contains an **enzyme,** or chemical, that helps break food down so saliva can change the food into nutrients. The enzyme in saliva helps change starches into sugars. That is why you may notice a sweet taste when you chew bread, crackers, and other starchy foods.

When you have finished chewing, your tongue moves the wet lump of food to the back of your mouth. You swallow, and the food enters a tube called the **esophagus.** Your bite of sandwich is now on its way to the next stop in the digestive system—your stomach.

Glossary

saliva (sə lī′və), the liquid in the mouth that makes chewed food wet and begins digestion

enzyme (en′zīm), a chemical that helps your digestive system change food into nutrients

esophagus (i sof′ə gəs), the tube that carries food and liquids from the mouth to the stomach

The starches in sandwich bread are made of sugars joined together. Saliva changes the starches into sugars. ▼

The Digestive System

The picture and captions on these two pages show what happens as food moves through the parts of the digestive system. As you read, use your finger to trace the path that food takes.

1 Mouth

As teeth tear, cut, and grind food, three pairs of glands make saliva. These salivary glands are located in front of the ears, under the lower jaw, and under the tongue. Tiny tubes carry the saliva from the salivary glands to the mouth.

2 Esophagus

The esophagus of an adult is about 25 centimeters long. Muscles in the esophagus contract and relax to push swallowed food down toward the stomach. The process is something like squeezing toothpaste out of a tube.

3 Stomach

The stomach is a baglike organ with muscular walls. Stomach muscles squeeze and mix food with digestive juice made in the stomach's lining. The juice changes the food, which stays in the stomach for two to four hours. When the food leaves the stomach, it is a thick liquid.

4 Small Intestine

*The liquid food is pushed into the **small intestine,** a curled-up tube. If stretched out, an adult's small intestine would be about 7 meters long. Most digestion takes place in the three to six hours that food stays in the small intestine. Juices made in the lining of the small intestine and other organs mix with food. The juices change the food into nutrients. The nutrients pass through the thin walls of blood vessels in the intestinal lining. Blood carries the nutrients to body cells.*

5 Large Intestine

The parts of food that cannot be digested move to the large intestine, along with some liquid. The large intestine removes much of the liquid and stores the resulting solid waste until it leaves the body. Read more about the large intestine on page D12.

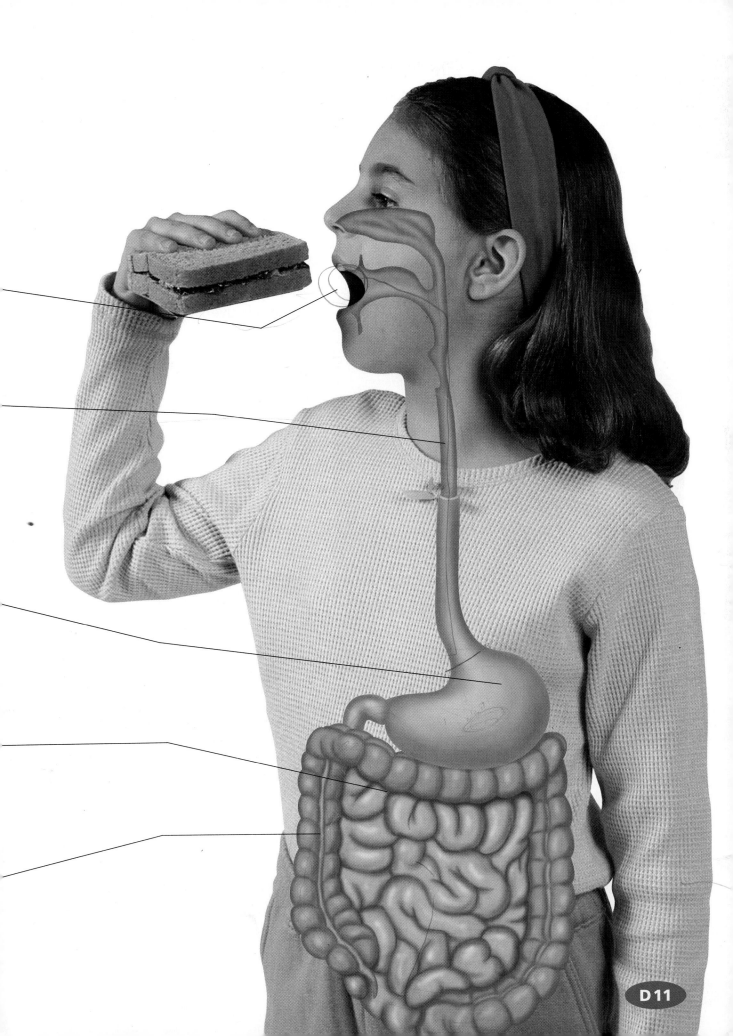

D11

You saw that the digestive system includes two intestines. Like the small intestine, the large intestine is a curled-up tube. Its name comes from the fact that it is more than twice as wide as the small intestine. However, the large intestine is only about one and a half meters long in an adult.

Not everything in food can be broken down into parts that the body can use. For example, the skins and seeds of fruits and vegetables cannot be digested. Undigested food, along with liquid left over from digestive juices, moves from the small intestine to the large intestine.

The large intestine removes much of the water from the mixture. The water is drawn through the thin walls of the large intestine into the blood. What is left in the large intestine is called solid waste. The X ray shows a large intestine with solid waste in it. Solid waste leaves the body after ten hours to a day or more in the large intestine.

▲ In this X ray, the backbone and hips look greenish-yellow in the background. The tube is the large intestine. Notice the brightly colored waste in the large intestine.

Lesson 1 Review

1. How does the digestive system help body cells?

2. What happens to food in the stomach?

3. Capacity
Your stomach produces about 2 liters of acid that helps digest food each day. How many milliliters of acid does your stomach produce?

Lesson 2

How Does the Circulatory System Work?

Put your hand on your chest. You can feel the steady **THUMP, THUMP** of your heart. In just one minute, your heart beats about ninety times, pumping blood all the way to the tips of your toes and back again.

Parts of Blood

Your heart, your blood, and the tubes that carry blood make up your circulatory system. This system takes nutrients, oxygen, and water to all your body cells. The system picks up wastes made by cells and carries the wastes to organs that get rid of them. Your circulatory system also helps keep you well.

Plasma is the watery part of blood. Nutrients, wastes, and blood cells float in plasma. Blood gets its color from **red blood cells,** shown in the picture. Red blood cells carry oxygen. **White blood cells** protect you from sickness. Some white blood cells surround and destroy germs. Others make chemicals that kill germs. **Platelets** are tiny parts of cells. When you get a cut, platelets help stop the bleeding.

What's the Big Idea?

You will learn:
- what the parts of blood are and what they do.
- about the three kinds of blood vessels.
- what the path of blood through your heart is.

Glossary

plasma (plaz′mə), the watery part of blood that carries nutrients, wastes, and blood cells

red blood cell, the kind of blood cell that carries oxygen to other body cells

white blood cell, the kind of blood cell that fights germs

platelet (plāt′lit), a tiny part of a cell that helps stop bleeding

Red blood cell

One kind of white blood cell

Platelet

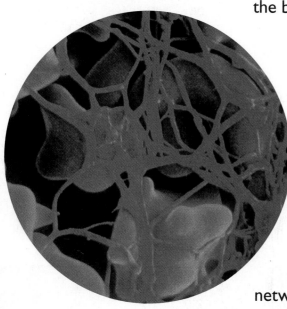

Glossary

artery (är′tər ē), the kind of blood vessel that carries blood away from the heart

When a blood vessel in the skin is cut, some blood leaks out. However, platelets soon clump together at the break in the blood vessel. The platelets give off a substance that causes a tangle of sticky fibers to form. Platelets, fibers, and trapped blood cells clump together to form a clot, as shown in the picture. The clot seals the break in the blood vessel. The bleeding stops.

After a while, the clot hardens to form a scab. The scab helps keep germs out of the cut. If germs do get in, white blood cells attack them. If there are a lot of germs, some white blood cells die in the attack. They form a thick, yellowish liquid called pus. Washing and bandaging a cut can help keep germs out while the cut heals.

▲ Platelets, sticky fibers, and trapped blood cells clump together to form a clot.

Kinds of Blood Vessels

Most of the time, blood flows through a network of blood vessels. Your circulatory system has three kinds of blood vessels. Each kind does a different job.

An **artery** is a blood vessel that carries blood away from the heart. Find the arteries in the large picture on the next page. Notice that the large arteries connected to the heart branch into smaller and smaller arteries.

If you place the tips of your fingers on the inside of your wrist and press firmly, you can feel a beat. You are pressing on an artery. You feel the beat because the walls of arteries stretch as the heart pumps blood through them.

Blood in the smallest arteries flows into tiny blood vessels called **capillaries,** shown in the small picture below. Capillaries are so narrow that red blood cells go through them in single file. Capillaries have thin walls. Oxygen and nutrients carried by the blood pass through capillary walls into body cells. Wastes from body cells pass through capillary walls into the blood.

A **vein** is a blood vessel that carries blood from the capillaries back to the heart. Blood in the capillaries flows into tiny veins. These veins join together to make larger and larger veins. The blood in veins flows more slowly than the blood in arteries. To keep the blood from flowing backward, many veins have valves that work like one-way doors.

Red blood cells move in single file through a capillary. ▼

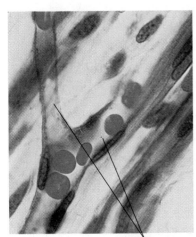

Capillaries

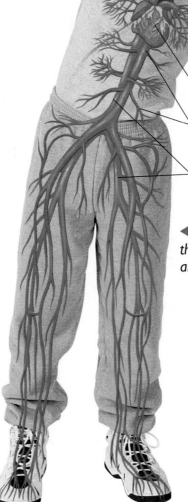

Heart

Arteries

Veins

◄ *Blood vessels carry blood from the heart to all parts of the body and then back to the heart.*

The Path of Blood Through the Heart

Your heart is a hollow, muscular organ that pumps blood every minute of every day. The inside of the heart is divided into four spaces. Each **atrium** receives blood from veins. Each **ventricle** pumps blood out of the heart through arteries. As you read the next page, trace the path of blood in the picture below.

Notice that a wall of muscle separates the right atrium and ventricle from the left atrium and ventricle. Blood moves through each side of the heart in one direction. Valves between each atrium and ventricle keep blood from flowing backward. ▶

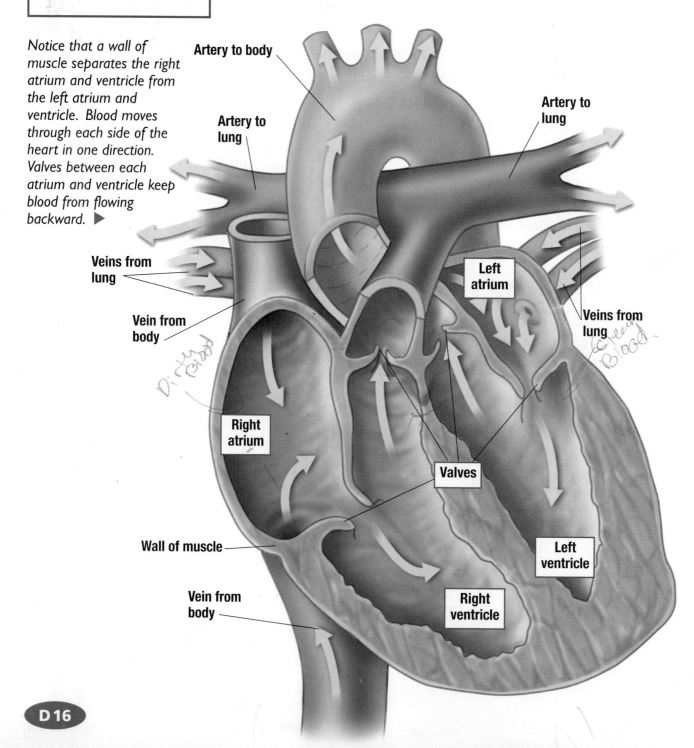

Artery to body

Artery to lung

Artery to lung

Veins from lung

Vein from body

Left atrium

Veins from lung

Right atrium

Valves

Wall of muscle

Left ventricle

Vein from body

Right ventricle

Find the two large veins from the body in the picture on page D16. These veins carry blood that has delivered oxygen to body cells. The oxygen-poor blood flows into the right atrium and then into the right ventricle. The right ventricle contracts, pumping the blood into a large artery. That artery divides into smaller arteries leading to the lungs. The blood picks up oxygen in the lungs.

Now find the veins that return oxygen-rich blood from the lungs to the heart. The blood flows into the left atrium and then into the left ventricle. The left ventricle contracts, pumping the blood into a large artery. That artery divides into smaller arteries leading to all parts of the body.

The two sides of the heart work in unison. For example, blood from the body enters the right atrium at the same time that blood from the lungs enters the left atrium. The right ventricle pumps blood to the lungs at the same time that the left ventricle pumps blood to all parts of the body.

Modern technology produced the special picture of a heart that you see on this page. Doctors use such pictures to decide whether a person's heart is working as it should.

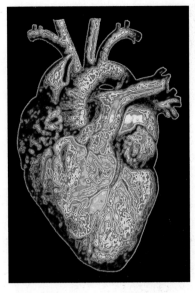

▲ A computer image of the heart can show how well the heart is pumping blood.

Lesson 2 Review

1. Name two parts of blood and their jobs.
2. What are the three kinds of blood vessels and what are their jobs?
3. Into which part of the heart does oxygen-poor blood flow?
4. **Graphic Sources**
   Use the picture on page D16 to make a graphic organizer showing how blood moves through the heart.

Investigating the Sense of Touch

Process Skills

- observing
- collecting and interpreting data
- inferring
- communicating

Materials

- safety goggles
- bobby pin
- metric ruler

Getting Ready

In this activity you will find out how the sense of touch varies.

Follow This Procedure

1 Make a chart like the one shown. Use your chart to record your observations.

	Felt 1 point when 1 point was used		Felt 2 points when 2 points were used	
	Yes	No	Yes	No
Neck				
Wrist				
Palm				
Finger				

2 Put on your safety goggles. Bend the bobby pin so the points are 5 mm apart (Photo A).

3 Lightly touch the back of another student's neck with either one or two points. Ask the student to **observe** how many points he or she feels. **Collect data** by making a mark in the appropriate place in your chart.

⚠ *Safety Note* Be very gentle when touching skin with the bobby pin.

4 Repeat step 3 until you have tested five times with one point and five times with two points. Do the test in a random way, so there is no pattern that the other student might recognize.

Photo A

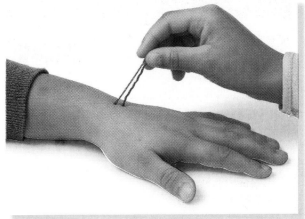

Photo B

5 Repeat the procedure on the back of a wrist (Photo B), on the palm of a hand, and on a fingertip. For each trial, have the student look away from you so he or she cannot see how many points are being tested.

Self-Monitoring
Have I correctly completed all the steps, including recording results in my chart?

Interpret Your Results

1. Find the total number of *Yes* answers for each body part. Then find the total number of *No* answers for each body part. For which body part did you record the highest number of *Yes* answers? the highest number of *No* answers?

2. Draw a conclusion. Which of the body parts tested were the most sensitive? the least sensitive?

3. Make an **inference.** What might be the advantage of having especially sensitive skin on some body parts that you tested? **Communicate** your ideas by writing a short paragraph.

 Inquire Further

What might happen if you tested other parts of the body, such as the upper arms, the calves of the legs, or the soles of the feet? Develop a plan to answer this or other questions you may have.

Self-Assessment

- I followed instructions to test another student's sense of touch.
- I **collected data** by recording my **observations** in a chart.
- I drew a conclusion about the sense of touch on different parts of the body.
- I made an **inference** about the advantages of having especially sensitive skin on some body parts that I tested.
- I **communicated** by writing about my inference.

What's the Big Idea?

You will learn:

- about the nervous system.
- what role the nerve endings in your skin play.
- how your eyes work.
- how your tongue and nose gather information.

Glossary

sense organ
(sens ôr′gən), a body part that has special nerve cells that gather information about the surroundings

nerve cell
(nėrv sel), a cell that gathers and carries information in the body

Lesson 3

How Does the Brain Get Information?

A friend has sent you a gift! It's in a sturdy box, so you can't tell what it is by squeezing or looking. You shake the box—gently at first, then harder. **RATTLE, RATTLE!** What can it be?

The Nervous System

You may be able to tell what the box holds just by listening. Chances are, though, you won't learn the secret until you look inside. Either way, you get information from your surroundings. Your brain decides what the information means and tells you what to do about it. Your brain and the other body parts that receive and send information make up your nervous system.

You notice your surroundings with your **sense organs.** Your ears, eyes, nose, tongue, and skin are sense organs. Each sense organ has special **nerve cells** that gather information from all around you.

See it! Hear it! Smell it! Taste it! Touch it! Your sense organs help you understand and enjoy the wonderful world around you. ▶

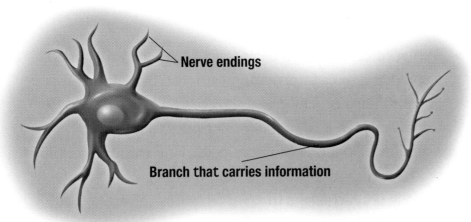

Nerve endings

Branch that carries information

◀ *Nerve cells gather information and carry it to other nerve cells.*

Nerve cells in the ears and eyes of the girl on page D20 gather information about sound and light. Nerve cells in the nose and tongue of the boy eating the apple gather information about scent and flavor. Skin has nerve cells that gather information about pressure, touch, pain, heat, and cold. What information might be gathered by the skin on the girl's hands as she holds her cat?

As you can see in the drawing above, nerve cells have a special shape. The tiny branches gather information from other nerve cells or from the outside world. These tiny branches are called **nerve endings.** The long branch of the nerve cell carries information to other nerve cells.

Glossary

nerve ending
(nėrv en′ding), a tiny branch of a nerve cell that gathers information

Glossary

Glossary

Glossary

spinal cord
(spī′nl kôrd), a thick bundle of nerves that connects the brain and nerves throughout the body

Nerve cells are the basic units of your entire nervous system. Information gathered by nerve cells in your sense organs travels along nerves to your brain. A nerve is a bundle of nerve cells. Your brain is made up of millions of nerve cells. Find these parts of the nervous system on the next page.

Your brain changes the messages it receives so that you can understand them. Suppose your ears catch sound waves coming from the mouth of the kitten shown on the next page. The ears send messages about the sound waves to your brain. You don't actually hear a "meow" sound until your brain tells you so.

Messages from most parts of your body travel through your spinal cord. The **spinal cord** is a bundle of nerves that connects your brain with nerves throughout your body. You can't see it in the picture on the next page, but a long chain of bones encloses and protects the delicate spinal cord. This chain of bones is called the backbone, or spine.

Nerve Endings in Your Skin

Your skin has many nerve endings in it. Different nerve endings gather information about touch, pressure, heat, cold, and pain. Find the different kinds of nerve endings in the cross section of skin below.

Nerve endings in the skin send messages to the brain, and the brain responds. For example, if someone lightly and repeatedly touches your bare foot, nerve endings for touch send a series of messages. The brain interprets the messages as tickling. The brain then sends messages that may cause you to laugh and try to pull away.

The different kinds of nerve endings are shown in the picture. ▼

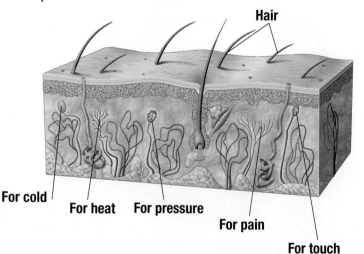

Hair

For cold

For heat   **For pressure**

For pain

For touch

The Nervous System

Your nervous system controls all the activities that you think about, from reading a book to playing with a pet. Your nervous system also controls body activities that you do not have to think about. ▶

Brain

The brain is a soft, wrinkly organ. The bones of your skull help protect your brain from injury.

Spinal Cord

The spinal cord extends from your brain down the length of your back. If you run your finger down the center of your back, you can feel the bones that protect the spinal cord.

Nerves

Many nerves branch off from the spinal cord. They divide again and again, reaching every part of your body. Nerves thread their way through all your body organs.

Iris

Optic nerve

Lens

Pupil

Retina

Clear covering

▲ *The clear covering at the front of the eye protects the eye and bends light. The eye is filled with a jellylike material that helps the eye keep its round shape.*

How Your Eyes Work

Most information about your world comes to you through your sense of sight. You can see people, animals, books, and other things because light reflects off them. Some of this light travels to your eyes.

The outer parts of the eye show clearly in the picture below. You can see the iris, which is the colored part of the eye, and the black-looking pupil in the center of the iris. Now look at the drawing on the left. Notice that the pupil is actually a hole that lets light inside the eye. The iris is a ring of muscle that changes the pupil's size to let in the right amount of light. The pupil gets smaller in bright light and larger in dim light.

A clear lens lies behind the pupil. The lens bends light to focus it on the retina. The retina is a thin layer of nerve cells at the back of the eye. The nerve cells gather information about the light that strikes them. They send a message to the brain along a nerve called the optic nerve. Your brain interprets the message, and you know what you are seeing.

◀ *The iris gives the eye its color. What color are your irises?*

The Tongue and Nose

Like your skin and eyes, your tongue and nose give you information about your surroundings. Sometimes these sense organs help protect you. The smell of smoke can warn you of a fire. The bad smell and taste of certain spoiled foods can warn you not to eat them. Mostly, though, your tongue and nose help you enjoy the tastes and smells of your world.

Your sense of taste comes from tiny taste buds on your tongue. The taste buds are grouped around the bases of the small bumps that you have on your tongue. Find those bumps in the enlarged picture on the right.

Taste buds have nerve cells that gather information about four tastes. The tastes are sweet, sour, salty, and bitter. All the flavors you know are combinations of those tastes. For example, when you eat an orange, taste buds for sweet and sour send messages to your brain. Your brain interprets the messages. As you can see in the labeled photograph, each kind of taste bud is located on a different part of the tongue.

Describe where the taste buds for sweet and for sour are located. ▶

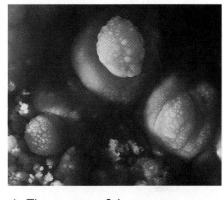

▲ *This section of the tongue has been enlarged eight times. Even so, you can't see the tiny taste buds clustered around each bump.*

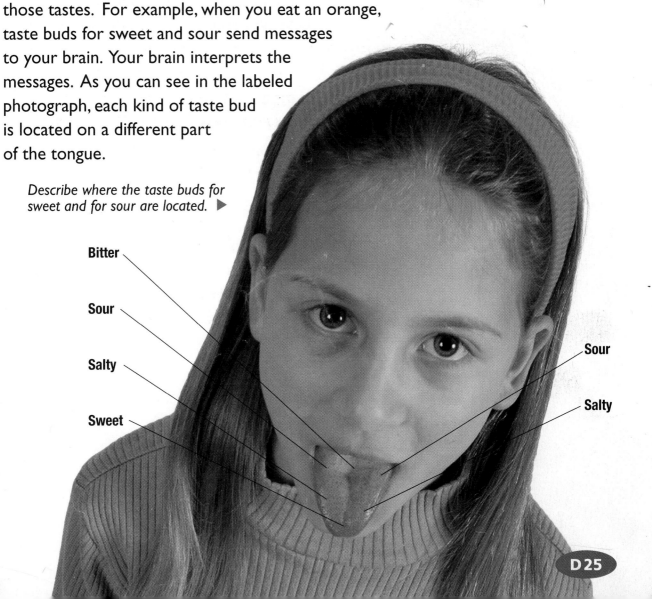

Bitter

Sour

Salty

Sweet

Sour

Salty

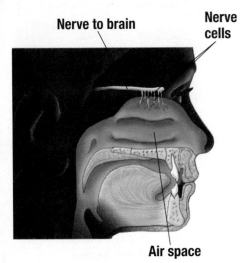

Nerve to brain **Nerve cells**

Air space

▲ As you breathe in air, smells also enter the nose.

Nerve cells in your nose gather information about all kinds of smells, both bad and good. ▼

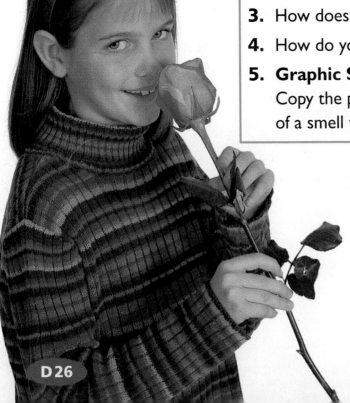

As you might guess, the nerve cells for your sense of smell are in your nose. When you breathe in through your nose, the air moves into a space. You can see in the drawing that nerve cells line the top of this space. Each nerve cell has nerve endings that are like tiny hairs. When a smell enters your nose, these nerve endings gather information about the smell. They send a message to your brain. Your brain tells you what you smell. Look at the picture. What do you suppose the girl's brain is telling her?

When it comes to eating, your nose and tongue work together. As you eat, both sense organs send information to your brain. The brain puts this information together and tells you the flavor of the food. When you have a stuffy nose, your brain does not get as much information as usual. Food seems to lack flavor. That's why you may not enjoy eating when you have a cold.

Lesson 3 Review

1. What do nerve cells do?

2. What do nerve endings in your skin do?

3. How does the retina help you see?

4. How do your tongue and nose work together?

5. **Graphic Sources**
   Copy the picture of the nose and trace the path of a smell through the nose.

Experimenting with the Sense of Smell

Materials

- 6 medicine cups with lids
- masking tape
- marker
- 1 graduated plastic cup
- water
- dropper
- mint extract
- plastic spoon
- large container

Process Skills

- formulating questions and hypotheses
- identifying and controlling variables
- experimenting
- collecting and interpreting data
- communicating

State the Problem

Do smell thresholds vary among students?

Formulate Your Hypothesis

The smell threshold is the lowest concentration of a substance that a person can smell. Do most students have a similar smell threshold or will there be variation? Write your **hypothesis**.

Identify and Control the Variables

The smell threshold of different students is the **variable** you will test. The same testing procedure must be performed for each student. Each student must smell the same concentrations of mint solution and a control that is unscented.

Test Your Hypothesis

Follow these steps to perform an **experiment**.

❶ Make a chart like the one on the next page. Use your chart to record your data.

❷ Use a marker and masking tape to label the medicine cups from 0 to 5. Fill medicine cup 0 with water. This will be a control, with no scent.

❸ Fill a graduated cup with 240 mL of water. Add 2 drops of mint extract (Photo A). Stir with a plastic spoon.

Photo A

Continued →

Photo B

Photo C

4 Open medicine cup 5 and fill it with mint solution. Replace the lid.

5 Pour mint solution out of the graduated cup into the large container until there is 120 mL remaining in the cup. Add water to the cup until it is filled to 240 mL. Stir with the plastic spoon. Fill medicine cup 4 with this solution. The mint concentration of cup 4 is now half the concentration of cup 5. Replace the lid.

6 Repeat step 5 for medicine cups 3, 2, and 1 (Photo B). Arrange the medicine cups from 0 (no scent) to 5 (highest mint concentration).

7 Open medicine cup 0 and have your partner sniff the control. Repeat with increasing concentrations of mint solution, starting with medicine cup 1, until the student can identify the smell as mint (Photo C). **Collect data** by recording the number of the identified concentration in your chart.

8 Repeat the test until all of your group members have been tested.

9 Obtain the test results from other groups and add them to your chart.

Collect Your Data

Student	Smell threshold concentration
1	
2	
3	
4	

Interpret Your Data

1. Label a piece of grid paper as shown. Use the data from your chart to make a bar graph on your grid paper.

2. Study your graph. Which concentration did most students identify as their smell threshold? Describe how the smell threshold varied, if it did, among students.

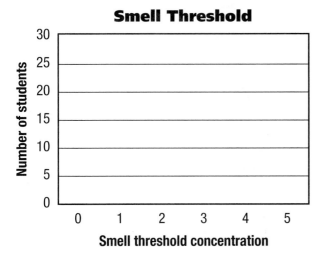

Smell Threshold

State Your Conclusions

How do your results compare with your hypothesis? **Communicate** your results. Write an explanation of how the smell threshold for mint does or does not vary among students.

Inquire Further

Would the smell threshold results be similar with other scents such as vanilla or lemon? Develop a plan to answer this or other questions you may have.

Self-Assessment

- I made a **hypothesis** about smell thresholds.
- I **identified** and **controlled variables.**
- I followed instructions to conduct an **experiment** to test students' smell thresholds for mint.
- I **collected** and **interpreted** data by making a chart and a graph.
- I **communicated** by writing my conclusion explaining how the smell threshold for mint does or does not vary among students.

Chapter 1 Review

Chapter Main Ideas

Lesson 1
• The digestive system changes food into nutrients that body cells use for energy, for growth and repair, and for working well.
• Food is broken down and chemically changed as it moves from the mouth through the esophagus to the stomach and small intestine.

Lesson 2
• The parts of blood are plasma, red blood cells, white blood cells, and platelets, and each part does a different job.
• The three kinds of blood vessels are arteries, capillaries, and veins, and each does a different job.
• Blood moves through each side of the heart in one direction, from the right atrium to the right ventricle and from the left atrium to the left ventricle.

Lesson 3
• Nerve cells are the basic units of the nervous system, which includes the brain, spinal cord, and nerves.
• Nerve cells in the skin gather information about touch, pressure, heat, cold, and pain and send messages to the brain.
• Nerve cells in the eyes gather information about light and send messages to the brain.

• Nerve cells in the tongue and nose gather information about taste and smell and send messages to the brain.

Reviewing Science Words and Concepts

Write the letter of the word or phrase that best completes each sentence.

a. artery
b. atrium
c. capillary
d. digestion
e. enzyme
f. esophagus
g. nerve cell
h. nerve ending
i. nutrient
j. plasma
k. platelet
l. red blood cell
m. saliva
n. sense organ
o. small intestine
p. spinal cord
q. vein
r. ventricle
s. white blood cell

1. A substance in food that the body uses for energy, for growth and repair, or for working well is a ___.
2. The changing of food into forms that body cells can use is called ___.
3. The liquid in the mouth that helps break down food is ___.
4. A chemical that helps the digestive system change food into nutrients is an ___.

5. The food you eat travels from your mouth to your stomach through the ___.

6. Most digestion of food takes place in the ___.

7. The watery part of blood is ___.

8. A blood cell that carries oxygen is a ___.

9. A blood cell that fights germs is a ___.

10. A tiny part of a cell that helps stop bleeding is a ___.

11. A blood vessel that carries blood away from the heart is an ___.

12. A tiny blood vessel with thin walls is a ___.

13. A blood vessel that carries blood to the heart is a ___.

14. A space in the heart that receives blood from veins is an ___.

15. A space in the heart that pumps blood out of the heart is a ___.

16. A body part, such as the nose, that gathers information about the surroundings is a ___.

17. A cell that gathers and carries information in the body is a ___.

18. A tiny branch of a nerve cell that gathers information is a ___.

19. The bundle of nerves that connects the brain with nerves throughout the body is the ___.

Explaining Science

Draw and label a diagram or write a paragraph to answer these questions.

1. How does food change as it moves through the digestive system?

2. How does the blood move through the heart?

3. How do you know when you are touching something soft?

Using Skills

1. Use what you've learned about **capacity** to answer this question: If your heart pumps 7,500 liters of blood each day, how many milliliters of blood does it pump in a day?

2. For fifteen minutes, **observe** your surroundings with all your sense organs. As you do this, make a list of everything you observe. Then arrange the items in your list according to which sense you used.

Critical Thinking

1. Without looking, you take a bite of food. At first, it tastes salty. After you chew the food, it tastes sweet. What might you **infer** about what the food is?

2. Suppose you eat a bite of apple while holding your nose. **Predict** whether the apple will taste the same as an apple usually does. Explain your reasoning.

Sip, Sip. Yum!

Aren't those little cardboard juice containers great? They can go anywhere— no need for a refrigerator! And every sip of that yummy juice helps keep your body systems healthy.

Chapter 2

Keeping Your Body Systems Healthy

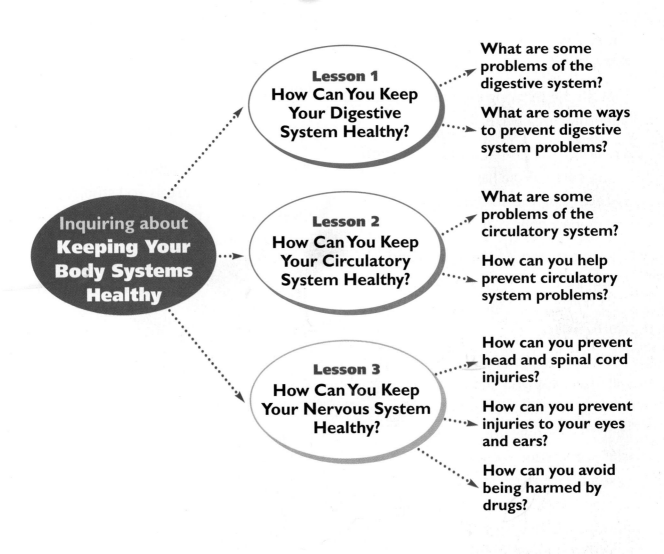

Inquiring about **Keeping Your Body Systems Healthy**

Lesson 1
How Can You Keep Your Digestive System Healthy?

What are some problems of the digestive system?

What are some ways to prevent digestive system problems?

Lesson 2
How Can You Keep Your Circulatory System Healthy?

What are some problems of the circulatory system?

How can you help prevent circulatory system problems?

Lesson 3
How Can You Keep Your Nervous System Healthy?

How can you prevent head and spinal cord injuries?

How can you prevent injuries to your eyes and ears?

How can you avoid being harmed by drugs?

Copy the chapter graphic organizer onto your own paper. This organizer shows you what the whole chapter is all about. As you read the lessons and do the activities, look for answers to the questions and write them on your organizer.

Exploring Food Labels

Process Skills

- collecting and interpreting data
- communicating

Materials

- masking tape
- marker
- 3 empty cereal packages

Explore

1 Use the masking tape and marker to label the cereals A, B, and C.

2 Study the Nutrition Facts section of the cereal A package. **Collect data** by recording the serving size, total fat, and dietary fiber.

3 Repeat step 2 for cereal B and cereal C.

Reflect

1. In this chapter, you will learn why you should eat little fat and lots of fiber for good health. **Interpret** your **data.** Based on fat and fiber content, does one cereal stand out as the most healthful choice? Why or why not?

2. Communicate. Discuss your findings with the class.

? Inquire Further

Are granola bars a more healthful food choice than the cereals you studied? Develop a plan to answer this or other questions you may have.

Identifying Cause and Effect

You know that your heart pumps blood through blood vessels in your body. The heart contracting causes the blood to be pushed out of the heart. The blood moving out of the heart through the blood vessels is the effect. As you read this chapter, look for examples of cause and effect.

Example

In Lesson 1, *How Can You Keep Your Digestive System Healthy?*, you will read about the causes and effects of digestive system problems. Make a chart like the one below to help keep track of the causes and effects of these problems. In the last row of your chart, list the ways you can help avoid the problems.

	Indigestion	Diarrhea	Constipation
Causes			
Effects			
Ways to Help			

Talk About It!

1. What can overeating cause to happen to your body?

2. What are some ways to prevent foods from spoiling?

▼ *Did you know that foods high in fiber are good for your digestive system?*

What's the Big Idea?

You will learn:

- about some problems of the digestive system.
- some ways to prevent digestive system problems.

Glossary

indigestion
(in/də jes/chən), one or more symptoms, such as stomachache, that occur when the body has difficulty digesting food

How Can You Keep Your Digestive System Healthy?

Birthday parties. Thanksgiving dinner. Family picnics. Saturday at the theme park. All these occasions mean food and fun. Sometimes, though, the fun ends with "UUHH! Why did I eat so much?"

Digestive System Problems

If you've ever eaten too much, as the girl in the picture has, you may have gotten a stomachache. Stomachaches are one form of indigestion. Indigestion is not a disease. Instead, **indigestion** includes various symptoms that you may feel when your digestive system has trouble doing its job. For example, you may have a burning feeling in your esophagus, or you may feel as if you are about to vomit, or "throw up."

◄ Sometimes eating too much can give you a stomachache.

In addition to overeating, causes of indigestion can include eating too fast and neglecting to chew food thoroughly. Eating foods and spices, such as those in the picture, can also cause indigestion. Another cause of indigestion might be eating when you are angry or otherwise upset.

Diarrhea is another problem that you may have had. Diarrhea occurs when the solid waste leaving the large intestine has too much water in it. Like stomachache, diarrhea is a symptom, not a disease. Emotional upset is one possible cause of diarrhea. Certain germs that get into the digestive system are another possible cause.

Sometimes, diarrhea is a symptom of food poisoning. A few foods, such as certain wild mushrooms, are naturally poisonous. Other foods can become poisonous when germs get in the food and spoil it. Freezing and canning are two methods that food companies use to try to keep foods from spoiling. However, germs can get in foods that are stored improperly.

Constipation is a different kind of digestive problem. It occurs when solid waste becomes dry and hard and difficult to eliminate from the body. Causes of constipation include not drinking enough water and not eating enough fiber. You will read more about fiber and water on pages D38 and D39.

Hot peppers and spices may taste good, but they can cause indigestion. ▼

Ways to Prevent Digestive Problems

You can prevent many digestive problems. For example, to help prevent indigestion, try not to overeat. Also, eat slowly and chew your food well. If spicy foods give you indigestion, avoid them. If you are very angry or otherwise upset, try to calm down before eating.

Food poisoning also can be prevented. Germs grow best in warm, moist places. Store foods such as meat, milk, cheese, eggs, fresh vegetables, and leftovers in the refrigerator to keep them cold. If any food looks or smells different than usual, do not taste it to decide whether it is spoiled. Tell an adult so that he or she can throw it away. To keep germs out of your digestive system, wash your hands with soap and water before you prepare or eat food. You should also wash fresh fruits and vegetables. Always use clean knives, forks, spoons, and dishes too. The pictures on these two pages show three more ways to help your digestive system work its best.

Foods that are low in fat and high in fiber are good for your digestive system. ▼

First, eat a healthful diet. Limit the amount of fried foods and other fatty foods that you eat. Instead, eat plenty of fruits, vegetables, and whole-grain breads and cereals. Those foods contain the material called fiber. Fiber helps food move through your digestive system properly. It helps prevent both constipation and diarrhea.

Second, drink plenty of water. Your entire body, including your digestive system, needs water to be healthy. In particular, water helps prevent constipation. Eating fruit, drinking fruit juices, and drinking low-fat or nonfat milk are other good ways to get water into your body.

Third, exercise regularly. Exercise helps keep your digestive system in good working order and helps prevent constipation. However, wait at least an hour after you eat before doing vigorous exercise. This will help prevent the painful tightening of the muscles known as cramps.

▲ Vigorous exercise is good for you, but not right after eating! During digestion, a lot of blood flows to the digestive organs. This means that less blood is available for other body parts, including muscles. Cramps may result. Mild activity, such as you might do during recess, shouldn't cause any problems after a meal.

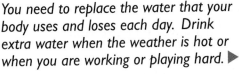

You need to replace the water that your body uses and loses each day. Drink extra water when the weather is hot or when you are working or playing hard. ▶

Lesson 1 Review

1. List three possible causes of indigestion.

2. Why is it important to eat plenty of fruits, vegetables, and whole-grain breads and cereals?

3. **Main Idea**
   What is the main idea of the first paragraph on this page?

How Can You Keep Your Circulatory System Healthy?

What's the Big Idea?

You will learn:

- about some problems of the circulatory system.
- how you can help prevent circulatory system problems.

Glossary

anemia (ə nē′mē ə), a condition in which the number of healthy red blood cells or the amount of hemoglobin is low

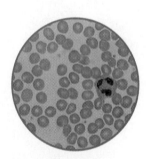

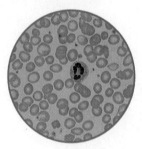

▲ Here you see healthy red blood cells (top) and the red blood cells of a person with one kind of anemia (bottom).

Only older people need to take care of their circulatory systems, right? Not really! Some circulatory problems can begin in childhood. The good news is that there's a lot you can do to prevent such problems.

Circulatory System Problems

Some circulatory problems affect the heart or the blood vessels. Other problems affect the blood. **Anemia** is a condition in which the number of healthy red blood cells is low or the amount of iron in the red blood cells is low. There are many different forms and causes of anemia.

The most common form of anemia occurs when a person's diet does not provide enough iron. The body needs this mineral to produce hemoglobin, the substance in red blood cells that carries oxygen. Too little iron means that the blood does not carry enough oxygen to body cells. Someone with this form of anemia may feel tired all the time and be very pale. The pictures show the difference between healthy red blood cells and red blood cells that do not have enough iron.

Lack of certain vitamins or exposure to dangerous chemicals also can cause anemia. Some kinds of anemia are inherited—that is, they are passed from parents to children.

High blood pressure is another problem of the circulatory system. In this disease, blood is pumped through the arteries with more force than is needed to move the blood through the body. Over a period of years, high blood pressure can damage the heart, brain, other organs, and blood vessels.

Most people with high blood pressure have no symptoms of the disease. A doctor or nurse usually finds the problem. Children rarely have high blood pressure. Still, it's a good idea to have your blood pressure measured as part of your regular health checkup, as the girl in the picture does.

In most cases of high blood pressure, doctors cannot tell the exact cause. People may inherit a tendency to have high blood pressure. In these people, being overweight, smoking, or eating too much salt may cause the disease to develop.

Glossary

Glossary

high blood pressure (presh′ər), a disease in which blood is pumped through the arteries with too much force

Blood pressure is the force of the blood on the walls of arteries as it is pumped through the arteries. Blood pressure is measured in the main artery of the arm. ▼

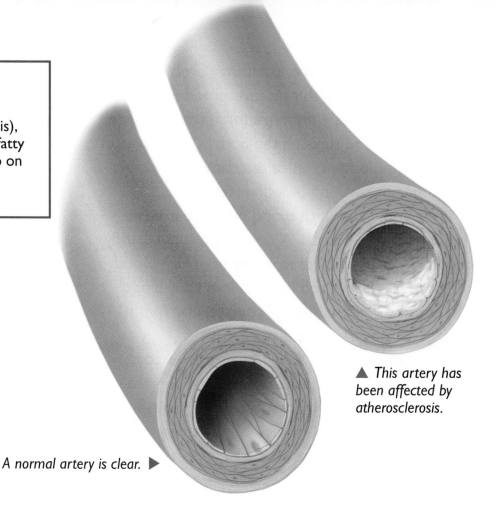

Glossary

Glossary

atherosclerosis
(ath′ər ō sklə rō′sis),
a disease in which fatty
substances build up on
the inside walls of
arteries

▲ *This artery has
been affected by
atherosclerosis.*

A normal artery is clear. ▶

A circulatory problem called **atherosclerosis**
occurs when fatty substances in the blood stick to the
inside walls of arteries. Some of the fatty substances
come from digested food. Over a period of years, the
arteries become partly or completely blocked. The
pictures above show a normal artery and one that is
partly blocked by fatty substances.

As atherosclerosis develops, the flow of blood
through the arteries decreases. As a result, some
body cells may not get enough oxygen. If an artery
carrying blood to the heart muscle becomes blocked,
some cells in the heart muscle may die from lack of
oxygen. This event is called a heart attack. If an artery
carrying blood to the brain becomes blocked, some
cells in the brain may die from lack of oxygen. This
event is called a stroke. Some people recover from a
heart attack or stroke. However, either event can
cause lasting damage and even death.

Ways to Prevent Circulatory System Problems

Anemia can affect people of all ages. Children usually do not have heart attacks or strokes, but children as young as age three have been found to have early signs of atherosclerosis. High blood pressure in adults may be triggered by habits that begin in childhood. It makes sense to do all you can to keep your circulatory system healthy—starting right now!

Your diet is a good place to begin. You can help prevent the most common form of anemia by eating foods rich in iron. Such foods include meat, poultry, fish, eggs, and dry beans. What iron-rich foods do you see in the picture?

Fat is a nutrient that you need for energy. However, you don't need a lot of it. You know that fatty substances can clog arteries. Too much fat in the diet also can make a person overweight, which puts a strain on the circulatory system. To reduce the fat in your diet, limit the amount of fried foods and high-fat foods from animals, such as meat and eggs. Choose low-fat or nonfat milk, cheese, and yogurt over other dairy products.

Fruits, vegetables, and grain products should make up most of your diet. You need only two or three daily servings of foods like meat, poultry, fish, and eggs. You also need only two or three daily servings of dairy products such as milk. ▼

◀ *This boy is doing a lot more than improving his basketball shot. He's helping his heart too! Playing active games such as basketball is a good way to exercise. Other good ways include bicycling, running, swimming, jumping rope, and cross-country skiing.*

You've read that too much salt may lead to high blood pressure in some people. Your body needs the sodium found in salt. However, a healthy diet contains all the sodium you need. It's a good idea to limit the amount of salt you add to food. Also, choose packaged foods whose labels show salt or sodium low on the list of ingredients.

Another way to help your circulatory system is to get plenty of exercise, as the child in the picture does. Regular, vigorous exercise strengthens the muscles, including the heart muscle. A strong heart can pump more blood with each beat and rest longer between beats. Also, exercise causes extra blood vessels to grow in the heart. This increases the blood supply to the heart.

Exercise has other benefits. Exercise helps maintain a normal body weight. It helps keep blood pressure low. It also helps keep fatty substances from building up inside arteries. Therefore, exercise may lower the risk of heart attacks and strokes.

A drug is a substance that causes changes in the way the body works. You can help keep your circulatory system healthy by avoiding drugs that harm it. One such drug is nicotine, which is found in cigarettes and other products made from tobacco. Nicotine strains the heart by making it beat too fast. Nicotine also narrows the blood vessels, which raises blood pressure and decreases the flow of blood through the body.

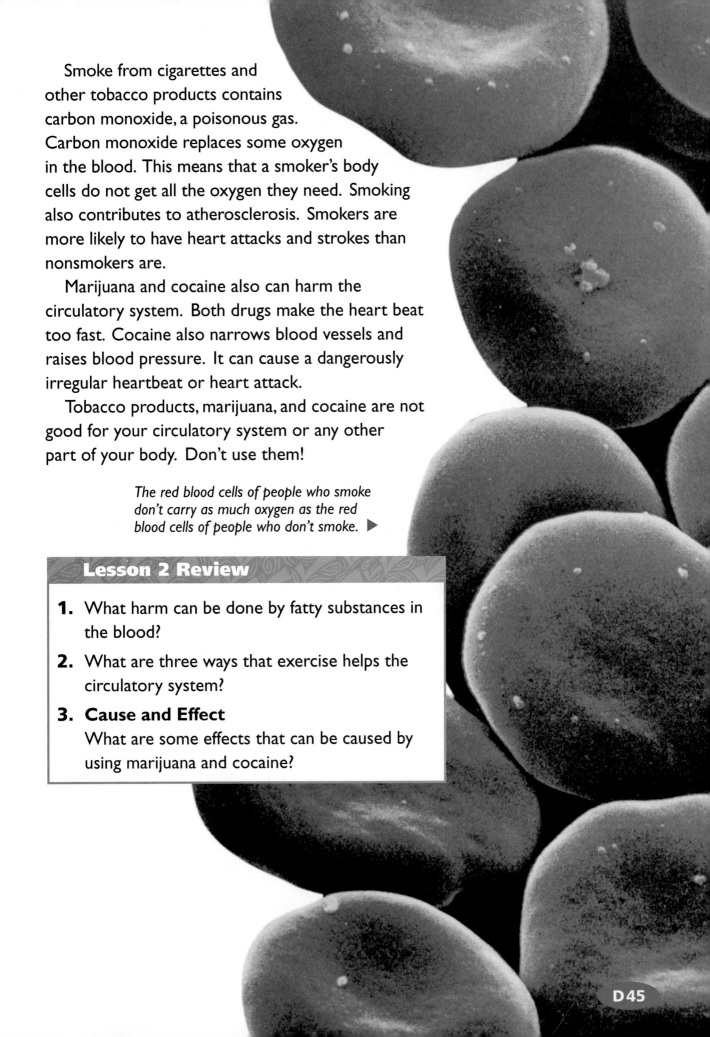

Smoke from cigarettes and other tobacco products contains carbon monoxide, a poisonous gas. Carbon monoxide replaces some oxygen in the blood. This means that a smoker's body cells do not get all the oxygen they need. Smoking also contributes to atherosclerosis. Smokers are more likely to have heart attacks and strokes than nonsmokers are.

Marijuana and cocaine also can harm the circulatory system. Both drugs make the heart beat too fast. Cocaine also narrows blood vessels and raises blood pressure. It can cause a dangerously irregular heartbeat or heart attack.

Tobacco products, marijuana, and cocaine are not good for your circulatory system or any other part of your body. Don't use them!

The red blood cells of people who smoke don't carry as much oxygen as the red blood cells of people who don't smoke. ▶

Lesson 2 Review

1. What harm can be done by fatty substances in the blood?

2. What are three ways that exercise helps the circulatory system?

3. **Cause and Effect**
   What are some effects that can be caused by using marijuana and cocaine?

Investigating How the Heart Works

Process Skills

Process Skills

- estimating and measuring
- observing
- inferring
- communicating

Materials

- clock with a second hand
- ball

Getting Ready

By trying to make your hand and arm muscles work at the same rate as your heart, you can appreciate how hard your heart works. You also can gain understanding of the importance of exercise.

Follow This Procedure

1 Make a chart like the one shown. Use your chart to record your measurements and observations.

Resting heart rate	
Length of time I was able to squeeze the ball	
Observations	

2 Place your arm on a desk, palm up. Place the first two fingers of your other hand against your upturned wrist near the base of your thumb (Photo A). Press gently until you can feel your pulse.

3 Watching the clock, count your pulse for ten seconds. Stop counting, write the number down, and multiply it by six. This **measurement** is your resting heart rate.

Photo A

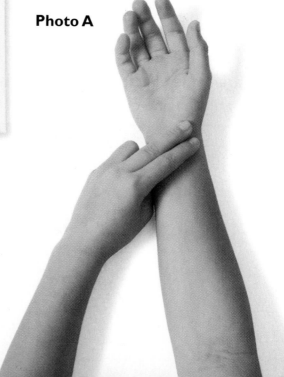

Photo B

4 Now hold the ball in one hand. Use your right hand if you are right-handed or your left hand if you are left-handed. Squeeze the ball hard (Photo B) and then relax your grip. This is about the amount of force your heart puts forth with each beat.

5 Again, watching the clock, try to squeeze the ball at the same rate as your heart rate. For example, if your heart rate is 80 beats per minute, squeeze the ball 80 times per minute. How long can you go without slowing? without stopping? Record your time. How do the muscles of your hand and arm feel when you do stop? Record your **observations**.

Self-Monitoring
Have I correctly completed all the steps?

Interpret Your Results

1. Make an **inference.** How is your heart muscle different from the muscles in your hands and arms?

2. A strong heart can pump more blood with each beat and rest longer between beats. Make an inference. If you began a regular exercise program today and continued for a month, how might your resting heart rate change?

3. Communicate. Imagine that your heart can talk. Write what it might say to persuade you to lower your resting heart rate.

 Inquire Further

Besides exercise, what other things affect a person's resting heart rate? Develop a plan to answer this or other questions you may have.

Self-Assessment

- I followed instructions to **measure** my resting heart rate.
- I followed instructions to try to make my hand and arm muscles work at the same rate as my heart rate.
- I recorded my **observations.**
- I made **inferences** about how my heart differs from other muscles and how regular exercise might affect my resting heart rate.
- I **communicated** by writing what my heart might say to encourage me to lower my resting heart rate.

You will learn:

- how to prevent head and spinal cord injuries.
- how to prevent injuries to your eyes and ears.
- how to avoid being harmed by drugs.

Lesson 3

How Can You Keep Your Nervous System Healthy?

The scene you see here couldn't have happened when your parents were your age. In-line skates hadn't been invented! Few, if any, skaters wore pads or helmets. **OOPS!** When they fell down, it could really hurt.

Preventing Head and Spinal Cord Injuries

Some people still don't understand why they need to wear a helmet for activities such as in-line skating. They believe their skull will protect them if they fall and hit their head. It's true that the bones of the skull do a good job of protecting the brain most of the time. However, a hard blow to an unprotected head still can cause harm. The skull may crack. Even if it doesn't, the blow may cause a sudden movement of the brain inside the skull. The brain may even be bruised.

◄ *Getting injured is no fun at all. That's why this boy protects his knees, elbows, wrists, and head when he goes in-line skating.*

A condition known as a **concussion** is one possible result of a sudden movement of the brain. In most cases of concussion, the person loses consciousness for a short time. Other possible symptoms include memory loss, headache, and blurred vision. The symptoms go away after a while.

More serious head injuries can cause lasting damage to the brain. Also, injuries to the spine can cause lasting damage to the spinal cord. The body cannot make new nerve cells to replace nerve cells that have been damaged or have died. Some head and spine injuries are so severe that they cause death.

Wear a helmet, such as the ones shown, when you do any activity in which you could be struck on the head or could fall and hit your head. Such activities include in-line skating, skateboarding, and bicycling. College and professional football and hockey players wear helmets, as do baseball and softball players when they go to bat. If you play those sports, you should wear a helmet too.

Do you like to swim and dive? If so, be sure to find out how deep the water is before you dive in. Do this whether you are at a pool or a natural body of water such as a lake. If you dive into water that is too shallow, you could hit the bottom. You could suffer a head or spine injury as a result. Also, if you are diving off a board or platform, be sure to jump in such a way that you do not hit your head, neck, or back on it.

Glossary

concussion
(kən kush′ən), a condition caused by a sudden movement of the brain inside the skull, usually involving a brief loss of consciousness

Glossary

Helmets can protect the brain from damage. ▼

D49

▲ *Buckle up your safety belt every time you ride in a car.*

Car accidents are a leading cause of injuries, including head and spine injuries. To be safe in a car, do as the girl at the left does. Always wear your safety belt. Wear it even if you are riding for only a short distance. If possible, sit in the back seat. You're less likely to be injured in the back seat if an accident does occur.

You can prevent head and spine injuries by making safety a part of your daily life. Like the children below, cross streets only at corners and crosswalks. When bicycling, ride on the right-hand side of the street and be sure to obey all traffic signs and signals.

Cross the street only when no traffic is coming. Look in all directions to be sure. If the corner has a traffic signal, wait for the walk sign or the green light to come on, check to be sure no traffic is coming, and then cross. ▼

Preventing Injuries to Eyes and Ears

The bones around your eyes help protect the eyes from blows. Your ability to blink and your eyelashes also help protect your eyes by keeping dust and other things out. Tears wash away some things that do get in the eyes.

You can do your part to protect your sense of sight. Chemicals, wood chips, and other things can harm your eyes. Like the students at the right, wear safety goggles when you do an experiment or other activity that might send something splashing or flying into your eyes.

Never throw sand, dirt, balls, or other objects toward anyone's eyes. Don't wave sharp objects around either. If you get something in your eyes, don't rub them. Get an adult's help right away.

Bright sunlight can also damage your eyes, so never look directly at the sun. Be sure to wear sunglasses with UV protection outdoors on sunny days. What else is the girl at the right doing to protect her eyes from the sun?

▲ Don't take chances with your eyesight. Wear safety goggles when you do science experiments, when you work with tools, and when you use chemicals, such as cleansers, at home.

She's cool—and smart! She knows that good-quality sunglasses and a hat with a brim protect her eyes from the sun's damaging rays. ▶

You also can do your part to protect your ears and your sense of hearing. Sudden loud sounds can harm your hearing. Being around loud sounds for a long time also can harm hearing. Avoid loud sounds as much as possible. For example, keep the volume down when you watch television or listen to music. This is especially important if you listen through headphones, as the child below is doing.

Getting hit on the ear can damage the delicate parts inside the ear that make hearing possible. In the picture at the left, notice the part of the batting helmet covering the ear. It faces the direction from which the ball will come. Wear a helmet like this if you play baseball or softball.

Do not clean your ears with small objects, such as cotton-tipped swabs. Damage could result. Tell an adult if you have trouble hearing or if your ears hurt. You may have an infection that needs to be treated by a doctor.

Turn it down! When you listen to music through headphones, keep the volume low enough that you can hear other sounds, such as people talking nearby. ▼

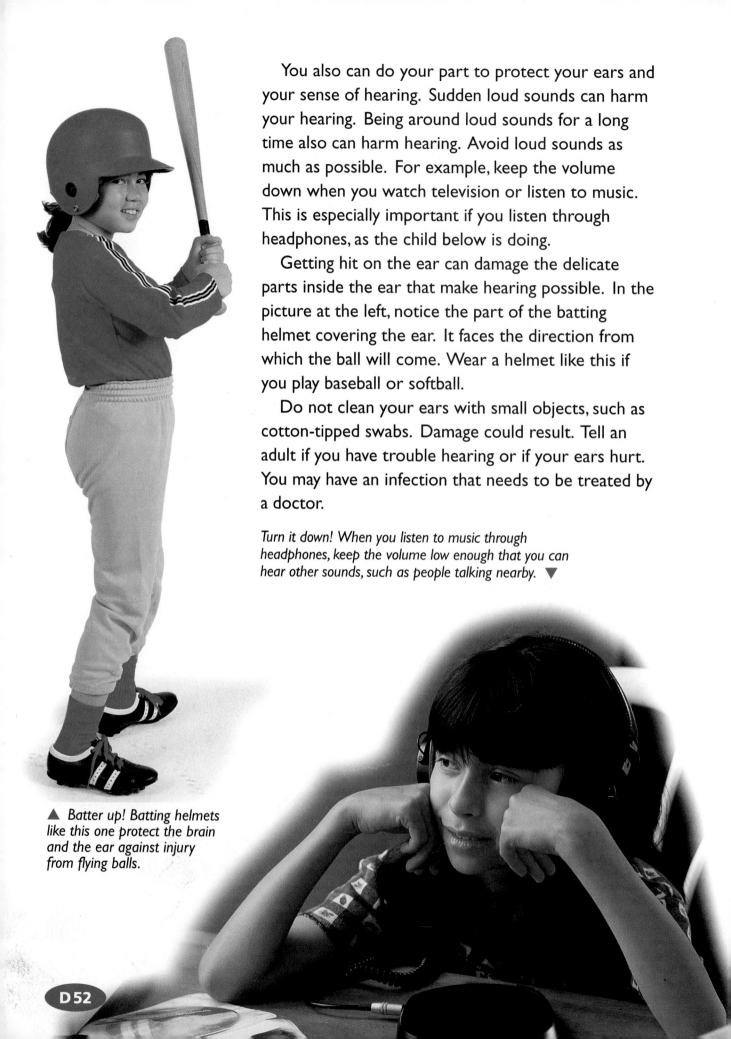

▲ *Batter up! Batting helmets like this one protect the brain and the ear against injury from flying balls.*

Saying No to Drugs

Many drugs can affect the brain. They can change the way a person thinks, feels, or acts. To keep your brain—and your whole body—healthy, you need to make wise decisions about drugs. For most drugs, your decision should be the same as the decision made by the girl in the picture: No!

Medicines are one kind of drug that can be helpful to health. Different medicines treat, cure, or prevent various health problems. An over-the-counter medicine is a medicine that people can buy without a doctor's order. People use such medicines for health problems that are not serious, such as a mild headache. A prescription medicine is a medicine that can be bought only with a doctor's order. A pharmacist carries out the order and gets the medicine ready.

Medicines are safe only when used correctly. You should take medicine only with the help of a doctor, a nurse, or an adult who is responsible for you. The adult should read and carefully follow all the directions on the medicine's label. The adult also should make sure that no one else takes a prescription medicine meant for you. The medicine could harm someone else.

The buttons on this girl's backpack make it clear how she feels about harmful drugs. ▼

Alcohol is a drug found in beer, wine, and liquor. Alcohol slows down the work of the brain. This in turn slows down other parts of the body. Someone who drinks alcohol may be unable to think, speak, or see clearly. He or she may walk unsteadily and feel dizzy or sleepy. If a drinker tries to drive a car or a bicycle, an accident may result. Over time, large amounts of alcohol can damage the brain, heart, and digestive organs.

It is against the law to sell alcohol to young people. Certain other drugs, such as marijuana and cocaine, are illegal for people of any age to sell, buy, or use. Marijuana and cocaine harm various parts of the body, including the brain. For example, marijuana users may have trouble learning because they cannot concentrate or remember facts.

You may wonder why people use drugs such as alcohol, marijuana, and cocaine. Some people start using drugs because they are bored. They may try a drug because their friends use it, and they want to feel part of the group. After a while, they may become dependent on a drug. They may believe they cannot get along without it.

Playing team sports such as soccer is just one way to be part of a group without using drugs. What other ways can you think of? ▼

◀ *These children have made a choice to be drug-free.*

One of the best decisions you can make in life is to say no to drugs such as alcohol, marijuana, and cocaine. That is what the children above have done. They know that there are many healthful ways to have fun and be part of a group. They don't use drugs to try to "belong."

Sometimes saying no is hard. You may fear that others will make fun of you or that you will lose your friends. Talking things over with your family can help you stand firm in your decision to refuse drugs. Also, your school or another organization in your community may offer a program to help you.

Lesson 3 Review

1. Why should you wear a helmet for activities such as in-line skating and bicycling?

2. List two ways to protect your eyes and two ways to protect your ears.

3. Why should you say no to alcohol?

4. **Main Idea**
   What is the main idea of the first paragraph on this page?

Conducting a Safety Survey

Process Skills

- collecting and interpreting data
- inferring
- communicating

Materials

- grid paper
- pencil

Getting Ready

In this activity you will conduct a survey to find out how often fourth graders wear helmets when bicycling.

Follow This Procedure

1 Make a chart like the one shown. Use your chart to record your data.

Use of bicycle helmets	Tally of students	Totals
Always		
Usually		
Sometimes		
Never		

2 Decide how many students to survey about their use of bicycle helmets. You might survey your entire class or more than one fourth-grade class. The more students you survey, the more reliable your data will be.

3 Decide how to word your survey question. Here is one possibility: "How often do you wear a helmet when bicycling: always, usually, sometimes, or never?" Write the question at the top of your survey form.

4 Ask each student in your survey group the question that you have written. **Collect data** by making a tally mark for each student's answer in the correct place on the survey form. Then calculate the total number of students that chose each answer.

Interpret Your Results

1. Label a piece of grid paper as shown. If your survey group is larger than 50, add numbers as needed. Use the data from your survey form to make a bar graph on the grid paper.

2. Study your graph. **Interpret data** by writing a paragraph that summarizes what the graph shows about the helmet-wearing practices of fourth graders.

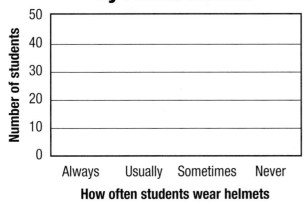

Bicycle Helmet Use by Fourth Graders

Number of students

50
40
30
20
10
0

Always Usually Sometimes Never

How often students wear helmets

3. Make an **inference.** What attitudes toward bicycle safety and helmets do fourth graders have? **Communicate.** Discuss your inference with classmates.

Inquire Further

How might the results of the survey be different after students see a presentation on bicycle safety, or participate in other bicycle safety activities? Develop a plan to answer this or other questions you may have.

Self-Assessment

- I followed instructions to conduct a survey about use of bicycle helmets.
- I **recorded** my **data** in a survey form and **interpreted** my **data** by making and studying a bar graph.
- I wrote a paragraph to summarize the data in the bar graph.
- I made an **inference** about the safety attitudes of fourth graders.
- I **communicated** by discussing my inference with the class.

Chapter 2 Review

Chapter Main Ideas

Lesson 1

• Problems of the digestive system can include indigestion, diarrhea, and constipation.

• Ways to prevent digestive system problems include not overeating, keeping germs out of food, eating foods low in fat and high in fiber, drinking plenty of water, and exercising regularly.

Lesson 2

• Problems of the circulatory system can include anemia, high blood pressure, and atherosclerosis.

• Ways to prevent circulatory system problems include eating foods rich in iron, limiting fat and salt in the diet, getting plenty of vigorous exercise, and avoiding harmful drugs such as nicotine.

Lesson 3

• Ways to prevent head injuries include wearing a helmet for activities such as bicycling, being careful when diving into water, and wearing a safety belt when riding in a car.

• Ways to prevent injuries to the eyes and ears include wearing sunglasses outdoors, wearing safety goggles for certain activities, avoiding loud sounds, and protecting the ears from flying objects.

• Ways to avoid being harmed by drugs include using medicines correctly and saying no to drugs such as alcohol, marijuana, and cocaine.

Reviewing Science Words and Concepts

Write the letter of the word or phrase that best completes each sentence.

a. anemia   **d.** high blood

b. atherosclerosis   pressure

c. concussion   **e.** indigestion

1. A symptom that occurs when the body has difficulty digesting food is known as ___.

2. A condition in which there is a low number of healthy red blood cells or a low amount of iron in the blood cells is ___.

3. A disease in which blood is pumped through the arteries with too much force is ___.

4. A buildup of fatty substances on the inside walls of arteries is known as ___.

5. A hard blow to the head can cause a ___.

Explaining Science

Draw and label a diagram or write a sentence or paragraph to answer these questions.

1. What are four things you can do to help your digestive system?

2. What are three steps you can take to keep your circulatory system healthy?

3. How can you protect your brain from the time you leave school today until you go to bed?

Using Skills

1. Use **cause** and **effect** to explain how the use of drugs can harm your circulatory system.

2. **Collect data** about ways to keep the digestive system and the circulatory system healthy. Make a Venn diagram. Label the left-hand circle *Ways to Help the Digestive System.* Label the right-hand circle *Ways to Help the Circulatory System.* Fill in the three sections of the diagram. **Interpret** the **data** to find out what ways help both the digestive system and the circulatory system.

3. One of your friends is tired all the time. She does not have the energy to play games like your other friends do. What might you **infer** about the condition of your friend's blood?

Critical Thinking

1. Your friend spends most of his free time watching TV and playing computer games. If he continues to do this, what might you **infer** about the health of his circulatory system as he grows up?

2. One Friday after school, a group of older children invite you to go to the park. They hint that someone will be there with cigarettes and beer for them. **Make a decision** about what you should do. Why?

3. When you arrive home after school one afternoon, you make an unpleasant discovery: You accidentally left a carton of milk out on the counter that morning. It's been sitting there all day. **Draw a conclusion.** What should you do? What should you not do?

Unit D Review

Reviewing Words and Concepts

Choose at least three words from the Chapter 1 list below.
Use the words to write a paragraph that shows how the words
are related. Do the same for Chapter 2.

Chapter 1
artery
capillary
plasma
red blood cell
vein
white blood cell

Chapter 2
anemia
atherosclerosis
concussion
high blood
 pressure
indigestion

Reviewing Main Ideas

Each of the statements below is false. Change the underlined
word or words to make each statement true.

1. A liquid called <u>nutrient</u> begins the process of digesting food.
2. Chewed food travels through the <u>enzyme</u> on its way from the mouth to the stomach.
3. Each <u>ventricle</u> in the heart receives blood from veins.
4. Nerve cells in your sense organs have tiny branches called <u>spinal cords,</u> which gather information.
5. Two sense organs—your tongue and your <u>skin</u>—work together to help you taste food.
6. Fruits and vegetables contain a material called <u>fat</u>, which helps food move through the digestive system properly.
7. By keeping the <u>intestines</u> clear of fatty substances, exercise may lower the risk of strokes.
8. Cigarettes contain <u>iron</u>, a drug that makes the heart beat fast and narrows the blood vessels.
9. To help prevent head injuries, wear a <u>hat</u> when in-line skating, skateboarding, or bicycling.
10. The sense of <u>sight</u> can be harmed by loud sounds.

Interpreting Data

Use the information on the food label below to answer the questions below. The label shows the amount of nutrients in one serving.

Total Fat	0 g
Saturated Fat	0 g
Cholesterol	0 mg
Sodium	340 mg
Total Carbohydrates	20g
Dietary Fiber	6 g
Sugars	2 g
Protein	8 g

1. How many grams of fat does one serving of the food contain?

2. Which does the food contain more of, fiber or sugar?

3. In what ways is this food a good choice for your circulatory system? your digestive system?

Communicating Science

1. Draw and label a diagram that shows the order in which these body parts are used during digestion: esophagus, large intestine, mouth, small intestine, stomach. Add a paragraph that summarizes the steps in digestion.

2. Write a paragraph to explain how your sense organs are like one another and different from one another.

3. Write a summary of how exercise can help the digestive system and the circulatory system.

4. Make a chart to show the benefits of saying no to alcohol, marijuana, and cocaine.

Applying Science

1. Imagine you can see inside the circulatory system. Write a "play-by-play" description—similar to a sportscaster's—telling what happens as blood makes its way through the heart, arteries, capillaries, and veins.

2. Make a list of rules for preventing food poisoning that you could post on the refrigerator at home. Try to write each rule so that any younger family members can understand it. Draw a picture to illustrate each rule.

3. List the different kinds of exercise you got during the past week. Include activities such as walking, bicycling, and doing active chores, as well as playing sports and games. Use what you have written to develop an exercise plan for next week. Plan to be active in some way every day, and plan for vigorous exercise on at least three days. Write how long you will exercise each day. If there are some new kinds of exercise you would like to try, include them in your plan.

Unit D
Performance Review

Body and Health Fair

Using what you learned in this unit, complete one or more of the following activities to be included in a Body and Health Fair. The fair will help students learn more about how various body systems work and how to keep those systems healthy. You may work by yourself or in a group.

Poetry

Imagine that a piece of popcorn could have feelings. How might it feel as it experiences a journey through the digestive system, from the mouth to the small intestine? Put your ideas into a poem or song titled something like "An Incredible Journey" or "What a Trip!" Plan to recite your poem or sing your song at the fair.

Graph

Measure and record your pulse several different times during one day. For example, measure it before you get out of bed, just after walking to school, while working at your desk, just after playing an active game, and while watching an exciting TV show. Show the results in a graph. Display the graph at the fair. Be prepared to offer explanations for any differences in your heart rate that the graph shows.

Drama

Plan a puppet show starring Harry the Heart and Susie the Stomach. Make a hand puppet to represent each character. Prepare a script in which Harry and Susie talk about their jobs, how their owners treat them, and how they wish they could treated. Present your puppet show at the fair. You may want to include recorded music, props, scenery, or special lighting in your show.

Research Report

Find out about animals that help people who are vision impaired and hearing impaired. Prepare a display about these animals for the fair. Your display might include photographs that you have taken, drawings you have made, or copies of pictures from books and magazines. Write descriptive labels for the various pictures. Include information about the animals' training and their daily lives with the people they help.

Health and Safety

You have been named safety officer for your school. Make one or more safety posters to present at the fair. Think of some slogans for staying safe while at school and while traveling to and from school. Include ideas for preventing cuts and head, eye, and ear injuries. Illustrate your safety slogans with pictures that you draw or cut out of old magazines.

Writing an Adventure Story or Play

An adventure story or play is an entertaining way to present information. To tell a good story, you need to put events in a logical order and create interesting characters.

Using Graphic Organizers

A graphic organizer is a visual device that helps make facts and ideas clearer. Word webs, flowcharts, and tables are different kinds of graphic organizers. The graphic organizer below is an example of a flowchart. A flowchart shows a series of events in the order in which they occur. This flowchart shows the path of food through your digestive system.

Make a Flowchart

In Chapter 1, you learned about the circulatory system and how blood moves through the heart and body. Use information from Lesson 2 to make a flowchart that traces the path of blood through the human heart.

Write an Adventure Story or Play

Use the information in your flowchart to write an adventure story or play in which the main character is a red blood cell. Your story or play should tell about the main character's adventures as it travels through the human heart. Try to be as descriptive as possible about what the blood cell might experience during this journey.

Remember to:

1. **Prewrite** Organize your thoughts before you write.

2. **Draft** Write your story or play.

3. **Revise** Share your work and then make changes.

4. **Edit** Proofread for mistakes and fix them.

5. **Publish** Share your story or play with your class.

mouth ·····▶ throat ·····▶ esophagus ·····▶ stomach ·····▶ intestines

Your Science Handbook

1

Safety in Science

Scientists know they must work safely when doing experiments. You need to be careful when doing experiments too. The next page shows some safety tips to remember.

Safety Tips

- Read each experiment carefully.

- Wear safety goggles when needed.

- Clean up spills right away.

- Never taste or smell substances
  unless directed to do so by your teacher.

- Handle sharp items carefully.

- Tape sharp edges of materials.

- Handle thermometers carefully.

- Use chemicals carefully.

- Dispose of chemicals properly.

- Put materials away when you finish
  an experiment.

- Wash your hands after each experiment.

Using the Metric System

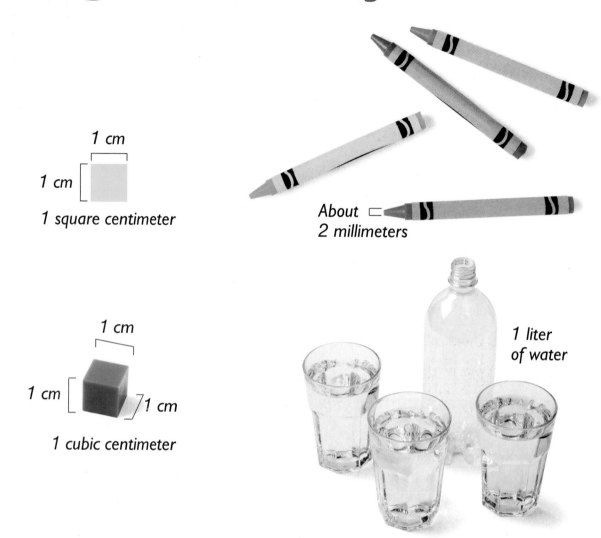

1 cm

1 cm

1 square centimeter

About 2 millimeters

1 cm

1 cm

1 cm

1 cubic centimeter

1 liter of water

11 football fields end to end is about 1 kilometer

4

About 1 centimeter

About 1 kilogram

Water boils
(100°C)

Normal body
temperature
(37°C)

Water freezes
(0°C)

About
1 meter

Observing

How can you make accurate observations?

The process of observing is the most important of all the process skills. Every scientific investigation requires you to make accurate observations.

You must use all your senses—sight, touch, hearing, smelling, and taste—to find out about objects and events. You can pick up objects, feel them, shake them, press them, smell them, look at them, listen to them. Doing all these things will help you find out about objects.

Observing requires that you notice things or events that are changing. You must compare the properties of the objects or events before, during, and after the change.

You may use tools or measuring instruments to make better observations. Limit your observations to things that are directly related to your senses.

Practice Observing

Materials
- pencil
- paper
- tape measure
- hand lens

Follow This Procedure

1. Observe your pencil with as many senses as possible. Do not taste your pencil.

2. List each sense that you used and list your observations.

3. Notice things that are changing. Compare properties before, during, and after the change. For example, use your hand lens to look carefully at the "lead" in your pencil. It is graphite. Then scribble on a piece of paper. Describe how the graphite looked before, during, and after you scribbled on the paper.

4. Use tools to make better observations. Use a tape measure to make observations of your pencil. Make as many measurements as you can.

5. Describe only what you observe directly with your senses. Look over your list of observations and tell what sense you used to make each observation.

Thinking About Your Thinking

List the steps that you used to make accurate observations. What could you have done to make better observations?

Communicating

How can you communicate by using descriptions?

You communicate when you share information through words, pictures, charts, graphs, and diagrams. Each of these is a different way to communicate.

If you want to communicate about something that has many things to describe, you can use several different ways to express your observations. For example, you might make a map like the one shown. The map shows how to locate a treasure that is hidden on the island in the picture.

Practice Communicating

Materials

- ruler
- pencil
- notebook

Follow This Procedure

1 Begin a letter to a friend from another school, telling him or her that you will be describing your classroom.

2 Describe the light in the classroom. Is it mostly from the windows? What time of day is the window light brightest? Are there ceiling lights?

3 Describe the smell of the air. Does it smell like an old shoe? like flowers? like mouthwash?

4 Describe the color and texture of the walls. Does tape stick to it? Is the floor rough or smooth? Is it slippery?

5 Draw a map of the classroom. Include the doors, windows, blackboards, desks, and closets. Draw and label any special activity areas. Label your assigned seat if you have one.

6 Measure and describe the classroom by the "steps" method. First measure the length of your step in centimeters. Count how many steps it takes to cross the length of the classroom. Then count how many steps it takes to cross the width. Calculate the length of the classroom by multiplying the length of your steps by the number of steps necessary to cross its length. Use the same calculation to find the width. Record your results. In the letter you are writing, describe how your measurements were obtained.

7 Compare your letter with the letter of another student to discover what you may not have communicated.

Thinking About Your Thinking

How did creating a map improve the communication in your letter? Could you have described a complex environment like your classroom as well without it? Would it have taken a lot more words?

Think about how important it is for people to communicate the methods and units of measurement they are using. Is the "steps" method precise enough to communicate how to build parts for an airplane? What other ways to measure might you have used?

Classifying

How can you classify objects in nature?

You classify objects by arranging or grouping them according to their common properties. Practice classifying things in nature. It is important to use an organized way to classify.

Look at the leaves on this page. How are these leaves alike and different? How would you group these leaves according to their common properties?

Practice Classifying

Materials

- collection of six leaves
- small magnifying glass
- pencil

Follow This Procedure

1. Classify your collection of leaves by their different characteristics. Make a list of the characteristics you used.

2. How many different ways did you sort your collection? Why did you choose those characteristics?

3. Plant scientists, or botanists, classify leaves in many ways. Look at each of your leaves. Are they thin and needle-like? Are they broad, or wide?

4. Look at a broad leaf. Notice the little stem at the bottom. The rest of the leaf is called the *blade*. Veins run from the little stem into the blade. You can see them with or without your hand lens. Do the veins alternate off of one big vein in the middle? Do they all branch off from the stem? Do they run in straight lines without touching?

5. Classify your broad leaves as one of the following.

   (1) having alternating veins
   (2) having branching veins
   (3) going in a straight line

Thinking About Your Thinking

Would you have thought about classifying leaves by their vein structure?

How else could you classify leaves? Could you have used color pattern? smell?

Estimating and Measuring

How can you estimate and measure a large number of objects?

An estimate is an intelligent, informed guess about an object's properties. Sometimes you may want to estimate how many objects are in a container without having to count or measure every object.

Suppose you were given the assignment to tell how many raisins were in a box of cereal. You surely wouldn't want to count every raisin. That would take too long. Instead you could decide on a plan to estimate and measure the cereal to come up with a reasonable answer.

Practice Estimating and Measuring

Materials
- 16 oz. box of raisin cereal
- measuring cup
- large bowl

Follow This Procedure

1. Work with a partner to estimate the number of raisins in the box of cereal.

2. Use the measuring cup to determine how many cups of cereal are in the box. Pour the cereal into the measuring cup and then put the cereal from the measuring cup into the bowl. Keep track of how many cups you poured into the bowl.

3. Divide the total number of cups in the box by 2. Round the answer up to the next whole number. Write down this number.

4. Use the measuring cup to take 2 cups of cereal back out of the bowl. Separate the raisins from the cereal. Count how many raisins were in the two cups of cereal.

5. Multiply the number of raisins in two cups of cereal by the number that you got in step 3. This will give you an estimate of the number of raisins in the whole box of cereal.

Thinking About Your Thinking

Can you think of another way to make a better estimate of the number of raisins in the box? Would taking a larger sample of cereal make any difference to the accuracy of your estimate? Try it to find out.

STAY HEALTHY!
Drink Orange Juice
Orange juice is good and it's good for you!
Get the— Vitamin C, Fiber, and Potassium that you need!

Inferring

How do you infer?

You infer when you make a reasonable guess, based on what you observe or on what you have experienced.

Observing with one or more of your senses—seeing, hearing, smelling, or touching—can be the reason for your inference. If you have done something in the past, what you learned can also help you make a good inference.

For example, when you watch TV or read a magazine, there are commercials or ads. You have seen these before and you know that someone is trying to sell you something. Watch a commercial. What do the advertisers want you to believe about their product?

Ad	Observation	Inference

Practice Inferring

Materials

- magazines or newspapers

Follow This Procedure

1. Make a chart like the one shown.

2. Look through a magazine or newspaper. Cut out several ads.

3. Read these ads carefully. List an observation and an inference that could be made about the ad.

4. Draw a conclusion about these ads. Is the message that the advertiser was trying to send accurate? Why or why not?

Thinking About Your Thinking

Watch several commercials on television. How do the commercials compare to the ads in the magazine or newspaper? Which type of advertising is more likely to make you want to buy a product—ads or TV commercials? Why do you think this is so?

Predicting

How can you make accurate predictions?

Predicting is an important process skill. There are five steps to making accurate predictions.

1. Make observations and measurements. Remember what you learned from doing something in the past.

2. Search for patterns in the data. Make inferences.

3. Make predictions about what may happen in the future. Use your inferences.

4. Test your predictions.

5. After testing, revise your predictions if necessary.

Practice Predicting

Materials

- meter stick
- small rubber ball

Follow This Procedure

1 Make a chart like the one below.

Drop	Predictions	Bounces
25 cm	X	
30 cm	X	
50 cm		
75 cm		
100 cm		

2 Work with a partner. Have your partner hold the meter stick with the 100 cm at the top.

3 Drop the ball from the 25 centimeter line on the meter stick. Have your partner count how many times the ball bounces.

4 Repeat this activity from the 30 centimeter line. Record the number of bounces.

5 Predict how many times the ball will bounce from the 50, 75, and 100 centimeter lines.

6 Do the activity and record the number of times the ball bounces from the 50, 75, and 100 centimeter lines.

Thinking About Your Thinking

How accurate were your predictions? What information did you use to make your predictions? If you dropped the ball from 200 centimeters, what would your prediction for the number of bounces be? Why?

Making Operational Definitions

How do you write an operational definition?

An operational definition is a definition or description of an object or an event based on your experience with it. As you gain experience with an object or event, your operational definition of it may become more effective. Keep your operational definition as simple as possible. Can you write an operational definition for the word "electricity"? Remember, use what you know already to write the definition. Do not look it up in a dictionary.

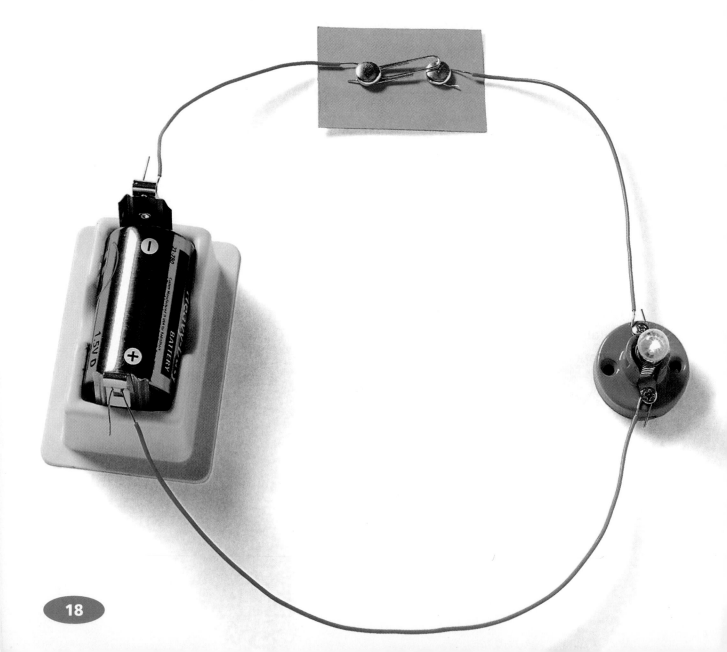

Practice Making Operational Definitions

Materials

- 1 D-cell battery
- 1 flashlight bulb
- insulated wire—both ends stripped

Follow This Procedure

1. Look at the diagram of the closed circuit. Set up the bulb, battery, and wire to make a closed circuit so the bulb lights.

2. Write your definition of a closed circuit based on what you did.

3. Look up *circuit* in your science book or the dictionary and write the definition given in the book.

4. How is your definition of a circuit different from the definition given in the book?

Thinking About Your Thinking

How did making a closed circuit help you define it? How did your definition communicate what the closed circuit did?

Making and Using Models

How can making a model help you understand a difficult concept?

There are many things to learn in your science book. Some of those things are easier to understand if you can see the object or event. You can make a model or copy of many of the objects or events in science.

For example, you can't go to a desert, forest, or prairie to see how animals live in these environments. However, you can build dioramas in shoeboxes or make posters of animals in their habitats. These models help you learn about animals and their habitats.

Practice Making and Using Models

Materials

- clear tape
- pictures of animals from magazines, web sites, or student drawings
- 4 different pieces of construction paper
- large poster board

Follow This Procedure

1 Cut out or draw pictures of 4 animals that go together in a food chain.

2 Tape these animals on the 4 different pieces of construction paper.

3 Put the pictures in order on the poster board.

4 Label the food chain, showing the direction that it goes.

5 Write a description of the food chain that you created for your class.

6 Create a series of questions that go with your food chain. Have your classmates answer these questions. Examples might be:

What is the source of energy for the ____?

What does the ____ eat?

Which animal or organism starts the food chain?

What do you think would happen to the ____ if it couldn't eat the ____?

Thinking About Your Thinking

Why do you think that the model that you made is called a "chain"? What other models could you make that might help explain what a food chain is?

Formulating Questions and Hypotheses

How do you formulate relevant questions and hypotheses?

The scientific process often begins when you ask yourself a question to solve a problem. You then formulate statements, or hypotheses, so you can test them. From the results of the test, you may be able to answer the question or to solve the problem.

When scientists form a possible answer to a question, they also form a hypothesis. For example, "If I do this … then this will happen."

Practice Formulating Questions and Hypotheses

Materials

- 6 straws
- scissors
- tape
- piece of construction paper

Follow This Procedure

1. Question: How does the length of the straw affect the pitch of the sound produced?

2. Cut one end of a straw to form a point and blow into this end of the straw to produce a sound. Observe the pitch of the sound produced (high or low).

3. Write a hypothesis about the length of the straw and its pitch.

4. Trim the 5 remaining straws to different lengths. Then cut one end of each straw to form a point. Blow into this end and observe the pitch of the sound produced.

5. Arrange your 6 straws in order from the highest to the lowest pitch and tape the straws on a piece of construction paper.

Thinking About Your Thinking

Did your investigation prove that your hypothesis is correct?

As you observe at school and home, think about questions you would like to find out about. Practice forming hypotheses to answer your questions. How would you test each hypothesis?

Collecting and Interpreting Data

How do you collect and interpret data accurately?

You collect and interpret data when you gather measurements and organize them into graphs, tables, charts, or diagrams. You can then use the information to solve problems or to answer questions.

When people take surveys, they ask many questions and collect a lot of useful data. This information is then put into charts and graphs so it's easier to understand. Have you ever taken a survey?

1. What color eyes do you have? _____

2. What color hair do you have? _____

3. How many brothers and sisters do you have? _____

Practice Collecting and Interpreting Data

Materials

- pencil
- paper

Follow This Procedure

1 Make a chart like the one below to record how many of your classmates have blue eyes, brown eyes, or green eyes.

Eye Color	Tally of Students	Totals
Blue		
Brown		
Green		

2 Make a chart like the one below to record how many of your classmates have blonde hair, red hair, brown hair, or black hair.

Hair Color	Tally of Students	Totals
Blonde		
Red		
Brown		
Black		

3 Take a survey to collect data on hair color and eye color from each of your classmates. Make a tally mark for each student's answer in the correct place on the charts. Then calculate the total number of students that chose each answer.

4 Which hair color do most students have? Which eye color do most students have?

Thinking About Your Thinking

What other questions might you have included on your survey? Is a chart the best way to show this data? Why or why not?

Systems

A system is a set of things that form a whole. Systems can be made of many different parts. All the parts depend on each other and work together. Systems can have living things and nonliving things.

The schoolyard on the next page is an example of a system that contains living things. Parts of the system that interact and depend on each other are the students, the grass, the bee, the clover plant, and the dandelion plant.

The circuit below is a nonliving system. The light bulb, the wires, the switch, and the energy source all make up the system.

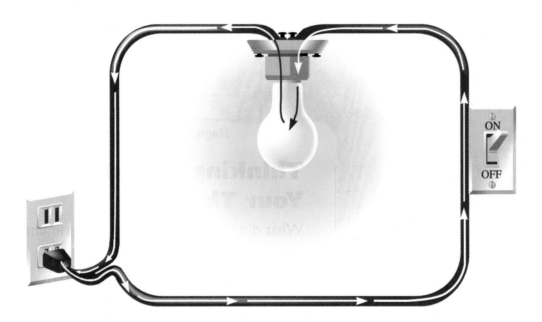

Layers of the Earth

Atmosphere

A blanket of air, called the atmosphere, surrounds the earth. The earth's atmosphere protects it from harmful sunlight and helps organisms on the earth survive.

Crust

The earth itself is made of layers. The outer layer, or crust, of the earth is made up of rocks and soil. The land you walk on and the land under the oceans are part of the crust.

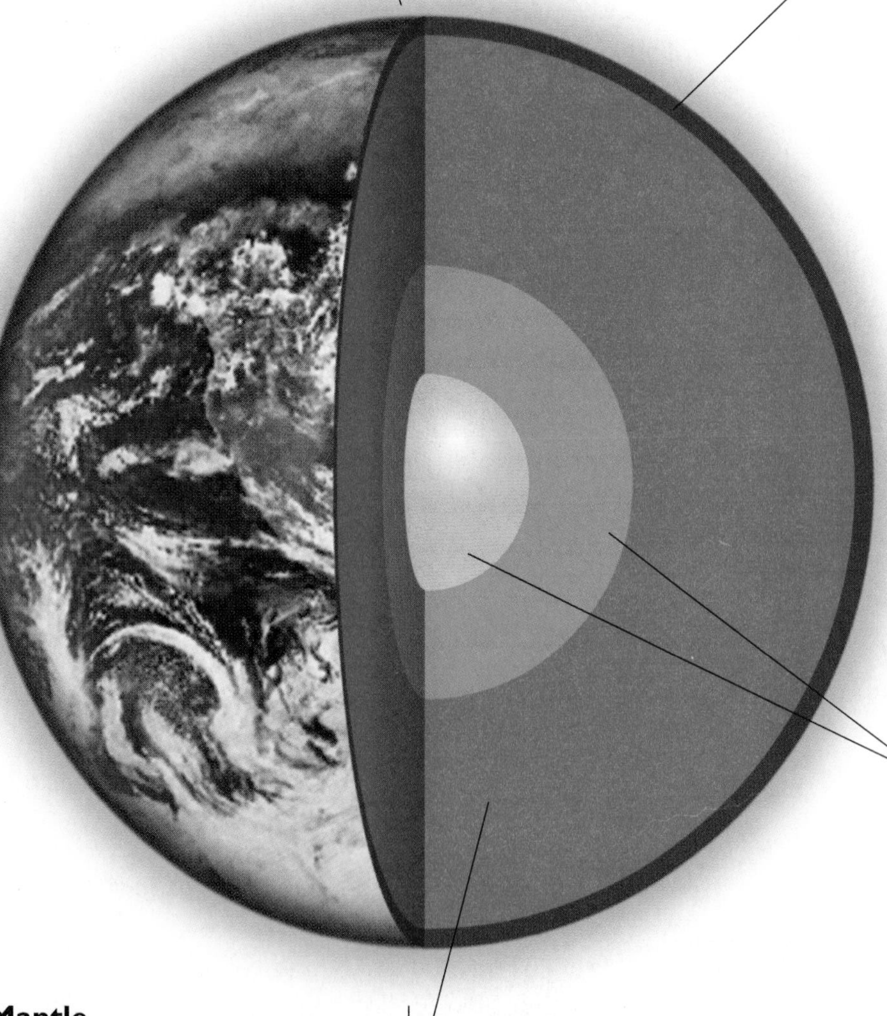

Core

The center of the earth—the core—is made mostly of iron. The outside part of the core has liquid iron. The inside part has solid iron. The core is the hottest part of the earth. The temperature of the core is almost as hot as the surface of the sun!

Mantle

The middle layer of the earth is called the mantle. The mantle is mostly made of rock. Some of the rock in the mantle is partly melted.

Climate Zones

A climate is the weather conditions which describe an area over many years. The earth has three basic climate zones—tropical, temperate, and polar. Areas within these zones can have different climates. Across the United States, climates vary because of differences in the amount of rainfall and temperature. There are no clear boundary lines between climate areas in the United States.

Highland climate
The highland climate mountain zones have very cold winters and cool summers.

Grassland climate
A grassland climate gets little rainfall during the year. This zone has very cold temperatures and snow in winter and hot temperatures in the summer.

Humid continental climate
A humid continental climate has warm summers with a lot of rain. Winters are very cold with a lot of snow.

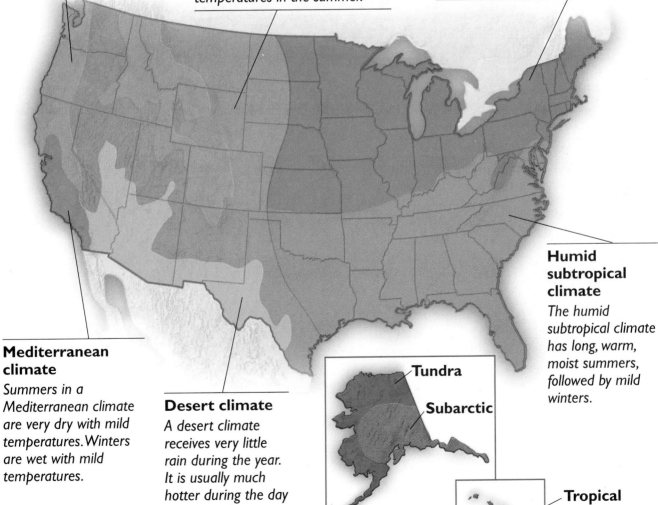

Humid subtropical climate
The humid subtropical climate has long, warm, moist summers, followed by mild winters.

Mediterranean climate
Summers in a Mediterranean climate are very dry with mild temperatures. Winters are wet with mild temperatures.

Desert climate
A desert climate receives very little rain during the year. It is usually much hotter during the day than at night.

Tundra

Subarctic

Tropical

The Rock Cycle

In the rock cycle, rocks form and change into other types of rock. Rocks form in three main ways. Over millions of years, each type of rock can change into another type of rock.

Rocks that form from melted material deep inside the earth are igneous rocks. Granite is an igneous rock.

As a result of weathering, rocks break down. Sand and small bits of rock sink beneath the water. Layers of material press together underwater and form sedimentary rocks. Sandstone is a sedimentary rock.

Metamorphic rock forms as very high heat and great pressure within the earth change igneous and sedimentary rocks. Gneiss is a metamorphic rock.

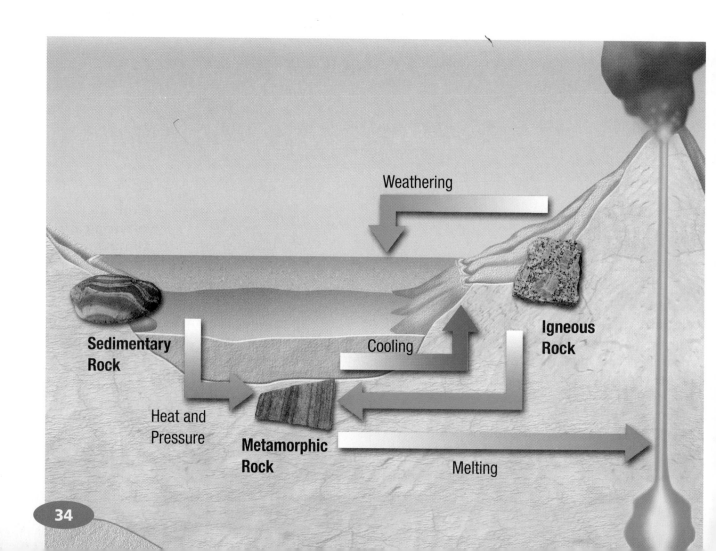

Weathering

Sedimentary Rock

Cooling

Igneous Rock

Heat and Pressure

Metamorphic Rock

Melting

Minerals

In 1822, Frederich Mohs created a scale that showed the hardness of certain minerals. On his scale, minerals with higher numbers are harder than minerals with lower numbers. You can tell how hard a mineral is by rubbing it against another mineral. The harder mineral will scratch the softer mineral. A diamond is the hardest mineral known. It will scratch any other mineral.

Mohs' Scale of Hardness

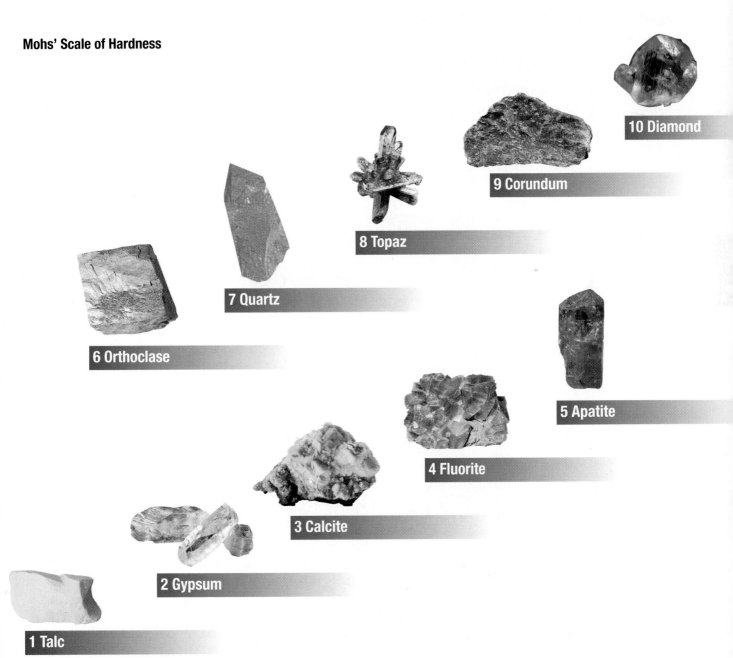

10 Diamond

9 Corundum

8 Topaz

7 Quartz

6 Orthoclase

5 Apatite

4 Fluorite

3 Calcite

2 Gypsum

1 Talc

Evidence of the Past

Many different types of organisms have existed on the earth throughout millions of years. Many types of organisms that lived millions of years ago are now extinct. Fossils of extinct organisms show that some plants and animals that lived long ago look very much like plants and animals that live today.

▲ *The woolly mammoth from thousands of years ago is similar to the elephant of today. The mammoth is now extinct.*

◄ *Scientists think that ferns date back hundreds of millions of years, making them some of the oldest types of plants on the earth.*

◀ In many ways, a tiger that lives today looks like a saber-toothed cat that lived thousands of years ago. The saber-toothed cat is now extinct.

◀ Cockroaches have been on the earth many millions of years. They look much the same now as their ancestors that lived long ago.

▲ Alligators that lived many millions of years ago may have been longer than alligators that live today. However, ancient alligators looked very much like alligators that live today.

Vertebrates and Invertebrates

The animal kingdom can be divided into two main groups. One group contains animals that have a backbone. Animals that have backbones are called vertebrates. The other group contains animals that do not have a backbone. These animals are called invertebrates.

▲ Crabs belong to a group called crustaceans.

Invertebrates

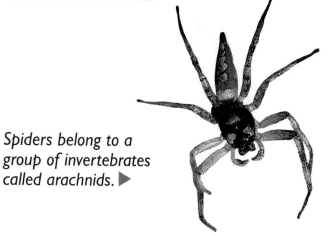

Spiders belong to a group of invertebrates called arachnids. ▶

Earthworms are annelids. ▼

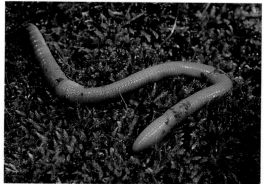

▲ Insects are the largest group of animals.

The group to which sponges belong is known as porifera. ▼

◀ Jellyfish are coelenterates.

Vertebrates

◀ *Snakes, turtles, and lizards belong to a group called reptiles.*

▲ *A hummingbird is one of many different birds.*

Koalas are mammals. ▶

Frogs are amphibians. ▶

Sharks are fishes. ▶

Life Cycles

Every living thing has a life cycle. In its life cycle, an organism goes through stages in which it grows, changes, and reproduces. Some young animals have the same body form as their parents. Others, such as frogs and butterflies, go through a metamorphosis, meaning they change form as they grow.

Life Cycle of a Frog

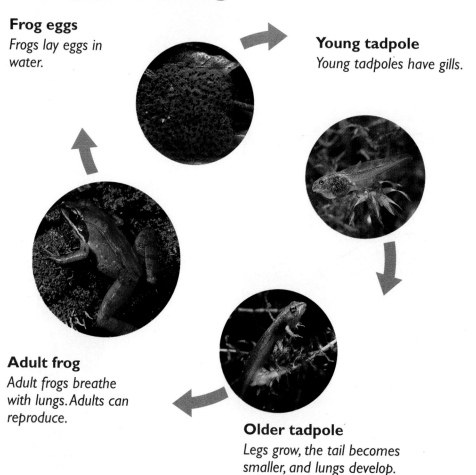

Frog eggs
Frogs lay eggs in water.

Young tadpole
Young tadpoles have gills.

Adult frog
Adult frogs breathe with lungs. Adults can reproduce.

Older tadpole
Legs grow, the tail becomes smaller, and lungs develop.

Life Cycle of a Butterfly

Egg
Butterflies lay their eggs on leaves.

Larva
The butterfly larva is also called a caterpillar.

Pupa
The larva wraps itself in a covering. The larva becomes a pupa. Its body changes form.

Butterfly
The covering opens and the butterfly comes out. After a time, the butterfly lays eggs. The cycle starts again.

Life Cycle of a Tree

Seeds
A seed falls to the ground.

Germination
A seed germinates when the tiny plant inside it begins to grow.

Seedling
A seedling is a young plant.

Fully grown tree
A fully grown plant makes flowers and seeds.

Cells, Tissues, Organs, and Body Systems

The human body is made of small units that join together to form larger and more complicated units.

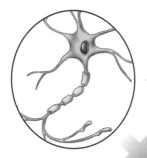

◄ *A cell is the basic unit of an organism. The body has many different kinds of cells. Each kind of cell does a different job. This cell is a nerve cell.*

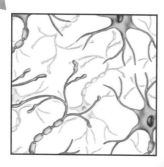

◄ *A group of the same kind of cells forms a tissue. A group of bone cells forms bone tissue, and a group of muscle cells forms muscle tissue. This diagram shows how nerve cells form nervous tissue.*

▶ *A group of many kinds of tissues forms an organ. The tissues in an organ work together to keep an organism alive. The brain is an organ that is made mainly of nervous tissue, but also has blood and other tissues.*

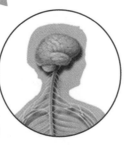

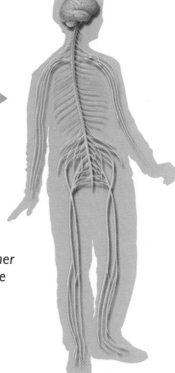

▶ *Different organs work together to do a job in the body. The organs that work together to do a special job make up a system. The brain, spinal cord, and nerves make up the nervous system.*

Body Systems

Each system in the human body has a special job to do.

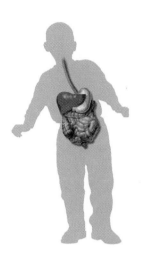

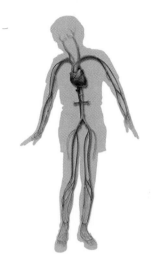

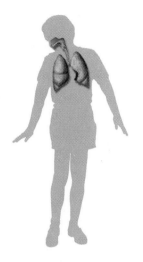

▲**Digestive System**
This system changes food into a form that body cells can use.

▲**Circulatory System**
This system brings oxygen and nutrients to cells and takes away wastes.

▲**Respiratory System**
This system brings oxygen into the body and gives off waste gases.

▲**Nervous System**
The brain and nerves control everything the body does.

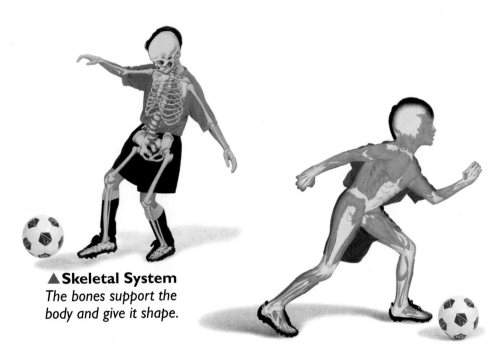

▲**Excretory System**
This system carries waste products out of the body.

▲**Skeletal System**
The bones support the body and give it shape.

▲**Muscular System**
Muscles make body parts move and give the body shape.

Plant and Animal Cells

A cell is the smallest part that makes up a living thing. Plant and animal cells are different in some ways and alike in others. An animal cell contains a cell membrane, a nucleus, and cytoplasm. A plant cell contains a cell membrane, a nucleus, cytoplasm, a cell wall, and chloroplasts.

Animal Cell

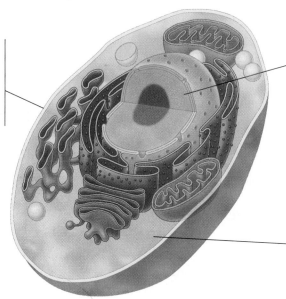

Cell Membrane
The cell membrane controls what goes in and out of the cell.

Nucleus
The nucleus directs the way the cell grows, develops, and divides.

Cytoplasm
Jellylike cytoplasm fills the cell and surrounds the nucleus.

Plant Cell

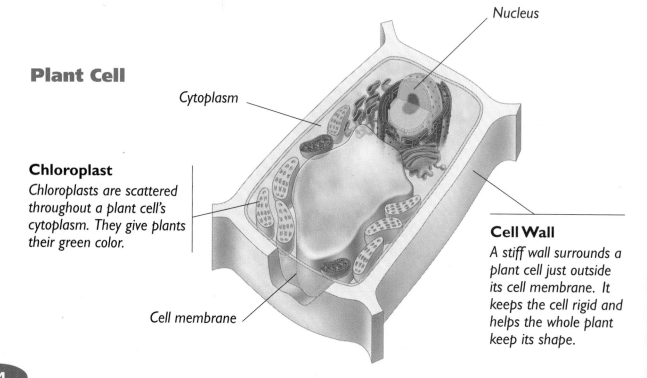

Nucleus

Cytoplasm

Chloroplast
Chloroplasts are scattered throughout a plant cell's cytoplasm. They give plants their green color.

Cell membrane

Cell Wall
A stiff wall surrounds a plant cell just outside its cell membrane. It keeps the cell rigid and helps the whole plant keep its shape.

Tools

Tools can make objects appear larger. They can help you measure volume, temperature, length, distance, and mass. Tools can help you figure out amounts and analyze your data. Tools can also provide you with the latest scientific information.

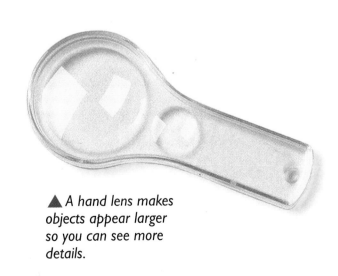

You can figure amounts using a calculator. ▶

▲ *Safety goggles protect your eyes.*

◀ *Microscopes have several lenses to make objects appear larger. You can see details of an object that you might not have been able to see with just your eyes.*

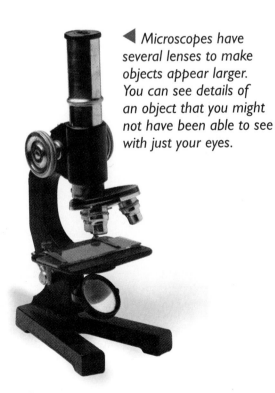

▲ *A hand lens makes objects appear larger so you can see more details.*

▲ Computers can quickly provide the latest scientific information.

▶ You use a thermometer to measure temperature. Many thermometers have both Farenheit and Celsius scales. Usually scientists only use the Celsius scale when measuring temperature.

Scientists use metric rulers and meter sticks to measure length and distance. Scientists use the metric units of meters, centimeters, and millimeters to measure length and distance. ▼

Pictures taken with a camera record what something looks like. You can compare pictures of the same object to show how the object might have changed. ▼

Clocks and stopwatches are used for measuring time. ▶

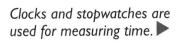

You can talk into a tape recorder to record information you want to remember. You can also use a tape recorder to record different sounds. ▲

▲ *You use a balance to measure mass.*

▲ *You can use a magnet to test whether an object is made of certain metals such as iron.*

▲ *A compass is used to indicate direction. The directions on a compass include north, south, east, and west.*

8000 B.C.	6000 B.C.	4000 B.C	2000 B.C.

Life Science

Physical Science

● **3000 B.C.**
The Egyptians develop geometry. They use it to re-measure their farmlands after floods of the Nile River.

Earth Science

● **8000 B.C.** Farming communities start as people use the plow for farming.

Human Body

4th century B.C.
Aristotle classifies
plants and animals.

3rd century B.C.
Aristarchus proposes that the
earth revolves around the sun.

4th century B.C.
Aristotle describes the
motions of falling
bodies. He believes that
heavier things fall faster
than lighter things.

260 B.C. Archimedes
discovers the principles of
buoyancy and the lever.

4th century B.C. Aristotle
describes the motions
of the planets.

200 B.C. Eratosthenes calculates
the size of the earth. His result is
very close to the earth's actual
size.

87 B.C.
Chinese report observing
an object in the sky that
later became known as
Halley's comet.

5th and 4th centuries B.C.
Hippocrates and other Greek
doctors record the symptoms of
many diseases. They also urge
people to eat a well-balanced diet.

Life Science

Physical Science

83 A.D. Chinese travelers use the compass for navigation.

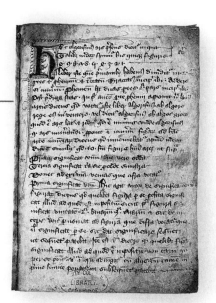

About 750–1250 Islamic scholars get scientific books from Europe. They translate them into Arabic and add more information.

Earth Science

140 Claudius Ptolemy draws a complete picture of an earth-centered universe.

132 The Chinese make the first seismograph, a device that measures the strength of earthquakes.

Human Body

2nd century Galen writes about anatomy and the causes of diseases.

1100s
Animal guide books begin to appear. They describe what animals look like and give facts about them.

1250
Albert the Great describes plants and animals in his book *On Vegetables and On Animals*.

1555
Pierre Belon finds similarities between the skeletons of humans and birds.

9th century
The Chinese invent block printing. By the 11th century, they had movable type.

1019
Abu Arrayhan Muhammad ibn Ahmad al'Biruni observed both a solar and lunar eclipse within a few months of each other.

1543
Nikolaus Copernicus publishes his book *On The Revolutions of the Celestial Orbs*. It says that the sun remains still and the earth moves in a circle around it.

1265
Nasir al-Din al-Tusi gets his own observatory. His ideas about how the planets move will influence Nikolaus Copernicus.

About 1000
Ibn Sina writes an encyclopedia of medical knowledge. For many years, doctors will use this as their main source of medical knowledge. Arab scientist Ibn Al-Haytham gives the first detailed explanation of how we see and how light forms images in our eyes.

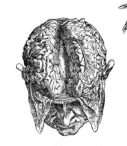

1543
Andreas Vesalius publishes *On the Makeup of the Human Body*. In this book he gives very detailed pictures of human anatomy.

1600	1620	1640	1660	1680

Life Science

1663 Robert Hooke first sees the cells of living organisms through a microscope. Antoni van Leeuwenhoek discovers bacteria with the microscope in 1674.

1679 Maria Sibylla Merian paints the first detailed pictures of a caterpillar turning into a butterfly. She also develops new techniques for printing pictures.

Physical Science

1600 William Gilbert describes the behavior of magnets. He also shows that the attraction of a compass needle toward North is due to the earth's magnetic pole.

1632 Galileo Galilei shows that all objects fall at the same speed. Galileo also shows that all matter has inertia.

1687 Isaac Newton introduces his three laws of motion.

Earth Science

1609–1619 Johannes Kepler introduces the three laws of planetary motion.

1610 Galileo uses a telescope to see the rings around the planet Saturn and the moons of Jupiter.

1669 Nicolaus Steno sets forth the basic principles of how to date rock layers.

1650 Maria Cunitz publishes a new set of tables to help astronomers find the positions of the planets and stars.

1693–1698 Maria Eimmart draws 250 pictures depicting the phases of the moon. She also paints flowers and insects.

1687 Isaac Newton introduces the concept of gravity.

Human Body

1628 William Harvey shows how the heart circulates blood through the blood vessels.

1735 Carolus Linnaeus devises the modern system of naming living things.

1759 Emile du Châtelet translates Isaac Newton's work into French. Her work still remains the only French translation.

1789 Antoine-Laurent Lavoisier claims that certain substances, such as oxygen, hydrogen, and nitrogen, cannot be broken down into anything simpler. He calls these substances "elements."

1704 Isaac Newton publishes his views on optics. He shows that white light contains many colors.

1729 Stephen Gray shows that electricity flows in a straight path from one place to another.

1781 Caroline and William Herschel (sister and brother) discover the planet Uranus.

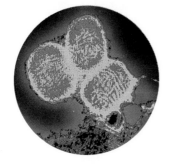

1784 French chemist Antoine-Laurent Lavoisier does the first extensive study of respiration.

1798 Edward Jenner reports the first successful vaccination for smallpox.

1721 Onesimus introduces to America the African method for inoculation against smallpox.

53

| 1805 | 1810 | 1815 | 1820 | 1825 | 1830 | 1835 |

Life Science

1808 French naturalist Georges Cuvier describes some fossilized bones as belonging to a giant, extinct marine lizard.

1838–1839 Matthias Schleiden and Theodor Schwann describe the cell as the basic unit of a living organism.

Physical Science

1800 Alessandro Volta makes the first dry cell (battery).

1820 H.C. Oersted discovers that a wire with electric current running through it will deflect a compass needle. This showed that electricity and magnetism were related.

1808 John Dalton proposes that all matter is made of atoms.

Earth Science

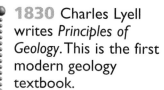

1830 Charles Lyell writes *Principles of Geology*. This is the first modern geology textbook.

1803 Luke Howard assigns to clouds the basic names that we still use today— cumulus, stratus, and cirrus.

Human Body

1842 Richard Owen gives the name "dinosaurs" to the extinct giant lizards.

1859 Charles Darwin proposes the theory of evolution by natural selection.

1863 Gregor Mendel shows that certain traits in peas are passed to succeeding generations in a regular fashion. He outlines the methods of heredity.

1847 Hermann Helmholtz states the law of conservation of energy. This law holds that energy cannot be created or destroyed. Energy only can be changed from one form to another.

1842 Christian Doppler explains why a car, train, plane, or any quickly moving object sounds higher pitched as it approaches and lower pitched as it moves away.

1866 Ernst Haeckel proposes the term "ecology" for the study of the environment.

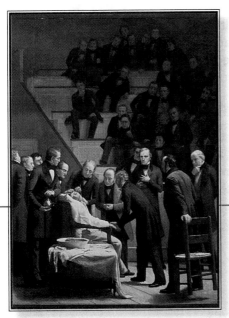

Early 1860s Louis Pasteur realizes that tiny organisms cause wine and milk to turn sour. He shows that heating the liquids kills these germs. This process is called pasteurization.

1840s Doctors use anesthetic drugs to put their patients to sleep.

1850s and 1860s Ignaz P. Semmelweis and Sir Joseph Lister pioneer the use of antiseptics in medicine.

1950	1955	1960	1965	1970

Life Science

1951 Barbara McClintock discovers that genes can move to different places on a chromosome.

1953 The collective work of James D. Watson, Francis Crick, Maurice Wilkins, and Rosalind Franklin leads to the discovery of the structure of the DNA molecule.

1972 Researchers find human DNA to be 99% similar to that of chimpanzees.

Physical Science

1969 UCLA is host to the first computer node of ARPANET, the forerunner of the internet.

1974 Opening of TRIUMF, the world's largest particle accelerator, at the University of British Columbia.

Earth Science

1957 The first human-made object goes into orbit when the Soviet Union launches *Sputnik I*.

1972 Cygnus X-1 is first identified as a blackhole.

1969 Neil Armstrong is the first person to walk on the moon.

1967 Geophysicists introduce the theory of plate tectonics.

1962 John Glenn is the first American to orbit the earth.

Human Body

1954–1962 In 1954, Jonas Salk introduced the first vaccine for polio. In 1962, most doctors and hospitals substituted Albert Sabin's orally administered vaccine.

1967 Dr. Christiaan Barnard performs the first successful human heart transplant operation.

1964 The surgeon general's report on the hazards of smoking is released.

NO SMOKING
American Cancer Society

1988 Congress approves funding for the Human Genome Project. This project will map and sequence the human genetic code.

1997 Scientists in Edinburgh, Scotland, successfully clone a sheep, Dolly.

1975 People are able to buy the first personal computer, called the Altair.

1996 Scientists make "element 112" in the laboratory. This is the heaviest element yet created.

1979 A near meltdown occurs at the Three Mile Island nuclear power plant in Pennsylvania. This alerts the nation to the dangers of nuclear power.

1976 National Academy of Sciences reports on the dangers of chlorofluorocarbons (CFCs) for the earth's ozone layer.

1995 The first "extra-solar" planet is discovered.

Early 1990s The National Severe Storms Laboratory develops NEXRAD, the national network of Doppler weather radar stations for early severe storm warnings.

1981 The first commercial Magnetic Resonance Imaging scanners are available. Doctors use MRI scanners to look at the non-bony parts of the body.

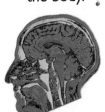

1982 Dr. Stanley Prusiner identifies a new kind of disease-causing agent—prions. Prions are responsible for many brain disorders.

1998 John Glenn, age 77, orbits the earth aboard the space shuttle *Discovery*. Glenn is the oldest person to fly in space.

Glossary

Full Pronunciation Key

The pronunciation of each word is shown just after the word, in this way: **ab·bre·vi·ate** (ə brē′vē āt).

The letters and signs used are pronounced as in the words below.

The mark ′ is placed after a syllable with primary or heavy accent, as in the example above.

The mark ′ after a syllable shows a secondary or lighter accent, as in **ab·bre·vi·a·tion** (ə brē′vē ā′shən).

a	hat, cap	g	go, bag	ō	open, go	ŦH	then,	zh	measure,
ā	age, face	h	he, how	ȯ	all, caught		smooth		seizure
â	care, fair	i	it, pin	ô	order	u	cup, butter		
ä	father, far	ī	ice, five	oi	oil, voice	u̇	full, put	ə	represents:
b	bad, rob	j	jam, enjoy	ou	house, out	ü	rule, move		a in about
ch	child, much	k	kind, seek	p	paper, cup	v	very, save		e in taken
d	did, red	l	land, coal	r	run, try	w	will,		i in pencil
e	let, best	m	me, am	s	say, yes		woman		o in lemon
ē	equal, be	n	no, in	sh	she, rush	y	young, yet		u in circus
ėr	term, learn	ng	long, bring	t	tell, it	z	zero,		
f	fat, if	o	hot, rock	th	thin, both		breeze		

A

absorb (ab sôrb′), to take in.

adaptation (ad′ap tā′shən), any structure or behavior that helps a living thing meet its need for survival.

air mass (âr mas), a large body of air that has about the same temperature and humidity throughout.

air pressure (âr presh′ər), the amount that air presses or pushes on anything.

amphibian (am fib′ē ən), one of a large group of animals with backbones that live part of their lives in water and part on land.

amplify (am′plə fī), to make stronger.

anemia (ə nē′mē ə), a condition in which the number of healthy red blood cells or the amount of hemoglobin is low.

anemometer (an′ə mom′ə tər), a tool that measures wind speed.

artery (ar′tər ē), the kind of blood vessel that carries blood away from the heart.

asteroid (as′tə roid′), a rocky object orbiting the sun between the planets.

atherosclerosis (ath´ər ō sklə rō´sis), a disease in which fatty substances build up on the inside walls of arteries.

atrium (ā´trē əm), one of two spaces in the top part of the heart that receive blood from veins.

axis (ak´sis), an imaginary line through a spinning object.

B

backbone, the main bone, made up of many small bones joined together, that runs along the middle of the back in some animals.

balance (bal´əns), an instrument used to measure an object's mass.

bar graph (graf), a graph that uses bars to show data.

barometer (bə rom´ə tər), a tool that measures air pressure.

behavior (bi hā´vyər), the way a living thing acts.

boiling (boi´ling) **point**, the temperature at which matter changes from a liquid to a gas.

bullhorn (bùl´hôrn´), an instrument with a built-in microphone that makes sound louder.

C

camouflage (kam´ə fläzh), any coloring, shape, or pattern that allows a living thing to blend into its surroundings.

capacity (kə pas´ə tē), the amount a container can hold.

capillary (kap´ə ler´ē), a tiny blood vessel with thin walls through which oxygen, nutrients, and wastes pass.

carbon dioxide (kär´bən dī ok´sīd), a gas found in air.

carnivore (kär´nə vôr), a consumer that eats other consumers.

cause (kȯz), a person, thing, or event that makes something happen.

centimeter (sen´tə mē´tər), a metric unit used to measure length; 1/100 of a meter.

chemical (kem´ə kəl) **change**, a change in matter that produces a different kind of matter.

chemical (kem´ə kəl) **energy**, energy that comes from chemical changes.

chlorophyll (klôr´ə fil), the green substance found in plants that traps energy from the sun and gives plants their green color.

classify (klas´ə fī), to sort into groups based on similarities and differences.

colony (kol′ə nē), a kind of animal group in which each member has a different job.

comet (kom′it), a frozen chunk of ice and dust that orbits the sun.

compass (kum′pəs), a small magnet that can turn freely.

complex machine (kom′pleks mə shēn′), a machine made of many simple and compound machines.

compound machine (kom′pound mə shēn′), a machine made of two or more simple machines.

concave lens (kon kāv′ lenz), a lens that is thinner in the middle than at the edges.

concussion (kən kush′ən), a condition caused by a sudden movement of the brain inside the skull, usually involving a brief loss of consciousness.

condense (kən dens′), to change from a gas to a liquid state.

conductor (kən duk′tər), a material through which electric current passes easily.

conifer (kon′ə fər), a plant that makes seeds inside cones.

constellation (kon′stə lā′shən), a group of stars that form a pattern.

consumer (kən sü′mər), a living thing that gets energy by eating plants and other animals.

context (kon′tekst), the parts directly before or after a word or sentence that influence its meaning.

continental (kon′tə nen′tl) **shelf**, the shallow part of the ocean at the edge of the continents.

continental (kon′tə nen′tl) **slope**, the edge of the continental shelf that extends steeply downward to the ocean floor.

control, the part of an experiment that does not have the variable being tested.

convex lens (kon veks′ lenz), a lens that is thicker in the middle than at the edges.

coral reef (kôr′əl rēf), a platform or ridge of coral at or near the ocean surface.

cubic meter (kyü′bik mē′tər), a unit for measuring the volume of a solid.

current (kėr′ənt), a riverlike flow of water in the ocean.

D

dark zone, the ocean water where sunlight does not reach.

decomposer (dē´kəm pō´zər), a consumer that puts materials from dead plants and animals back into the soil, air, and water.

density (den´sə tē), how much mass is in a certain volume of matter.

dicot (dī´kot) **seed**, a seed that has two seed leaves that contain stored food.

digestion (də jes´chən), the changing of food into forms that the body can use.

dormant (dôr´mənt), the resting stage of a seed.

dune (dün), a pile of sand formed by the wind.

E

earthquake (ėrth´kwāk´), the shaking of the ground caused by rock movement along a fault.

ecosystem (ē´kō sis´təm), all the living and nonliving things in an environment and how they interact.

effect (ə fekt´), whatever is produced by a cause; a result.

electric signal (i lek´trik sig´nəl), a form of energy.

electrical (i lek´trə kəl) **energy**, energy that comes from the flow of electricity.

electromagnet (i lek´trō mag´nit), a magnet made when an electric current flows through a wire.

ellipse (i lips´), the shape of a flattened circle.

embryo (em´brē ō), a tiny part of a seed that can grow into a new plant.

endangered (en dān´jərd), having a population that is falling low in number and that is in danger of becoming extinct.

energy (en´ər jē), the ability to do work.

enzyme (en´zīm), a chemical that helps your digestive system change food into nutrients.

erosion (i rō´shən), the moving of weathered rocks and soil by wind, water, or ice.

esophagus (i sof´ə gəs), the tube that carries food and liquids from the mouth to the stomach.

exoskeleton (ek´sō skel´ə tən), a hard outer covering that supports and protects some animals without backbones.

extinct (ek stingkt´), no longer existing.

F

fault (fȯlt), a crack in the earth's crust along which rocks move.

fertilization (fėr´tl ə zā´shən), the combination of sperm from a pollen grain with an egg to form a seed.

food chain, the flow of energy through a community.

food web, all the food chains in a community.

force (fôrs), a push or a pull on an object that can cause it to change motion.

forecast (fôr´kast´), a prediction of what the weather will be like.

fossil (fos´əl), any mark or remains of a plant or animal that lived a long time ago.

freezing (frē´zing) **point,** the temperature at which matter changes from a liquid to a solid.

friction (frik´shən), a force that slows the motion of moving objects.

front (frunt), the line where two air masses meet.

G

generator (jen´ə rā´tər), a machine that uses an energy source and a magnet to make electricity.

gills, organs for breathing found in fish and amphibians.

graduated cylinder (graj´ü ā´tid sil´ən dər), a tool used to measure the volume of liquids.

gram, the basic unit for measuring mass.

graphic source (graf´ik sôrs), a drawing, photograph, table, chart, or diagram that shows information visually.

gravity (grav´ə tē), a force that pulls any two objects toward one another, such as you toward the center of the earth.

H

habitat (hab´ə tat), a place where an animal or a plant lives.

hearing aid, an instrument used to help people with a hearing problem hear better.

herbivore (hėr´bə vôr), a consumer that eats plants.

hibernation (hī´bər nā´shən), a long, deep sleep in which an animal's heart rate and breathing are much slower than normal.

high blood pressure (presh´ər), a disease in which blood is pumped through the arteries with too much force.

high-pressure area (hī´presh´ər âr´ē ə), a place where cool air sinks and pushes down on the earth's surface with more pressure.

host (hōst), a plant or animal that is harmed by a parasite.

humidity (hyü mid´ə tē), the amount of water vapor in the air.

hygrometer (hī grom´ə tər), a tool that measures humidity.

I

indigestion (in′də jes′chən), one or more symptoms, such as stomachache, that occur when the body has difficulty digesting food.

inertia (in ėr′shə), the tendency of a moving object to stay in motion or a resting object to stay at rest.

instinct (in′stingkt), a behavior that an animal is born with and does not need to learn.

insulator (in′sə lā′tər), a material through which electric current does not pass easily.

K

kilogram (kil′ə gram), a metric unit of mass equal to 1,000 grams.

kinetic (ki net′ik) **energy**, energy of motion.

L

landform, a shape of the land, such as a mountain, plain, or plateau.

large intestine (in tes′tən), the last organ of the digestive system, which removes water and stores the waste material.

light zone, the sunlit waters of the ocean.

line graph (graf), a graph that connects point to show how data change over time.

liter (lē′tər), a unit for measuring volume.

low-pressure area (lō′presh′ər âr′ē ə), a place where warm air rises and pushes down on the earth's surface with less pressure.

M

magnet (mag′nit), anything that pulls iron, steel, and certain other metals to it.

magnetic (mag net′ik) **field**, the space around a magnet where magnetism acts.

magnetism (mag′nə tiz′əm), the force around a magnet.

mammal (mam′əl), an animal with a backbone that usually has hair on its body and feeds milk to its young.

mass (mas), the amount of material that an object has in it.

matter (mat′ər), anything that has mass and takes up space.

mechanical (mə kan′ə kəl) **energy**, the kind of energy an object has because it can move or because it is moving.

median (mē′dē ən), the middle number when the data are put in order.

melting (mel´ting) **point,** the temperature at which matter changes from a solid to a liquid.

meteor (mē´tē ər), a piece of rock or dust from space burning up in Earth's air.

meteorite (mē´tē ə rīt´), a rock from space that has passed through Earth's air and landed on the ground.

meteorologist (mē tē ə rol´ə jist), a person who studies weather.

meter (mē´tər), a unit for measuring length.

microphone (mī´krə fōn), an instrument used to amplify voices, music, and other sounds.

migration (mī grā´shən), the movement of an animal from one location to another as the seasons change.

milliliter (mil´ə lē´tər), a unit for measuring volume equal to 1/1000 of a liter.

mineral (min´ər əl), nonliving, solid matter from the earth.

mixture (miks´chər), two or more substances that are mixed together but can be easily separated.

mode (mōd), the number that occurs most often in the data.

molt (mōlt), to shed an animal's outer covering.

monocot (mon´ə kot) **seed,** a seed that has one seed leaf and stored food outside the seed leaf.

N

National Weather Service (nash´ə nəl weTH´ər sér´vis), a government agency that collects information about weather.

nerve cell (nèrv sel), a cell that gathers and carries information in the body.

nerve ending (nèrv en´ding), a tiny branch of a nerve cell that gathers information.

nutrient (nü´trē ənt), a substance in food that the body uses for energy, for growth and repair, or for working well.

O

ocean basin (bā´sn), the floor of the deep ocean.

omnivore (om´nə vôr´), a consumer that eats both plants and other consumers.

opaque (ō pāk´), does not allow light to pass through.

orbit (ôr´bit), the path of an object around another object.

ovary (ō´vər ē), the bottom part of the pistil in which seeds form.

ovule (ō´vyül), the inner part of an ovary that contains an egg.

P

parallel circuit (par´ə lel sėr´kit), a circuit that connects several objects in a way that the current for each object has its own path.

parasite (par´ə sīt), a plant or animal that feeds off another living thing and harms it.

photosynthesis (fō´tō sin´thə sis), a process by which plants change light energy from the sun and use it to make sugar.

physical (fiz´ə kəl) **change**, a change in matter that changes physical properties, but does not produce a different kind of matter.

pistil (pis´tl), part of a flower that makes the eggs that grow into seeds.

pitch (pich), the highness or lowness of a sound.

plasma (plaz´mə), the liquid part of blood that carries nutrients, wastes, and blood cells.

platelet (plāt´lit), a small part of a blood cell that helps blood clot and stops bleeding.

pole (pōl), a place on a magnet where magnetism is strongest.

pollen (pol´ən), tiny grains that make seeds when combined with a flower's egg.

pollination (pol´ə nā´shən), the movement of pollen from a stamen to a pistil.

pollution (pə lü´shən), anything harmful added to the air, land, or water.

potential (pə ten´shəl) **energy**, energy that an object has because of position.

precipitation (pri sip´ə tā´shən), moisture that falls from clouds to the ground.

predator (pred´ə tər), an animal that hunts and kills other animals for food.

predict (pri dikt´), to tell what will happen next based on what has already happened.

prey (prā), the animals that predators hunt.

producer (prə dü´sər), a living thing that uses sunlight to make sugar.

R

rain gauge (gāj), a tool that measures precipitation.

range (rānj), the difference between the highest and lowest number in the data.

recycle (rē sī´kəl), to use the same materials over and over again.

red blood cell, the kind of blood cell that carries oxygen to other body cells.

reflect (ri flekt´), to bounce back.

reflex (rē´fleks), a simple, automatic behavior.

reproduce (rē´prə düs´), to make more of the same kind.

reptile (rep´tīl), an animal with a backbone that has a dry, scaly skin.

resistance (ri zis´təns), a measure of how much a material opposes the flow of electric current and changes electric current into heat energy.

response (ri spons´), a behavior caused by a stimulus.

revolution (rev´ə lü´shən), the movement of an object around another object.

ridge (rij), the highest part of a chain of underwater mountains.

rotation (rō ta´shən), one full spin of an object around an axis.

S

saliva (sə lī´və), the liquid in the mouth that makes chewed food wet and begins digestion.

satellite (sat´l īt), an object that revolves around another object.

scavenger (skav´ən jər), an animal that eats dead animals.

sense organ (sens ôr´gən), a body part that has special nerve cells that gather information about the surroundings.

sepal (sē´pəl), one of the leaflike parts that protects a flower bud and that is usually green.

series circuit (sir´ēz sėr´kit), a circuit that connects several objects one after another so that the current flows in a single path.

simple machine (sim´pəl mə shēn´), a machine made of one or two parts.

small intestine (in tes´tən), the organ of the digestive system in which most digestion takes place.

solar system (sō´lər sis´təm), the sun, the nine planets and their moons, and other objects that orbit the sun.

solution (sə lü´shən), a mixture in which one substance spreads evenly throughout another substance.

spinal cord (spī´nl kôrd), a thick bundle of nerves that connects the brain and nerves throughout the body.

spore (spôr), a tiny cell that can grow into a new plant.

stamen (stā´mən), part of a flower that makes pollen.

stethoscope (steth´ə skōp), an instrument used to hear the sounds of body organs.

stimulus (stim´yə ləs), the cause of a behavior.

symbiosis (sim´bē ō´sis), a special way in which two different kinds of living things live together.

T

tide, the rise and fall of the surface level of the ocean.

translucent (tran slü´snt), allows light to pass through but scatters it so that whatever is behind it cannot be clearly seen.

transmit (tran smit´), to allow to pass through.

transparent (tran spâr´ənt), allows light to pass through so that whatever is behind can be seen.

trench, a deep, narrow valley in the ocean floor.

V

vein (vān), the kind of blood vessel that carries blood back to the heart.

ventricle (ven´trə kəl), one of two spaces in the bottom part of the heart that pump blood out of the heart.

vibrate (vī´brāt), to move quickly back and forth.

visible spectrum (viz´ə bəl spek´trəm), light energy that can be seen and can be broken into the colors of the rainbow.

volcano (vol kā´n... by hardened lava w... ntain formed through which lava, ash... ening other materials come out... s, and

volume (vol´yəm), the amount ...space that matter takes up; the loudness... softness of a sound.

W

wave, the up-and-down movement of ocean water caused by the wind.

wavelength (wāv´lengkth´), the distance from a point on a wave to the same point on the next wave.

weathering (weTH´ər ing), the breaking and changing of rocks.

wind vane (vān), a tool that shows wind direction.

work (wėrk), the result of a force moving an object.

Index

Acknowledgments

Illustration
Borders Patti Green; **Icons** Precison Graphics

Front Matter J.B. Woolsey

Unit A 20, 27d, 74, 78, 108 Precision Graphics; 22, 27a-d J.B. Woolsey; 39c Ka Botzis; 70a Walter Stuart

Unit B 50 Walter Stuart; 78, 100, 101, 108, 109a, 112, 113, 117, 121 J.B. Woolsey

Unit C 9, 12, 13, 14, 27, 99, 100, 103b, 104 J.B. Woolsey; 40a, 53, 66, 67, 68, 79, 81 Precision Graphics

Unit D 11, 15, 23 Precision Graphics; 16, 21, 22, 24, 26 J.B. Woolsey; 42 Christine D. Young

Photography
Unless otherwise credited, all photographs are the property of Scott Foresman, a division of Pearson Education. Page abbreviations are as follows: (T) top, (C) center, (B) bottom, (L) left, (R) right, (INS) inset.

Cover: Lynette Cook/SPL/Photo Researchers; **iv** PhotoDisc, Inc.; **v** T Joe McDonald/DRK Photo; **v** B Michael Fogden/Animals Animals/Earth Scenes; **viii-ix** Background Leo L. Larson/Panoramic Images

Unit A
1 Spencer Jones/Bruce Coleman Inc.; 2 T Vincent O'Bryne/Panoramic Images; 2 CL Arie deZanger for Scott Foresman; 2 CR Arie deZanger for Scott Foresman; 2 Inset Nick Caloyianis; 3 C John Pade/Nelson/Pade Multimedia; 3 B Michael Stuwe; 8 David Young-Wolff/PhotoEdit; 9 William M. Smithey, Jr./Planet Earth Pictures (Seaphot Ltd.); 9 Inset John Neubauer/PhotoEdit; 10 B PhotoDisc, Inc.; 12 T Bill Beatty/Animals Animals/Earth Scenes; 13 T Runk/Schoenberger/Grant Heilman Photography; 13 T-Inset Runk/Schoenberger/Grant Heilman Photography; 14 TR Breck P. Kent/Animals Animals/Earth Scenes; 14 B Jim Corwin/Photo Researchers; 18 William J. Weber/Visuals Unlimited; 20 B Runk/Schoenberger/Grant Heilman Photography; 21 BL Mary Goljenboom/Ferret Research, Inc.; 21 BC Mary Goljenboom/Ferret Research, Inc.; 21 BR Mary Goljenboom/Ferret Research, Inc.; 38 Tom Bean/Tony Stone Images; 39 T Superstock, Inc.; 39 R. Maler/IFA/Bruce Coleman Inc.; 40 T Zig Leszczynski/Animals Animals/Earth Scenes; 40 B Bob and Clara Calhoun/Bruce Coleman Inc.; 41 T Chris McLaughlin/Animals Animals/Earth Scenes; 41 C E. S. Ross; 41 B Chris McLaughlin/Animals Animals/Earth Scenes; 42 Bill Beatty/Visuals Unlimited; 42 Inset L. West/Photo Researchers; 43 T Jane Burton/Bruce Coleman Inc.; 43 C Frans Lanting/Minden Pictures; 43 B Tom McHugh, 1973, Steinhart Aquarium/Photo Researchers; 45 BR John Gerlach/Dembinsky Photo Assoc. Inc.; 45 TL James P. Rowan/DRK Photo; 45 CL Scott Camazine/Photo Researchers; 45 CR E. R. Degginger/Bruce Coleman Inc.; 45 BL Kramer/Stock Boston; 45 TR D. Lyons/Bruce Coleman Inc.; 46 PhotoDisc; 47 T Gary Meszaros/Dembinsky Photo Assoc. Inc.; 47 B Mark Moffett/Minden Pictures; 48 T Joe McDonald/DRK Photo; 48 B Wayne Lankinen/DRK Photo; 49 TR Mitsuaki Iwago/Minden Pictures; 49 CR Wolfgang Bayer/Bruce Coleman Inc.; 49 CL Frans Lanting/Minden Pictures; 49 BR Marty Cordano/DRK Photo; 50 T PhotoDisc, Inc.; 50 B Art Wolfe/Tony Stone Images; 51 T Stephen Dalton/Animals Animals/Earth Scenes; 51 BL Dr. E. R. Degginger/Color-Pic, Inc.; 51 BR D. Cavagnaro/Visuals Unlimited; 52 Chuck Davis/Tony Stone Images; 53 T Renee Stockdale/Animals Animals/Earth Scenes; 53 C Julian Barker/National Gerbil Society; 53 B Julian Barker/National Gerbil Society; 54 Robert Maier/Animals Animals/Earth Scenes; 55 Leen Van Der Slik/Animals Animals/Earth Scenes; 56 T Steve Maslowski/Photo Researchers; 56 B Michio Hoshino/Minden Pictures; 57 T Leroy Simon/Visuals Unlimited; 58 Ralph Reinhold/Animals Animals/Earth Scenes; 59 Pat & Tom Leeson/DRK Photo; 63 Art Wolfe/Tony Stone Images; 68 L-Inset C. C. Lockwood/Animals Animals/Earth Scenes; 68 B PhotoDisc, Inc.; 68 R-Inset John Gerlach/DRK Photo; 75 Jose Carillo/PhotoEdit; 77 Lee Rentz/Bruce Coleman Inc.; 78 B Patti Murray/Animals Animals/Earth Scenes; 78 T Kim Taylor/Bruce Coleman Inc.; 79 T M.H. Sharp/Photo Researchers; 79 BR PhotoDisc, Inc.; 79 BL Zig Leszczynski/Animals Animals/Earth Scenes; 79 CR Norman Owen Tomalin/Bruce Coleman Inc.; 80 CL Tim Laman/Wildlife Collection; 80 TL Joe McDonald/Visuals Unlimited; 82 R Rod Planck/TOM STACK & ASSOCIATES; 82 L Michael Gadomsky/Photo Researchers; 83 BL-inset Larry West/Photo Researchers; 83 R-Inset David Northcott/Superstock, Inc.; 83 Background Peter Cade/Tony Stone Images; 84 T Rod Planck/TOM STACK & ASSOCIATES; 84 CL Michael Gadomsky/Photo Researchers; 84 CR John Cancalosi/TOM STACK & ASSOCIATES; 84 B Tom Vezo/Wildlife Collection; 85 TL © Heather Angel; 85 TC Larry West/Photo Researchers; 85 CL Lynn M. Stone; 85 TCR David Northcott/Superstock, Inc.; 85 CC Stephen J. Krasemann/DRK Photo; 85 CR Michael Durham/ENP Images; 85 BL Dwight R. Kuhn/DRK Photo; 85 BR Stephen J.

Krasemann/DRK Photo; 86 C Tony Freeman/PhotoEdit; 86 BL Michael Gadomsky/Photo Researchers; 86 BR Rod Planck/TOM STACK & ASSOCIATES; 87 L Larry West/Photo Researchers; 87 R David Northcott/Superstock, Inc.; 88 T David W. Harp Photographer; 88 BR Norman Tomalin/Bruce Coleman Inc.; 88 CL Frans Lanting/Minden Pictures; 89 T Patti Murray/Animals Animals/Earth Scenes; 89 CL Steve Winter/National Geographic; 89 CR Steve Winter/National Geographic; 93 Lee Rentz/Bruce Coleman Inc.; 98 R Peter Feibert/Liaison Agency; 98 L Bill Gallery/Stock Boston; 99 T Clifton Carr/Minden Pictures; 99 B Ken Cole/Animals Animals/Earth Scenes; 100 T HPH Photography/Wildlife Collection; 100 B Bruce Coleman Inc.; 101 T © Heather Angel ; 101 C John W. Matthews/DRK Photo; 101 B Michael Fogden/Animals Animals/Earth Scenes; 102 T Jim Brandenburg/Minden Pictures; 102 B Dr. Paul A. Zahl/Photo Researchers; 103 TR Frans Lanting/Minden Pictures; 103 CL Frans Lanting/Minden Pictures; 103 BR Jim Brandenburg/Minden Pictures; 104 B Fred Bavendam/Minden Pictures; 104 T Patti Murray/Animals Animals/Earth Scenes; 105 Scott Camazine/Photo Researchers; 106 B HPH Photography/Wildlife Collection; 106 T Erwin and Peggy Bauer/Bruce Coleman Inc.; 107 B ZEFA-Bauer/Stock Market; 107 T Mitsuaki Iwago/Minden Pictures; 108 L Francois Gohier/Photo Researchers; 108 C Patti Murray/Animals Animals/Earth Scenes; 108 R Dave B. Fleetham Marine Photographer/Visuals Unlimited; 109 T Jeff Foott/Bruce Coleman Inc.; 109 B Wayne Lankinen/Bruce Coleman Inc.; 110 TL Bradley Simmons/Bruce Coleman Inc.; 110 TR E.R. Degginer/Animals Animals/Earth Scenes; 110 BL F. Stuart Westmorland/Animals Animals/Earth Scenes; 110 BR M.C. Chamberlain/DRK Photo; 111 T Art Wolfe Inc.; 111 B Zig Leszczynski/Animals Animals/Earth Scenes; 114 Owen Franken/Stock Boston; 115 T Townsend P. Dickinson/Image Works; 115 B Warren Williams/Planet Earth Pictures (Seaphot Ltd.); 116 Background Johnathan Nourok/PhotoEdit; 116 TR Michael Newman/PhotoEdit; 116 B Tony Freeman/PhotoEdit; 116 TL Richard Hutchings/Photo Researchers; 117 T Bob Daemmrich/Stock Boston; 117 B Greg Vaughn/TOM STACK & ASSOCIATES; 118 Mark J. Thomas/Dembinsky Photo Assoc. Inc.; 119 John Obata/The National Tropical Botanical Garden, Lawai, Kauai, Hawaii; 119 C J. Beckett/American Museum of Natural History/Department of Library Services, Neg. No. 5367(4); 119 T Tom McHugh/Photo Researchers; 121 T Field Museum of Natural History, Chicago, IL/Neg.#GE086127C, photograph by John Weinstein; 121 B David M. Dennis/TOM STACK & ASSOCIATES; 123 HPH Photography/Wildlife Collection; 125 PhotoDisc, Inc.

Unit B
1 Tom Pantages; 2 T Vincent O'Bryne/Panoramic Images; 2 C Geoff Tompkinson/SPL/Photo Researchers; 3 B Alan L. Detrick/Photo Researchers; 3 C Dennis Potokar/Photo Researchers; 7 Kim Brownfield; 24 PhotoDisc, Inc.; 25 TL Binney & Smith; 25 TR Richard T. Nowitz/National Geographic; 25 CL Richard T. Nowitz/National Geographic; 25 CR Richard T. Nowitz/National Geographic; 29 NASA; 36 Al Bello/Tony Stone Images; 37 Milt & Joan Mann/Cameramann International, Ltd.; 38 Myrleen Ferguson/PhotoEdit; 42 Tony Freeman/PhotoEdit; 45 Jim Shippee/Unicorn Stock Photos; 48 Robert Clay/Visuals Unlimited; 77 Pekka Parviainen/SPL/Photo Researchers; 93 Michael Giannechini/Photo Researchers; 94 Michael Giannechini/Photo Researchers; 95 B Bruce Coleman Inc.; 95 C Robert E. Daemmrich/Tony Stone Images; 97 Background Lowell Georgia/Science Source/Photo Researchers; 97 TR-Inset Alfred Pasieka/Science Photo Library/Photo Researchers; 97 BR-inset Will and Deni McIntyre/Photo Researchers; 101 L Jeremy Horner/Tony Stone Images; 103 T Richard Megna/Fundamental Photographs; 103 C Richard Megna/Fundamental Photographs; 108 Mark Richards/PhotoEdit; 109 Myrleen Ferguson/PhotoEdit; 111 T Tony Stone Images; 112 T Harold Hoffman/Photo Researchers; 112 B Flip Nicklin/Minden Pictures; 118 Tom McCarthy/PhotoEdit; 119 BR Milt & Joan Mann/Cameramann International, Ltd.; 119 TR David Young-Wolff/Tony Stone Images; 120 T Hulton Deutsch Collection Ltd.; 120 B Hulton-Deutsch Collection/Corbis Media; 121 BR Jane Shemilt/Science Photo Library/Photo Researchers; 121 TL Jane Shemilt/Science Photo Library/Photo Researchers; 121 TR G. Thomas Bishop/Custom Medical Stock Photo

Unit C
1 Frank Siteman/PhotoEdit; 2 T Vincent O'Bryne/Panoramic Images; 2 CL NASA/Science Source/Photo Researchers; 3 B NASA; 3 C Hank Morgan/Rainbow; 8 PhotoDisc; 10 Greg Vaughn/Tony Stone Images; 15 T Felicia Martinez/PhotoEdit; 16 Barry L. Runk/Grant Heilman Photography; 17 Michael von Ruber/International Stock; 18 Craig Aurness/Corbis-Westlight; 19 T David R. Frazier/Photo Researchers; 19 BL John Lemker/Animals Animals/Earth Scenes; 20 T Mary Fulton/Tony Stone Images; 20 BL PhotoDisc, Inc.; 20 BR Johnny Johnson/DRK Photo; 27 Background Warren Faidley/International Stock; 28 L GOES Image/NOAA; 28 R GOES Image/NOAA; 29 Inset European Space Agency/Photo Researchers; 29 Ken Biggs/Tony Stone Images; 30 B Warren Faidley/International Stock; 30 T Charles Doswell III/Tony Stone Images; 31 Margaret Durrance/Photo Researchers; 37 Richard J. Green/Photo Researchers; 38 Leo L. Larson/Panoramic Images; 39 T Werner Forman/Corbis Media; 41 C Roger Werth/Woodfin Camp & Associates; 41 B Richard J. Green/